107 11265

Proletarianization and Family History

STUDIES IN SOCIAL DISCONTINUITY

Under the Consulting Editorship of:

CHARLES TILLY
New School for Social Research

EDWARD SHORTER
University of Toronto

In preparation

Michael Timberlake (Ed.). Urbanization in the World-Economy

Published

David Levine (Ed.). Proletarianization and Family History

Susan Walsh Sanderson. Land Reform in Mexico: 1910–1980

Manuel Gottlieb. A Theory of Economic Systems

Robert Max Jackson. The Formation of Craft Labor Markets

Michael B. Katz. Poverty and Policy in American History

Arthur L. Stinchcombe. Economic Sociology

Jill S. Quadagno. Aging in Early Industrial Society: Work, Family, and Social Policy in Nineteenth-Century England

J. Dennis Willigan and Katherine A. Lynch. Sources and Methods of Historical Demography

Dietrich Gerhard. Old Europe: A Study of Continuity, 1000–1800

Charles Tilly. As Sociology Meets History

Maris A. Vinovskis. Fertility in Massachusetts from the Revolution to the Civil War

Juan G. Espinosa and Andrew S. Zimbalist. Economic Democracy: Workers' Participation in Chilean Industry 1970–1973: Updated Student Edition

Alejandro Portes and John Walton. Labor, Class, and the International System

James H. Mittelman. Underdevelopment and the Transition to Socialism: Mozambique and Tanzania

John R. Gillis. Youth and History: Tradition and Change in European Age Relations, 1770–Present: Expanded Student Edition

Samuel Kline Cohn, Jr. The Laboring Classes in Renaissance Florence

Richard C. Trexler. Public Life in Renaissance Florence

Paul Oquist. Violence, Conflict, and Politics in Colombia

The list of titles in this series continues at the end of this volume.

PROLETARIANIZATION AND FAMILY HISTORY

Edited by
David Levine

Department of History and Philosophy of Education
The Ontario Institute for Studies in Education
Toronto, Ontario, Canada

1984

ACADEMIC PRESS, INC.

(Harcourt Brace Jovanovich, Publishers)

Orlando   San Diego   New York   London
Toronto   Montreal   Sydney   Tokyo

ACADEMIC PRESS, INC.
Orlando, Florida 32887

United Kingdom Edition published by
ACADEMIC PRESS, INC. (LONDON) LTD.
24/28 Oval Road, London NW1 7DX

Library of Congress Cataloging in Publication Data

Main entry under title:

Proletarianization and family history.

(Studies in social discontinuity)
Includes index.
1. Labor and laboring classes--Great Britain--History.
2. Family--Great Britain--History. 3. Proletariat--
History. I. Levine, David, Date   . II. Series.
HD8388.P76 1984   305.5'62'0941   84-6301
ISBN 0-12-444980-8 (alk. paper)

PRINTED IN THE UNITED STATES OF AMERICA

84 85 86 87   9 8 7 6 5 4 3 2 1

Contents

2. Production, Reproduction, and the Proletarian Family in England, 1500–1851
David Levine

3. Peasant, Plebeian, and Proletarian Marriage in Britain, 1600–1900
John R. Gillis

4. Policing the Early Modern Proletariat, 1450–1850
Catharina Lis and Hugo Soly

5. Social Formation and Class Formation in North America, 1800–1900

Bryan D. Palmer

Contributors

Numbers in parentheses indicate the pages on which the authors' contributions begin.

John R. Gillis (129), Department of History, Rutgers University, New Brunswick, New Jersey 08903

David Levine (87), Department of History and Philosophy of Education, The Ontario Institute for Studies in Education, Toronto, Ontario M5S 1V6, Canada

Catharina Lis (163), Department of Pre-Industrial History, Erasmus Universiteit Rotterdam, Rotterdam, The Netherlands

Bryan D. Palmer[1] (229), Department of History, Simon Fraser University, Burnaby, British Columbia V5A, 1S6, Canada

Hugo Soly (163), Department of Social and Economic History, University of Ghent, Ghent, Belgium

Charles Tilly[2] (1), Departments of History and Sociology, University of Michigan, Ann Arbor, Michigan 48104

[1] Present address: Department of History, Queen's University, Kingston, Ontario K7L 3N6, Canada.

[2] Present address: Center for Studies of Social Change, New School for Social Research, New York, New York 10003.

Preface

The five essays in this volume are concerned with the social implications of the birth of capitalism and industrial society. Each was written especially for this collection and covers a long time span. The collection itself is meant as a reflection, 30 years later, of the "transition debate." While earlier historians focused their attention on the economic and juridical aspects of this process, more recent students have been concerned with the impact of these changes upon society in general and the family in particular. It might be said that this switch in emphasis itself reflects a rather different appreciation of the feedback mechanisms involved in the process of social change. Moreover, the extended chronology in these essays makes it quite clear that all of the contributors agree that we are discussing a process, not an event. For this reason, pride of place is given to the English experience, which was at the cutting edge of capitalist development. Once the English economy broke free of the restrictions imposed by social and political regulation, the industrial Prometheus was unbound, and all other countries had to adjust themselves to this new reality. The North American experience is therefore particularly interesting because we see in it a compaction of the chronological process: at one and the same time, after the Civil War, the emergence of "machinofacture" coincided with the colonization of the hinterlands. In none of these essays is there an attempt to smooth over the rough edges of historical change; in fact, a subtext of the volume is the uneven character of this change. Finally, each of the chapters is presented as a personal summation of and reflection upon contemporary research. Each reflects the contributor's point of view, and, again, we have made no attempt to smooth over these rough edges. Indeed, the strains and tensions between the various chapters all direct attention to the gaps in our knowledge and the inevitability of new and revised hypotheses. We all welcome that prospect.

The contributors owe a special debt of gratitude to Harvey Waterman and his colleagues in the Office of Graduate Studies, Rutgers University, which sponsored a small, vital colloquium, ''Proletarianization Past and Present,'' in May 1983. Not only did we proffer our essays for intensive analysis, but we also had the opportunity to discuss mutual interests in an intimate setting.

1

Demographic Origins
of the European Proletariat

Charles Tilly

A PROLETARIAN WORLD

We live in a proletarian world. Depending on how we classify workers in various sorts of socialist states, either a majority or a fat majority of the world's labor force are people who work for wages, using means of production over whose disposition they have little or no control. They are proletarians. In this broad but authentic sense of the word, almost all of us are proletarians. Yet quite recently—only a few hundred years ago—very few people anywhere worked for wages. Most people lived in households that exercised considerable control over their means of production, however meager those means. In the past few hundred years, the world has become proletarianized.

That proletarianization was arguably the most far-reaching change in the quality of everyday life to occur in the modern era. It had a more profound impact than did urbanization, secularization, bureaucratization, or any of the other "izations" that occurred in its company. The growth of wage labor at expropriated means of production transformed family life, altered the structure of local communities, created whole new

1

varieties of politics, and overturned the conditions determining the life chances of individuals and households. What is more, the process of proletarianization is continuing in the already quite proletarian Western world and accelerating outside the West. A majority of the world's physicians, for example, now work for wages in large organizations, especially state-run organizations. Dreams and struggles over workers' control, over land reform, and over the growth of alienated labor under socialism all attest to the pressure of proletarianization today.

Given all this profound transformation, it is astounding to turn to social-scientific writings on large-scale social change. For most of academic social science, proletarianization is a phantom. Amid the tons of writing on industrialization and on the growth of "modern" attitudes, we are lucky to find a few ounces on the emergence of the proletariat. And those rare discussions, for the most part, treat proletarianization as a special case or an incidental consequence. Of what? Of occupational differentiation, of industrialization, or of increase in the scale of production.

Recently, it is true, students of the labor process such as Harry Braverman, Richard Edwards, and Michael Burawoy have opened up important inquiries into management's strategies of expropriation, and labor historians such as David Montgomery, Michael Hanagan, and Klaus Tenfelde have paid attention to the ways that artisans and skilled workers became increasingly subject to capitalist work discipline. Furthermore, European agricultural historians, as well as students of cottage industry and related forms of production have for some time been enriching our understanding of expropriation and wage labor in the villages of Europe. My later discussion will draw extensively on their research. Yet these varied inquiries focus on the experiences of workers who were (or are) already essentially proletarian: dependent for survival on the sale of their labor power to capitalists of one sort or another. In any case, social scientists lack a general analysis of proletarianization to complement and modify their many analyses of industrialization or urbanization, whereas historians lack a general account of the processes by which the essentially nonproletarian population of a few hundred years ago turned into the largely proletarian population of today.

The lack is visible even in the one area in which we might have expected a general historical account to fall into place: the growth of the European proletariat since 1500 or so. There, the increase of landless labor has stirred recurrent concern; the relevant evidence is abundant if scattered; and bitter scholarly controversies have borne on such questions as whether English enclosures created a rural proletariat.

Adam Smith addressed the question more than two centuries ago:

"The demand for those who live by wages," wrote Smith in *The Wealth of Nations*, "naturally increases with the increase of national wealth, and cannot possibly increase without it."[1] "Those who live by wages" is a short definition of the proletariat. "The liberal reward of labor, therefore," said Smith later on, "as it is the effect of increasing wealth, so it is the cause of increasing population. To complain of it is to lament over the necessary effect and cause of the greatest public prosperity."[2] In Adam Smith's analysis, the increasing division of labor resulted from the rational disposition of the factors of production—land, labor, and capital—by those who controlled each of them. Since the increasing division of labor enhanced productivity, it increased the return to all factors of production, including labor. Indirectly, the rational disposition of resources led to the growth of that part of the population that lived from wages alone. It led to the growth of the proletariat.

But how did that growth occur? So far as I know, Adam Smith never analyzed the historical process in detail.[3] Perhaps it seemed too obvious: wage laborers multiplied because the demand for their labor increased. Parson Malthus's pessimistic gloss on Smith, after all, does little more than elaborate that basic relationship. Both Adam Smith and Thomas Robert Malthus lived in a world in which landless laborers were already numerous. In that world, it was common bourgeois practice to wring hands over the decline of independent craftsmen and yeomen and to deplore the reckless breeding of the poor—without doing anything substantial to reverse either one.[4] Smith's innovation was to treat the growth of the proletariat as an inevitable, perhaps even desirable, consequence of increasing wealth.

MARX VERSUS MALTHUS

Writing a century later, however, Karl Marx considered the historial process of proletarianization to be both fundamental and problematic. Chapters 25 to 32 of his *Capital* discuss at length the formation of the English proletariat. Marx denied emphatically that the smooth operation of demand accounted for the proletarianization of the English labor force. "The proletariat created by the breaking up of the bands of feudal retainers and by the forcible expropriation of the people from the soil," he wrote, "this 'free' proletariat could not possibly be absorbed by the nascent manufactures as fast as it was thrown upon the world."[5]

Note that Marx concentrated on rural, and especially agricultural, workers; only since his time has the term *proletarian* taken on its current connotation of large-shop manufacturing. Although Marx did present the factory wage slave as the extreme case of proletarianization, his own analysis of proletarianization dealt largely with rural workers.

In general, Marx portrayed proletarianization as the forcible wresting of control over the means of production from artisans and, especially, from peasants. "In the history of primitive accumulation," he declared at the end of Chapter 26:

> All revolutions are epoch-making that act as levers for the capitalist class in course of formation; but, above all, those moments when great masses of men are suddenly and forcibly torn from their means of subsistence, and hurled as free and "unattached" proletarians on the labor-market. The expropriation of the agricultural producer, of the peasant, from the soil, is the basis of the whole process.[6]

Thus the central fact was the creation of a rural proletariat, working mainly for wages in agriculture, but available at bargain rates for industrial production.

Insofar as he discussed the changing size of the proletariat at all, Marx described two contradictory processes. He followed the classical economists, including Adam Smith, in seeing a general association between capital accumulation and the growth of the proletariat. Although Marx did not specify the population processes involved, a plausible reading of his text is that an increase in the total volume of wages permitted more children of existing proletarians to survive. In this reading, the death rate serves as the gatekeeper. It guards the gate both from and to the proletariat. When death relaxes its cold grip on the gate, the proletariat grows. At one point, however, Marx suggested that the substitution of child labor for adult labor encouraged the poor to marry young and to bear many children. If so, changes in the marriage and birth rates mattered as well.

Marx's main argument, in any case, ran in the other direction. Under capitalism, he argued, employers extracted surplus value from the labor power they hired, essentially by squeezing more value in production from workers than it cost to hire them. Then the capitalists reinvested their surplus in the means of production. As a result, the fixed capital represented by the means of production necessarily increased faster than did the variable capital directly committed to the employment of labor. Economies of scale alone would have produced that effect of capital accumulation. Both the centralization of capital in large firms and the imposition of more intensive labor discipline accelerated it. In consequence, according to Marx, the demand for labor power increased much more slowly than capital accumulated.

As workers became increasingly redundant, the famous Industrial Reserve Army—whose existence presumably guaranteed the holding near subsistence of the wages for those who worked—came into being. That was, to Marx's eyes, the central demographic process of capitalism. It was, he said, a cruel peculiarity of the system:

> The laboring population therefore produces, along with the accumulation of capital produced by it, the means by which itself is made relatively superfluous, is turned into a relative surplus-population; and it does this to an always increasing extent. This is a law of population peculiar to the capitalist mode of production; and in fact every special historic mode of production has its own special laws of population, historically valid within its limits alone.[7]

Later in the same chapter, Marx briefly mentioned the declining rate of growth of the whole English population as if it supported his analysis. In general, however, Marx seems to have reasoned differently: first, the important increases in the number of proletarians occurred in bursts of expropriation such as the enclosures. Second, once people were proletarians, they more or less reproduced themselves: proletarians begat proletarians, in roughly constant numbers. If that is the case, the growth of the proletariat directly measures both the progress of expropriation and the current extent of exploitation.

In his notebooks of 1857 and 1858, the famous *Grundrisse*, Marx heaped scorn on Malthus. Malthus, Marx complained, had confused the specific conditions of capitalism with a general law of population growth:

> It is Malthus who abstracts from these specific historic laws of the movement of popuation, which are indeed the history of the nature of humanity, the *natural* laws, but natural laws of humanity only at a specific historical development, with a development of the forces of production determined by humanity's own process of history.[8]

In his discussion, nevertheless, Marx appeared to accept a hedged version of Malthus's thesis: that under capitalism population did, indeed, tend to grow faster than the means of subsistence did and thus to encounter devastating positive checks. If so, Marx was admitting implicitly that natural increase played a significant part in the proletariat's growth.

In any case, Marx's main argument was that "overpopulation" was not an objective external condition that somehow weighed on the system of production, but a consequence of the social organization linking different sorts of people to the existing means of production. "Never a relation to a *non-existent* absolute mass of means of subsistence," he wrote in his notebook,

> but rather relation to the conditions of production, of the production of these means, including likewise the *conditions of reproduction of human beings*, of the total population. This surplus purely relative: in no way related to the *means of subsistence* as such, but rather to the mode of producing them.[9]

Then he bent the discussion back to an analysis of the tendency of capitalism to separate increasing numbers of workers from the means of production. Thus Marx was clear enough about the structural conditions favoring the growth of a proletariat, but vague about the demographic processes involved.

A CHANCE FOR SYNTHESIS

Marx's analysis and his apparent indecision about the relevant demographic mechanisms provide a prime opportunity for complementary work by historians, demographers, and other social scientists. There is the opportunity to verify the main lines of Marx's analysis; for example, the idea of spurts of proletarianization as the consequence of massive expropriation. There is the opportunity to specify the different paths by which people moved from artisanal or peasant production into various forms of wage labor. There is the opportunity to assign relative weights to those paths: Which ones bore the most traffic? There is the opportunity to integrate them into a general account of the flows of people by which the largely peasant and artisanal European population of 1500 or 1600 became the overwhelmingly proletarian European population of 1900 and later.

How and why did that great shift occur? Why in Europe rather than elsewhere? In the century since Marx's death, one version or another of that double question has dominated the agenda of modern European economic and social history. Some of the debate has pivoted on the facts: How many yeomen, for example, did the enclosures actually displace? Some of the debate has concerned the proper way to state the questions: Weber and Tawney differed over the appropriate *Problemstellung* as much as over the historical facts. And much of the debate has dealt with explanations: why did capitalism flourish earlier in Britain than in Prussia?

Since the questions are vast and compelling, fragments of the debate on proletarianization, including the debate on the population changes involved, appear in widely scattered literatures. Historians of industrialization (especially British industrialization), for example, have carried on a long discussion of labor supply in the industrial revolution. The discussion pivots on the demographic origins of the proletariat.[10]

Demographers who have looked to the European experience for guidance in understanding the transition from high to low fertility and mortality throughout the world have repeatedly asked one another whether massive proletarianization was by-product, cause, or countercurrent of that transition in Europe.[11] Local and regional historians have edged into the demographic problem by discovering, in place after place, similar transformations of the labor force: the disproportionate increase of proletarian occupations and industries.[12] Students of poverty and of control over the poor have necessarily brushed against the problem of proletarianization but have not posed the demographic changes very directly or effectively.[13]

Analysts who have sought self-consciously to trace the process of proletarianization have commonly come from the ranks not of historians but of economists and sociologists. They have focused, by and large, on the expropriating and disciplining of wage workers, rather than on the development of wage labor itself.[14] Finally, the builders and critics of Marxist schemata concerning the general development of capitalism have had to commit themselves to one view or another of the origins of the proletariat.[15] These many overlapping enterprises offer the student of proletarianization a rich, broad, vigorous literature. The literature's richness, breadth, and vigor, however, make the task of synthesis mindbreaking.

I do not claim to have surveyed all the relevant sources, much less to have synthesized them. In this chapter, I aim merely to tidy up a small but crucial corner of this vast space: the demographic corner. The chapter discusses where population processes fit into general accounts of Europe's proletarianization. It specifies which features of those population processes have to be explained and why they are problematic. It offers a limited review of existing knowledge concerning those processes and proposes some tentative explanations of the particular paths taken by European proletarianization. On its way, the chapter spends more time on concepts and techniques than any reader will enjoy; conceptual and technical questions, it turns out, comprise a significant obstacle to understanding how proletarianization occurred.

Nevertheless, the chapter's main point is to pursue into the demographic sphere two of Marx's central insights concerning proletarianization: that the basic population processes respond to the logic of capitalism instead of being somehow exogenous to it and that the strategies of capitalists themselves determine the form and pace of proletarianization.

COMPONENTS OF GROWTH

A dull, routine sociological procedure promises to help the search for the origins of the European proletariat. It is to break the search into three parts: (1) analysis of components of growth, (2) explanation of individual components and their interactions, and (3) integration of those partial explanations into a general account of the process. Let me stress at once that these are logical subdivisions of the task, not distinct temporal stages. If we do not begin with a piece of the third part—with a tentative account of the entire process of proletarianization—we are quite likely to wander through the analysis of components and to stumble through the explanation of individual components and their interactions. The secret is to begin with a tentative account that is clearly verifiable, falsifiable, and correctible—or better yet, two or three competing accounts that are clearly verifiable, falsifiable, and correctible: accounts built, let us say, on the arguments of Adam Smith and Karl Marx.

Components of growth? At its simplest, the analysis consists of defining precisely the change being analyzed, preparing a logically exhaustive list of the components of that change, and estimating the contribution of each component to the change as a whole. In the case of European proletarianization, we must begin with working definitions of *Europe* and *proletarian*. That means deciding what to do with Iceland, Constantinople, Malta, the Azores, and so on. It also means deciding whether it is possible to be a little bit proletarian—for example, whether the independent weaver who hires himself out for the harvest qualifies as a proletarian, as one-quarter of a proletarian, or as no proletarian at all. What about his young children? Uninteresting decisions, these, except that they significantly affect the results of the analysis.

These tedious but crucial decisions made, we can begin to ask how the absolute number and the proportion of the European population in the category *proletarian* changed from, say, 1500 to 1900. We shall come back to guesses at the real numbers later. For now, the thing to notice is that we can break down those numbers into geographic, temporal, and, most important, logical components. We may ask *where* the transformation of nonproletarian populations into proletarian populations occurred. Did it happen mainly in areas of advanced capitalism? We may ask *when* the transformation occurred. Did the process accelerate greatly with the expansion of large-scale manufacturing after 1800? We may also ask *how* it happened. But the how, in this case, concerns the change's logical components.

If we turn to standard demographic accounting procedures, we shall find three logical possibilities. Each is, in turn, the result of two possible changes. The three logical possibilities are social mobility, natural increase, and net migration. Marx stressed social mobility: the movement of a particular social unit from one category to another as a consequence of an alteration in its own characteristics or relationships. If individuals are our social units, all persons who, in their own lifetimes, lose control over their means of production and move into wage labor add to the toll of proletarianization. In fact, the same individuals often oscillate between the two categories throughout their lifetimes. The net effect of all such moves across the boundary is the component of social mobility.

Natural increase is the result of births and deaths. If I read him aright, Marx implicitly assumed that natural increase was an unimportant component of the European proletariat's growth: the deaths more or less balanced out the births, and the net enlargements of the proletariat depended on new entries by people who began life as nonproletarians. This is where the components-of-growth analysis gets interesting, for several alternative possibilities exist. Given their vulnerability to infectious disease, starvation, and war, proletarians sometimes underwent a natural *decrease:* deaths exceeded births. The question is: how often and how much? If natural decrease were the normal situation of proletarians, the proletarian population would be in something like the situation of most preindustrial cities: they would have to recruit substantial numbers of newcomers merely to maintain their current size. To grow, they would have to recruit very large numbers indeed.

The birthrates of proletarians could also normally have run above their death rates. In that case, the proletarian population could grow without any new recruitment of nonproletarians. If the proletarian rate of natural increase were higher than that of the rest of the population, the proletarian share of the total population would tend to rise—even in the absence of lifetime mobility from nonproletarian to proletarian. With additional permutations of fertility and mortality, still further alterations are quite possible. For example, the proletarian rate of natural increase could have risen over time.

The third component—*net migration*—likewise offers multiple possibilities. If we are considering the European population as a whole, the migration that matters consists of moves of proletarians into and out of the continent. Because that component, too, sums up numerous losses and gains, its overall effect may have been nil, a substantial addition to the proletariat, a substantial subtraction from the proletariat, or something else. If we start considering migration into and out of the proletarian populations of different European regions, instead of reckoning for Europe as a whole, the problem becomes more complex and interesting.

To recapitulate: as in any population change, we can break down the increase of the European proletarian population from 1500 to 1900 (or for any other interval) in terms of a standard accounting equation:

$$P_2 = P_1 + (IC - OC) + (B - D) + (IM - OM) + e$$

where P_1 and P_2 are the population at the beginning and end of the interval; IC and OC are the numbers of persons who make lifetime moves into and out of the category; B and D are the births and deaths of members of the category; IM and OM are in-migration and out-migration; and e is the measurement error summed over all these observations.

THE IMPORTANCE OF GROWTH COMPONENTS

Why should anyone care about these hypothetical numbers? For more reasons than one. First, if we are to attempt any general account of Europe's proletarianization, we have no choice but to formulate hypotheses about the components of growth. The hypotheses may be implicit, and they may be very crude; they may consist, for example, of assigning an indefinitely large positive value to the net effect of lifetime moves and zero values to all the other components. That is the tone of Marx's analysis. Adam Smith, on the other hand, wrote as if natural increase were the only component differing significantly from zero. Thus in the absence of any exact numbers, simple knowledge of which components were positive or negative, large or small, would give us the means of judging whether Marx's formulation, Smith's formulation, or some modification of one or the other, was more adequate.

The choice is not merely hypothetical. Although the problem has often been badly posed, how the proletariat grew figures somehow in every account of industrialization and every history of the working class. Speaking of Sweden from 1750 to 1850, Christer Winberg points out that the peasantry increased by about 10%, whereas the landless classes of the countryside more than quadrupled. "The dominant interpretation of this development," he comments,

> can be summarized as follows: An important part is played by the "autonomous death-rate", i.e. a death-rate that remains relatively autonomous in relation to the economic development. Particularly from c. 1810 onwards, the decline of the death-rate was due to a series of exogenous factors, such as smallpox vaccination, the peace period from 1814 onwards and the cultivation of the potato. The result was a rapid increase in population that led to a subsequent proletarianization.[16]

"This interpretation," Winberg continues, "is not based on any coherent theory." He counters with an argument having five important elements:

1. On the whole, the landless population of the early eighteenth century did not constitute a distinct social class, since it consisted

largely of widowed old people and other non-producers; the separate class formed mainly after 1750.
2. The peasant population of the eighteenth century generally maintained an implicit system of population control in which, for example, declines in mortality normally produced a visible narrowing of opportunities for employment, which in turn led young people to delay marriage and to have fewer children.
3. After 1750, widespread reorganization of rural estates by their landlords turned many peasants into landless laborers.
4. Peasant villages themselves became increasingly stratified, with many smallholders likewise becoming landless laborers.
5. In the process, the rural population as a whole broke out of the older, implicit system of population control and moved toward strategies of relatively early marriage and high fertility.

Winberg documents these generalizations by means of a close study of a sample of Swedish rural parishes. In those parishes, he finds a general tendency for the landless to marry later and have fewer children than do the full-fledged peasantry. He also finds a small movement from landless labor into landholding and a very large move in the opposite direction. The bulk of the rural proletariat's increase, in his analysis, resulted from the unequal balance between these flows. Thus Winberg ends up assigning central importance to social mobility. Yet he by no means eliminates natural increase from the picture. Swedish villages, however, are not the whole of Europe. We must find out how generally Winberg's model of proletarianization applies elsewhere.

We have a second reason for concern about the three components of growth, as their relative weight and direction make a genuine difference to our understanding of the historical experience of proletarianization. To the extent that lifetime moves into the proletariat comprised the dominant process, we might expect a good deal of proletarian action to consist of efforts to retain or recapture individual control over the means of production. On the other hand, the same extensive recruitment through lifetime moves would make it more difficult to account for the persistence of an autonomous proletarian culture, enduring from one generation to the next.

To the extent that natural increase was the main source of growth in the proletariat, on the other hand, we would find find it easy to understand autonomous, persistent proletarian culture, but hard to account for artisanal and peasant themes in that culture. To the extent, finally, that net migration was the primary source, we might expect the proletariat to be the locus not only of alienation but also of aliens, and to be correspondingly resistant to unification. The contrasting portraits of proletarian experience that come to us from, say, E. P. Thompson and Louis Chevalier may result in part from their having studied populations differing significantly in these regards or from their having implicitly assumed differing configurations of social mobility, natural increase, and net migration.

Third, the *composition* of each of the three major components matters as well. Zero net migration over a long period may result from no moves in either direction, from large but exactly equal flows of definitive in-migrants and definitive out-migrants, from numerous circular migrants who spend some time at the destination and then return to their points of origin, and from a number of other equalizing migration patterns. These are very different social situations and have very different implications for social control, proletarian culture, class conflict, and the recruitment of an industrial labor force.

Positive or negative net migration may likewise result from a wide variety of migratory patterns, each affecting life at the destination in different ways. The same observation holds for the subcomponents of social mobility: temporary or definitive moves into the proletariat. Clearly it holds for births and deaths as well. Consider the difference between (1) slight natural increase due to high fertility almost balanced by high mortality and (2) slight natural increase due to low fertility matched with even lower mortality. That is the difference between the death-ridden experience of the sixteenth century and the long life of the twentieth. If we want to understand the quality of proletarian experience, we have to make that distinction very clearly.

Components of growth matter, finally, because their relative magnitudes bear directly on two continuing debates in European history. The two debates overlap. The first concerns the source of labor supply in the industrial revolution, the second the reasons for Europe's rapid population growth in the eighteenth and nineteenth centuries.[17] The debate about labor supply echoes the differences between Smith and Marx; it pits explanations in which the expropriation of peasants and artisans figures prominently against explanations in which population growth is a relatively smooth, automatic response to new opportunities for employment.

The debate on population growth begins with the fact that over Europe as a whole, natural increase accelerated markedly during the eighteenth century and continued rapidly into the nineteenth. The debate pivots on the extent to which declines in mortality due to life-saving technical improvements in medicine, sanitation, or nutrition (as opposed to more general improvements in the standard of living, temporary increases in fertility, or other alternatives) explain the acceleration of natural increase.

In both debates, the changes in places of mortality and fertility in the growth of landless labor are questions of central importance. If, for example, the growth of the proletariat was due mainly to decreasing mortality attributable to an improving standard of living, both the expropriation theory of labor supply and the fertility-increase interpretation of population growth become less credible. To make such distinctions, we do not need the precise numbers. But we do need to consider the full set of components of growth.

It is a good thing we do not need the precise numbers. If we did, the task would be impossible in our lifetimes. Although the methods of archeology, paleobotany, and historical demography may one day converge on fine estimating procedures for the European population, at present we have only a crude sense of the grand totals.

What is more, we have no large-scale estimates of the proletarian population. We face one of those recurrent historiographical ironies: the ideas of "labor force" and "employment" are at once essential to keeping the sorts of statistics we need and contingent on the very process we hope to trace, proletarianization. In the absence of capitalized firms and extensive wage labor, no one bothers to do the requisite bookkeeping. Generally speaking, we cannot look to the statistical reports of national states before the full bloom of nineteenth-century proletarianization. For earlier periods, we must combine analysis of trends in small areas that historians have studied intensively, with indirect inferences from evidence concerning other processes that are somehow connected with proletarianization.

PRINCIPLES OF PROLETARIANIZATION

Before examining trends and making inferences, however, we had better get straight some definitions and principles. Let us seek definitions that are broad enough to permit solid comparisons across time and space, supple enough to capture matters of degree, and yet precise enough to call forth reliable measurement.

Whatever practical separation of proletarians from nonproletarians that we adopt, we must keep in mind that the process of proletarianization has two logically distinct components: (1) separation of workers from control of the means of production (*expropriation*, for short), and (2) increasing dependence of workers on the sale of their labor power (*wage work*, for short). To concretize these abstract components, we might imagine computing the following items for some specific population:

T: total hours per year spent in productive labor
L: hours per year spent in labor controlling the means of production
D: hours per year spent in dependent labor, defined as $T - L$
W: hours per year spent in labor for wages
e: level of expropriation, defined as D/T
w: wage dependence, defined as W/T
P: level of proletarianization, defined as $e \times w$
$\dot{P}$: rate of proletarianization, defined as $\dot{e} + \dot{w}$

Thus an increase in either the proportion of all work time spent in dependent labor or the proportion of all work time spent in labor for wages raises, by definition, the level of proletarianization. Since the degree of control over the means of production actually forms a continuum rather than a simple either/or, in a practical application we would no doubt have to weight D—hours per year in dependent labor—for the extent of control exerted by workers.

Although expropriation and wage work have a strong historical connection—that is, after all, one of this chapter's premises—in some important circumstances they moved in different directions. The enserfment of European peasants, for example, certainly reduced their control of the land they tilled; they spent increasing shares of their total labor time in dependent labor. But enserfment did not ordinarily increase their dependence on wages for survival. Instead, landlords commonly assigned households to subsistence plots and forced each household to deliver some combination of monetary dues, agricultural products, and labor services. Expropriation increased, but wage work may well have declined.

In recent times, mine and factory workers who were already fully dependent on wages have often confronted bosses who were seeking to weaken the workers' control of the pace or quality of production by subdividing tasks, imposing time discipline, or applying piece rates. In these cases, dependent labor increased as a share of all labor; expropriation occurred without an increase in wage work.

The opposite case also occurred, although it was surely rarer: In nineteenth-century Europe, for instance, landlords frequently liquidated their rights to forced labor of villagers in the landlords' fields in favor of cash payments which they then used to hire labor in those same fields. Such a shift increases wage work without decreasing the workers' control over the means of production.

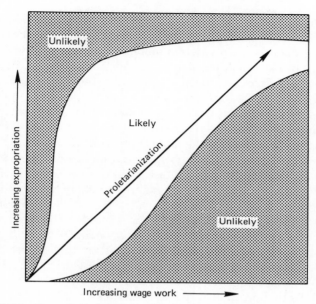

FIGURE 1.1   The components of proletarianization and their likely covariation.

In principle, then, the two components of proletarianization—expropriation and wage work—vary in partial independence from each other. The extent and pace of proletarianization are, by definition, results of the two. Figure 1.1 lays out the definition schematically and also sketches four rough hypotheses concerning the extent and character of the two components' covariation under capitalism:

1. In general, expropriation and wage work increase together.
2. However, considerable expropriation sometimes occurs without changes in wage work.
3. Except at low levels of proletarianization, wage work rarely increases (or, for that matter, decreases) without corresponding changes in expropriation.
4. At the extreme, nevertheless, it is less likely—even under capitalism—that workers will be completely dislodged from control over the means of production than that they will become entirely dependent on wages.

My reasoning is simple: employers do not value wage work for its own sake. They impose it as a means of accomplishing expropriation, but not vice versa. To the extent that they can seize control of labor power without paying wages, they do so. The major exception to the rule comes at low levels of proletarianization, at which landlords and capitalists sometimes prefer the payment of a money wage to the provision of subsistence in kind; English farmers who had live-in hands, for example, tended to expel them from bed and board when food became expensive.[18]

The reasoning continues: employers seek to minimize the price they pay for labor power, as the standard Marxist analysis says, in order to maximize their return from the labor applied to production.[19] But they expropriate all factors of production, including labor power, in order to control the deployment of those factors in the service of increased return. Extensive proletarianization is therefore likely to occur only when the payment of wages is a relatively attractive means of expropriating labor power—because the need for labor is highly variable, because neither custom nor force will suffice, or for some other reason. At the extreme, however, the requirements of production themselves set greater limits on expropriation than they do on wage work: the costs of subdividing and degrading complex tasks eventually become prohibitive, and the worker whose skill and discretion make a difference to the quantity and quality of the product always has some vestige of bargaining power.[20]

Note how this approach works. Note especially how it does *not* work. It does not equate impoverishment or immiseration with proletarianization. So far as the definition is concerned, the rise or fall of real income is irrelevant to the extent of proletarianization. Nor does wealth as such figure in the definition of the proletariat; to the extent that household wealth consists of nonproductive goods—television sets, automobiles, and so on—many households are wealthy but proletarian. Nor do style of life, education, skill, or locus of employment, in themselves, become criteria of proletarianization. There is no requirement of consciousness: In principle, an expropriated wage worker might well think of himself or herself as a full-time member of the bourgeoisie.

In this approach, the idea of a "new working class" consisting of skilled technicians, professionals, and researchers in science-sector industries is no contradiction in terms. The concept does not require that proletarians be factory workers or even be producing commodities. Not that income, wealth, life-style, education, skill, locus of employment, consciousness, or productive position are trivial matters; far from it. But the concepts adopted here make the relationships of these important aspects of social life to proletarianization into questions of fact rather than matters of definition.

The treatment of proletarianization as a result of expropriation and wage work neither assumes that the process continues indefinitely in one direction nor ties the proletariat, by definition, to capitalism. Both the continuity of the trend and the extent of its dependence on capitalism become questions for theory and for research. Worker-participation schemes, for example, do sometimes increase slightly the workers' control of production decisions and occasionally reduce the dependence of workers on wages.[21] To that small extent, they move the work force's average position toward the lower left-hand corner of our diagram; they deproletarianize. But one could reasonably argue, on the other hand, that socialist regimes such as that of the Soviet Union have adopted capitalists' methods with a vengeance, using the full power of the state to accelerate expropriation and extend wage work in the name of the workers; they have been great proletarianizers.

Proletarianization within ostensibly noncapitalist states has led many observers to conclude that proletarianization has no special tie to capitalism but results inevitably from any form of industrialization. In my view, however,

1. Over the past few centuries, the association between the development of capitalism and the growth of proletarianization has been strong enough to indicate that in general, one causes the other.
2. The association between capital concentration and proletarianization in agriculture as well as other forms of nonindustrial production makes dubious the idea that "industrialization" is proletarianization's necessary condition.
3. On the whole, capitalists acquire a greater interest in expropriation and wage work than do other sorts of powerholders.
4. When socialists push proletarianization, they do so in imitation of capitalists.

Fortunately for the pursuit of this chapter's purposes, only the first two propositions matter greatly to the search for the demographic origins of the European proletariat. During most of the European experience since 1500, capitalists have stood at the center of the proletarianizing process.

My approach, to be sure, rests on a guiding hypothesis: over the long run, expropriation and wage work were, and are, more fundamental than income, wealth, life-style, and so on.

More fundamental? I mean that changes in expropriation and in dependence on wages have wider ramifications in everyday social life than do changes in income, wealth, et cetera. I also mean that to an important degree, changes in expropriation and wage dependence *cause* changes in income, wealth, life-style, and so on. At this point we move out of the simple, arbitrary world of concepts. We begin working with arguments that are open to empirical challenge, and to theoretical scrutiny as well.

EXPLAINING PROLETARIANIZATION

Remember the crude expression for the rate of proletarianization $\dot{P}$:

$$\dot{P} = \dot{w} + \dot{e},$$

where $\dot{w}$ is the rate of change of wage dependence and $\dot{e}$ is the rate of change of expropriation. If the sum of the two rates is positive, the population is proletarianizing. If it is negative, the population is deproletarianizing. If it stands at or near zero, the population's structure is remaining about the same. My general argument is elementary, perhaps obvious: The rate of proletarianization is a direct function of changes in each of the following variables: (1) the demand for goods and services; (2) the cost of establishing new units; (3) the concentration of capital; and (4) the coercive power of employers. The *mechanisms* by which these variables affect the increase of expropriation and wage dependence are mainly matters of the number, size, and internal organization of the producing units: concentration or deconcentration of control over production decisions within producing units, growth or decline in the average size of producing units, elimination or consolidation of the producing units that already exist, limits on the creation of new producing units, and increases or decreases in the amount of labor drawn from the average worker.

The most obvious illustrations of these mechanisms at work come from periods and places in which a small number of producers were expanding their scale of production at the expense of their neighbors. In his old but still useful analysis of the growth of a rural proletariat in England, William Hasbach gave center stage to engrossing: the building up of large farms by a few active landlords. Here is his summary of the background conditions for engrossing:

> They were, first, the more luxurious standard of life adopted by the landlord class, and their consequent need of a larger income; secondly, the enclosures, for the most part results of that need; then the increased price of provisions, to which the enclosures contributed; next the system of the large farm, pioneered about this same period; and finally the new method of cultivation, which demanded men of a differnt class and larger capital. But besides these there were other forces at work. There was the attraction which the great industry, then just developing, exercised on capacity, enterprise and capital. And

there were the indirect taxes, imposed to pay the interest on the growing national debt rolled up by trade wars and colonial wars, which of course increased the cost of living.[22]

Under these conditions, according to Hasbach, those who had the power increased their holdings, invested and reinvested their capital, and shifted to labor-efficient farming techniques. In the process, they squeezed smallholders, tenants, and squatters off the land into agricultural or industrial wage labor.

In our terms, then, engrossing directly and strongly reduced the number of nonproletarian positions in rural areas: The size of producing units increased, their number declined, production decisions concentrated, existing units disappeared, and the possibility of creating new units decreased. Behind these changes lay all the general conditions for proletarianization we have already reviewed: rising demand for goods and services, increasing cost of establishing new units, concentration of capital, and growing coercive power of employers.

We begin with the obvious part: changes in the demand for goods and services directly affect the rate at which new producing units come into being and the rate at which existing units change scale. Changes in demand, however, likewise affect the rate of population growth, and thereby the rate of change in total labor supply. As a result, they have no necessary effects on the rate of proletarianization. Although economies of scale may well result from expanded demand, those economies have no reliable effects on the division of labor between proletarian and nonproletarian producers. All other things being equal, the system merely reproduces itself on a larger scale. In modern Europe, for example, household production proved itself enormously elastic in response to the demand for textiles, woodworking, metal crafting, and similar goods. Beyond some point of expansion, on the other hand, the cost of establishing new units often rises, since established producers squeeze the newcomers, the costs of materials and equipment rise, and/or the quality of available resources declines. The theorem of diminishing marginal returns in agriculture rests on just such an observation of the effects of bringing marginal land into cultivation.

From the perspective of proletarianization, however, the central process is the concentration of capital. When small producers become capitalists and when petty capitalists become big capitalists, they increase the share of all means of production they control, and expand the amount of labor power they buy from others. Enclosing landlords, manufacturers who drive artisanal competitors out of business, local authorities who restrict the number of available farms, peasants who take on additional hired hands, masters who expand the numbers of their journeymen or apprentices, and merchants who build up networks of dependent domestic producers all are agents of proletarianization.

Broadly speaking, anyone who has an interest in buying labor power also has an interest in proletarianization. Buying is by no means the only way to control labor; coercing, bartering, and using kinship ties or patron-client networks also make labor available under some circumstances. Buying becomes attractive when those who control the means of production require large amounts of labor and when that requirement is discontinuous—for example, when the demand for agricultural labor swings importantly from season to season. The transformation of workers into proletarians serves the employer in several different ways: by expanding the employer's power to redirect the factors of production in search of maximum return, by increasing the employer's ability to capture the existing returns from labor, by externalizing some of the costs of maintaining the work force, and by facilitating the employer's removal of unwanted labor power.

Each of these advantages to the employer, however, means disadvantages for other parties, especially the workers themselves. Workers have investments in their skills, and they therefore have the most to gain from allocations of production that differ from those that most favor the employer. Political authorities often have an interest in maintaining existing uses of land, labor, or commodities in order to ensure their revenues from taxation. Rentiers often have an interest in reliable rents from the very same land that capitalists want to commit to new uses. Workers have a direct interest in holding onto the returns from their labor. And the externalization of maintenance costs—supplying food, finding revenue in times of unemployment, caring for the ill, and so on—is likely to shift the burden to workers' households as well as to the community at large. Even if a giant neoclassical cost–benefit analysis gives the net advantage to proletarianization, therefore, the immediate interests of most of the parties directly involved dictate determined resistance. The employer's interest does not automatically prevail.

As North and Thomas (who have, in fact, conducted something like a giant neoclassical cost–benefit analysis of capitalist property relations) suggest, one of the most important conditions promoting the growth of wage labor is the emergence of a state that supports the consolidation of property into disposable bundles and guarantees the owner a major part of the return from that property's use.[23] I am not so sure as North and Thomas are that in the two leading examples, the Netherlands and England, the property-confirming state developed *before* capitalist property relations prevailed. Indeed, Macfarlane has argued that a version of capitalist property was already quite visible in thirteenth-century England.[24] Yet the Dutch and English states surely did favor the consolidation of property into disposable bundles.

More generally, any conditions that augment the coercive power of employers favor proletarianization; and coincidence of economic and political power in the same capitalist hands, the outlawing of workers' organizations, the monopolization of food or land by employers, and the presence of surplus labor all make it easier to expropriate workers. But with this last item—the presence of surplus labor—we pass to the other side of the dependent/independent labor ratio and enter an area of intense controversy.

The question is: How and why does the total work force increase? For practical purposes, we may concentrate on why the population as a whole increases. That simplification glides past several fascinating questions:

1. How does the changing age structure produced by alterations in fertility and mortality affect the proportion of the population in prime working ages?
2. Under what conditions do children and old people participate in productive labor?
3. What governs the extent of female labor force participation?
4. What part do household strategies play in the supply of different sorts of labor?
5. How do employers squeeze additional labor out of a given amount of labor power?[25]

However, the largest component by far of increase in the work force— and the only one on which we can hope to assemble information for Europe as a whole—is growth in the base population from which the work force comes. Let us think about that growth.

Many students of European history have treated population change as an essentially autonomous variable, a product of such "accidents" as plagues and crop failures. The rate of population growth figures as an exogenous variable—a very important one—in the North-Thomas account of European economic history. In his famous analysis of labor supply in the industrial revolution, J. D. Chambers proposed a general distinction between the period of slow growth before the mid-eighteenth century and the great acceleration thereafter. Chambers allowed for the possibility that after 1750 industrial employment encouraged earlier marriage, which in turn accelerated fertility. But on the whole his analysis treated the rate of population growth as a powerful external determinant of labor supply. As Christer Winberg points out, a similar argument has dominated historians' thinking about changes in the

Swedish labor force. Over Europe as a whole, most historians have been willing to consider population growth a crucial but exogenous variable in economic change.

Yet we have grounds for being skeptical: for doubting that the rate of population increase was independent of the pace of proletarianization. The most important ground for skepticism is the association, in region after region of Europe, of rapid accelerations in population growth with visible increases in landless labor; we shall review a number of cases later on.

Such an association could, of course, result from the application, over and over again, of the rule that population pressure produces proletarians. In fact, most such regions probably did begin their proletarianization with a stock of underemployed, cheap labor; that made them attractive to entrepreneurs. But once the process had begun, rates of marriage, childbearing, and migration all seem to have responded actively to employment opportunities. By that point, the growth of the work force was at least partly dependent on the tempo of its proletarianization.

I suggest, then, that four major variables governed the rate of increase in the total population:

1. changes in the demand for goods and services;
2. changes in the opportunity cost of childbearing;
3. previous proletarianization of the population, whose effect operated with a lag corresponding to the average age at which children began productive labor; and
4. an exogenous component combining the effects of "natural" fluctuations of fertility and mortality due to alterations in disease, nutrition, disaster, and other factors external to the system.

I suggest, further, that as proletarianization proceeded, the first three variables—the demand for goods and services, the opportunity cost of childbearing, and previous proletarianization—became increasingly dominant. Natural fluctuations declined in importance. The portmanteau "exogenous" component, to be sure, introduces a touch of magic into the analysis: Many irregularities will disappear into the portmanteau. The point of this formulation, however, is not to provide a comprehensive explanation of population growth but merely to indicate that with proletarianization, population growth responded increasingly to the economic situation of the proletarianized population.

Set down in tabular form and marked to indicate whether the general relationship is supposed to be positive (+), negative (−), or indeterminate (±), the variables I have proposed to explain the rate of proletarianization are shown in Table 1.1. Without specification of the effects

TABLE 1.1 Determinants of the Rate of Proletarianization

Determinants of increase in wage labor	Determinants of increase in potential work force
Demand for goods and services (+)	Demand for goods and services (+)
Cost of establishing new production units (+)	Opportunity cost of childbearing (−)
Concentration of capital (+)	Existing level of proletarianization (+)
Coercive power of employers (+)	Natural fluctuations (±)

of changing demand for goods and services, we have no reason to think that the growth or decline of demand will, in itself, affect the population's proletarianization; effects on the two sides are likely to cancel each other. But the lists say that everything else being equal, the following conditions will promote proletarianization:

1. increases in the cost of establishing new producing units;
2. concentration of capital;
3. increases in the coercive power of employers;
4. declines in the opportunity cost of childbearing, and
5. previous proletarianization.

As a model of the actual process, this is very crude. As a guide to searching through the historical experience of proletarianization, however, it will serve us well. We look for times and places in which capitalists are consolidating their power over production and in which the alternatives open to the local population are diminishing. That is, I think, a credible general description of the most common circumstances of proletarianization in Europe.

WHERE AND WHEN?

Concretely, where and when did these general conditions for proletarianization converge in modern Europe? Did they, in fact, reliably produce increases in expropriation and wage work? Despite innumerable fragments of the necessary evidence, we do not know. As a way of sorting out the evidence, we might try distinguishing some very different social settings:

Estate systems (example: East Prussia), in which large landlords produced grain for the market by means of servile labor, whose subsistence came mainly from small plots assigned to their households. The consolidation of landlord control ordinarily occurred at the expense of peasants who had been more or less independent producers; in those same areas, the nineteenth-century emancipation of servile laborers produced a temporary movement away from the proletariat, but the unfavorable conditions for access to the land pushed more and more of the freedmen into wage labor.[26]

Large-farm systems (example: East Anglia), in which large landlords or their tenants likewise produced grain for the market, but with wage labor. They grew variously from estate systems, from specialized farming, and from peasant farming. They expanded by adding more wage laborers. In most cases, however, small independent producers disappeared as the large farms grew.[27]

Specialized farming (example: coastal Flanders), in which peasants specialized in cash-crop production and nonproducing landlords were unimportant. It did not necessarily promote proletarianization. In the case of grain production, for instance, independent family units actually took up a larger share of the world market during the nineteenth and twentieth centuries.[28] Elsewhere, however, some specialists commonly expanded their holdings, accumulated capital, and hired their own wage laborers (e.g., the northern Netherlands).[29] In those cases, specialization also proletarianized the population.

Peasant farming (example: western France), in which landlords lived from rents and peasants lived from various combinations of owned, rented, and sharecropped land. Peasant farming, as such, tended to block proletarianization as long as it lasted. But peasant farming sometimes turned into specialized farming, as peasants took up more and more cash-crop production, sometimes gave way to large-farm or estate agriculture as landlords seized their advantage, sometimes succumbed to the increasing subdivision of inheritances which eventually became too small to support households, and sometimes—when the available labor was underemployed and markets for industrial products were more accessible than were markets for cash crops—hosted proletarianizing cottage industry.

Cottage industry (example: Lancashire), in which petty entrepreneurs parceled out industrial production among households that also devoted some of their labor to small-scale subsistence farming and/or seasonal wage labor in agriculture. Cottage industry always grew up on an agricultural base. It began as a complement to some sort of farming and as an alternative to less attractive and remunerative forms of labor, such as military and domestic service. But when cottage industry flourished, it tended to squeeze out other activities and to become an aggressive proletarianizer.[30]

Urban craft production (example: north Italian cities), in which masters of small shops controlled the labor of journeymen and apprentices lodged in their masters' households. Like peasant farming, urban craft production tended to resist proletarianization so long as it retained its pure form. But masters sometimes used the structure of the craft to expand the numbers of journeymen and, especially, apprentices under their control. When the masters succeeded, they helped create a proletarian large-shop and factory system.[31]

Large-shop and factory production (example: the Rhineland after 1850), in which capitalists assembled and coordinated the labor of many wage workers in the same place. This system has the reputation of being the great proletarianizer. In our time, it is no doubt the setting in which the work force has come closest to being entirely expropriated and completely dependent on wages. Yet several features of large shop/factory production qualify its claims to being the primary site of European proletarianization. First is its tardiness: Prior to the twentieth century, large shops and factories were relatively rare; before then, most industrial expansion occurred through the proliferation of small shops and even of household production. Second, in skilled trades the earlier grouping of workers in large shops often involved little change in the technology of production and in the relationship of the worker to the means of production, although it did eventually facilitate the owner's imposition of timing and work discipline. Third, in many industries the large-shop and factory work force came largely from workers who were already involved in household or small-shop production within the same industry. All three of these features mitigate the historical impact of large shops and factories as the settings of European proletarianization. Nonetheless, when large shops and factories did grow fast, they had unparalleled power to proletarianize. Only mining (which came to share many organizational features with factory production) rivaled them.

The categories are neither tight nor exhaustive. On the one hand, the types overlap, and on the other, they leave out such important configurations as the smallholding cash-crop production that commonly appeared in Europe's winegrowing areas. Still, the typology suggests the sort of variation that any systematic analysis of proletarianization must take into account and identifies the chief settings in which European proletarianization actually did take place.

Given the general conditions for proletarianization enumerated earlier—increases in the cost of establishing new producing units, concentration of capital, increases in the coercive power of employers, declines in the opportunity cost of childbearing, and previous proletarianization—some of these settings stand out as prime candidates. The very creation of estate systems, large-farm systems, cottage industry, and large shop/factory production entailed the creation or recruitment of local proletariats. Specialized farming, peasant farming, and urban craft production, in contrast, did not necessarily proletarianize. Which of the first four were the dominant settings for proletarianization changed over time. The two agricultural settings were probably the dominant sites of European proletarianization before the eighteenth century; cottage industry became increasingly important after 1700; and large shop/factory production did not play the major role before the end of the nineteenth century.

In considering these alternative modes of production, let us flee from technological determinism. The seven settings did not differ in importance as precipitators of proletarianization because expropriated wage labor was technically essential to some of them and technically incompatible with others. The settings differed because of their varying association with the proletarianizing conditions we enumerated earlier: increasing costs of new productive units, concentration of capital, growing employer coercive power, declines in the opportunity cost of child-bearing, and previous proletarianization. The expansion of cottage industry, for example, favored proletarianization, not because of any intrinsic affinity between expropriated wage labor and weaving or woodworking, but because (1) the concentration of capital in the hands of entrepreneurs and the domination of access to markets by those same entrepreneurs radically narrowed workers' room for maneuver, and (2) the opportunity cost of childbearing sank so dramatically—since young children could make significant contributions to household income, and older children became less expensive to "place" in adult positions—as to favor the production of more and more new proletarians. Ultimately, then, the search for general explanations of European proletarianization should concentrate less on such matters as the demand for textiles or wheat than on the conditions favoring the reorganization of relations of production. Perhaps we can gain insight into those conditions by breaking with the abstract, deductive approach to the problem that I have followed so far. Let us ask when, where, and in what quantities European proletarianization actually occurred.

HOW MANY PROLETARIANS?

Considering how much discussion has gone into the subject, we have amazingly little knowledge of the timing and loci of European proletarianization. For Britain, John Saville has ventured this general sketch:

(1) the development of commercial farming during mediaeval times and the existence, by the beginning of the sixteenth century, of a class of capitalist farmers;

(2) the slow disappearance of the peasantry as a substantial element in rural society over the three centuries from 1500 to 1800 . . . ,

(3) the presence in the countryside, from the sixteenth century onwards . . . of a class of landless labourers; their swelling numbers in the eighteenth century, in part the result of the further decline of the peasant class, in part the product of natural population growth;

(4) the growth of the large farm . . . ,

(5) the growing concentration of land in the ownership of the landlord class from the middle of the seventeenth century onwards . . . ,

(6) accompanying the social changes in the agrarian structure went the technical transformation of farming methods.[32]

Saville's lucid distillation of a murky literature suggests that the timing of the major agrarian changes—hence the growth of an agricultural proletariat—is well known. It is not. Think, for example, about one of the easiest numbers to establish: the proportion of landless laborers in Britain's agricultural population. Table 1.2 presents commonly cited sources for estimates of the share of landless labor in the agricultural population as a whole at various times from about 1600 to 1851.

A glance at the table identifies two major difficulties: First, the numbers oscillate implausibly from one period to the next; second, the categories and base populations fluctuate almost as wildly. A comparison of Gregory King's high figure for 1688 with the Census of 1831 permitted J. H. Clapham to make his notorious "demonstration" that the scale of agricultural production had risen only modestly over the period of the enclosures and to conclude that enclosures could not have played a major part in the creation of the agricultural proletariat.

One reason that Massie's figures record an apparent drop in the proletarian share of the agricultural population between 1688 and 1760 is simply that in 1688 King saw no need to distinguish rural industrial workers from the rest of the laborers, whereas in 1760 Massie enumerated 100,000 families who were "Manufacturers of Wood, Iron, etc.," likewise in the country. Their inclusion in agricultural labor would bring Massie's proportion up to 66%: exactly the same as King's. But that correction would be risky; after all, the differences between Massie's estimates and King's could have registered a genuine increase in rural industry.

Again, Massie mentioned no "vagrants" in 1760; he was estimating the likely return from taxes on chocolate, and vagrants mattered little for that purpose. Gregory King, on the other hand, listed 30,000 vagrants for 1688, and Patrick Colquhoun counted a full 234,000 of them in 1803. Many "vagrants" were indubitably unemployed agricultural

TABLE 1.2 Estimates of the Percentage of the English, English & Welsh, British,
or British and Irish Agricultural Population Consisting of Laborers

Date	Percentage	Reference agricultural population	Author of estimate	Citation
c. 1600	25–33	Entire rural popula- tion, England and Wales	Alan Everitt	Everitt, 1967: 398
1688	66	English families[a]	Gregory King	Mathias, 1957: 45
1760	59	Families, England and Wales[b]	Joseph Massie	Mathias, 1957: 45
1803	62	Families, England and Wales[c]	Patrick Colquhoun	Colquhoun, 1806: 23
1812	49	Males in agriculture, Great Britain and Ireland	Patrick Colquhoun	Colquhoun, 1815: 124–125
1831	76	Males 20 and over in agriculture, Great Britain	1831 Census	Abstract: xiii
1841	76	All persons classified	1841 Census	Spackman, 1847: 143
1851	80	All persons classified[d]	1851 Census	Census, 1851: 148
1851	79	Total in agriculture[e]	1851 Census	Bellerby, 1958: 3
1911	64	Total in agriculture[e]	1911 Census	Bellerby, 1958: 3
1931	59	Total in agriculture[e]	1931 Census	Bellerby, 1958: 3
1951	54	Total in agriculture[e]	1951 Census	Bellerby, 1958: 3

[a] Includes nobility, gentry, freeholders, farmers, laboring people, outservants, cottagers, and paupers. I have taken "labouring people, outservants, cottagers and paupers" as laborers. From the total for those categories I have subtracted my best estimate of the proportion of the total population of England and Wales in places of 20,000 or more—11.0% in 1688—to allow for the urban location of that share of general laborers.

[b] Reference population includes nobility, gentry, freeholders, farmers, husbandmen, and laborers. In this case, I have counted all "husbandmen and labourers" as agricultural laborers.

[c] Reference population includes nobility, gentry, freeholders, farmers, laborers in husbandry, pauper laborers, and pensioners who work. Here "labourers in husbandry, pauper labourers, and pensioners who work" count as agricultural laborers. I have, however, subtracted my best estimate of the proportion of the total population of England and Wales in places of 20,000 or more—17.4% in 1803—from the total for pauper laborers and pensioners, to allow for the urban location of that share of general laborers.

[d] Excluding persons listed as wives, children, and relatives of farmers and graziers.

[e] Excluding "relatives occupied on the farm."

laborers on the road. Should they, too, be included in the agricultural proletariat? Judgments on such matters depend on knowledge of the very trends and processes one might have hoped to derive from the comparison of Everitt, King, Massie, and Colquhoun.

We can, I fear, draw no more than a few tentative, meager conclusions from the series:

1. During most of the seventeenth and eighteenth centuries a large

share—most likely a majority—of Britain's agricultural labor force consisted of landless laborers.

2. Since the population of England and Wales may well have risen from 4 to 5 million people during the seventeenth century and from 5 to 9 million during the eighteenth, even a relatively constant proportion of proletarians implies a substantial increase in their absolute number.

3. During the early nineteenth century, both the absolute number and the proportion of agricultural laborers grew considerably.

4. After the middle of the nineteenth century, laborers left British agriculture so rapidly that the total agricultural labor force contracted, and the share of farmers rose significantly.

As Deane and Cole put this last point:

> Apart from a fall of about 8 1/2 per cent in the 1870's, and a rise of about 13 per cent between 1911 and 1921, the number of British farmers has shown remarkably little tendency to vary. Farmers (excluding relatives) thus accounted for about 15 per cent of the occupied population in agriculture in 1851, about 20 per cent in 1911 and about 27 per cent in 1951.[33]

Thus the century after 1851 witnessed a deproletarianization of British agriculture, at a time when the industrial labor force was proletarianizing rapidly. But when and how the earlier proletarianization of agriculture occurred does not leap out at us from the available national figures.

To locate any figures on proletarianization at a regional or national scale, we must cross over to the Continent. In his survey of changes in agrarian class structure at a number of locations across the continent, Slicher van Bath offers multiple examples of the disproportionate growth of smallholders, cottars, and laborers. (Slicher himself, I hasten to add, interprets the changes as illustrating "the influence that a rise in population had on the distribution of the various groups in rural society."[34]) In the Dutch province of Overijssel, he reports the pattern of increase among heads of household shown in Table 1.3. Two things were happening in Overijssel: First, a great expansion of cottage textile production was swelling the number of weavers and spinners in the countryside. Second, the agricultural population itself was proletarianizing. The net effect of the two was a substantial proletarianization of Overijssel's population in the seventeenth and, especially, the eighteenth century.

We have already noticed the changes in Sweden's rural population— a full nine-tenths of the total population—between 1750 and 1850. There, the rural proletariat grew more than 30 times as fast as the peasantry did. (One consequence of that expansion was an overall decline in real wages for Swedish agricultural workers over the century after 1750.[35])

TABLE 1.3   Growth Rates of Various Overijssel Populations, 1601–1795[a]

Category	Base period	Annual rate of growth
Total population	1675–1795	0.7
Nonagricultural population	1675–1795	0.9
Agricultural population	1602–1795	0.3
Farmers on family-sized farms	1602–1795	0.1
Cottars on small holdings	1601–1795	0.2
Cottars and day laborers	1602–1795	0.4

[a] Computed from Slicher van Bath, 1977:130.

From about 30% of the rural population in 1750, the proletariat grew to about 60% in 1850. If we were to extrapolate that sort of change to the European scale, it would imply an increase from about 35 million rural proletarians in 1750 to about 90 million in 1850; the increase rate for the whole continent would be lower than that for Sweden, because in Europe as a whole the rural population only increased by about a third, whereas in Sweden it doubled. Still, an increase of 55 million rural proletarians would represent the great majority of the continent's total population increase (which was on the order of 85 million people) between 1750 and 1850.

Now, Sweden is most likely an extreme case because of its large rural population, its relative lack of rural manufacturing, and its fairly late industrialization. However, a similar computation based on one of Europe's old industrial areas, the Kingdom of Saxony, produces an estimate in the same general range: about 51 million of the total 85 million increase in population consisting of expansion in the continent's rural proletariat.[36]

Let us look more closely at Saxony, since it is the only large area of Europe for which we have reliable estimates of the proletarian population running back to the sixteenth century. For the years 1550, 1750, and 1843, Karlheinz Blaschke provides us with counts of the following categories of the Saxon population:

Urban	Rural
Bürger (full citizens)	Bauern (peasants)
Inwohner in Städten (dependent urban workers)	Gärtner and Häusler (gardeners, cottars)
Geistlichkeit (professionals, intellectuals, etc.)	Inwohner in Dörfern (village labor)
	Grundherren (noble landlords)

The classification into "urban" and "rural" is my own, but aside from the rural residence of a few parsons and professionals (*Geistlichkeit*) and the urban residence of a few noble landlords (*Grundherren*), it looks like a fairly accurate division. On the urban side, the *Inwohner*, or in-dwellers, were essentially proletarians: servants, journeymen, apprentices, and others. On the rural side, the *Gärtner* and *Häusler* (gardeners and cottars) join the *Inwohner* in the proletarian category. *Gärtner* had their own garden plots, *Häusler* nothing but their dwellings. *Gärtner* is sometimes also translated as "smallholder"—but in either translation designates a worker who had to sell a substantial part of his labor power to survive. Table 1.4 gives Blaschke's counts of the numbers of workers in each of these categories from 1550 to 1843.

Blaschke's figures tell an important story. Throughout the three centuries after 1550, according to this classification, the Saxon countryside was more proletarian than the cities were; even in 1550, gardeners, cottars, and village labor made up 25.6% of the rural work force, and dependent workers comprised 15.5% of the urban total. Within both the urban and the rural sectors, the proletarian share rose dramatically. Both from 1550 to 1750 and from 1750 to 1843, gardeners and cottars—the all-

TABLE 1.4   Distribution of the Workforce of Saxony in 1550, 1750, and 1843, According to Blaschke[a]

Category	Year		
	1550[b]	1750	1843
Urban			
Full citizens	82.0	54.0	47.5
Dependent workers	15.5	44.8	51.7
Professionals, etc.	2.5	1.2	0.7
	100.0	100.0	99.9
Number	141,500	370,500	631,000
Rural			
Peasants	73.5	38.6	20.4
Gardeners, cottars	6.8	47.9	70.9
Village labor	18.8	12.7	8.2
Noble landlords	0.8	0.8	0.5
	99.9	100.0	100.0
Number	292,400	647,500	1,225,000

[a] Source: Blaschke, 1967:190–191.
[b] The 1550 figures omit the region of Oberlausitz.

TABLE 1.5 Growth Rates of Various Saxon Populations, 1550–1843

Category	1550–1750	1750–1843
Full citizens	0.2	0.4
Dependent urban workers	1.0	0.7
Professionals, etc.	0.1	0.0
Peasants	0.1	0.0
Gardeners, cottars	1.4	1.1
Village labor	0.2	0.2
Noble landlords	0.4	0.1
Total	0.4	0.6

purpose wage workers of the countryside—grew the fastest. Translated into annual rates of increase, the comparison is shown in Table 1.5. The numbers of professionals and peasants hardly increased over three centuries, a fact that probably reflects the implicit fixing of quotas for each of them. Full-fledged burghers, regular village labor, and landlords did not increase much faster. The dynamic categories were the proletarian ones. In terms of rates alone, those categories grew faster before 1750 than after. The fact that they made up an increasing share of the total, however, meant that their impact on total growth expanded later; as a result, the overall rate of growth in the work force accelerated after 1750: 0.6% per year from 1750 to 1843, as opposed to 0.4% from 1550 to 1750.

We are not staring at the ripples of a backwater. The Kingdom of Saxony contained such major industrial centers as Leipzig and Dresden. With 46% of its labor force in manufacturing by 1849 and 53% in manufacturing by 1861, the Kingdom of Saxony moved at the leading edge of German industrialization.[37] The kingdom's "potential labor force" (the population 15 and over, less housewives, dependent daughters, students, invalids, and certain other categories) grew by an average of 1.5% per year between 1822 and 1849 and by 1.2% per year between 1849 and 1864; those rates were higher than those elsewhere in Germany.[38] The kingdom was the only major region of Germany gaining from migration more or less continuously from 1817 to 1865.[39] In fact, Wolfgang Köllmann offers the Kingdom of Saxony as a principal example of the overrunning of employment opportunities by population growth—in his view, the crucial process that depressed wages in the old crafts, drove workers out of those old crafts, and provided a labor force for expanding large-scale industry. We do not have to accept Kollmann's whole analysis of proletarianization to recognize Saxony as a good base for the analysis of European proletarianization as a whole.

Table 1.6 shows the results of imagining that the entire European pop-

TABLE 1.6   Estimates of the European Proletarian Population in 1550, 1750, and 1843, Based on Blaschke's figures for Saxony[a]

Year and category	Total population	Proletarian population	Nonproletarians	Percentage proletarian
1550				
Rural	61,175	15,661	45,514	25.6
Urban	10,325	1,600	8,725	15.5
	71,500	17,261	54,239	24.3
1750				
Rural	113,100	68,539	44,561	60.6
Urban	18,150	8,131	10,019	44.8
	131,250	76,670	54,580	58.4
1843				
Rural	146,453	115,844	30,609	79.1
Urban	63,194	32,671	30,523	51.7
	209,647	148,515	61,132	70.8

[a] In thousands. I have changed Bairoch's estimate of total population for 1500 (85 million), which is implausibly high, to a more conventional 56 million. The adjustment diminishes the estimate of the proletarian population in 1550 from 24.5 to 24.3%. Sources: Blaschke, 1967:190–191; Bairoch 1977: 42.

ulation (except for Russia) behaved like Saxony. The procedure is simple: Adopt Paul Bairoch's estimates of rural and urban population, interpolate values for 1550, 1750, and 1843, and then apply the percentages of proletarians that Blaschke finds in Saxony's rural and urban sectors to the whole European population. Although this approach multiplies suppositions by approximations, it suggests orders of magnitude for the growth of the European proletariat.

If Europe behaved like Saxony, both rural and urban proletarianization were massive. The totals show the proletarian population increasing more than eightfold, whereas the nonproletarian population increased by a mere 13% and the population as a whole rose from 71 million to 210 million people. The estimated absolute increase in the proletarian population from 1550 to 1843 was 131 million, nearly equivalent to the total increase in Europe's population; the computations suggest that the nonproletarian population hardly increased at all. Of the 131 million increase, furthermore, the estimates show 100 million as occurring within the rural sector, only 31 million in the cities. That was especially true for the period before 1750, when only a small share of Europe's proletarianization *could* have occurred in the cities. After 1750 (and, in fact, especially after 1800) the balance shifted toward urban proletarianization: in short, a massive proletarianization of the population, occurring first and foremost in the countryside.

No one region can sum up the experience of the whole continent. Yet, in the absence of other series as ample in space and time, we have no reason to shrug off the experience of the region of Leipzig, Chemnitz, and Dresden as an inappropriate model for Europe. The orders of magnitude are likely to be correct, and if so, we can reasonably adopt three working hypotheses: (1) that the increase in Europe's proletarian population was on the order of its *total* population increase; the nonproletarian population barely increased; (2) that over the sixteenth to the mid-nineteenth centuries, most of Europe's proletarianization took place in village and country; and (3) that with the nineteenth century, cities became increasingly important as the sites of proletarianization. These hypotheses call for careful verification.

Given a broad definition of the proletariat, the second and third hypotheses become more plausible as we examine the temporal pattern of Europe's urbanization. Figure 1.2 graphs Bairoch's estimates of changes since 1500 in the European population by size of place. It reminds us that the great majority of the population lived in rural areas until quite recently. More important, it shows that Europe did not urbanize significantly between 1500 and 1800. Indeed (if you accept my reduction of Europe's total population in 1500 from 85 million to a more plausible 56 million), the estimates suggest that Europe as a whole *de*-urbanized slightly over those three centuries. Here are the percentages: 1500, 16.1%; 1700, 13.0%; 1800, 14.4%; 1900, 41.3%; 1970, 62.4%. Only after 1800, according to these figures, did the frenzied urbanization with which we are familiar begin.

In absolute terms, the rural population never actually declined. But by the middle of the nineteenth century, with about 150 million people, it had come close to its limit. From that point on, almost the whole of the European population increase occurred in urban areas.

The site of proletarianization shifted as the locus of the population growth changed. Blaschke's figures simply show that shift to have occurred a bit earlier in relatively industrial Saxony than in Europe as a whole. My grafting of Blaschke's figures onto Bairoch's estimates for urban and rural population adjusts for the difference in timing. But both sets of figures indicate that the nineteenth century swung the active loci of European proletarianization toward the cities.

If we start our inquiry at 1500, we will be dealing with a total of about 56 million people. If we end it in 1900, we will arrive at a total of around 285 million people. That is an increase of some 230 million people in the four centuries. At the beginning (to extrapolate from the estimates we

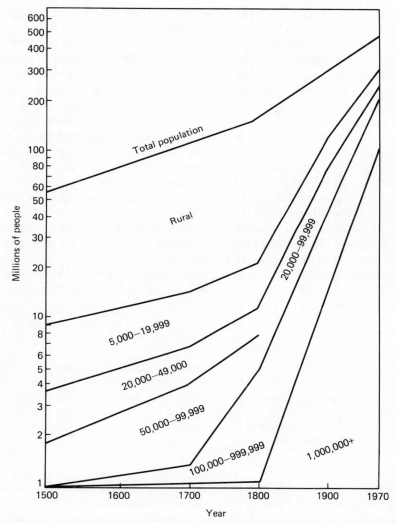

FIGURE 1.2   Bairoch's estimates of the European population by size of place, 1500–1970.
Excludes Russia and Turkey. Source: Bairoch, 1977:42.

have squeezed from the combination of Blaschke with Bairoch), perhaps
17 million of the 56 million total were proletarians of one kind or another. By 1900, on the order of 200 million out of the 285 million total
were proletarians. That gives us an increase of around 180 million proletarians to account for, and it also gives us a smaller increase—perhaps

45 million—of nonproletarians to explain. If those are the numbers, then we must ask when, where, and how the increase occurred.

The timing of population growth sets important limits on the possible timetable of proletarianization. Since the population of Europe (not including Russia and Turkey) rose from about 150 million to 285 million during the nineteenth century, a large part of the net increase in the proletariat must also have occurred in the nineteenth century. Nevertheless, given the significant eighteenth-century expansion of wage labor in such widely scattered areas as England, Poland, and Spain, it is quite possible that by 1800 something like 100 million Europeans were already proletarian workers and members of their households. Notice again the implications of Bairoch's estimates for 1800: Only 20 million or so Europeans then lived in urban areas. At least three-quarters of the proletariat must have lived in small towns, villages, and open countryside. In tracing the proletarianization of Europe before 1800, we have to give priority to farms and villages, but from the nineteenth century onward, cities start occupying our attention.

Let me sum up these speculations and approximations. We are thinking of components of growth within a population that broke down something like this (in millions):

	1500	1800	1900
Total population	56	150	285
Nonproletarians	39	50	85
Proletarians in cities	1	10	75
Rural proletarians	16	90	125

To avoid any misunderstanding, let me repeat: These numbers are no more than thoughtful guesses, orders of magnitude, and hypotheses to verify. Their revision stands high on the agenda of historical demography. If they hold up to further investigation, the numbers will have important implications. They suggest a 75-fold increase in the proletarian population of European cities from 1500 to 1900, an eightfold increase of the rural proletariat during the same period. They concentrate the great bulk of European proletarianization in rural areas before 1800 and in cities after then. With these orders of magnitude in mind, let us return to the components of growth: social mobility, natural increase, and net migration.

SOCIAL MOBILITY

Speaking of the sixteenth- and seventeenth-century Netherlands, Jan de Vries distinguishes between two models of rural social organization: a peasant model and a specialization model. Peasants produce enough to survive at a conventional level of well-being and to meet their basic outside obligations. They work to insulate themselves from the market's volatility while avoiding as much as possible purchases of goods and services. They seek, in general, to maintain all their offspring on the land. With natural increase, that strategy produces a subdivision of holdings and intensified cultivation of the available land. The result is that per-capita income almost never rises; it remains constant or declines.

Specialists, on the other hand, exploit the market by concentrating on profitable crops. They specialize in agricultural production and purchase those goods and services they cannot produce profitably. They accumulate capital and reinvest it in land and equipment. Such children as they cannot profitably employ on the land they place in other forms of enterprise. Over the long run, their per-capita income tends to rise. Specialists are capitalists, peasants are noncapitalists. In fact, the peasants are often anticapitalists.

The two models identify two quite different exits from the peasantry. The peasant path leads eventually to wage labor in agriculture or industry. The specialization path leads to cash-crop farming. The peasant strategy proletarianizes, whereas the specialization strategy—if successful—capitalizes. The peasant strategy leads to wage labor for two reasons: first, because its internal logic results sooner or later in the overrunning of the household's capacity to support itself from the land it controls and, second, because in the meantime capitalists are expanding *their* control over the land and over other means of production. English enclosures and Polish "refeudalization" are variants of that second pattern.

Whether the new proletarians remained in agricultural wage labor, moved into manufacturing, or took up some combination of the two varied significantly as a function of the local labor requirements of agriculture and the market for local manufactures. In the Swiss mountain areas studied by Rudolf Braun, cottage textile manufacturing oriented toward Zurich displaced the subsistence agriculture of the highlands. In the Leicestershire agricultural villages studied by David Levine, cottage industry provided the context for proletarianization where the landlord tolerated it, but dairy farming produced a later, slower, and more subtle form of proletarianization where the landlord would not tolerate manufacturing. In the Flanders studied by Franklin Mendels, the proletarianizing populations of the coast moved into agricultural wage labor, whereas those of the interior moved into a mixture of agriculture and textile industry and shifted their weight from one to the other as a function of the available wage.

This last example serves as a reminder that the specialists' strategy also fostered a certain amount of proletarianization. Although those who succeeded in specializing became petty capitalists, those who failed moved into the proletariat. Moreover, the more successful cash-crop farmers became employers of wage laborers from among their skidding neighbors and from nearby regions of mixed agriculture and industry. Mendels has pointed out, in fact, that small-scale industrial production tended to expand especially in regions having nearby sources of part-time and seasonal agricultural employment, which reduced the industrial employer's minimum maintenance costs for labor. The interdependence of Flanders's coastal cash-crop areas and internal cottage-industry areas illustrates the point very well.[40]

Parallel paths to those of peasants and specialists led away from the world of artisans. Artisans slipped into the proletariat as cheaper production processes reduced the demand for their wares and as entrepreneurs assumed control over the means of production. But a few artisans climbed into the bourgeoisie by becoming successful entrepreneurs. Herbert Kisch gives us the contrast between Silesia and the Rhineland.[41] In both places the growth of rural textile production undercut the urban craft guilds. But in Silesia the process was one of almost pure proletarianization: A small number of chartered merchants worked with large landlords who were happy to have the weaver serfs contributing to the incomes of their estates. In the Rhineland, proletarianization was likewise the main trend, but a few master craftsmen in Cologne, Barmen, Aachen, and elsewhere accumulated capital and made themselves pivotal figures in textile production. Although Kisch does not give us the details of labor force recruitment, lifetime movement from artisan to proletarian must have been a common experience in both regions. In neither case, however, is it likely that social mobility was the main component of the proletariat's growth. Natural increase and migration must have been important in both Silesia and the Rhineland.

NATURAL INCREASE

Natural increase or decrease is the net effect of births and deaths. The proletariat grows through natural increase when in any given period, more proletarians are born than die. Perhaps we should distinguish between the proletarian children of nonproletarian parents and the proletarian children of proletarians. In the first case we stand midway between social mobility and natural increase: if at a given succession a peasant holding fragments into pieces too small to support the heirs, we may debate how much of that family's move into the proletariat is due to natural increase. The same is true of the "extra" child of a peasant family who spends his or her life as a servant or day laborer. Yet at least some of the resulting expansion of the proletariat is attributable to natural increase.

The least ambiguous and most important case is somehow the most ignored. It is the natural increase of full-fledged proletarians. If, on the average, the natural increase of wage laborers were greater than that of peasants and artisans, that fact alone would suffice to produce a relative growth of the proletariat without any skidding of peasants or artisans and without any in-migration of proletarians. I suggest that differential natural increase was the principal component in the relative growth of the European proletariat from 1500 to 1900. More precisely, I suggest that the principal component was a natural increase resulting from the difference between fairly high mortality and very high fertility.

To be even more exact (and at the risk of being ponderous), I propose the following hypothesis: on the average, proletarians responded to economic expansion with greater declines in mortality and greater increases in fertility than nonproletarians did and responded to economic contraction with greater increases in mortality but no greater declines in fertility than nonproletarians did. The consequence was a disproportionate natural increase of proletarians in good times, not completely compensated by the natural decrease of bad times. Since the period we are considering was on the whole an era of economic expansion, such a system would have produced a significant tendency for the proletariat to increase more rapidly than the rest of the population. My hypothesis is that it did.

In its main lines, the hypothesis generalizes to the entire proletarian population the model of demographic change that Mendels developed to deal with the "proto-industrialization" of Flanders and elsewhere.[42] The hypothesis does not mean that proletarians always had higher fertility than nonproletarians did. We have already seen that the opposite was true among the Swedish villagers studied by Winberg and can find similar evidence elsewhere. The hypothesis does mean that the demographic responses of proletarians and nonproletarians to economic expansion and contraction differed significantly. To put it schematically, nonproletarians responded to changing opportunities for the placement of their household capital, whereas proletarians responded to changing opportunities for wage labor.

In one muted form or another, the hypothesis has been around a long time. In his pioneering study of the Vale of Trent, Chambers noted the higher natural increase of parishes with rural industry between 1670 and 1800. Although they lack crucial evidence concerning the components of growth, Blaschke's analysis of Saxony, Klíma's discussion of Bohemia, and Braun's portrayal of the Zurich highlands all bring out a similar contrast between the slow-growing regions of peasant agriculture and the fast-growing regions of rural industry.[43] In his direct attack on the problem, Levine identifies a relationship between the rising natural increase and rural industrial growth in eighteenth-century Shepshed and between the rising natural increase and agricultural proletarianization in nineteenth-century Bottesford. Levine also provides a plausible interpretation of the demographic ups and downs of the famous village of Colyton, Devon, as a consequence of the rise and fall of rural industry.[44]

Following the same line of inquiry, Wrightson and Levine trace the population growth of Terling, Essex, to the proletarianizing effects of a large-farm system.[45] Kussmaul has made a good case for a sequence in which English farmers expelled live-in servants during periods of rising food prices; servants became day laborers; day laborers married younger and in greater numbers; and fertility rose.[46] Elsewhere, and with very fine evidence, Gaunt has argued for a similar tuning of natural increase to opportunity among Swedish rural proletarians.[47]

If such a relationship holds, it reverses conventional wisdom. We commonly think of rural proletarianization as a *consequence* of rapid population growth—too many people for the available land. But the possibility we see here is that proletarianization may induce rapid population growth. Of course, both may be true. Then a process of proletarianization initiated by some such action as enclosure will tend to perpetuate itself up—or, rather, down—to the limit set by starvation. At the limit and in this special case, Malthusian models begin to work fairly well. (Even in the case of widespread famine, however, the usual circumstance is not usually an absolute shortfall in available food per capita, but a maldistribution due to the lack of fit between needs and entitlements.)[48]

How and why would the natural increase of proletarians tend to exceed that of nonproletarians? The critical relationships link fertility, marriage, and the availability of employment. In a world in which most households control their own means of production, the chief opportunities for young adults are to inherit positions within their own households or to enter other households. In the world of European artisans and peasants, the capital of a household set stringent limits on the number of persons it could sustain; household capital thereby limited the number of children who could remain at home into adulthood, and especially into marriage and parenthood. The only way to enter another household as a full-fledged adult was to marry into it. Persons who entered as servants, apprentices, day laborers, and the like ordinarily acquired no control over the household means of production and no right to marry or to procreate. Opportunities to marry, to have children, and to place one's children in full-fledged adult positions thus depended on the rate at which senior positions in households were opening up. Mortality was the chief determinant of that rate. But sometimes out-migration or the putting of new land into cultivation also provided adult opportunities. To an important degree, the system regulated itself: Nuptiality and fertility adapted to changing opportunity, and total population remained fairly constant over the medium run.[49]

Under these circumstances, couples adjusted both their marriages and their childbearing to the probable availability of adult positions and to the probability that their newborn children would survive to adulthood. As a result, marriage and fertility surged after famine or pestilence wiped out many adults and slowed when mortality declined. Or so it seems. In the present state of our knowledge, any hypothesis implying widespread, deliberate fertility control before the nineteenth century and outside the Westernized industrial countries is controversial.[50]

The idea of deliberate fertility control of any great extent before the nineteenth century counters a set of ideas that demographers cherish:

1. that in general human populations have lived under a regime of "natural" fertility, without imposing deliberate, self-conscious controls over conception;
2. that variations in the fertility of populations outside the wealthy nations of our own era have resulted from differences over which people did not exert deliberate control, at least not for the purpose of controlling conception, such as marriage customs, sexual taboos, breast-feeding practices, nutrition, illness, and so on;
3. that once the members of a population *do* begin to control births, they keep at it, with the consequence that a fertility decline begun in earnest leads unerringly to a stable low fertility; and
4. that such a decline requires a fundamental shift in attitudes away from ignorance, passivity, and short-run gratification.

Students of European population changes who subscribe to these views point to several different sorts of evidence. First, following Louis Henry, they commonly insist that deliberate fertility control will show up in the record as differential age-specific fertility: At a given age, women who

have been married longer and/or who have had more children will bear
children at a lower rate than will other women in the same population;
solid evidence of those age-specific differentials is, in fact, quite rare for
periods before the nineteenth century. Second, they draw attention to
the fact that when strong evidence of deliberate fertility control does
appear, it tends to increase irreversibly with time. Third, the broad similarity in the timing of fertility decline in different parts of Europe, despite drastic differences in levels of income, urbanization, and
industrialization, couples with an apparent tendency of culturally ho-
mogeneous regions to behave as units within the fertility decline: some
sort of diffusion and cultural change is suggested.

Yet there is evidence on the other side. First, there *are* well-docu-
mented "preindustrial" cases that meet the stringent tests of parity-
dependence.[51] Second, there are many more cases in which the
evidence is less direct and compelling, but in which differentials in nuptiality and fertility by class and time period correspond closely to variations in economic interest.[52] Third, Ronald Lee's exacting time-series
analyses of the best national data available for the long run of English
history display a significant tendency for both nuptiality and fertility to
rise and fall as a function of real wages.[53]

The main relationships are hard to disentangle empirically from the
contrary effects. It is likely, for example, that improvement in nutrition
simultaneously boosted fertility and depressed mortality.[54] It is quite
possible, as William Langer has suggested, that the expanding cultivation of American plants, such as the potato, significantly improved life
expectancy and thus contributed to natural increase without any necessary rise in fertility. Yet the general hypothesis that people adjusted
marriage and fertility to the availability of adult places in crafts and on
the land is not absurd. In one form or another, it has been around since
Malthus. And it is compatible with many forms of fertility control short
of the self-conscious efficacy of twentieth-century contraception.

Proletarians faced a set of circumstances different from that for peasants and artisans. To the extent that the world around them was proletarian, they had both the incentive and the opportunity to marry and
form their own households early. They could acquire at quite a young
age the means of survival as adults. The characteristic organization of
work and the characteristic lifetime curve of earnings—rising rapidly
with adolescence, falling steadily from young adulthood—provided further encouragements to marriage and fertility.

On balance, these generalizations hold more clearly for employment
in rural industry than for employment in agriculture. In agriculture,
landlords' great control over the opportunities for wage labor, coupled

with their characteristic political authority, gave them strong influence over the possibility that young people could settle, marry, and bring up children. The rise of wage labor in agriculture—as rural Sweden has already taught us—sometimes *diminished* opportunities for marriage. Industrial employment, mediated by small merchants, gave householders more independence. Indeed, it sometimes promoted marriage.

Especially in the many variants of domestic industry, the standard labor unit was not a single individual but a household: for example, a weaver plus several spinners and tenders.[55] To work in these arrangements, it was almost essential to form a household. Speaking of the region of Charleroi (now in southern Belgium) during the eighteenth century, Hervé Hasquin declares, "Thus, in these working-class settings, *all* members of the family worked, since *all* wages were welcome. The women and girls made spun goods; at a very young age, the boys were pushed hard; they were not spared the most demanding work."[56] Hasquin shows that the birthrate rose in the towns in which industry was expanding—by now, a classic finding. He concludes that "having children resulted increasingly from deliberate intention."[57]

In his more general analysis of the Belgian fertility decline, Lesthaege adopts a similar argument:

> With the accelerated growth of employment outside the family-related artisanal workshops or agricultural enterprises during the Industrial Revolution, an even larger section of the population became both economically independent and capable of establishing a household at an earlier age. The precariousness of the wage-earners' sustenance ceased to be related to their age, and they had no more grounds for postponing their marriages.[58]

So long as employment opportunities, however marginal, were expanding, a proletarian strategy of early marriage and high fertility made sense. At least it made sense in the short run.

The findings from Wrigley's and Schofield's reconstruction of English population dynamics from 1541 to 1871 deserve special attention. The English evidence shows clearly that well before the decisive nineteenth-century decline in fertility, rates of marriage and birth more than once had risen and fallen significantly. In general, nuptiality and fertility rose with real wages, at a lag of about 40 years. That relationship grew stronger over time as the link between the aggregate population growth and food prices grew weaker. (Wrigley himself, I must admit, considers the nuptiality-wage link to have remained substantially uniform from the sixteenth to nineteenth centuries and regards the downturn in nuptiality after the downturn of real wages after about 1780 as "fatal" to the view that proletarianization promoted nuptiality.)[59]

In the medium and long runs, furthermore, death rates did not depend on real wages. The results strike a blow against a strict Malthusian interpretation of English experience, since the English seem to have avoided the positive check of heightened mortality in response to excessive population growth. The results also strike a blow against the notion of population pressure, since the rate of population growth apparently had little independent effect on mortality, fertility, or nuptiality. But these results are at least compatible with the emergence of a wage-driven demographic system. David Weir has shown that as a whole, similar dynamics operated in France from 1740 to 1829. Both countries give evidence of having tuned marriage and childbirth to employment opportunities.

NET MIGRATION

Migration figured in the formation of the European proletariat in two rather different ways. From the perspective of Europe as a whole from 1500 to 1900, migration's chief contribution was negative: The Continent shipped out many more migrants than it took in, and the bulk of the out-migrants were proletarian. Before 1750 the net outflows were small: colonists to the Americas, Slavs into continental Asia, trickles of settlers into other parts of the world. With the accelerating population growth of the later eighteenth century, out-migration speeded up as well. A plausible estimate for the period from 1800 to World War I is a net loss of 50 million Europeans to extracontinental migration. Before 1900, those out-migrants came disproportionately from the British Isles. From 1846 to 1890, for example, an estimated 48% of all European out-migrants came from England, Scotland, Wales, or Ireland.[60] The loss of migrants was equivalent to a fifth or a sixth of the Continent's entire nineteenth-century population growth.

Most of those millions were proletarians. A prototype of the transatlantic migration was the outflow from seventeenth-century Tourouvre-au-Perche.[61] The roughly 300 migrants from Tourouvre and vicinity and their numerous descendants played a major part in the settlement of Quebec. Labor recruiters intervened in a local but very active system of migration, in which wage laborers already predominated. The recruiters drew a high proportion of young men in their twenties, most of them apparently servants and day laborers. In Canada, to be sure, their grants of land transferred them out of the proletariat. In the European reckoning, nevertheless, they amounted to a loss of a few hundred proletarians.

Or take one of the best-documented flows after 1800: from Denmark to America.[62] Denmark's nineteenth-century population ran in the vicinity of 2 million people. That small country sent almost 300,000 migrants to North America between 1840 and 1914. The bulk of the migrants were servants, wage laborers, and other proletarians. The ideal candidates for emigration seem to have been young people who had already made the move from farms and villages to a nearby, slow-moving regional center. Many—probably the great majority—moved within chains of friends, neighbors, and kinspeople who kept information about American opportunities flowing back to Denmark and who helped the migrants find passage money, jobs, and housing. The chains also made it easier for those who disliked America to return home; almost 100,000 emigrants went back to Denmark. But their main effect was to facilitate the flow of emigrants from Denmark. Their demographic consequence was a net loss of some 200,000 Danish proletarians.

Migration also influenced the growth of the proletariat indirectly through its effect on social mobility and natural increase. One of the most valuable by-products of recent European historical demography has been the accumulating evidence of high mobility levels before the period of large-scale industrialization. Contrary to the idea of an immobile preindustrial world, historians of many different parts of Europe turn up village after village with annual migration rates of 10% or more.[63] Americans of the last century considered themselves exceptionally mobile because in the average year about 20% of the population changed residence—and a great many of them moved within the same community. Comparable levels of mobility are showing up in many parts of Europe before massive industrialization.

That high preindustrial mobility, however, requires several qualifications: first, that earlier Europe was not preindustrial in any strict sense of the term. Dispersed, small-scale manufacturing played an important part in rural and small-town life, occupying a significant share of the population at least part time. People working in small-scale industry were a relatively mobile segment of the population. They also comprised an important fraction of the European proletariat. Second, most of the moves were quite local, consisting largely of exchanges of labor among nearby villages and of a small city's recruitment of youngsters from its immediate hinterland. Third, the most active migrants were proletarians. Proletarianization itself produced migration, as when a household displaced by enclosures left the land or when an extra child of a peasant family trudged off to work as a mercenary soldier or domestic servant. In addition, the proletarian worker had the least to tie him to any particular locality and the greatest incentive to follow the scent of better wages into a new labor market. The local authorities of seventeenth-century England considered the ever-present wanderers as potential workers in good times, but as "vagrants" in bad times.[64] In good times or bad, they were quintessential proletarians.

Long-distance migration probably became an increasingly common context of proletarianization during the nineteenth century. The average distances moved increased, the definitiveness of the departure from home probably increased as well, and the growth in the scale of production diminished the likelihood that an expanding firm could draw its new workers from its region's existing proletarians. Furthermore, as Abel Châtelain has pointed out, the innumerable circuits of seasonal migration that permitted people to lead a nonproletarian existence at least part of the year finally began to disintegrate during the nineteenth century. Two opposite movements—short-distance commuting and definitive long-distance migration—began replacing them. Nevertheless, even during the nineteenth century the new industrial labor force came largely from the small towns and rural areas in which small-scale industrial production was declining.[65] If so, small towns and rural areas continued to serve as important way stations on the road to the proletariat.

The pattern of proletarian geographic mobility affected the way that social mobility and natural increase performed as a component of the proletariat's growth. The existence of well-established flows of migrants probably facilitated the proletarianization of the population in two ways. First, it helped produce a whole series of intermediate positions between the full artisan or peasant and the full proletarian—the alpine peasant who walked off to be a peddler in the winter, the weaver who followed the harvest in the fall, and so on.[66] Temporary expedients imperceptibly became a proletarian life. Second, the existence of well-established migratory flows withdrew the proletarianizing populations from the communities in which they had rights and solidarity and placed them in communities in which they had neither.

If the choice had been sharper and more dramatic in either regard, one might suppose that the proletarians would have resisted their fate with greater determination and effectiveness. When the choice was sharp and the proletarianizing populations were still embedded in their communities, they did often fight back against expropriation, by attacking others who were seizing control of the means of production. They also fought by adopting family strategies that limited the strain on household resources: strategies of late marriage, low fertility, regrouped inheritance, and so on. That fight against proletarianization pervades eighteenth-century peasant struggles against the enclosures and alienation of common rights, nineteenth-century artisanal struggles against work discipline, and twentieth-century winegrowers' struggles against big producers. It was a losing battle, but passionately fought.

WEIGHING THE COMPONENTS

Anyone who has watched how the evidence has leaked into and out of this discussion will realize that I am in no position to build estimates of the components of proletarianization that will hold water. For the sake of refocusing the inquiry, however, we may as well speculate about the relative weights of social mobility, natural increase, and net migration. Remember first the approximations of the European proletariat's size. In millions, the numbers run:

	1500	1800	1900
Total population	56	150	285
Nonproletarians	39	50	85
Proletarians	17	100	200

Remember also that the likely effect of net migration on the proletarian population of the Continent was a small loss before 1800 and a large loss—on the order of 50 million—during the nineteenth century. If we set the loss from 1500 to 1800 at a modest 10 million (a mere 33,000 per year) and retain the estimate of 50 million for between 1800 and 1900, we shall arrive at guesses of the amounts of change attributable to the sum of social mobility and natural increase:

	1500–1800	1800–1900
Total population	+ 104 (0.3)	+ 185 (0.8)
Nonproletarians	+ 11 (0.1)	+ 35 (0.5)
Proletarians	+ 93 (0.6)	+ 150 (0.9)

(The figures in parentheses represent the implied annual rates of growth.) For the three centuries from 1500 to 1800, the figures indicate a mild increase for the nonproletarian population and a significant increase for the proletarians. In the nineteenth century, they indicate substantial increases in both categories, with the proletariat growing almost twice as fast as the nonproletarian population did.

Imagine a nonproletarian population with zero natural increase: a population that simply reproduced itself over the four centuries under examination. That would be consistent with the models of peasant and artisanal demographic behavior reviewed earlier. With a zero natural increase in the nonproletarian population, the figures would imply that (1) the net increase of 11 million nonproletarians between 1500 and 1800 was entirely due to social mobility out of the proletariat, and (2) the European proletariat added 104 million via natural increase and lost 11 million of them to social mobility. Those implications are, to say the least, unconventional. For the nineteenth century, the same assumption of zero natural increase among nonproletarians would suggest an even more surprising pair of conclusions: that (3) from 1800 to 1900 the net effect of social mobility was not to create massive numbers of new proletarians but to move 35 million people out of the proletariat into nonproletarian positions, and (4) that the natural increase of the proletarian population was on the order of 185 million people, about 1.1% per year over the century as a whole.

Note that we are imagining *net* effects. For example, a net gain of 11 million nonproletarians via social mobility could easily mean that 25 million proletarians moved into nonproletarian positions, and 14 million non-proletarians moved into the proletariat. Likewise, the nineteenth-century transfer from proletariat to nonproletariat could result from, say, 60 million moves out of the proletariat balanced by 25 million moves into the proletariat. From a technical point of view, there is nothing implausible about the levels of natural increase that the figures suggest; for example, an average crude birthrate of 35 coupled with an average crude death rate of 24 would produce the sort of natural increase indicated for proletarians in the nineteenth century.

For the sake of a contrasting argument, let us imagine equal rates of natural increase among proletarians and nonproletarians. The rates of natural increase are equal to the annual rates of growth of the total European population plus the migration rate: 0.4% per year from 1500 to 1800 and 0.8% per year from 1800 to 1900. Again, these figures are perfectly acceptable from a strictly technical point of view. Under the assumption of an equal natural increase, our general figures imply an accounting of the following order: (1) that between 1500 and 1800 nonproletarians had a natural increase of 72 million people, counterbalanced by social mobility into the proletariat of 61 million; (2) that in the same period proletarians experienced a natural increase of 32 million people,

TABLE 1.7 Components of Growth in the Total, Nonproletarian, and Proletarian Population of Europe, 1550–1900, under Alternative Assumptions[a]

Component	Total	Nonproletarian	Proletarian
Number in 1500	56	39	17
Number in 1800	150	50	100
Change, 1500–1800	+94	+11	+83
Estimate of net migration, 1500–1800	−10	0	−10
Estimated sum of social mobility and natural increase, 1500–1800	+104	+11	+93
Implied annual percentage increase	0.4	0.1	0.6
Natural increase under zero hypothesis	+104	0	+104
Social mobility under zero hypothesis	0	+11	−11
Natural increase under equal hypothesis	+104	+72	+32
Social mobility under equal hypothesis	0	−61	+61
Number in 1900	285	85	200
Change, 1800–1900	+135	+35	+100
Estimate of net migration, 1800–1900	−50	0	−50
Estimated sum of social mobility and natural increase, 1800–1900	+185	+3⁵	+150
Implied annual percentage increase	0.8	0.5	0.9
Natural increase under zero hypothesis	+185	0	+185
Social mobility under zero hypothesis	0	+35	−35
Natural increase under equal hypothesis	+185	+62	+123
Social mobility under equal hypothesis	0	−27	+17

[a]In millions of people. Zero hypothesis: Nonproletarians have zero natural increase (fertility is equal to mortality). Equal hypothesis: Nonproletarians and proletarians have equal rates of natural increase (i.e., rate of increase of total population, net of migration).

received 61 million newcomers via social mobility, and lost 10 million through migration from Europe; (3) that during the nineteenth century the nonproletarian population added 62 million people through natural increase and lost 27 million to social mobility; and (4) that during the same century the proletariat augmented its 27-million-person gain from social mobility with a natural increase of 123 million people but exported 50 million of its members overseas. (See Table 1.7.)

We have, then, two extreme models: one with zero natural increase for nonproletarians and the other with nonproletarians experiencing the same natural increase as proletarians did. The "zero increase" model suggests some departure of proletarians from the proletariat before 1800, a massive movement out of the proletariat during the nineteenth century. The "same increase" model suggests a huge transfer of nonproletarians into the proletariat before 1800 and a more modest transfer in the same direction from 1800 to 1900.

Figure 1.3 locates the zero and equal hypotheses within the range of likely combinations of natural increase and social mobility. Using Figure 1.3, we can construct any number of other hypotheses. Yet the graph makes clear that if my assumptions about net migration and the magnitude of increase in the proletariat are correct, the plausible hypotheses all will lie within a fairly narrow range. The zero hypothesis, as the graph shows, marks an extreme; it requires exceptional rates of proletarian

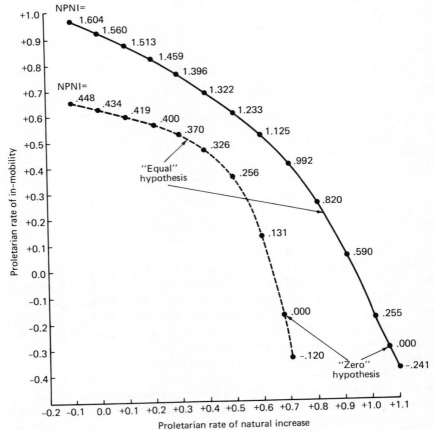

FIGURE 1.3 Proletarian rate of in-mobility and nonproletarian rate of natural increase (NPNI) as a function of proletarian rate of natural increase for Europe as a whole: 1500–1800 (broken line) and 1800–1900 (solid line). All rates in percentage change per year.

natural increase and of mobility out of the proletariat, especially after 1800. The equal hypothesis positions itself on more plausible terrain. Before 1800, however, it requires a very high rate of social mobility into the proletariat: about 0.5% per year. If we were willing to contemplate even higher rates of social mobility, the graph would show the possibility of a truly extreme hypothesis: that nonproletarian natural increase ran substantially ahead of proletarian natural increase.

The reality and all useful models of it lie between the two extremes. We could, for example, reasonably argue that natural increase declined earlier among nonproletarians than among proletarians and that we should therefore shift from the same increase model toward the zero increase model as time moves on. That suggests, however, a zigzag: huge moves into the proletariat before 1800 and large moves out of the proletariat between 1800 and 1900. Unconventional? Yes. Absurd? Perhaps. Yet that very absurdity has its value, for it clears the way to the real challenge: to fashion these crude estimates and fragile models into genuine portrayals of the proletariat's growth.

If forced to sum up the arguments and evidence of this chapter (and allowed to rely on some strong guesses), I would sketch a model midway between the equal and zero hypotheses. That would imply something like the following levels:

Period	Nonproletarian natural increase	Proletarian natural increase	Mobility into proletariat
1500–1800	0.25	0.50	0.40
1800–1900	0.60	0.90	0.10

These are plausible levels with interesting implications. They imply, for example, a marked slowing of individual mobility into the proletariat from the eighteenth to the nineteenth century—a circumstance that would be consistent with Marx's suggestion of a massive and early displacement of the rural population, although the pattern as a whole would still challenge his apparent assumption of a zero natural increase among proletarians. The hypothetical numbers provide a means of following up the implications of alternative theories and of weighing the significance of empirical observations concerning real European populations. Yet I must insist that the numbers come from nothing more than informed speculation.

Still, the speculative reasoning we have just gone through actually imposes serious constraints on those portrayals. For instance:

1. By any reasonable argument, natural increase must have played the major role in the growth of the European proletariat since 1500, and especially since 1800.
2. Well-grounded estimates of fertility, mortality, and their trends among specific European populations will set serious limits on the part that social mobility could have played in the proletarianization of those populations; to the extent that the patterns and trends are similar from one population to another, they will set limits on the possible role of social mobility in the growth of the whole European proletariat.
3. Earlier, I sketched the argument that nonproletarians tend to adjust their fertility to the availability of land and capital, whereas proletarians adjust their fertility to the availability of wages. That argument can be verified, modified, and refined through the examination of local populations. To the extent that it applies in a similar fashion throughout Europe, it limits the assumptions we can plausibly make concerning the trends in natural increase among proletarian and nonproletarian populations from 1500 to 1900.

Thus reasoning about the broad trends for Europe as a whole clarifies what sorts of conclusions we need to draw from the local studies of demographic processes that are now proliferating.

Let me stress that outcome. The numbers with which we have been working are temporary constructions, useful mainly as shelter while we catch our bearings. But in the long run, they will not withstand the historical wind. Two sorts of new building are essential. First, the broad estimates must be verified, revised, and refined. Even if the numbers I have proposed were precise and reliable, they would leave us far from the historical reality we are trying to understand. Most pressing is the need to specify the actual flows into and out of the proletariat that leave the net effects we have been discussing. How many people, for example, spent their lives straddling the line between proletarian and nonproletarian existence, by alternating between wage labor and independent production? How many proletarian emigrants actually realized the recurrent migrant dream: to accumulate capital at their destinations and then return home as peasants, artisans, rentiers, or capitalists?

Second, the sharp distinctions among migration, natural increase, and social mobility will eventually have to give way. We must examine their combinations and interactions. How often were the people who made the lifetime move from nonproletarian to proletarian households "extra" children of peasants and artisans, thus in some sense creatures of natural increase? How frequently did social mobility occur as a correlate or consequence of long-distance migration? Was the exclusion of squatters and tenants from common rights, and thus from the village, the potent proletarianizer it seems to have been? For such questions, more reliable estimates of the components of growth on a continental scale will be of little help. We need precise, textured local analyses.

CONCLUSIONS

In hacking out the contours of this massive problem, then, I have neglected all the graceful refinements that make the problem interesting. For example, the detailed timetable of proletarianization matters a good deal. Cottage industry and agricultural wage labor seem to have expanded much more rapidly in the seventeenth and, especially, the eighteenth century than before. Yet there was a good deal of population increase in Europe during the sixteenth century. Is it possible that during the sixteenth century, peasants, artisans, and other nonproletarians increased more rapidly than did the general population and that it was therefore a century of *de*proletarianization?

The geography of proletarianization likewise cries out for attention. At a minimum we need contrasts among the legal enserfment of essentially landless laborers on the large estates of eastern Europe, the creation of a legally free proletarian labor force in England, and the emergence of landowning peasants and cash-crop farmers in important parts of western Europe.

Finally, a historically useful portrayal cannot stop with the tabulation of social mobility, natural increase, and net migration as separate components; it must specify their interplay. And all this requires a more refined analysis than I have provided here.

Qualifications, hesitations, and apologies duly registered, what provisional conclusions may we draw? Where did the European proletariat come from? One answer recurs through the arguments and evidence of this chapter: *Cherchez le capitaliste.* The activity of capitalists, not the abstract mechanics of population growth, lay behind all the components of the proletariat's growth. On the side of social mobility, we have encountered the old processes of capitalist expropriation, although less frequently than the simplest Marxist accounts lead us to expect. More often, the piece-by-piece consolidation of land and capital by small producers gradually but inexorably edged their neighbors into the proletariat.

In migration, the capitalist's hand is gloved, but no less powerful: to the extent that capitalists accomplished expropriation and the ·imposition of control over labor by transferring capital from one work site to another and thus attracted proletarianizing flows of migrants, they did the work more subtly and effectively.

The most surprising implication of this chapter's analysis, however, is the importance of capitaists to natural increase. Perhaps there was some "exogenous" decline in mortality due to climatic shifts, extinction of the natural carriers of the plague, and so on. But the alterations in nutrition that are the strongest candidates for explanations of involuntary long-term changes in fertility and mortality before the nineteenth century surely depended to an important degree on the activities of merchants and agricultural capitalists. And—most important—the pattern of proletarian natural increase in response to the availability of wage labor we have encountered depended entirely on the capitalists' provision of employment. Specialist farmers who offered work to day laborers and petty entrepreneurs who built cottage industry thereby incited the disproportionate natural increase of the proletariat. Not that they plotted to do so or ceased to condemn the heedless breeding of their workers: The power of a system like capitalism is that it does not require malevolent, or even self-conscious, agents to do its work.

For all its Marxist accent, to be sure, such an analysis revises an important element of Marx's own analysis and makes significant concessions to Malthus. Whereas Marx implicitly treated the lifetime mobility of workers and their households from nonproletarian to proletarian positions as the principal component of the proletariat's growth, my account gives far greater weight to the movement between generations and to differential natural increase. Expropriation and the extension of wage labor occurred widely, all right, but they happened to whole populations rather than to individuals. The stress on natural increase, with the fluctuations in fertility driven largely by fluctuations in marriage, has a Malthusian edge. Parson Malthus saw clearly enough that the poor English people of the later eighteenth century had strong incentives to marry and multiply and that the old system of enforced celibacy for large numbers of servants and laborers was disintegrating as wage labor expanded. His errors, then, were to inflate the particular circumstances of capitalist expropriation into general laws, to misunderstand the incentives to high fertility, and to neglect the importance of capitalist farmers, merchants, and manufacturers to the increase of the proletariat.

Back at the start of this long discussion, I said that there were three steps to the appropriate sociological procedure: the delineation of the components of growth, the separate explanation of each of the components, and the integration of those explanations into a comprehensive account of the whole process. We have not, by any means, completed that entire program. Yet the fragmentary observations we have made point to the utility of a modified Marxist account of European proletarianization. The most important modification consists of the large significance attributed to natural increase within the existing proletariat. Marx implicitly made lifetime entries of nonproletarians—that is, social mobility—the major component of the proletariat's increase. The modification fits nicely with that brand of Marxist analysis, typified by E. P. Thompson, which emphasizes the continuity of working-class culture from one generation to the next.

APPENDIX: THE RATE OF PROLETARIANIZATION, ITS COMPONENTS, AND ITS LIKELY DETERMINANTS

T: total hours per year spent in productive labor
L: hours per year spent in labor controlling the means of production
D: hours per year spent in dependent labor $= T - L$
W: hours per year spent in labor for wages
e: level of expropriation $= D/T$; $\dot{e}$: rate of change in e
w: wage dependence $= W/T$; $\dot{w}$: rate of change in w
P: level of proletarianization $= e \times w$
$\dot{P}$: rate of proletarianization $= \dot{e} + \dot{w}$

Determinants of Increase in Wage Labor	Determinants of Increase in Potential Work Force
Demand for goods and services (+)	Demand for goods and services (+)
Cost of establishing new production units (+)	Opportunity cost of childbearing (−)
Concentration of capital (+)	Existing level of proletarianization (+)
Coercive power of employers (+)	Natural fluctuations (±)

Proletarianization is likely to occur under these conditions:

1. increases in the cost of establishing new producing units,
2. concentration of capital,
3. increases in the coercive power of employers,
4. declines in the opportunity cost of childbearing, and
5. previous proletarianization.

NOTES

1. Book 1, Chapter 8. Given the many editions of this work, I am citing by chapter for the convenience of readers.
2. Book 1, Chapter 8.
3. For indirect confirmation, see A. W. Coats, "The Classical Economists and the Labourer," in E. L. Jones and G. E. Mingay, eds., *Land, Labour and Population in the Industrial Revolution. Essays Presented to J. D. Chambers* (London: Arnold 1967); and J. J. Spengler, "Adam Smith on Population," *Population Studies*, 2d ser., 17 (1970):377–388.
4. For a convenient review, see Carl Jantke, "Zur Deutung des Pauperismus," in Carl Jantke and Dietrich Hilger, eds., *Der deutsche Pauperismus und die Emanzipationskrise in Darstellung der zeitgenossischen Literatur* (Munich: Karl Alber, 1965).
5. *Capital*, Chapter 26. Again, I am citing by chapter for the convenience of readers.
6. *Ibid.*, Chapter 26.
7. *Ibid.*, Chapter 25.
8. Karl Marx, *Grundrisse. Foundations of the Critique of Political Economy (rough draft)* (London: Allen Lane, 1973), p. 606.
9. *Ibid.*
10. For example, J. D. Chambers, "Enclosure and the Labour Supply in the Industrial Revolution," *Economic History Review*, 2d ser., 5 (1953): 319–343; Jon S. Cohen and Martin L. Weitzman, "Enclosures and Depopulation: A Marxian Analysis," in William N. Parker and Eric L. Jones, eds., *European Peasants and Their Markets* (Princeton, N.J.: Princeton University Press, 1975); D. C. Coleman, "Labour in the English Economy of the Seventeenth Century," *Economic History Review*, 2d ser., 8 (1955–1956): 280–295; J. P. Cooper, "The Social Distribution of Land and Men in England, 1436–1700," *Economic History Review*, 2d ser., 20 (1967): 419–440; Ingrid Eriksson and John Rogers, *Rural Labor and Population Change* (Stockholm: Almqvist & Wiksell, 1978); H. J. Habakkuk, *Population Growth and Economic Development Since 1750* (Leicester: Leicester University Press, 1971); Gerd Hohorst, *Wirtschaftswachstum und Bevölkerungsentwicklung in Preussen 1816–1914* (New York: Arno Press, 1977); E. L. Jones, "The Agricultural Labour Market in England, 1793–1872," *Economic History Review*, 2d ser., 17 (1964): 322–338; Hermann Kellenbenz, *Agrarisches Nebengewerbe und Formen der Reagrarisierung im Spätmittelalter und 19./20. Jahrhundert* (Stuttgart: Gustav Fischer, 1975); William Lazonick, "Karl Marx and Enclosures in England," *Review of Radical Economics* 6 (1974):1–59; Yves Lequin, *Les ouvriers de la région lyonnaise (1848–1914)*, 2 vols. (Lyon: Presses Universitaires de Lyon, 1977); Sture Martinius, *Befolkningsrörlighet under industrialismens inledningsskede i Sverige* (Gothenberg: Elanders, 1967); Horst Matzerath, "Industrialisierung, Mobilität und sozialen Wandel am Beispiel der Stadte Rheydt und Rheindalen," in Hartmut Kaelble et al., eds., *Probleme der Modernisierung in Deutschland* (Opladen: Westdeutschen Verlag, 1978); Alan S. Milward and S. B. Saul, *The Economic Development of Continental Europe, 1780–1870* (London: Allen & Unwin, 1973); John Saville, "Primitive Accumulation and Early Industrialization in Britain," *Socialist Register* (1969): 247–271; Lawrence Schofer, *The Formation of a Modern Labor Force. Upper Silesia, 1865–1914* (Berkeley and Los Angeles: University of California Press, 1975); Louise A. Tilly, "Urban Growth, Industrialization and Women's Employment in Milan, Italy, 1881–1911," *Journal of Urban History*, 3 (1977): 467–484; Richard Tilly and Charles Tilly, "An Agenda for European Economic History in the 1970s," *Journal of Economic History* 31 (1971): 184–197; E. A. Wrigley, *Industrial Growth and Population Change* (Cambridge: Cambridge University Press, 1961).
11. For example, Lutz Berkner and Franklin F. Mendels, "Inheritance Systems, Family

Structure, and Demographic Patterns in Western Europe, 1700-1900," in Charles Tilly ed., *Historical Studies of Changing Fertility* (Princeton, N.J.: Princeton University Press, 1978); David Gaunt, "Pre-Industrial Economy and Population Structure: The Elements of Variance in Early Modern Sweden," *Scandinavian Journal of History* 2 (1977): 183-210; Michael Haines, *Fertility and Occupation. Population Patterns in Industrialization* (New York: Academic Press, 1979); John Knodel and Etienne van de Walle, "Lessons from the Past: Policy Implications of Historical Fertility Studies," *Population and Development Review* 5 (1979): 217-245; Wolfgang Köllmann, "Zur Bevölkerungsentwicklung der Neuzeit," in Reinhart Koselleck ed., *Studien zum Beginn der Modernen Welt.* Stuttgart: Klett-Cotta, 1977); Peter Kriedte, Hans Medick, and Jürgen Schlumbohm, *Industrialisierung vor der Industrialisierung. Gewerbliche Warenproduktion auf dem Land in der Formationsperiode des Kapitalismus* (Göttingen: Vandenhoeck & Ruprecht, 1977); Ron J. Lesthaege, *The Decline of Belgian Fertility, 1800-1970* (Princeton, N.J.: Princeton University Press, 1977); Edward E. McKenna, "Marriage and Fertility in Postfamine Ireland: A Multivariate Analysis," *American Journal of Sociology* 80 (1974): 688-705.

12. For example, Kurt Ågren et al., *Aristocrats, Farmers, Proletarians. Essays in Swedish Demographic History* (Uppsala: Almqvist & Wiksell, 1973); Sune Åkerman, Hans Christian Johansen, and David Gaunt, eds., *Chance and Change: Social and Economic Studies in Historical Demography in the Baltic Area* (Odense: Scandanavian Universities Press, 1978); J. Bourget, "Prolétarisation d'une commune de l'agglomération parisienne: Colombes," *La Vie Urbaine* n.s. nos. 3 and 4 (1954): 185-194; Rudolf Braun, *Industrialisierung und Volksleben* (Zurich: Rentsch, 1960); Rudolf Braun, *Sozialer und kultureller Wandel in einem ländlichen Industriegebiet* (Zurich: Rentsch, 1965); J. D. Chambers, *The Vale of Trent, 1670-1800. A Regional Study of Economic Change* (Cambridge: Cambridge University Press, 1957); Alain Corbin, *Archaisme et modernité en Limousin au XIXe siècle.* 2 vols. (Paris: Marcel Rivière, 1975); Paul Deprez, "The Demographic Development of Flanders in the Eighteenth Century," in D. V. Glass and D. E. C. Eversley, eds., *Population in History* (Chicago: Aldine, 1965); John Foster, *Class Struggle and the Industrial Revolution. Early Industrial Capitalism in Three Towns* (London: Weidenfeld & Nicolson, 1974); David Gaunt, "Familj, Hushall och Arbetsintensitet," *Scandia* 42 (1976): 32-59; Franz Gschwind, *Bevölkerungsentwicklung und Wirtschaftsstruktur der Landschaft Basel im 18. Jahrhundert* (Liestal: Kantonal Drucksachen- und Materialzentrale, 1977); Hervé Hasquin, *Une mutation. Le "Pays de Charleroi" aux XVIIe et XVIIIe siècles* (Brussels: Editions de l'Institut de Sociologie, Université Libre de Bruxelles, 1971); Karlbernhard Jasper, *Der Urbanisierungsprozess dargestellt am Beispiel der Stadt Köln* (Cologne: Rheinisch-Westfälischen Wirtschaftsarchiv zu Köln, 1977); Herbert Kisch, *Die Hausindustriellen Textilgewerbe am Niederrhein vor der industriellen Revolution. Von der ursprünglichen zur kapitalistischen Akkumulation* (Göttingen: Vandenhoeck & Ruprecht, 1981); Arnost Klíma, "The Role of Rural Domestic Industry in Bohemia in the Eighteenth Century," *Economic History Review* 27(1974): 48-56; David Levine, *Family Formation in an Age of Nascent Capitalism* (New York: Academic Press, 1977); David Levine, "Proto-Industrialization and Demographic Upheaval," in David Levine et al., *Essays on the Family and Historical Change* (College Station, Tex.: A&M Press, 1983); Sven Lundqvist, *Folkrörelserna i det svenska samhallet, 1850-1920* (Stockholm: Almqvist & Wiksell, 1977); Bo Ohngren, *Folk i rörelse. Samhallsutveckling, flyttningsmonster och folkrörelser i Eskilstuna 1870-1900* (Uppsala: Almqvist Wiksell, 1974); Jaroslav Purš, "Struktur und Dynamik der industriellen Entwicklung in Böhmen im letzten Viertel des 18. Jahrhunderts," *Jahrbuch für Wirtschaftsgeschichte* (1965): 160-196; Jaroslav Purš, "Die Aufhebung der Hörigkeit und die Grundentlastung in den böhmischen Ländern," *Second International Conference of Economic History. Aix en Provence 1962* (Paris: Mouton, 1965); Jane Schneider and Peter Schneider, *Culture and Political*

Economy in Western Sicily (New York: Academic Press, 1976); Joan W. Scott, *The Glassmakers of Carmaux. French Craftsmen and Political Action in a Nineteenth Century City* (Cambridge, Mass.: Harvard University Press, 1974); Margaret Spufford, "Peasant Inheritance Customs and Land Distribution in Cambridgeshire from the Sixteenth to the Eighteenth Centuries," in Jack Goody, Joan Thirsk and E. P. Thompson, eds., *Family and Inheritance. Rural Society in Western Europe, 1200–1800* (Cambridge: Cambridge University Press, 1976); Pierre Vilar, *La Catalogne dans l'Espagne moderne*, 3 vols. (Paris: SEVPEN, 1962); Jan de Vries, "Peasant Demand Patterns and Economic Development: Friesland, 1550–1750," in William N. Parker and Eric L. Jones, eds., *European Peasants and Their Markets* (Princeton, N.J.: Princeton University Press, 1975); Keith Wrightson and David Levine, *Poverty and Piety in an English Village. Terling, 1525–1700* (New York: Academic Press, 1979).

13. For example, Wilhelm Abel, *Massenarmut und Hungerkrisen im vorindustriellen Europa* (Hamburg and Berlin: Paul Parey, 1974); A. W. Coats, "The Relief of Poverty, Attitudes to Labour and Economic Change in England, 1660–1782," *International Review of Social History* 21 (1976): 98–115; Natalie Zemon Davis, "Poor Relief, Humanism and Heresy: The Case of Lyon," *Studies in Medieval and Renaissance History* 5 (1968): 217–275; Pierre Deyon, "A propos du paupérisme au milieu du XVIIe siècle: Peinture et charité chrétienne," *Annales: Economies, Sociétés, Civilisations* 22 (1967): 137–153; Jean-Pierre Gutton, *La société et les pauvres en Europe, XVIe-XVIIIe siècles*, (Paris: Presses Universitaires de France, 1974); Olwen Hufton, The Poor of Eighteenth-Century France, 1750–1789 (Oxford: Clarendon Press); Jeffrey Kaplow, *The Names of Kings. The Parisian Laboring Poor in the Eighteenth Century* (New York: Basic Books 1972); Catharina Lis and Hugo Soly, *Poverty and Capitalism in Pre-Industrial Europe* (Atlantic Highlands, N.J.: Humanities Press, 1979); Jill Quadagno, *Aging in Early Industrial Society. Work, Family, and Social Policy in Nineteenth-Century England* (New York: Academic Press, 1982); Paul A. Slack, "Vagrants and Vagrancy in England, 1598–1664," *Economic History Review*, 2d ser., 27 (1974): 360–379.

14. For example, Stanley Aronowitz, "Marx, Braverman, and the Logic of Capital," *Insurgent Sociologist* 8 (1978): 126–146; Reinhard Bendix, *Work and Authority in Industry. Ideologies of Management in the Course of Industrialization* (New York: Wiley, 1956); Michael Burawoy, "Towards a Marxist Theory of the Labor Process: Braverman and Beyond," *Politics and Society* 8 (1979): 247–312; Michael Burawoy, *Manufacturing Consent. Changes in the Labor Process under Monopoly Capitalism* (Chicago: University of Chicago Press, 1979); Duncan Gallie, *In Search of the New Working Class. Automation and Social Integration Within the Capitalist Enterprise* (Cambridge: Cambridge University Press, 1978); David Gartman, "Marx and the Labor Process: An Interpretation," *Insurgent Sociologist* 8 (1978): 97–108; Herbert Gintis, "The Nature of Labor Exchange and the Theory of Capitalist Production," *Review of Radical Political Economy* 8 (1976): 36–54; Gerd H. Hardach, Der soziale Status des Arbeiters in der Frühindustrialisierung (Berlin: Duncker & Humblot, 1969); Stephen A. Marglin, "What Do Bosses Do? The Origins and Functions of Hierarchy in Capitalist Production," *Review of Radical Political Economics* 6 (1974): 60–112; David Montgomery, *Workers' Control in America* (Cambridge: Cambridge University Press, 1979); Wilbert E. Moore and Arnold S. Feldman, eds., Labor Commitment and Social Change in Developing Areas (New York: Social Science Research Council, 1960); Bernard Mottez, *Systèmes de salaire et politiques patronales* (Paris: Centre National de la Recherche Scientifique, 1966); Luciano Pellicani, "La rivoluzione industriale e il fenomeno della proletarizzazione," *Rassegna Italiana di Sociologia* 14 (1973): 63–84; François Perroux, *Aliénation et société industrielle* (Paris: Gallimard, 1970); Katherine Stone, "The Origins of Job Structures in the Steel Industry," *Review of Radical Political Economics* 6 (1974): 113–173; E. P. Thompson, "Time, Work-Discipline, and Industrial Capitalism," *Past and Present* 38 (1967): 56–97; Michael Vester, *Die Entstehung des Proletariats als Lernprozess. Die Entstehung anti-*

kapitalistischer Theorie und Praxis in England, 1792-1848 (Frankfurt am Main: Europäische Verlaganstalt, 1970); Hartmut Zwahr, "Zur Konstituierung des Proletariats als Klasse. Strukturuntersuchung über das leipziger Proletariat während der industriellen Revolution," in Horst Bartel and Ernst Engelberg, eds., *Die grosspreussisch-militarische Reichsgründung 1871,* Band I (Berlin: Akademie Verlag, 1971.)

15. For example, Perry Anderson, *Lineages of the Absolutist State* (London: NLB, 1974); Fernand Braudel, *Civilisation matérielle, économie et capitalisme, XVe–XVIIIe siècles.* 3 vols. (Paris: Colin, 1979); Robert Brenner, "Agrarian Class Structure and Economic Development in Pre-Industrial Europe," *Past and Present* 70 (1976): 30–75; Robert Brenner, "The Origins of Capitalist Development. A Critique of Neo-Smithian Marxism," *New Left Review* 104 (1977): 25–92; Pierre Chaunu, *La civilisation de l'Europe classique* (Paris: Arthaud, 1970); Patricia Croot and David Parker, "Agrarian Class Structure and Economic Development," *Past and Present* 78 (1978): 37–46; Maurice Dobb, *Studies in the Development of Capitalism* (London: Routledge & Kegan Paul, 1963); Hermann Kellenbenz, *The Rise of the European Economy. An Economic History of Continental Europe from the Fifteenth to the Eighteenth Century* (London: Weidenfeld & Nicolson, 1976); David S. Landes, *The Unbound Prometheus. Technological Change and Industrial Development in Western Europe from 1750 to the Present* (Cambridge: Cambridge University Press, 1969); Emmanuel Le Roy Ladurie, "Pour un modèle de l'économie rurale française au XVIIIe siècle," *Cahiers d'Histoire* 29 (1974): 5–27; Barrington Moore, Jr., *Social Origins of Dictatorship and Democracy. Lord and Peasant in the Making of the Modern World* (Boston: Beacon Press, 1966); Fritz Redlich and Herman Freudenberger, "The Industrial Development of Europe: Reality, Symbols, Images," *Kyklos* 17 (1964): 372–401; Emilio Sereni, *Il capitalismo nelle campagne (1860-1900)* (Turin: Einaudi, 1948); Gabriel Tortella Cesares, *Los origines del capitalismo en España: Banca, industria y ferocarria en el siglo XIX* (Madrid: Editorial Jernos, 1973); Jan de Vries, *The Economy of Europe in an Age of Crisis, 1600-1750* (Cambridge: Cambridge University Press, 1976); Immanuel Wallerstein, *The Modern World System.* 2 vols. (New York: Academic Press, 1974 and 1980); E. A. Wrigley, "The Process of Modernization and the Industrial Revolution in England," *Journal of Interdisciplinary History* 3 (1972): 225–259.

16. Christer Winberg, *Folkökning och proletarisering kring den sociala strukturomvandlingen på Sveriges landsbygd under den agrara revolutionen* Gothenberg: Historiska Institutionen i Göteborg, 1975), 331; see Gustaf Utterstrom, *Jordbrukets arbetare,* vol. 1 (Stockholm: Tidens Forlag, 1957), 68.

17. For summaries of the debates, see H. J. Habakkuk, *Population Growth and Economic Development Since 1750* (Leicester: Leicester University Press, 1971); and Thomas McKeown, *The Modern Rise of Population* (New York: Academic Press, 1976).

18. Ann Kussmaul, *Servants in Husbandry in Early Modern England* (Cambridge: Cambridge University Press, 1981), 97–119.

19. Gartman, *op cit.;* Gintis, *op cit.*

20. See Stanley Aronowitz, "Marx, Braverman, and the Logic of Capital," *Insurgent Sociologist* 8 (1978):126–146.

21. See Juan G. Espinosa and Andrew S. Zimbalist, *Economic Democracy. Workers' Participation in Chilean Industry 1970-1973* (New York: Academic Press, 1978); Walter Korpi, *The Working Class in Welfare Capitalism. Work, Unions, and Politics in Scandinavia* (London: Routledge & Kegan Paul, 1978); Evelyne Huber Stephens, *The Politics of Workers' Participation* (New York: Academic Press, 1980).

22. William Hasbach, *A History of the English Agricultural Labourer* (London: P. S. King, 1920), 103–104.

23. Douglass C. North and Robert Paul Thomas, *The Rise of the Western World. A New Economic History* (Cambridge: Cambridge University Press, 1973).

24. Alan Macfarlane, *The Origins of English Individualism* (Cambridge: Cambridge University Press, 1978).

25. On these issues, see John D. Durand, *The Labor Force in Economic Development. A Comparison of International Census Data, 1946–1966.* Princeton, N.J.: Princeton University Press, 1975); Richard Edwards, ''Social Relations of Production at the Point of Production,'' *Insurgent Sociologist* 8 (1978): 109–125; Louise A. Tilly and Joan W. Scott, *Women, Work and Family* (New York: Holt, Rinehart & Winston, 1978).

26. Jerome Blum, *The End of the Old Order in Rural Europe* (Princeton, N.J.: Princeton University Press, 1978).

27. See for example, Habakkuk, *op cit.*

28. Harriet Friedmann, ''World Market, State, and Family Farm: Social Bases of Household Production in the Era of Wage Labor,'' *Comparative Studies in Society and History* 20 (1978): 545–586.

29. Jan de Vries, *The Dutch Rural Economy in the Golden Age, 1500–1700* (New Haven, Conn.: Yale University Press, 1974).

30. For example, Rudolf Braun, ''Early Industrialization and Demographic Change in the Canton of Zurich,'' in Charles Tilly, ed., *Historical Studies of Changing Fertility* Princeton, N.J.: Princeton University Press, 1978).

31. For example, Kisch, *op. cit.*

32. John Saville, ''Primitive Accumulation and Early Industrialization in Britain,'' *Socialist Register* (1969):251–252.

33. Phyllis Deane and W. A. Cole, *British Economic Growth, 1688–1959. Trends and Structure* (Cambridge: Cambridge University Press, 1967),143–144.

34. B. H. Slicher van Bath, ''Agriculture in the Vital Revolution,'' in E. E. Rich and C. H. Wilson, eds., *Cambridge Economic History of Europe V. The Economic Organization of Early Modern Europe* (Cambridge: Cambridge University Press, 1977),127.

35. Lennart Jorberg, ''The Development of Real Wages for Agricultural Workers in Sweden During the 18th and 19th Centuries,'' *Economy and History* 15 (1972): 41–57.

36. Computed from Karlheinz Blaschke, *Bevölkerungsgeschichte von Sachsen bis zur industriellen Revolution* (Weimar: Böhlhaus, 1967),190–191; Paul Bairoch, *Taille des villes, conditions de vie et développement économique* (Paris: Ecoles des Hautes Etudes en Sciences Sociales, 1977),42.

37. Wolfgang Köllmann, *Bevölkerung in der industriellen Revolution* (Göttingen: Vandenhoeck & Ruprecht, 1974),88–90.

38. *Ibid.*, 74.

39. *Ibid.*, 70.

40. Franklin L. Mendels, ''Aux origines de la proto-industrialisation,'' *Bulletin du Centre d'Histoire Economique et Sociale de la Région Lyonnaise* no. 2 (1978):1–25.

41. Kisch, *op. cit.*

42. For an extensive review of the evidence on protoindustrial demography, see Kriedte, Medick, and Schlumbohm *op. cit.*, especially pp. 155–193; for an empirical challenge, see Gerd Hohorst, *op cit.*, especially pp. 208–227; and Gerd Hohorst, ''Protoindustrialisierung im Übergang zum industriellen Kapitalismus: Die demoökonomische Entwicklung im Kreis Hagen 1817 bis 1863,'' in Pierre Deyon and Franklin L. Mendels, eds., *Protoindustrialisation: Théorie et réalité* (Lille: Université des Arts, Lettres, et Sciences Humaines, 1982).

43. Blaschke, *op cit.*; Klíma, *op cit.*; Braun, *op cit.* 1978.

44. Levine, *op cit.*, pp. 103–115; for a skeptical commentary, see E. A. Wrigley, ''The Changing Occupational Structure of Colyton over Two Centuries,'' *Local Population Studies* 18 (1977): 9–21.

45. Wrightson and Levine, *op cit.*

46. Kussmaul, *op cit.*

47. Gaunt, *op cit.*, 1977.

48. See Amartya Sen, *Poverty and Famines. An Essay on Entitlement and Deprivation* (Oxford: Clarendon Press, 1981).

49. See Ronald Lee, "Models of Pre-Industrial Population Dynamics, with Application to England," in Charles Tilly, eds., *Historical Studies of Changing Fertility* (Princeton, N.J.: Princeton University Press, 1978).

50. See John C. Caldwell, "Towards a Restatement of Demographic Transition Theory," *Population and Development Review* 2 (1976): 321–366; John C. Caldwell, *Theory of Fertility Decline* (New York: Academic Press, 1982); John Knodel, "Natural Fertility in Pre-Industrial Germany," *Population Studies* 32 (1978): 481–510; Knodel and van de Walle *op cit.*

51. Rudolf Andorka, "Family Reconstitution and Types of Household Structure," in Jan Sundin and Eric Soderlund, eds., *Time, Space and Man* (Stockholm: Almqvist & Wiksell International, 1979); Gaunt *op. cit.* 1977; Levine *op. cit.* 1977; E. A. Wrigley, "Family Limitation in Pre-Industrial England" *Economic History Review* n.s., 19 (1966): 82–109.

52. For a review of many such cases, see Charles Tilly, "The Historical Study of Vital Processes," in Charles Tilly, ed., *Historical Studies of Changing Fertility* (Princeton, N.J.: Princeton University Press, 1978).

53. Ronald Lee, "An Historical Perspective on Economic Aspects of the Population Explosion: The Case of Pre-Industrial England," unpublished paper, National Bureau of Economic Research; Ronald Lee, *op. cit.* 1978; E. A. Wrigley and R. S. Schofield, *The Population History of England, 1541–1871: A Reconstruction* (London: Arnold, 1981).

54. McKeown, *op. cit.*; Lee, *op. cit.* 1978.

55. L. Tilly and J. Scott, *op. cit.*, chap. 2.

56. Hasquin, *op. cit.*, pp. 292–293.

57. *Ibid.*, 292.

58. Lesthaege, *op. cit.*, p. 69, citing Hofstee as the argument's source.

59. E. A. Wrigley, "The Growth of Population in Eighteenth-Century England: A Conundrum Resolved," *Past and Present* 98 (1983): 121–150.

60. Leszek A. Kosínski, *The Population of Europe. A Geographical Perspective* (London: Longmans, 1970),57.

61. Hubert Charbonneau, *Tourouvre-au-Perche aux XVIIe et XVIIIe siécles* (Paris: Presses Universitaires de France, 1974).

62. Kristian Hvidt, *Flight to America. The Social Background of 300,000 Danish Emigrants* (New York: Academic Press, 1975).

63. For example, C. J. Bukatsch, "The Constancy of Local Population and Migration in England before 1800," *Population Studies* 5 (1951): 62–69; Julian Cornwall, "Evidence of Population Mobility in the Seventeenth Century," *Bulletin of the Institute of Historical Research* 40 (1967): 143–152; Eriksson and Rogers, *op. cit.*; Carl Hammer, "The Mobility of Skilled Labour in Late Medieval England. Some Oxford Evidence," *Vierteljahrschrift für Sozial- und Wirtschaftsgeschichte* 63 (1976): 194–210; T. H. Hollingsworth, "Historical Studies of Migration," *Annales de Demographie Historique* (1970): 87–96; Martinius, *op. cit.*; John Patten, *Rural-Urban Migration in Pre-Industrial England* (Oxford: School of Geography, 1973); Jean-Pierre Poussou, "Introduction à l'étude des mouvements migratoires en Espagne, Italie et France méditerranéenne au XVIIIe siècle," In M. Aymard et al., eds., *Les migrations dans les pays méditerranéens au XVIIIème au début du XIXème* (Nice: Centre de al Méditerranée Moderne et Contemporaine, 1974); David Sabean, "Household Formation and Geographic Mobility: A Family Register Study in a Wurttemburg Village 1760–1900," *Zeitschrift für Agrargeschichte und Agrarsoziologie* 14 (1971): 137–175.

64. Slack, *op. cit.*

65. Abel Châtelain, *Les migrants temporaires en France de 1800 à 1914: Histoire économique et sociale des migrants temporaires des campagnes françaises du XIXe siècle au début du XXe siècle*, 2 vols. (Lille: Publications de l'Université de Lille, 1976). See also Braun, *op. cit.*, 1965; Kellenbenz *op. cit.*, 1975; Lequin, *op. cit.*; L. Tilly, *op. cit.*, 1977.

66. See Châtelain, *op. cit.*, for numerous examples.

ACKNOWLEDGMENTS

Previous versions of this chapter have taken shape as an address to the American Historical Association (1976) as "Sociology, History and the Origins of the European Proletariat" (CRSO Working Paper 148, 1976) and as "Demographic Origins of the European Proletariat" (CRSO) Working Paper 207, 1979; revised version CRSO Working Paper 286, 1983). The reactions of audiences at the University of Michigan, the University of Missouri, the University of Utah, Emory University, the California Institute of Technology, and a number of other places have stimulated some of that incessant revision. Searching criticism, coupled with encouragement to keep on revising, have come from Ron Aminzade, Rod Aya, John Knodel, David Levine, Franklin Mendels, Richard Tilly, Jan de Vries, and David Weir. I am especially grateful to Knodel for challenging my demographic thinking and to Mendels, de Vries, and Weir for saving me from technical blunders. A major part of the formalization derives from advice given me by Mendels; I have not, however, adopted his intriguing idea of incorporating the intensity of work directly into the definition of proletarianization. I owe thanks to Martha Guest, Cecilia Brown, Joan Skowronski, Dawn Hendricks, and Phil Soergel for help with the bibliography and to Rose Siri and Sheila Wilder for help in producing the paper. The Horace Rackham School of Graduate Studies (University of Michigan) and the National Science Foundation have supported the work on European social change that lies behind this chapter.

BIBLIOGRAPHY

In addition to each item cited in the text, I have included a number of historical surveys that shed light on the creation of the European proletariat, a few relevant theoretical essays, and a great many local or regional studies that contain evidence on one aspect of proletarianization or another. For syntheses and bibliographies of major literatures on which the paper draws, see especially Blum 1978, Braverman 1974, Cipolla 1976, Goody, Thirsk, and Thompson 1976, Kellenbenz 1976, Kriedte, Medick and Schlumbohm 1977, Landes 1969, Lis and Soly 1979, McKeown 1976, Milward and Saul 1973, Slicher van Bath 1977, C. Tilly 1975, 1978a, 1978b, 1979, 1982, L. Tilly and J. Scott 1978, R. and C. Tilly 1971, and de Vries 1976.

Wilhelm Abel
1974 *Massenarmut und Hungerkrisen im Vorindustriellen Europa.* Hamburg and Berlin: Paul Parey.
Gerhard Adelmann
1979 "Die ländlichen Textilgewerbe des Rheinlandes vor der Industrialisierung," *Rheinische Vierteljahrsblätter* 43:260–288.
Kurt Ågren, Sune Åkerman, Ingrid Erikson, David Gaunt, Anders Norberg, and John Rogers

1973   *Aristocrats, Farmers, Proletarians. Essays in Swedish Demographic History.* Uppsala: Almqvist & Wiksell. Studia Historica Upsaliensia, 47.

Sune Åkerman, Hans Christian Johansen, and David Gaunt, eds.
1978   *Chance and Change: Social and Economic Studies in Historical Demography in the Baltic Area.* Odense: Scandinavian Universities Press.

Eric L. Almqvist
1979   "Pre-Famine Ireland and the Theory of European Proto-industrialization: Evidence from the 1841 Census," *Journal of Economic History* 39:699–718.

Perry Anderson
1974   *Lineages of the Absolutist State.* London: NLB.

Rudolf Andorka
1979   "Family Reconstitution and Types of Household Structure," in Jan Sundin and Eric Soderlund, eds., *Time, Space and Man.* Stockholm: Almqvist & Wiksell International.

Stanley Aronowitz
1978   "Marx, Braverman, and the Logic of Capital." *Insurgent Sociologist* 8:126–146.

Lothar Baar
1968   "Probleme der industriellen Revolution in grossstädtischen Industriezentren. Das Berliner Beispiel," in Wolfram Fischer, ed., *Wirtschafts- und sozialgeschichtliche Probleme der frühen Industrialisierung.* Berlin: Colloquium Verlag.

Klaus J. Bade
1982   "Transnationale Migration und Arbeitsmarkt im Kaiserreich. Vom Agrarstaat mit stärker Industrie zum Industriestaat mit stärker agrarischen Basis," in Toni Pierenkemper and Richard Tilly, eds., *Historische Arbeitsmarktforschung. Entstehung, Entwicklung und Probleme der Vermarktung von Arbeiskraft.* Göttingen: Vandenhoeck & Ruprecht.

Paul Bairoch
1977   *Taille des villes, conditions de vie et développement économique.* Paris: Ecole des Hautes Etudes en Sciences Sociales.

Paul Bairoch and J. M. Limbor
1968   "Changes in the Industrial Distribution of the World Labour Force, by Region, 1880–1960," *International Labor Review* 98:311–336.

A. L. Beier
1978   "Social Problems in Elizabethan London," *Journal of Interdisciplinary History* 9:203–221.

J. R. Bellerby
1958   "The Distribution of Manpower in Agriculture and Industry 1851–1951," *Farm Economist* 9:1–11.

Reinhard Bendix
1956   *Work and Authority in Industry. Ideologies of Management in the Course of Industrialization.* New York: Wiley.

Lutz Berkner
1977   "Peasant Household Organization and Demographic Change in Lower Saxony (1689–1766)," in Ronald Lee, ed., *Population Patterns in the Past.* New York: Academic Press.

Lutz Berkner and Franklin F. Mendels
1978   "Inheritance Systems, Family Structure, and Demographic Patterns in Western Europe, 1700–1900," in Charles Tilly, ed., *Historical Studies of Changing Fertility.* Princeton, N.J.: Princeton University Press.

Karlheinz Blaschke
   1967   *Bevölkerungsgeschichte von Sachsen bis zur industriellen Revolution*. Weimar:
              Böhlhaus.
Grethe Authén Blom, ed.
   1977   *Industrialiseringens første fase*. Olso: Universitetsforlaget. Urbaniseringspro-
              sessen i Norden, 3.
Jerome Blum
   1978   *The End of the Old Order in Rural Europe*. Princeton, N.J.: Princeton University
              Press.
Willi A. Boelcke
   1967   "Wändlungen der dorflichen Sozialstruktur während Mittelalter und Neu-
              zeit," in Heinz Haushofer and Willi A. Boelcke, eds., Wege und Forschun-
              gen der Agrargeschichte. Frankfurt a/Main: DLG Verlag.
Ingomar Bog
   1975   "Über Arme und Armenfürsorge in Oberdeutschland in der Eidgenossen-
              schaft im 15. und 16. Jahrhundert," *Jahrbuch für fränkische Landesforschung*
              34/35:983–1001.
Douglas E. Booth
   1978   "Karl Marx on State Regulation of the Labor Process: The English Factory
              Acts," *Review of Social Economy* 36:137–158.
Peter Borscheid
   1978   *Textilarbeiterschaft in der Industrialisierung. Soziale Lage und Mobilität in Würt-
              temberg* (19. Jahrhundert). Stuttgart: Klett-Cotta.
J. Bourget
   1954   "Prolétarisation d'une commune de l'agglomération parisienne: Colombes,"
              La Vie Urbaine. Urbanisme et Habitation n.s. nos. 3 et 4:185–194.
Samuel Bowles and Herbert Gintis
   1975   "Class Power and Alienated Labor," *Monthly Review* 26:9–25.
Robert Boyer
   1979   "Wage Formation in Historical Perspective: The French Experience," *Cam-
              bridge Journal of Economics* 3:99–118.
Fernand Braudel
   1979   *Civilisation matérielle, économie et capitalisme, XVe–XVIIIe siècles*. 3 vols. Paris:
              Colin.
Rudolf Braun
   1960   *Industrialisierung und Volksleben*. Zurich: Rentsch.
   1965   *Sozialer und Kultureller Wandel in einem ländlichen Industriegebiet*. Zurich:
              Rentsch.
   1978   "Early Industrializaton and Demographic Change in the Canton of Zurich,"
              in Charles Tilly, ed., *Historical Studies in Changing Fertility*. Princeton, N.J.:
              Princeton University Press.
Harry Braverman
   1974   *Labor and Monopoly Capital. The Degradation of Work in the Twentieth Century*.
              New York: Wiley.
Robert Brenner
   1976   "Agrarian Class Structure and Economic Development in Pre-Industrial Eu-
              rope," *Past and Present* 70:30–75.
   1977   "The Origins of Capitalist Development. A Critique of Neo-Smithian Marx-
              ism," *New Left Review* 104:25–92.
John D. Buissink

1971   "Regional Differences in Marital Fertility in the Netherlands in the Second Half of the Nineteenth Century," *Population Studies* 25:353–374.

C. J. Bukatsch
1951   "The Constancy of Local Population and Migration in England Before 1800," *Population Studies* 5:62–69.

Larry L. Bumpass
1969   "Age at Marriage As a Variable in Socio-economic Differentials in Fertility." *Demography* 6:45–54.

Michael Burawoy
1979a   *Manufacturing Consent. Changes in the Labor Process Under Monopoly Capitalism.* Chicago: University of Chicago Press.
1979b   "Towards a Marxist Theory of the Labor Process: Braverman and Beyond," *Politics and Society* 8(3–4):247–312.

John C. Caldwell
1976   "Towards a Restatement of Demographic Transition Theory," *Population and Development Review* 2:321–366.
1981   "The Mechanisms of Demographic Change in Historical Perspective," *Population Studies* 35:5–27.
1982   *Theory of Fertility Decline.* New York: Academic Press.

Gösta Carlsson
1970   "Nineteenth Century Fertility Oscillations," *Population Studies* 24:413–422.

N. Caulier-Mathy
1963–   "La composition d'un prolétariat industriel. Les cas de l'entreprise Cock-
1964   erill." *Revue d'Histoire de la Sidérurgie* 4:207–222.

Pierre Cayez
1981   "Une proto-industrialisation décalée: la ruralisation de la soierie lyonnaise dans la première moitié du XIXème siècle," *Revue du Nord* 63:95–104.

J. D. Chambers
1953   "Enclosure and the Labour Supply in the Industrial Revolution," *Economic History Review*, 2d ser., 5:319–343.
1957   *The Vale of Trent, 1670–1800. A Regional Study of Economic Change.* Cambridge: Cambridge University Press. Economic History Review Supplements, 3.
1965   "Three Essays on the Population and Economy of the Midlands," in D. V. Glass and D. E. C. Eversley, eds., *Population in History.* Chicago: Aldine.

J. D. Chambers and G. E. Mingay
1966   *The Agricultural Revolution, 1750–1880.* London: Batsford.

Hubert Charbonneau
1974   *Tourouvre-au-Perche aux XVIIe et XVIIIe siècles.* Paris: Presses Universitaires de France. Institut National d'Etudes Demographiques, Travaux et Documents, cahier 55.

Serge Chassagne
1981   "Aspects des phénomènes d'industrialisation et de désindustrialisation dans les campagnes françaises au XIXème siècle," *Revue du Nord* 63:35–58.

Abel Châtelain
1976   *Les migrants temporaires en France de 1800 à 1914: Histoire économique et sociale des migrants temporaires des campagnes françaises du XIXe siècle au début du XXe siècle.* 2 vols. Lille: Publications de l'Université de Lille.

Pierre Chaunu
1970   *La civilisation de l'Europe classique.* Paris: Arthaud.

A. V. Chayanov
    1966   *The Theory of Peasant Economy*. Homewood, Ill.: Richard D. Irwin.
Louis Chevalier
    1958   *Classes laborieuses et classes dangéreuses*. Paris: Plon.
Helena Chojnacka
    1976   "Nuptiality Patterns in an Agrarian Society," *Population Studies* 30:203–226.
Carlo Cipolla
    1976   *Before the Industrial Revolution. European Society and Economy, 1000–1700*. New
                York: Norton.
J. H. Clapham
    1923   "The Growth of an Agrarian Proletariat, 1688–1832, A Statistical Note,"
                Cambridge Historical Journal 1:92–95.
L. A. Clarkson
    1971   *The Pre-Industrial Economy in England 1500–1750*. London: Batsford.
Hugh D. Clout
    1977   "Industrial Development in the Eighteenth and Nineteenth Centuries," in
                Hugh D. Clout, ed., *Themes in the Historical Geography of France*. New York:
                Academic Press.
Ansley Coale
    1969   "The Decline of Fertility in Europe from the French Revolution to World War
                II," in S. J. Behrman, ed., *Fertility and Family Planning*. Ann Arbor: Univer-
                sity of Michigan Press.
    1983   "Recent Trends in Fertility in Less Developed Countries," *Science* 221:828–
                832.
A. W. Coats
    1967   "The Classical Economists and the Labourer," in E. L. Jones and G. E. Min-
                gay, eds., *Lands, Labour and Population in the Industrial Revolution. Essays Pre-
                sented to J. D. Chambers*. London: Arnold.
    1976   "The Relief of Poverty, Attitudes to Labour and Economic Change in Eng-
                land, 1660–1782," *International Review of Social History* 21:98–115.
Jon S. Cohen and Martin L. Weitzman
    1975   "Enclosures and Depopulation: A. Marxian Analysis," in William N. Parker
                and Eric L. Jones, eds., *European Peasants and Their Markets*. Princeton, N.J.:
                Princeton University Press.
D. C. Coleman
    1955–1956   "Labour in the English Economy of the Seventeenth Century," *Economic
                History Review*, 2d ser., 8:280–295.
E. J. T. Collins
    1969   "Labour Supply and Demand in European Agriculture 1800–1880," in E. L.
                Jones and S. J. Woolf, eds., *Agrarian Change and Economic Development. The
                Historical Problems*. London: Methuen.
Patrick Colquhoun
    1806   *A Treatise on Indigence*. London: J. Hatchard.
    1815   *Treatise on the Wealth, Power and Response of the British Empire*. London: Joseph
                Mawman.
J. P. Cooper
    1967   "The Social Distribution of Land and Men in England, 1436–1700," *Economic
                History Review*, 2d ser., 20:419–440.
Julian Cornwall
    1967   "Evidence of Population Mobility in the Seventeenth Century," *Bulletin of
                the Institute of Historical Research* 40:143–152.

Alain Corbin
1975   *Archaisme et modernité en Limousin au XIXe siècle.* 2 vols. Paris: Marcel Rivière.
Marcel Couturier
1969   *Recherches sur les structures sociales de Chateaudun.* Paris: SEVPEN.
Patricia Croot and David Parker
1978   "Agrarian Class Structure and Economic Development," *Past and Present* 78:37–46.
Herman E. Daly
1971   "A Marxian-Malthusian View of Poverty and Development," *Population Studies* 25:25–37.
Mike Davis
1975   "The Stop Watch and the Wooden Shoe: Scientific Management and the Industrial Workers of the World," *Radical America* 9:69–85.
Natalie Zemon Davis
1968   "Poor Relief, Humanism and Heresy: The Case of Lyon," *Studies in Medieval and Renaissance History* 5:217–275.
Alan Dawley
1976   *Class and Community. The Industrial Revolution in Lynn.* Cambridge, Mass.: Harvard University Press.
Phyllis Deane and W. A. Cole
1967   *British Economic Growth, 1688–1959. Trends and Structure.* Cambridge: Cambridge University Press.
Paul Deprez
1965   "The Demographic Development of Flanders in the Eighteenth Century," in D. V. Glass and D. E. C. Eversley, eds., *Population in History.* Chicago: Aldine.
Bernard Desrouet
1980   "Une démographie différentielle: Clés pour un système autorégulateur des populations rurales d'Ancien Régime," *Annales: Economies, Sociétés, Civilisations* 35:3–41.
Pierre Deyon
1967a   *Amiens capitale provinciale. Etude sur la société urbaine au 17e siècle.* Paris: Mouton.
1967b   "A propos du paupérisme au milieu du XVIIe siècle: Peinture et Charité chrétienne," *Annales: Economies, Sociétés, Civilisations* 22:137–153.
1979a   "L'Enjeu des discussions autour du concept de 'protoindustrialisation'," *Revue du Nord* 61:9–15.
1979b   "La diffusion rurale des industries textiles en Flandre française à la fin de l'Ancien Régime et au début du XIXe siècle," *Revue du Nord* 61:83–95.
1981   "Un modèle à l'épreuve, le développement industriel de Roubaix de 1762 à la fin du XIXème siècle," *Revue du Nord* 61:59–66.
H. van Dijk
1980   *Wealth and Property in the Netherlands in Modern Times.* Rotterdam: Centrum voor Maatschappijgeschiednis.
Maurice Dobb
1963   *Studies in the Development of Capitalism.* Rev. ed. London: Routledge & Kegan Paul.
Folke Dovring
1969   "Eighteenth-Century Changes in European Agriculture: A Comment," *Agricultural History* 43:181–186.
Michael Drake

1969   *Population and Society in Norway, 1735–1865.* Cambridge: Cambridge University Press.

Robert S. DuPlessis and Martha C. Howell
1982   "Reconsidering Early Modern Urban Economy: The Cases of Leiden and Lille," *Past and Present* 94:49–84.

John D. Durand
1975   *The Labor Force in Economic Development. A Comparison of International Census Data 1946–1966.* Princeton, N.J.: Princeton University Press.

Stale Dyrvik
1972   "Historical Demography in Norway, 1660–1801: A Short Survey," *Scandinavian Economic History Review* 20:27–44.

Richard A. Easterlin
1978   "The Economics and Sociology of Fertility: A Synthesis," in Charles Tilly, ed., *Historical Studies of Changing Fertility.* Princeton, N.J.: Princeton University Press.

Richard Edwards
1978   "Social Relations of Production at the Point of Production," *Insurgent Sociologist* 8:109–125.

Mohamed El Kordi
1970   *Bayeux aux XVIIe et XVIIIe siècles.* Paris: Mouton.

Rudolf Endres
1975   "Das Armenproblem im Zeitalter des Absolutismus," *Jahrbuch für Frankische Landesforschung* 34–35:1003–1020.

Ingrid Eriksson and John Rogers
1978   *Rural labor and Population Change. Social and Demographic Development in East-Central Sweden during the Nineteenth Century.* Stockholm: Almqvist & Wiksell; Studia Historica Upsaliensia, 100.

Juan G. Espinosa and Andrew S. Zimbalist
1978   *Economic Democracy. Workers' Participation in Chilean Industry 1970–1973.* New York: Academic Press.

Alan Everitt
1967   "Farm Labourers," in H. P. R. Finberg, ed., The Agrarian History of England and Wales IV. 1500–1640. Cambridge: Cambridge University Press.

J. A. Faber, H. K. Roessingh, B. H. Slicher van Bath, A. M. van der Woude, and H. J. van Xanten
1965   "Population Changes and Economic Developments in the Netherlands: A Historical Survey," *A. A. G. Bijdragen* 12:47–114.

Wolfram Fischer
1963   "Soziale Unterschichten im Zeitalter der Frühindustrialisierung," *International Review of Social History,* 8:415–435.

Michael W. Flinn
1970   *British Population Growth, 1700–1850.* London: Macmillan.
1981   *The European Demographic System, 1500–1820.* Baltimore: Johns Hopkins University Press.

Michael Fores
1981   "The Myth of a British Industrial Revolution," *History* 66:181–198.

John Foster
1974   *Class Struggle and the Industrial Revolution. Early Industrial Capitalism in Three Towns.* London: Weidenfeld & Nicolson.

Etienne François

1975   "Unterschichten und Armut in rheinischen Residenzstädten des 18. Jahrhunderts," *Vierteljahrschrift für Sozial- und Wirtschaftsgeschichte,* 62:433–464.

Gunther Franz
1970   *Geschichte des deutscher Bauernständes vom frühen Mittelalter bis zum 19. Jahrhundert.* Stuttgart: Ulmer. Deutsche Agrargeschichte. Edited by Gunther Franz. Vol. 4.

Rainer Fremdling and Richard Tilly, eds.
1979   *Industrialisierung und Raum. Studien zur regionalen Differenzierung im Deutschland des 19. Jahrhunderts.* Stuttgart: Klett-Cotta.

Herman Freudenberger
1960   "Industrialization in Bohemia and Moravia in the Eighteenth Century," *Journal of Central European Affairs* 19:347–356.
1968   "Die Struktur der frühindustriellen Fabrik im Umriss (mit besonderer Berüksichtigung Böhmens)," in Wolfram Fischer, ed., *Wirtschafts-und sozialgeschichtliche Probleme der frühen Industrialisierung.* Berlin: Colloquium Verlag.

Gunnar Fridlizius
1975   "Some New Aspects of Swedish Population Growth," *Economy and History* 18:3–33, 126–154.

Dov Friedlander
1973   "Demographic Patterns and Socioeconomic Characteristics of the Coal-Mining Population in England and Wales in the Nineteenth Century," *Economic Development and Cultural Change* 22:39–51.

Harriet Friedmann
1978   "World Market, State, and Family Farm: Social Bases of Household Production in the Era of Wage Labor," *Comparative Studies in Society and History* 20:545–586.

Fridolin Fürger
1927   *Zum Verlagssystem als Organisationsform des Frühkapitalismus im Textilgewerbe.* Stuttgart: W. Köhlhammer. Beihefte zur Vierteljahrschrifte für Sozial- und Wirtschaftsgeschichte, vol. 11.

Giorgio Gagliani
1981   "How Many Working Classes?" *American Journal of Sociology* 87:259–285.

D. Gallie
1978   *In Search of the New Working Class. Automation and Social Integration Within the Capitalist Enterprise.* Cambridge: Cambridge University Press.

Maurice Garden
1970   *Lyon et les Lyonnais au XVIIIe siècle.* Paris: Les Belles Lettres.

David Gartman
1978   "Marx and the Labor Process: An Interpretation," *Insurgent Sociologist* 8:97–108.

David Gaunt
1976   Familj, Hushall och arbetsintensitet," *Scandia* 42:32–59.
1977   "Pre-Industrial Economy and Population Structure: The Elements of Variance in Early Modern Sweden," *Scandinavian Journal of History* 2:183–210.

B. Geremek
1968   "La popolazione marginale tra il medioeve e l'era moderne," *Studi Storici* 9:623–640.

Herbert Gintis
1976   "The Nature of Labor Exchange and the Theory of Capitalist Production," *Review of Radical Political Economy* 8:36–54.

Jack Goody
  1973   "Strategies of Heirship," *Comparative Studies in Society and History* 15:3–20.
Jack Goody, Joan Thirsk, and E. P. Thompson, eds.
  1976   *Family and Inheritance: Rural Society in Western Europe 1200–1800.* Cambridge:
            Cambridge University Press.
David M. Gordon, Richard Edwards, and Michael Reich
  1982   *Segmented Work, Divided Workers. The Historical Transformation of Labor in the
            United States.* Cambridge: Cambridge University Press.
Pierre Goubert
  1968   *Cent mille provinciaux au XVIIe siècle. Beauvais et le Beauvaisis de 1600 à 1730.*
            Paris: Flammarion.
            L'Ancien Régime. I. La Société. Paris: Colin.
Franz Gschwind
  1977   *Bevölkerungsentwicklung und Wirtschaftsstruktur der Landschaft Basel im 18. Jahr-
            hundert.* Liestal: Kantonal Drücksachen- und Materialzentrale.
Philippe Guignet
  1979   "Adaptations, mutations et survivances proto-industrielles dans le textile du
            Cambrésis et du Valenciennois du XVIIIème au début du XXème siècle,"
            Revue du Nord 61:27–59.
Gay L. Gullickson
  1981   "The Sexual Division of Labor in Cottage Industry and Agriculture in the
            Pays de Caux: Auffay, 1750–1850," *French Historical Studies* 12:177–199.
  1982   "Proto-industrialization, Demographic Behavior and the Sexual Division of
            Labor in Auffay, France, 1750–1850," *Peasant Studies* 9:106–118.
Myron P. Gutmann and René Leboutte
  1979   "Early Industrialization and Population Change. Rethinking Protoindustrial-
            ization and the Family," Austin: Texas Population Research Center, Papers.
Jean-Pierre Gutton
  1974   *La société et les pauvres en Europe, XVIe–XVIIIe siècles.* Paris: Presses Univer-
            sitaires de France.
H. J. Habakkuk
  1955   "Family Structure and Economic Change in Nineteenth-Century Europe,"
            Journal of Economic History 15:1–12.
  1965   "La disparition du paysan anglais," *Annales: Economies, Sociétés, Civilisations*
            20:649–663.
  1971   *Population Growth and Economic Development Since 1750.* Leicester: Leicester
            University Press.
Michael Haines
  1979   *Fertility and Occupation. Population Patterns in Industrialization.* New York: Ac-
            ademic Press.
John Hajnal
  1982   "Two Kinds of Preindustrial Household Formation System," *Population and
            Development Review* 8:449–494.
Carl Hammer
  1976   "The Mobility of Skilled Labour in Late Medieval England. Some Oxford
            Evidence," *Vierteljahrschrift für Sozial- und Wirtschaftsgeschichte* 63:194–210.
Michael Hanagan
  1980   *The Logic of Solidarity. Artisans and Industrial Workers in Three French Towns,
            1871–1914.* Urbana: University of Illinois Press.
Gerhard Hanke
  1969   "Zur Sozialstruktur der ländlichen Siedlungen Altbayerns im 17. und 18.

Jahrhundert," in *Gesellschaft und Herrschaft. Forschungen zur sozial- und landgeschichtlichen Problemen vornehmlich in Bayern.* Munich: C. H. Beck.

Gerd H. Hardach
1969   *Der soziale Status des Arbeiters in der Frühindustrialisierung.* Berlin: Duncker & Humblot.

Hartmut Harnisch
1975   "Bevölkerung und Wirtschaft. Uber Zusammenhänge zwischen sozialökonomischen Struktur und demographischer Entwicklung im Spätfeudalismus," *Jahrbuch für Wirtschaftsgeschichte* 2:57–87.

1978   "Produktivkräfte und Produktionsverhältnisse in der Landwirtschaft der Magdeburger Börde von der Mitte des 18. Jh. bis zum Beginn der Zuckerüberanbaus in der Mitte der dreissiger Jahre des 19. Jr.," in Hans-Jürgen Rach and Bernhard Weissel, eds., *Landwirtschaft und Kapitalismus.* Berlin: Akademie Verlag.

William Hasbach
1920   *A History of the English Agricultural Labourer.* London: P. S. King.

Hervé Hasquin
1971   *Une mutation. Le "Pays de Charleroi" aux XVIIe et XVIIIe siècles.* Brussels: Editions de l'Institut de Sociologie, Université Libre de Bruxelles.

Friedrich-Wilhelm Henning
1977   "Der Beginn der modernen Welt im agrarischen Bereich," in Reihhart Koselleck, ed., *Studien zum Beginn der modernen Welt.* Stuttgart: Klett-Cotta.

1978   "Humanisierung und Technisierung der Arbeitswelt. Über den Einfluss der Industrialisierung auf die Arbeitsbedingungen im 19. Jahrhundert," in Jürgen Reulecke and Wolfhard Weber, eds., *Fabrik, Familie, Feierabend.* Wuppertal: Peter Hammer.

David G. Hey
1969   "A Dual Economy in South Yorkshire," *Agricultural History Review* 17:108–119.

Christopher Hill
1952   "Puritans and the Poor," *Past and Present* 2:32–50.

1967   "Pottage for Freeborn Englishmen: Attitudes to Wage Labour in the Sixteenth and Seventeenth Centuries," in C. H. Feinstein, ed., *Socialism, Capitalism and Economic Growth. Essays Presented to Maurice Dobb.* Cambridge: Cambridge University Press.

R. H. Hilton
1975   *The English Peasantry in the Later Middle Ages.* Oxford: Oxford University Press.

Kurt Hinze
1963   *Die Arbeiterfrage zu Beginn des modernen Kapitalismus in Brandenburg-Preussen, 1685–1806.* 2d ed. Berlin: Walter de Gruyter.

E. J. Hobsbawm
1980   "Scottish Reformers of the Eighteenth Century and Capitalist Agriculture," in E. J. Hobsbawm *et al., Peasants in History. Essays in Honour of Daniel Thorner.* Calcutta: Oxford University Press.

E. W. Hofstee
1968   "Population Increase in the Netherlands," *Acta Historiae Neerlandica* 3:43–125.

Erland Hofsten and Hans Lundstrom
1976   *Swedish Population History. Main Trends from 1750 to 1970.* Stockholm: Statistika Centralbyran Urval, no. 8.

Gerd Hohorst

1977   *Wirtschaftswachstum und Bevölkerungsentwicklung in Preussen 1816–1914.* New
        York: Arno Press.

1982   "Protoindustrialisierung im Übergang zum industriellen Kapitalismus: Die
        demoökonomische Entwicklung im Kreis Hagen 1817 bis 1863," in Pierre
        Deyon and Franklin Mendels, eds., *Protoindustrialisation: Theorie et réalité.*
        Lille: Université des Arts, Lettres, et Sciences Humanaines.

B. A. Holderness
1972   " 'Open' and 'Close' Parishes in England in the Eighteenth and Nineteenth
        Centuries," *Agricultural History Review* 22:126–138.

T. H. Hollingsworth
1971   "Historical Studies of Migration," *Annales de Demographie Historique*
        1970:87–96.

David W. Howell
1978   *Land and People in Nineteenth-Century Wales.* London: Routledge & Kegan Paul.

Olwen H. Hufton
1974   *The Poor of Eighteenth-Century France, 1750–1789.* Oxford: Clarendon Press.

Volker Hunecke
1978   *Arbeiterschaft und Industrielle Revolution in Mailand 1859–1892.* Gottingen: Van-
        denhoeck & Ruprecht.

James P. Huzel
1980   "The Demographic Impact of the Old Poor Law: More Reflexions on Mal-
        thus," *Economic History Review* n.s. 33:367–381.

Kristian Hvidt
1975   *Flight to America. The Social Background of 300,000 Danish Emigrants.* New York:
        Academic Press.

V. K. Iatsunsky
1965   "Formation en Russie de la grande industrie textile sur la base de la pro-
        duction rurale," *Second International Conference of Economic History. Aixen-
        Provence 1962.* Paris: Mouton. Vol. 2: 365–376.

1971   "Le rôle des migrations et de l'accroissement naturel dans la colonisation
        des nouvelles régions de la Russie," *Annales de Démographie Historique*
        1970:302–312.

Arthur Erwin Imhof
1976   *Aspekte der Bevölkerungsentwicklung in den nordischen Ländern 1720–1750.* 2 vols.
        Bern: Francke Verlag.

Maths Isacson
1979   *Ekonomisk tillvaxt och social differentiering 1680–1860. Bondeklassen i By Socken,
        Kopparbergs lan.* Stockholm: Almqvist & Wiksell International.

Carl Jantke
1965   "Zur Deutung des Pauperismus," in Carl Jantke and Dietrich Hilger, eds.,
        *Die Eigentumslösen. Der deutsche Pauperismus und die Emanzipationskrise in Dar-
        stellung der zeitgenossischen Literatur.* Munich: Karl Alber.

Karlbernhard Jasper
1965   *Der Urbanisierungsprozess dargestellt am Beispiel der Stadt Köln.* Cologne: Rhein-
        isch-Weistfälischen Wirtschaftsarchiv zu Köln. Schriften zur Rheinisch-
        Westfälischen Wirtschaftsgeschichte, 30.

Hans Christian Johansen
1975   *Befolkningsudvikling og familie Struktur: Det 18. arhundrede.* Odense: Odense
        University Press.

Arthur Henry Johnson
1909   *The Disappearance of the Small Landowner.* Oxford: Clarendon Press.

Robert Eugene Johnson
1979   *Peasant and Proletarian. The Working Class of Moscow in the Late Nineteenth Century.* New Brunswick, N.J.: Rutgers University Press.
E. L. Jones
1964   "The Agricultural Labour Market in England, 1793–1872," *Economic History Review* 17:322–338.
1968   "The Agricultural Origins of Industry," *Past and Present* 40:58–71.
Lennart Jorberg
1972a   "The Development of Real Wages for Agricultural Workers in Sweden During the 18th and 19th Centuries," *Economy and History* 15:41–57.
1972b   *A History of Prices in Sweden 1732–1914.* 2 vols. Lund: Gleerup.
Etienne Juillard, ed.
1976   *Apogée et crise de la civilisation paysanne.* Paris: Seuil. *Histoire de la France rurale.* Edited by Georges Duby and Armand Wallon. t. 3.
Eino Jutikkala
1975   "Large-Scale Farming in Scandinavia in the Seventeenth Century," *Scandinavian Economic History Review* 23:159–166.
Ann-Sofie Kalvemark
1977   "The Country That Kept Track of Its Population," *Scandinavian Journal of History* 2:211–230.
Jeffrey Kaplow
1972   *The Names of Kings. The Parisian Laboring Poor in the Eighteenth Century.* New York: Basic Books.
Hermann Kellenbenz
1965   "Ländliches Gewerbe und bauerliches Unternehmertum in Westeuropa von Spätmittelalter bis ins XVIII. Jahrhundert," *Second International Conference of Economic History. Aix en Provence 1962.* Paris: Mouton. Vol. 2:377–428.
1975   *Agrarisches Nebengewerbe und Formen du reagrarisierung im Spätmittelatter und 19./20 Jahrhundert.* Stuttgart: Gustav Fischer. *Forschungen zur Sozial- und Wirtschaftsgeschichte, 21.*
1976   *The Rise of the European Economy. An Economic History of Continental Europe from the Fifteenth to the Eighteenth Century.* London: Weidenfeld & Nicolson.
J. Thomas Kelly
1977   *Thorns on the Tudor Rose. Monks, Rogues, Vagabonds, and Sturdy Beggars.* Jackson: University Press of Mississippi
Hubert Kiesewetter
1980   "Bevölkerung, Erwerbstätige und Landwirtschaft im Königreich Sachsen 1815–1871," in Sidney Pollard, ed., *Region und Industrialisierung. Studien zur Rolle der Region in der Wirtschaftsgeschichte der letzten zwei Jahrhunderte.* Göttingen: Vandenhoeck & Ruprecht.
Gregory King
1936   "Naturall and Politicall Observations and Conclusions upon the State and
[1696]   Condition of England," in G. E. Barnett, ed., *Two Tracts by Gregory King.* Baltimore: Johns Hopkins University Press. First published in 1696.
Bernard Kirchgassner
1974   "Der Verlag im Spannungsfeld von Stadt und Umland," in Eric Maschke and Jurgen Sydow, eds., *Stadt und Umland. Protokoll der X. Arbeitstagung des Arbeitskreises für sudwestdeutsche Stadtgeschichtsforschung.* Stuttgart: Köhlhammer. *Veröffentlichungen der Kommission für Geschichtliche Landeskunde in Baden-Württemberg, Reihe B, 82.* Pp. 72–128.
Herbert Kisch

1981   *Die Hausindustriellen Textilgewerbe am Niederrhein vor der industriellen Revolu-
            tion. Von der ursprünglichen zur kapitalistischen Akkumulation.* Göttingen: Van-
            denhoeck & Ruprecht.

Arnost Klíma
1965   "The Domestic Industry and the Putting-out System (Verlags-System) in the
            Period of Transition from Feudalism to Capitalism," *Second International
            Conference of Economic History, Aix en Provence 1962.* Paris: Mouton. Vol.
            2:477–82.
1968   Die Entstehung der Arbeiterklasse und die Anfänge der Arbeiterbewegung
            in Böhmen," in Wolfram Fischer, ed., *Wirtschafts- und sozialgeschichtliche
            Probleme der frühen Industrialisierung.* Berlin: Colloquium Verlag.
1974   "The Role of Rural Domestic Industry in Bohemia in the Eighteenth Cen-
            tury," *Economic History Review* 27:48–56.

John Knodel
1977   "Family Limitation and the Fertility Transition: Evidence from the Age Pat-
            terns of Fertility in Europe and Asia," *Population Studies* 3:481–521.
1978   "Natural Fertility in Pre-Industrial Germany," *Population Studies* 32:481–510.
1979   "From Natural Fertility to Family Limitation: The Onset of Fertility Transi-
            tion in a Sample of German Villages," *Demography* 16:493–521.
1982   "Demographic Transitions in German Villages," Research Reports, Popu-
            lation Studies Center, University of Michigan.

John Knodel and C. Wilson
1981   "The Secular Increase in Fecundity in German Village Populations: An Anal-
            ysis of Reproductive Histories of Couples Married 1750–1899," *Population
            Studies* 35:53–84.

John Knodel and Etienne van de Walle
1979   "Lessons from the Past: Policy Implications of Historical Fertility Studies,"
            Population and Development Review 5:217–245.

Wolfgang Köllmann
1974   *Bevölkerung in der industriellen Revolution.* Göttingen: Vandenhoeck & Ru-
            precht. *Kritische Studien zur Geschichtswissenschaft,* 12.
1977   "Zur Bevölkerungsentwicklung der Neuzeit," in Reinhart Koselleck, ed.,
            Studien zum Beginn der Modernen Welt. Stuttgart: Klett-Cotta.

Walter Korpi
1978   *The Working Class in Welfare Capitalism. Work, Unions and Politics in Scandinavia.*
            London: Routledge & Kegan Paul.

Leszek A. Kosinski
1970   *The Population of Europe. A Geographical Perspective.* London: Longmans.

J. T. Krause
1967   "Some Aspects of Population Change, 1690–1790," in E. L. Jones and G. E.
            Mingay, eds., *Land, Labour and Population in the Industrial Revolution.* London:
            Arnold.

Peter Kriedte
1982   "Die Stadt im Prozess der europäischen Proto-Industrialisierung," in Pierre
            Deyon and Franklin Mendels, eds., *Proto-industrialisation: Théorie et réalité.*
            Lille: Université des Arts, Lettres, et Sciences Humaines.

Peter Kriedte, Hans Medick, and Jürgen Schlumbohm
1977   *Industrialisierung vor der Industrialisierung. Gewerbliche Warenproduktion auf dem
            Land in der Formationsperiode des Kapitalismus.* Göttingen: Vandenhoeck & Ru-
            precht.

Jürgen Kuczynski

1965 "Industrieller Kapitalismus und Arbeiterklasse," *Second International Conference of Economic History. Aix en Provence 1962.* Paris: Mouton. Vol. 2:25–29.

Witold Kula

1980 "Money and the Serfs in Eighteenth Century Poland," in E. J. Hobsbawm *et al., Peasants in History. Essays in Honour of Daniel Thorner.* Calcutta: Oxford University Press.

Ann Kussmaul

1981 *Servants in Husbandry in Early Modern England.* Cambridge: Cambridge University Press.

David S. Landes

1969 *The Unbound Prometheus. Technological Change and Industrial Development in Western Europe from 1750 to the Present.* Cambridge: Cambridge University Press.

William Langer

1972 "Checks on Population Growth, 1750–1850," *Scientific American* (February):93–99.

Peter Laslett

1968 "Le brassage de la population en France et en Angleterre aux XVIIe et XVIIIe siècles," *Annales de Démographie Historique* 1968:99–109.

V. M. Lavrovskii

1940 *Parlamentskaia Ogorozhivaniia obschinn'ix Zemel' v Anglii kontsa xvii–nachala xix vv.* Moscow: Izdatel'stvo Akademii Nauk SSSR.

William Lazonick

1974 "Karl Marx and Enclosures in England," *Review of Radical Political Economy* 6:1–59.

François Lebrun

1971 *Les hommes et la mort en Anjou aux 17e et 18e siècles.* Paris: Mouton.

Robert Lee

1972 "Introduction: Population Growth, Economic Development and Social Change in Europe, 1750–1970," in W. R. Lee, ed., *European Demography and Economic Growth.* London: Croom Helm.

Ronald Lee

1976 "An Historical Perspective on Economic Aspects of the Population Explosion: The Case of Pre-Industrial England." Unpublished paper, National Bureau of Economic Research.

1977 "Methods and Models for Analyzing Historical Series of Births, Deaths, and Marriages," in Ronald Lee, ed., *Population Patterns in the Past.* New York: Academic Press.

1978 "Models of Pre-Industrial Population Dynamics, with Application to England," in Charles Tilly, ed., *Historical Studies of Changing Fertility.* Princeton, N.J.: Princeton University Press.

Pierre Léon, François Crouzet, and Raymond Gascon, eds.

1972 *L'Industrialisation en Europe au XIXe siècle. Cartographie et Typologie.* Paris: Editions du Centre National de la Recherche Scientifique

Yves Lequin

1977 *Les ouvriers de la région lyonnaise (1848–1914).* 2 vols. Lyon: Presses Universitaires de Lyon.

Emmanuel Le Roy Ladurie

1966 *Les paysans de Languedoc.* 2 vols. Paris: SEVPEN.

1974 "Pour un modèle de l'économie rurale française au XVIIIe siècle," *Cahiers d'histoire* 29:5–27.

1977   "Les masses profondes: la paysannerie," in Fernand Braudel et Ernest La-
        brousse, eds., *Histoire économique et sociale de la France. I, 2: De 1450 à 1660.
        Paysannerie et Croissance.* Paris: Presses Universitaires de la France.

Emmanuel Le Roy Ladurie, ed.
1975   *L'âge classique des paysans, 1340-1789.* Paris: Seuil. *Histoire de la France rurale.*
        Edited by Georges Duby and Armand Wallon. t. 2.

Ron J. Lesthaege
1977   *The Decline of Belgian Fertility, 1800-1970.* Princeton, N.J.: Princeton Univer-
        sity Press.

Giovanni Levi
1971   "Mobilità della popolazione e immigrazione a Torino nella prima metà del
        settecento," *Quaderni storici* 17:510-554.
1974   "Sviluppo urbano e flussi migratori nel Piemonte nel 1600," in M. Aymard,
        ed., *Les Migrations dans les pays méditerranéens au XVIIIème et au début du XIX-
        ème.* Nice: Centre de la Méditerranée Moderne et Contemporaine.

David Levine
1977   *Family Formation in an Age of Nascent Capitalism.* New York: Academic Press.
1983   "Proto-Industrialization and Demographic Upheaval," in David Levine,
        Leslie Page Moch, Louise A. Tilly, John Modell, and Elizabeth Pleck, *Essays
        on the Family and Historical Change.* College Station: Texas A&M Press.

Ulrich Linse
1972   "Arbeiterschaft und Gebürtenentwicklung im Deutschen Kaiserreich von
        1871," *Archiv für Sozialgeschichte* 12:205-272.

Catharina Lis
1976   "Sociale politiek in Antwerpen (1779). Het controleren van de relatieve ov-
        erbevolking en het reguleren van de arbeidsmarkt," *Tijdschrift voor Sociale
        Geschiedenis* 5:146-166.

Catharina Lis and Hugo Soly
1979   *Poverty and Capitalism in Pre-Industrial Europe.* Atlantic Highlands, N.J.: Hu-
        manities Press.

Orvar Lofgren
1978   "The Potato People. Household Economy and Family Patterns Among the
        Rural Proletariat in Nineteenth Century Sweden," in Sune Åkerman, ed.,
        *Chance and Change. Social and Economic Studies in Historical Demography in the
        Baltic Area.* Odense: Odense University Press.

Sven Lundqvist
1977   *Folkrörelserna i det svenska samhallet, 1850-1920.* Stockholm: Almqvist & Wik-
        sell.

Alan Macfarlane
1978   *The Origins of English Individualism.* Cambridge: Cambridge University Press.

Stephen A. Marglin
1974   "What Do Bosses Do? The Origins and Functions of Hierarchy in Capitalist
        Production," *Review of Radical Political Economics* 6:60-112.

Sture Martinius
1967   *Befölkningsrörlighet under industrialismens inledningsskede i Sverige.* Göteborg:
        Elanders. Meddelanden fran Economisk-Historiska Institutionen vid Göte-
        borgs Universitet, 8.
1977   *Peasant Destinies: The History of 552 Swedes Born 1810-1812.* Stockholm:
        Almqvist & Wiksell International.

Karl Marx
1970   *Capital. A Critique of Political Economy.* 3 vols. London: Lawrence & Wishart.

1973   *Grundrisse. Foundations of the Critique of Political Economy* (rough draft). London: Allen Lane.
Peter Mathias
1957   "The Social Structure in the Eighteenth Century: A Calculation by Joseph Massie," *Economic History Review* 10:30–45.
Albert Mathiez
1930   "Notes sur l'importance du prolétariat en France à la veille de la Révolution," *Annales Historiques de la Révolution Française* 7:487–524.
P. C. Matthiessen
1970   *Some Aspects of the Demographic Transition in Denmark.* Copenhagen: Kobenhavns Universitets Fond til Tilvejebringelse af Laeremidler.
Horst Matzerath
1978   "Industrialisierung, Mobilität und sozialen Wandel am Beispiel der Städte Rheydt und Rheindalen," in Hartmut Kaelble, ed., *Probleme der Modernisierung in Deutschland.* Opladen: Westdeutscher Verlag.
Edward E. McKenna
1974   "Marriage and Fertility in Postfamine Ireland: A Multivariate Analysis," *American Journal of Sociology* 80:688–705.
Thomas McKeown
1976   *The Modern Rise of Population.* New York: Academic Press.
Franklin Mendels
1972   "Proto-industrialization: The First Phase of the Industrialization Process," *Journal of Economic History* 32:241–261.
1975   "Agriculture and Peasant Industry in Eighteenth-Century Flanders," in William N. Parker and Eric L. Jones, eds., *European Peasants and Their Markets.* Princeton, N.J.: Princeton University Press.
1978   "Aux origines de la proto-industrialisation," *Bulletin du Centre d'Histoire Economique et Sociale de la Région Lyonnaise* no. 2: 1–25.
1981a   "Les temps de l'industrie et les temps de l'agriculture. Logique d'une analyse régionale de la proto-industrialisation," *Revue du Nord* 63:21–33.
1981b   *Industrialization and Population Pressure in Eighteenth-Century Flanders.* New York: Arno Press.
1982   "Faut-il modifier le modèle flamand?" in Pierre Deyon and Franklin Mendels, eds., *Proto-industrialisation: Theorie et realité.* Lille: Université des Arts, Lettres, et Sciences Humaines.
Andrea Menzione
1971   "Storia sociale quantitativa: alcuni problemi della ricerca per i Secoli XVI–XVIII," *Studi Storici* 12 (July-September):585–596.
Pierre Merlin, ed.
1971   *L'Exode rural, suivi de deux études sur les migrations.* Paris: Presses Universitaires de France. Institut National d'Etudes Demographiques, Travaux et Documents, Cahier 59.
John Merrington
1975   "Town and Country in the Transition to Capitalism," *New Left Review* 93:71–92.
Alan S. Milward and S. B. Saul
1973   *The Economic Development of Continental Europe, 1780–1870.* London: Allen & Unwin.
Dennis Mills
1976   "A Social and Demographic Study of Melbourn, Cambridgeshire c. 1840," *Archives* 12:115–120.

Sidney W. Mintz
1974   "The Rural Proletariat and the Problem of Rural Proletarian Consciousness,"
        Journal of Peasant Studies 1:291–325.
Joel Mokyr
1976   *Industrialization in the Low Countries, 1795–1850.* New Haven, Conn.: Yale
        University Press.
David Montgomery
1976   "Workers' Control of Machine Production in the Nineteenth Century," *Labor
        History Review* 17:485–509.
1979   *Workers' Control in America.* Cambridge: Cambridge University Press.
Barrington Moore, Jr.
1966   *Social Origins of Dictatorship and Democracy: Lord and Peasant in the Making of
        the Modern World.* Boston: Beacon Press.
Wilbert E. Moore and Arnold S. Feldman, eds.
1960   *Labor Commitment and Social Change in Developing Areas.* New York: Social
        Science Research Council.
R. B. Morrow
1978   "Family Limitation in Pre-Industrial England: A Reappraisal," *Economic History Review* 31:419–428.
Bernard Mottez
1966   *Systèmes de salaire et politiques patronales.* Paris: Centre National de la Recherche Scientifique.
L. L. Murav'eva
1971   *Derevensckaia prom'ishlennost' tsentral'noi Rossii vtoroi polovin'i xvii v.* Moscow:
        Izdatel'stvo Nauka.
A. E. Musson
1978   *The Growth of British Industry.* New York: Holmes & Meier.
Douglass C. North and Robert Paul Thomas
1973   *The Rise of the Western World. A New Economic History.* Cambridge: Cambridge
        University Press.
P. K. O'Brien, D. Heath, and C. Keyder
1977   "Agricultural Efficiency in Britain and France, 1815–1914," *Journal of European Economic History* 6:339–391.
Bo Ohngren
1974   *Folk i rörelse. Samhallsutveckling, flyttningsmonster och folkröresler i Eskilstuna
        1870–1900.* Uppsala: Almquist & Wiksell. Studia Historica Upsaliensia, 55.
Martha Paas
1981   *Population, Labor Supply and Agriculture in Augsburg, 1480–1618: A Study of
        Early Demographic-Economic Interaction.* New York: Arno Press.
John Patten
1973   *Rural-Urban Migration in Pre-Industrial England.* Oxford: School of Geography. Research Papers, no. 6.
Luciano Pellicani
1973   "La rivoluzione industriale e il fenomeno della proletarizzazione," *Rassegna
        Italiana di Sociologia* 14:63–84.
Alfred Perrenoud
1970   "Les migrations en Suisse sous l'Ancien Régime: Quelques problèmes," *Annales de Démographie Historique* 1970:251–259.
François Perroux
1970   *Aliénation et société industrielle.* Paris: Gallimard.

Jan Peters
1967   "Ostelbische Landarmut. Sozialökonomisches (sic) über landlöse und landärme Agrarproduzenten im Spätfeudalismus," Jahrbuch für Wirtschaftsgeschichte t. 3–4:255–302.
Jean Pitié
1971   Exode rural et migrations intérieures en France. L'exemple de la Vienne et du Poitou-Charentes. Poitiers: Norois.
Carlo Poni
1982   "Protoindustrializzazione: un commento," Studi Storici 51:1103–1112.
Jean-Pierre Poussou
1971   "Les mouvements migratoires en France et à partir de la France de la fin du XVe siècle au début de XIXe siècle. Approches pour une synthèse," Annales de Démographie Historique 1970:11–78.
1974   "Introduction à l'étude des mouvements migratoires en Espagne, Italie et France méditerranéenne au XVIIIe siècle," in M. Aymard, ed., Les migrations dans les pays méditerranéens au XVIIIème et au début de XIXème. Nice: Centre de la Méditerranée Moderne et Contemporaine.
Walter Prochaska
1956   "Die wirtschaftliche und kulturelle Entwicklung auf dem Eichsfelde von 1648 bis 1848," in Walter Prochaska, ed., Eichsfelder Heimatsbuch. Heiligenstadt: Rat des Kreises Heiligenstadt.
Adam Przeworski
1977   "Proletariat into a Class: The Process of Class Formation from Karl Kautsky's The Class Struggle to Recent Controversies," Politics and Society 7:343–401.
Jaroslav Purš
1965a   "Struktur und Dynamik der industriellen Entwicklung in Böhmen im letzten Viertel des 18. Jahrhunderts," Jahrbuch für Wirtschaftsgeschichte:160–196.
1965b   "Die Aufhebung der Hörigkeit und die Grundentlastung in den böhmischen Ländern." Second International Conference of Economic History. Aix en Provence 1962. Paris: Mouton
Jill Quadagno
1982   Aging in Early Industrial Society. Work, Family, and Social Policy in Nineteenth-Century England. New York: Academic Press.
Hans-Jürgen Rach and Bernhard Weissel, eds.
1978   Landwirtschaft und Kapitalismus. Zur Entwicklung der ökonomischen und sozialen Verhältnisse in der Magdeburger Börde vom Ausgang des 18. Jahrhunderts bis zum Ende des ersten Weltkrieges. 1. Halbband. Berlin: Akademie Verlag.
Arthur Redford
1964   Labour Migration in England, 1800–1850. 2d. ed. Manchester: Manchester University Press.
Fritz Redlich and Herman Freudenberger
1964   "The Industrial Development of Europe: Reality, Symbols, Images," Kyklos 17:372–401.
Alan R. Richards
1979   "The Political Economy of Commercial Estate Labor Systems: A Comparative Analysis of Prussia, Egypt, and Chile," Comparative Studies in Society and History 21:483–518.
Toni Richards
1977   "Fertility Decline in Germany: An Econometric Appraisal," Population Studies 31:537–553.

H. K. Roessingh
    1970   "Village and Hamlet in a Sandy Region of the Netherlands in the Middle of
              the 18th Century. An Application of the Guttman Scalogram Technique to
              Socio-historical Research," *Acta Historiae Neerlandica* 4:105–129.
    1979   "Tobacco Growing in Holland in the Seventeenth and Eighteenth Centuries:
              A Case Study of the Innovative Spirit of Dutch Peasants," *Acta Historiae
              Neerlandica* 11:18–54.
John Rogers, ed.
    1980   *Family Building and Family Planning in Pre-Industrial Societies.* Uppsala: Family
              History Group, University of Uppsala.
Harald Runblom and Hans Norman, eds.
    1976   *From Sweden to America. A History of the Migration.* Minneapolis: University
              of Minnesota Press.
Diedrich Saalfeld
    1966   "Die Produktion und Intensität der Landwirtschaft in Deutschland und an-
              grenzenden Gebieten um 1800," *Zeitschrift für Agrargeschichte und Agrarso-
              ziologie* 14:137–175.
David Sabean
    1971   "Household Formation and Geographic Mobility: A Family Register Study
              in a Wurttemburg Village 1760–1900," *Annales de Démographie Historique*
              1978:275–294.
    1976   "Aspects of Kinship Behavior and Property in Rural Western Europe Before
              1800," in Jack Goody, Joan Thirsk and E. P. Thompson, eds., *Family and
              Inheritance. Rural Society in Western Europe, 1200–1800.* Cambridge: Cambridge
              University Press.
Osamu Saito
    1981   "Labour Supply Behaviour of the Poor in the English Industrial Revolution,"
              Journal of European Economic History 10:633–652.
John Saville
    1957   *Rural Development in England and Wales, 1851–1951.* London: Routledge & Ke-
              gan Paul.
    1969   "Primitive Accumulation and Early Industrialization in Britain," *Socialist Reg-
              ister* 1969:247–271.
Jane Schneider and Peter Schneider
    1976   *Culture and Political Economy in Western Sicily.* New York: Academic Press.
Lawrence Schofer
    1975   *The Formation of a Modern Labor Force. Upper Silesia, 1865–1914.* Berkeley and
              Los Angeles: University of California Press.
Lennart Schon
    1972   "Västernorrland in the Middle of the Nineteenth Century. A Study in the
              Transition from Small-scale to Capitalistic Production," *Economy and History*
              15:83–111.
Bernd Schöne
    1977   *Kultur und Lebensweise Lausitzer Bandweber (1750–1850).* Berlin: Akademie Ver-
              lag.
Joan W. Scott
    1974   *The Glassworkers of Carmaux. French Craftsmen and Political Action in a Nine-
              teenth Century City.* Cambridge, Mass.: Harvard University Press.
Wally Seccombe
    1983   "Marxism and Demography," *New Left Review* 137:22–47.

Domenico Sella
1975   "Les deux faces de l'économie Lombarde au XVIIe siècle," in Paul M. Hoh-
        enberg and Frederick Krantz, eds., *Transition du féodalisme à la société indus-
        trielle: l'échec de l'Italie de la Renaissance et des Pays Bas du XVIIe siècle.* Montréal:
        Centre Interuniversitaire d'études européennes.
1979   *Crisis and Continuity. The Economy of Spanish Lombardy in the Seventeenth Cen-
        tury.* Cambridge, Mass.: Harvard University Press.

Amartya Sen
1981   *Poverty and Famines. An Essay on Entitlement and Deprivation.* Oxford: Clar-
        endon Press.

Emilio Sereni
1948   *Il capitalismo nelle campagne (1860–1900).* Turin: Einaudi.

Alan Sharlin
1978   "Natural Decrease in Early Modern Cities: A Reconsideration," *Past and
        Present* 79:126–138.

June A. Sheppard
1961   "East Yorkshire's Agricultural Labour Force in the Mid-Nineteenth Cen-
        tury," *Agricultural History Review* 9:43–54.

Paul A Slack
1974   "Vagrants and Vagrancy in England, 1598–1664," *Economic History Review,*
        2d. ser., 27:360–379.

B. H. Slicher van Bath
1969   "Eighteenth-Century Agriculture on the Continent of Europe: Evolution or
        Revolution?" *Agricultural History* 43:169–180.
1977   "Agriculture in the Vital Revolution," in E. E. Rich and C. H. Wilson, eds.,
        *Cambridge Economic History of Europe V. The Economic Organization of Early Mod-
        ern Europe.* Cambridge: Cambridge University Press.

Adam Smith
1910   *The Wealth of Nations.* 2 vols. London: J. M. Dent.
[1776]

Daniel Scott Smith
1977   "A Homeostatic Demographic Regime: Patterns in West European Family
        Reconstitution Studies," in Ronald Lee, ed., *Population Patterns in the Past.*
        New York: Academic Press.

Richard Smith
1981   "Fertility, Economy and Household Formation in England over Three Cen-
        turies," *Population and Development Review* 7:595–622.
1983   "On Putting the Child Before the Marriage: Reply to Birdsall," *Population
        and Development Review* 9:124–136.

K. D. M. Snell
1981   "Agricultural Seasonal Unemployment, the Standard of Living, and Wom-
        en's Work in the South and East, 1690–1860," *Economic History Review,* 2d.
        ser., 34:407–437.

Johan Söderberg
1982   "Causes of Poverty in Sweden in the Nineteenth Century," *Journal of Eu-
        ropean Economic History* 11:369–402.

H. Soly
1975   "Economische ontwikkeling en sociale politiek in Europa tijdens de over-
        gang van middeleeuwen naar nieuwe tijden," *Tijdschrift voor Geschiednis,*
        88:584–597.

Werner Sombart
  1909–1911 "Verlagssystem (Hausindustrie)," *Handwörterbuch der Staatswissenschaften* 8:233–261.
William Frederick Spackman
  1847 *An Analysis of the Occupations of the People . . .* London: The Author.
J. J. Spengler
  1945 "Malthus's Total Population Theory: A Restatement and Reappraisal," *Canadian Journal of Economics and Political Science* 11:83–110, 234–264.
  1970 "Adam Smith on Population," *Population Studies*, 2d ser., 17:377–388.
Margaret Spufford
  1976 "Peasant Inheritance Customs and Land Distribution in Cambridgeshire from the Sixteenth to the Eighteenth Centuries," in Jack Goody, Joan Thirsk, and E. P. Thompson, eds., *Family and Inheritance. Rural Society in Western Europe, 1200–1800.* Cambridge: Cambridge University Press.
David Stark
  1980 "Class Struggle and the Transformation of the Labor Process: A Relational Approach," *Theory and Society* 9:89–130.
Evelyne Huber Stephens
  1980 *The Politics of Workers' Participation.* New York: Academic Press.
Katherine Stone
  1974 "The Origins of Job Structures in the Steel Industry," *Review of Radical Political Economics* 6(Summer):113–173.
Albrecht Ströbel
  1972 *Agrarverfassung im Übergang. Studien zur Agrargeschichte des badischen Breisgaus vom Beginn des 16. bis zum Ausgang des 18. Jahrhunderts.* Freiburg: Albers.
W. Stys
  1957 "The Influence of Economic Conditions on the Fertility of Peasant Women," *Population Studies* 11–12:136–148.
Albert Tanner
  1982 *Spulen—Weben—Sticken. Die Industrialisierung in Appenzell Ausserrhoden.* Zurich: Juris Druck.
R. H. Tawney
  1967 *The Agrarian Problem in the Sixteenth Century.* New York: Harper Torchbooks.
Arthur J. Taylor, ed.
  1975 *The Standard of Living in Britain in the Industrial Revolution.* London: Methuen.
Klaus Tenfelde
  1977 *Sozialgeschichte der Bergarbeiterschaft an der Ruhr im 19. Jahrhundert.* Bonn/Bad Godesberg: Neue Gesellschaft.
Didier Terrier and Philippe Toutain
  1979 "Pression demographique et marché du travail à Comines au XVIIIeme siècle," *Revue du Nord* 61:19–25.
Joan Thirsk
  1961 "Industries in the Countryside," in F. J. Fisher, ed., *Essays in the Economic and Social History of Tudor and Stuart England in Honor of R. H. Tauney.* Cambridge: Cambridge University Press.
  1970 "Seventeenth-Century Agriculture and Social Change," *Agricultural History Review* 18 (Supplement):148–177.
Malcolm I. Thomis
  1974 *The Town Labourer and the Industrial Revolution.* London: Batsford.
E. P. Thompson
  1963 *The Making of the English Working Class.* London: Gollancz.

1967   "Time, Work-Discipline, and Industrial Capitalism," *Past and Present* 38:56–97.
1978   "Eighteenth-Century English Society: Class Struggle Without Class?" *Social History* 3:133–165.
Francis M. L. Thompson
1966   "The Social Distribution of Landed Property in England Since the Sixteenth Century," *Economic History Review*, 2d ser., 19:505–517.
1969   "Landownership and Economic Growth in England in the Eighteenth Century," in E. L. Jones and S. J. Woolf, eds., *Agrarian Change and Economic Development. The Historical problems.* London: Methuen.
Charles Tilly
1975   "Food Supply and Public Order in Modern Europe," in Charles Tilly, ed., *The Formation of National States in Western Europe.* Princeton, N.J.: Princeton University Press.
1978a   "The Historical Study of Vital Processes," in Charles Tilly, ed., *Historical Studies of Changing Fertility.* Princeton, N.J.: Princeton University Press.
1978b   "Migration in Modern European History," in William H. McNeill, ed., *Human Migration: Patterns, Implications, Policies.* Bloomington: Indiana University Press.
1979   "Did the Cake of Custom Break?" in John Merriman, ed., *Consciousness and Class Experience in Nineteenth Century Europe.* New York: Holmes & Meier.
1982   "Proletarianization and Rural Collective Action in East Anglia and Elsewhere, 1500–1900," *Peasant Studies* 10:5–34.
1983   "Flows of Capital and Forms of Industry in Europe, 1500–1900," *Theory and Society* 12:123–143.
Louise A. Tilly
1977   "Urban Growth, Industrialization and Women's Employment in Milan, Italy, 1881–1911," *Journal of Urban History* 3:467–484.
Louise A. Tilly and Joan W. Scott
1978   *Women, Work and Family.* New York: Holt, Rinehart & Winston.
Richard Tilly and Charles Tilly
1971   "An Agenda for European Economic History in the 1970s," *Journal of Economic History* 31:184–197.
Gabriel Tortella Cesares
1973   *Les origines del capitalismo en España: Banca, industria y ferrocarria en el siglo XIX.* Madrid: Editorial Ternos.
G. N. von Tunzelmann
1978   *Steam Power and British Industrialization to 1860.* Oxford: Clarendon Press.
Gustaf Utterström
1957   *Jordbrukets arbetare.* 2 vols. Stockholm: Tidens Forlag.
Christiaan Vandenbroeke
1981   "Mutations économiques et sociales en Flandre au cours de la phase proto-industrielle, 1650–1850," *Revue du Nord* 63:73–94.
1982   "Analyse critique de la phase proto-industrielle en Flandre: Evolution sociale et comportement démographique aux XVIIème-XIXème siècles," in Pierre Deyon and Franklin Mendels, eds., *Proto-industrialisation: Théorie et réalité.* Lille: Université des Arts, Lettres, et Sciences Humaines.
Herman Van der Wee
1975   "Structural Changes and Specialization in the Industry of the Southern Netherlands, 1100–1600," *Economic History Review* 28:203–221.

Herman Van de Wee and Eddy van Cauwenberghe, eds.
1978   *Productivity of Land and Agricultural Innovation in the Low Countries (1250–1800)*. Louvain: Louvain University Press.

Benoit Verhaegen
1961   *Contribution à l'histoire économique des Flandres*. 2 vols. Louvain: Nauwelaerts.

Michael Vester
1970   *Die Enstehung des Proletariats als Lernprozess. Die Enstehung antikapitalistischer Theorie und Praxis in England, 1792–1848*. Frankfurt am Main: Europaïsche Verlaganstalt.

Jaime Vicens Vives
1969   *An Economic History of Spain*. Princeton, N.J.: Princeton University Press.

Pierre Vilar
1962   *La Catalogne dans l'Espagne moderne*. 3 vols. Paris: SEVPEN.

Ia. E. Vodarskii
1972   Prom'ishlienn'ie seleniia tsentral'noi Rossii v period genezisa i razvitiia kapitalizma. MOSCOW: Izdatel'stvo Nauka.
1973   *Naselienie Rossii za 400 let (xvi–nachala xx v.v.)*. Moscow: "Prosveschchenie".
1977   "Naselenie Rossii v. kontsee xvii–nachalie xviii veka (problem'i, metodika issledovaniia, rezul'tat'i)," in R. N. Pullat, ed., *Problem'i istoricheskoidemograffi SSSR*. Tallinn: Institute of History, Academy of Sciences.

Günter Vogler
1965   *Zur Geschichte der Weber und Spinner von Nowaes, 1751–1785*. Potsdam: Bezirksheimatmuseum.

Jan de Vries
1974   *The Dutch Rural Economy in the Golden Age, 1500–1700*. New Haven, Conn.: Yale University Press.
1975   "Peasant Demand Patterns and Economic Development: Friesland, 1550–1750," in William N. Parker and Eric L. Jones, eds., *European Peasants and Their Markets*. Princeton, N.J.: Princeton University Press.
1976   *The Economy of Europe in an Age of Crisis, 1600–1750*. Cambridge: Cambridge University Press.
1981   "Patterns of Urbanization in Pre-Industrial Europe, 1500–1800," in H. Schmal, ed., *Patterns of European Urbanisation Since 1500*. London: Croom Helm.
1982   "Hierarchy Formation in the European Urban System, 1500–1800." Paper presented to the Social Science History Association, Bloomington, Indiana.

Etienne Van de Walle
1974   *The Female Population of France in the Nineteenth Century. A Reconstruction of 82 Departments*. Princeton, N.J.: Princeton University Press.

Immanuel Wallerstein
1974   *The Modern World-System. Capitalist Agriculture and the Origins of the European World-Economy in the Sixteenth Century*. New York: Academic Press.
1980   *The Modern World System. Vol. II: Mercantilism and the Consolidation of the European World-Economy, 1600–1750*. New York: Academic Press.

Susan Cott Watkins
1981   "Regional Patterns of Nuptiality in Europe, 1870–1960," *Population Studies* 35:199–215.

Max Weber
1950   *General Economic History*. Glencoe, Ill.: Free Press.
[1927]

1972   *Wirtschaft und Gesellschaft.* 5th ed. Tübingen: Mohr.
[1921]

David Weir
1982   "Fertility Transition in Rural France, 1740–1829." Ph.D. diss., Stanford University.

Christer Winberg
1975   *Folkökning och proletarisering kring den sociala struckturomvandlingen på Sveriges landsbygd under den agrara revolutionen.* Gothenburg: Historiska Institutionen i Göteborg.
1978   "Population Growth and Proletarianization. The Transformation of Social Structures in Rural Sweden During the Agrarian Revolution," in Sune Åkerman, ed., *Chance and Change. Social and Economic Studies in Historical Demography in the Baltic Area.* Odense: Odense University Press.

Nils Richard Wohlin
1909   *Den Jordbruksidkande befolkningen i Sverige 1751–1900. Statistik-demografisk studie på Grundval af de svenska yrkesrakningarna.* Stockholm: Emigrationsutredningen, Bil. IX.

Hermann Wopfner
1938   "Guterteilung und Obervölkerung tirolischer Landbezirk im 16., 17. und 18. Jahrhundert. *Südostdeutsche Forschungen* 3:202–232.

Keith Wrightson and David Levine
1979   *Poverty and Piety in an English Village. Terling, 1525–1700.* New York: Academic Press.

E. A. Wrigley
1961   *Industrial Growth and Population Change.* Cambridge: Cambridge University Press.
1966   "Family Limitation in Pre-Industrial England," *Economic History Review* 19:82–109.
1967   "A Simple Model of London's Importance in Changing English Society and Economy," *Past and Present* 37:44–70.
1972   "The Process of Modernization and the Industrial Revolution in England," *Journal of Interdisciplinary History* 3:225–259.
1977   "The Changing Occupational Structure of Colyton over Two Centuries," *Local Population Studies* 18:9–21.
1978   "Fertility Strategy for the Individual and the Group," in Charles Tilly, ed., *Historical Studies of Changing Fertility.* Princeton, N.J.: Princeton University Press.
1981   "Marriage, Fertility and Population Growth in Eighteenth-Century England," in R. B. Outhwaite, ed., *Marriage and Society. Studies in the Social History of Marriage.* London: Europa.
1983   "The Growth of Population in Eighteenth-Century England: A Conundrum Resolved," *Past and Present* 98:121–150.

E. A. Wrigley and R. S. Schofield
1981   *The Population History of England, 1541–1871: A Reconstruction.* London: Arnold.

Hartmut Zwahr
1971   "Zur Konstituierung des Proletariats als Klasse. Strukturuntersuchung über das Leipziger Proletariat während der industriellen Revolution," in Horst Bartel and Ernst Engelberg, eds., *Die grosspreussisch-militarische Reichsgründung 1871, Band I.* Berlin: Akademie Verlag.

2

Production, Reproduction, and the Proletarian Family in England, 1500–1851

David Levine

The higher soldiers or statesmen are in the pyramid of authority, the farther they must be from its base which consists of those ordinary men and women whose lives are the actual stuff of history; and, consequently, the smaller the effect of the words and acts of such remote personages, despite all their theoretical authority, upon that history.

Isaiah Berlin, *The Hedgehog and the Fox*

INTRODUCTION

My presentation is concerned with accommodating Marxist and Malthusian hypotheses on proletarianization and population growth within a single framework. Although neither Marx nor Malthus provides us with explanations that are sufficient in themselves, they both highlight significant aspects of these processes. My argument, then, seeks to integrate Marxist concerns with expropriation and the Malthusian preoccupation with the "home economics" of demography.

87

PROLETARIANIZATION
AND FAMILY HISTORY

I shall describe the formation and growth of the English proletariat between the early sixteenth and the middle nineteenth centuries in terms of the changing domestic organization of production and reproduction.[1] Let us begin by considering the magnitude of these changes. In 1524–1525 a subsidy was levied on Henry VIII's subjects to pay for one of his foreign wars. This graduated wealth tax suggests that about one-quarter of the adult male population was not assessed on property at all, but rather on their wages.[2] Because it is unlikely that all or even the majority of those adult males assessed on wages were lifelong proletarians, we would be making a generous allowance if we proposed that there were something like 600,000 proletarians and their dependents in a total population that might have numbered 2.4 million.[3] If we shift our attention foward some 11 or 12 generations, to the middle of the nineteenth century, we find that four out of five members of the labor force were either "employees" or domestic servants. This crude estimation suggests that from a population of 18 million at the time of the Crystal Palace Exhibition in 1851, there were likely to have been about 14 million proletarians and their dependents.[4] Between the end of the medieval period in the 1520s and the heyday of its capitalist successor, the English population rose over seven times. During these same 11 or 12 generations, the proletariat grew much faster—it rose more than 23-fold.

WAGE WORK

The nature of wage work was affected by unique local conditions, and we could strongly argue that it is wrong even to talk of a proletariat until the final years of the period under discussion. But it is my contention that perhaps overscruplous attention to the question of class as an entity in itself has had a distracting effect, by drawing too much scholarly investigation to the later stages of the transition from feudalism to capitalism. The emergent working class of the Industrial Revolution had long and deep roots in English history,[5] and unfortunately, the fissiparous tendency of academic historiography has segmented a protracted process and, by compartmentalizing its parts, has obscured the whole. Seen at the generalized level of our long-term chronology and somewhat abstracted from specific historical circumstances, this basic cultural continuity of wage work is an integrating and compelling factor. The perdurance of wage work runs like an Ariadne's thread through our three centuries.

Between the subsidy assessment of 1524–1525 and the end of the seventeenth century, when Gregory King analyzed the socioeconomic structure of England, the population doubled and the wage-labor force quadrupled.[6] King estimated that nearly 50% of English subjects were cottagers, laborers, squatters, and vagrants—groups that were to a greater or lesser extent dependent on wage work for their survival. To a mercantalist like King, these people decreased the wealth of the kingdom because they needed public money to make ends meet.[7]

THE ADVANTAGES OF PRIVATE ENTERPRISE AND ENCLOSURE

In rural England there were two major forces generating this process of social stratification: first, the shift away from subsistence farming to commercial cropping based on private enterprise and, second, the enclosure of the common fields. These forces separated small producers from the land so that in a period of population growth, the independent family farmer became less common. Surplus labor therefore became wage labor, and the social pyramid grew at its base. With almost monotonous regularity, scholars have shown that in widely separated villages and regions, the smaller peasantry was forced off the land, and the ranks of wage labor and vagrants swelled. The years 1570–1630 seem to have been the most violent, when a vicious cycle of famine and epidemic disease dealt a series of deathblows to the lesser peasantry. In the 1590s, disastrous harvests led to the forcible eviction of small tenants and the dramatic decline in the chances of life-cycle mobility.

The complexion of the landscape changed as the smaller peasants were expropriated and the common fields were enclosed. The countryside became a crazy quilt of individually operated farms, with separate fields under private management. Some locales held out, although the course of events and, particularly after the 1650s, the weight of the political authorities, was on the side of the encloser and the engrosser.[8] Common lands—heaths, woodlands, meadows, and fens—were reclaimed from their natural state and incorporated into the natural stock of farmland. The reorganization of the field systems was at the heart of the agricultural revolution of this period. Land was switched from arable to pasture and back again, and the main consideration became commercial gain and not popular usage. Arable systems were themselves being transformed as convertible husbandry superseded the traditional three-field rotation that had been geared to subsistence farming and was maintained by the persistent undercapitalization of farmers. The new techniques were predicated on private enterprise, commercial cropping, and large inputs of labor and capital. Nitrogen-fixing legumes and vast increases in the animal population contributed to the fertility of the soil and consequent increases in yield. Specialization and an agricultural re-division of labor led to a dramatic reordering of the agrarian economies across the length and breadth of the country.[9] Successful entrepreneurs did not behave like traditional subsistence peasants, and the inflationary spiral of these years allowed the entrepreneurs to find huge profits in the reorganization of agricultural production. In order to cope with the increased commercial activity, the transportation network became more intensive as roads and navigable rivers crisscrossed the land. Geograph-ical isolation was broken down, and by the first decades of the eigh-teenth century a national food market had been established. The modern-ization of the English agrarian sector meant that famine was expunged from the lives of the meanest and the poorest a century or more before it was banished from the lives of French people.[10]

From the last years of Henry VIII to the first of the American Revo-lution, from about 1540 to 1770, landowners enjoyed a vast profit infla-tion as wages rose three and one-half times, whereas rental values increased 20-fold.[11] Tenant farmers, like remora fish, swam along with their landlords, also enjoying the gains. The massive redistribution of income toward those with capital—either working or rental—under-wrote the purchases of new forms of consumer goods. Rural England was rebuilt with sturdy half-timbered houses to replace the mud-and-wattle shacks of the peasantry.[12] Inside these houses was material evi-dence of the trappings of their inhabitants' wealth—linen, pewter, and oak furniture became common household items. For the yeoman farm-ers and the newly rich graziers, the length and complexity of their post-mortem inventories bear witness to their prosperity.

THE DISADVANTAGES OF PRIVATE ENTERPRISE AND ENCLOSURE

The observe of this process of enclosure and private expenditure was a massive upsurge in public squalor. Ungoverned villages became rural slums holding the overflow from the process of expropriation. Home-steads were built without any visible means of support. In the wood pasture and forest districts, settlements of squatters colonized the wastelands. The population of vagrants, wayfarers, and sojourners grew at a pace that alarmed contemporaries. The urban centers mushroomed. Later-medieval England had a miniscule urban population; yet six gen-erations afterward, London and its suburbs contained something like 500,000 inhabitants, and most of the provincial centers had long since ceased to be overgrown villages.[13] Beneath a patina of bourgeois culture and Protestant civilization, there was a pullulating mass of paupers, proletarians, and plebeians. In the working-class East End of London more than half of the population were judged to be too poor to pay the Hearth Tax in the early years of the restored monarchy of Charles II. In the third quarter of the seventeenth century, in Leicester, Worcester, and Salisbury, there was an equal number of poor people.[14]

Early modern cities were a refuge for those who had been uprooted from the land: migrants came from all over England to settle in London. The smaller towns mirrored this process in their own ways. It should not be thought, however, that this movement and turnover was unidirectional. In the villages of Clayworth, Nottinghamshire, and Cogenhoe, Bedfordshire, for example, one-half of the villagers vanished in the course of a decade.[15] By and large it was the landowning elements who remained in place while all around them was flux. Slack was termed much of this movement "subsistence migration," and it became particularly noticeable whenever the harvest failed and proletarianization received another turn of the ratchet.[16] In the later 1590s, for instance, the barns of the capitalist farmers were often the last refuge of poor wayfaring strangers. In the parish churchyard of Terling, Essex, a number of these unfortunate creatures were given a pauper's burial.

EFFECT ON PUBLIC SPHERE

Geographical turbulence was but one aspect of social disintegration. Thomas and Macfarlane have argued that intravillage struggles arose from the *ressentiment* of those who were left behind by the advancing commercialization of social ties.[17] In place of the reciprocal peasant community, a series of class-based institutions was erected in the nascent capitalist village. Parochial office was almost exclusively the preserve of the village elite, who were thus in a position to enforce political control over their social subordinates. The distribution of welfare to a landless and underemployed populace became a method of enforcing deference and subservience.[18] At the same time, the church courts attempted to enact new codes of morality and enforce strict sexual behavior. The emergence of a regime of labor discipline at first took on a religious visage. The village's resident Puritan clergyman (if it had one) in his sermon weekly reiterated the theme of God's arbitrary election of his chosen people at the same time as the godly parishioners implored their laborers to suffer and be still. The village alehouse was controlled and its hours were regulated—tippling became a crime, and a tavern keeper could have his license revoked for serving clients an extra beer during their working hours.[19]

Like a giant centrifuge, the dominant forces in this period created a huge cultural gap between the classes and the masses. Literacy, rationality, and the emergence of bureaucratic forms of social organization largely left the plebeians behind.[20] Illiterate and superstitious, these plebians moved through a world under the unpredictable sway of the Four Horsemen—war, famine, pestilence, and death. Historians are only now recapturing the ramifications of this process of intellectual and moral distancing, which grew apace in the eighteenth century and which had its roots in the early modern social and economic distancing engendered by enclosures and engrossing, pauperization and proletarianization. By the end of the seventeenth century, an economically, socially, and culturally distinct rural proletariat had grown out of the reorganization of agricultural practices, which created a demand for a new species of labor that was different in form as well as content from its medieval predecessor.

EFFECT ON PRIVATE SPHERE

Within this transformed public world, the private sphere was also transformed. The family lives of the working population were attuned to a set of imperatives different from the domestic arrangements of their economic masters and social superiors. The nuclear family was the predominant form of household organization at least as early as the sixteenth century.[21] The separateness of the individual household complemented the notable lack of integration, with the extended family and the larger kinship group living outside the nuclear family's residence.[22] Laslett's insistence that over time the nuclear family stood alone masks important class-specific variations in household organization over this period. Although the household of a gentleman might contain a dozen or even 20 people, the common laborer usually lived in a mean cottage with his wife and their younger children. The older children left home when their childhood ended, for a period of time in service— either in the employ of the local gentleman or one of the tenant farmers. It is estimated that almost every youth of the laboring classes spent considerable time—sometimes up to a dozen years—living away from his or her immediate family.[23]

Upon leaving service there were few options; a number of young adults were able to amass sufficient capital to purchase a lease and stock a small family farm, but because these were fast disappearing, most married and returned to the agricultural proletariat. They lived by means of a combination of wage work and foraging on the remaining common lands, while eking out some supplementary income from their garden plot. Thus, there was a massive labor transfer from the homes of the poorer villagers to those of the wealthier ones. Moreover, the poorer families undertook a great deal of the "human capital formation" in this system and only benefited in noneconomic ways. Finally, when the children of the poor left their parents' home, they left their father's discipline. The ideology of the time demanded household discipline, but the farm and domestic servants were caught up in a system of control exerted by a nonfamily patriarch. Servants-in-husbandry who lived in their masters' homes were subjected to a labor discipline that was both economic and personal. Patriarchalism was not a vestigial force; it continued and declined only slowly.[24] Not surprisingly, the political commentators of the mid-seventeenth century considered the wage-laboring population to be dependent and therefore unfree. For contemporaries, freedom was proscribed for the proletarians because they lived by means of the direct sale of their labor and were thus as dependent on another man's will as if they lived in his house.[25]

CLASS VARIATIONS IN DEMOGRAPHY

Demographic behavior also showed class-specific variations. If we block out the role of epidemics (which are overrated as a long-term force in the population history of early modern England) and look at what might be called "background mortality," it seems that even though the rich died in startling numbers, the poor suffered even more. The lower orders were liable to a constellation of debilitating illnesses that accompanied their miserable working conditions, squalid housing, and inadequate diets. It is evident from Shorter's recent research that the women of the poorest families suffered an array of gynecological problems that were poverty induced. Deformed pelvises, a result of rickets, were associated with inadequate diet and made childbirth a fearsome experience. Legal sanctions also discriminated against the lower classes; for example, during plague outbreaks it was illegal for the poor to flee. They were ordered by law to await their fates while the disease flared around them.[26] For all, life was nasty and brutish, even when it was not unduly short.

Social differences in the birthrate were perhaps more pronounced. For example, women of the higher social strata married earlier.[27] Cottagers' and laborers' brides were somewhat older than the women who married landowners, tenant farmers, and the urban bourgeoisie, although the brides of proletarians were younger than the women who married peasants. Here we see a pronounced time lag in operation, the unevenness of the historical process, since the full implications of proletarianization were inhibited by the operation of institutional forces in the countryside. In the traditional system of marriage there was an interplay between the achievement of economic independence, marriage, and the allotment of niches in a relatively stable local agrarian economy. In this arrangement, marriage was usually deferred until a niche became vacant or a dowry was forthcoming.[28] This institutional brake acted more forcefully in backward regions than in the more commercialized parts of the country around London. Thus, within the rural laboring population, marital strategies were a blend of modern and traditional factors, and it was not until the later eighteenth century that the full-scale implications of rural proletarianization burst forth. In the first half of our period, then, the rural proletarians' brides were older, although there were sizable variations within the national marriage patterns. In the Leicestershire village of Shepshed, women of the cottager class were, on the average, nearly 28 when they married, whereas in the Essex village of Terling, the laborers' brides averaged 23—about 5 years younger than their midlands counterparts in the seventeenth century.[29]

In turning from marriage to fertility, we find that the rate of reproduction was again lower among the poorer segments of the population. Breast-feeding practices seem to have played a major role in this disparity. Rich women suckled their own children less frequently and then only for a short time.[30] For those poorer women who acted as wet nurses, the combination of breast-feeding their own and other women's infants meant that the resumption of ovulation was retarded, and hence, conceptions were spaced farther apart.[31] For the individual, breast feeding is a risky form of birth control, but for the group, the efficacy of prolonged, if uncertain, anovulatory periods in preventing closely spaced births has been substantiated by researchers.[32] So, the inequality of wealth influenced the reproductive structure in that the added burdens of motherhood caused fertility within marriage to be lower, and poverty and dependency were intimately connected with a later age of marriage.[33]

There are two other factors that must be mentioned in discussing the social differences in the replacement rates of the poorer and wealthier elements in the kingdom. Neither has, to the best of my knowledge, been studied systematically, but both are of real importance. From my acquaintance with local poor-law records, it seems clear that substantial numbers of lower-class women were deserted by their husbands. To the extent that such women were left during their childbearing years, their total fertility did not approach its potential. The other factor that limited the reproductive capacity of the poor is, in some ways, the obverse of marital desertion—social sanctions were exerted against the poor who wished to marry. As has already been mentioned, the rural economy did not have a completely free market with regard to labor, and I have discussed the ways in which wealthier households tended to subsume the labor of proletarian youths. Another important factor was the parochial authorites' control over settlement. In practice, the parish officers had the power to encourage "surplus" people to leave, and after 1662 the parish gave its emigrants a ticket acknowledging parochial responsibility in the event that the displaced person become a welfare recipient in his or her new residence. Such supervisory powers obviously encroached on the intimate decisions of young adults, and some were completely frustrated in their wish to marry. Others were forbidden to marry by poor-law wardens who feared that the children of these unions would become a burden on the parish and so swell the tax rolls.[34] These two aspects of plebeian marriage cannot be quantified, but it would be a serious mistake to underestimate the extent to which they contributed to the later marriage age and the lower replacement rate of the poorer sections of the English population.

The crucial point of the foregoing discussion is that although the number of agricultural proletarians rose dramatically, most of this increase was due to the forces of expropriation and not internal forces of self-replacement. In the first half of our period, the rural proletariat's demographic growth was severely cramped by the retention of vestigial forms of patriarchal social control. These forces restricted access to marriage, and as Schofield and Wrigley underscored in *The Population History of England*, the demographic growth that did occur was largely driven by changes in marriage patterns.

EMERGENCE OF THE INDUSTRIAL PROLETARIAT

Turning to the emergence of the industrial proletarian population is to shift from an arena of slow change to one of rapid development. So far our discussion of English history before 1700 has not acknowledged that this was a society in the throes of proto-industrialization. After the middle of the sixteenth century, England underwent a virtual revolution in handicraft production, and so the sleepy isle of Thomas More was rapidly transformed into the bustling world of Daniel Defoe and Adam Smith.[35] On Tyneside, the Grand Lease mines in Whickham parish employed as many as 500 face workers at a single colliery complex.[36] As the region was honeycombed with pit villages and mining was heavily labor intensive, it is easy to see how this massive increase in production led to the proliferation of other employment in ancillary activities— transport workers, carpenters, boat builders, and an army of staithmen, keelmen, wherrymen, and others who loaded coal onto coastal ships. Besides those involved in the extraction and transport of the black gold of Newcastle, there was a major spin-off from the alum, glass, soap, and other industries that proliferated with the availability of cheap fuel. To take a different example, when Daniel Defoe rode through the West Riding of Yorkshire in the 1720s, he was astonished by the size of the manufacturing communities. In regard to Halifax parish, with some 50,000 inhabitants, he remarked:

> So still the nearer we come to Halifax, we found the houses thicker, and the villages greater in every bottom . . . we found the country, in short, one continuous village, though mountainous every way, as before; hardly a house standing out at a speaking distance from another, and . . . we could see that at almost every house there was a tenter and on almost every tenter a piece of cloth, or kersie, or shalloon, for they are the three articles of that country's labour . . . yet look which way we would, high to the tops, and low to the bottoms, it was all the same innumerable houses, and a white piece upon every tenter.[37]

Defoe's *Tour* is a guidebook to England's manufacturing centers. In many of these places, production was organized on the dispersed pattern described for Halifax, but in others—such as the Devon town of Tiverton—the workers were gathered into large workshops, which might almost be called "proto-factories."[38]

London, the capital, was also the largest city of proto-industrial manufacturing, with a proliferation of small workshops producing an astonishing variety of articles—shoes, stockings, furniture, iron goods, jewlery, and so on. London's industries were peculiar in that they encompassed both luxury and common goods, although the genius of English capitalism was that its market was continually being expanded as fashionable goods were produced, in inferior quality, for the mass market. A chorus of complaints from social conservatives bewailing the passing of social hierarchy, marked by sumptuary divisions, testifies to the successful enfranchisement of the lower classes in a consumer economy based on democratic access and, of course, money—that lubricant of pretension and social disorder.[39]

At this stage, industrial organization varied tremendously and with it the conditions under which men and women sold their labor. The salient point, however, is that although the proletariat more than quadrupled between 1500 and 1700, a good half of this increase was absorbed by cottage industries in the countryside and the larger cities. The distinction between proto-industrial labor and agricultural labor was not hard and fast. In fact, Mendels pointed out when he coined the term *proto-industry*, there was a marked degree of symbiosis. Here I have found it convenient for argument and emphasis to ride roughshod over the subtle local variations.[40]

These proto-industrial developments were, I think, of great importance, for they began a series of changes that ultimately freed the plebeian family from the patriarchal control of its social superiors and economic masters. Although, we should note, there was no significant change in the household structure of the cottage industrialists—almost everyone still lived in nuclear family units—there were important changes within the home itself. In the proto-industrial centers the household became a focus for production in a way that it never was for the agricultural laborers. Domestic outwork gave the worker control over the pace of production and, to a considerable extent, ownership of the means of production. Household units, like those Defoe found in Halifax, were multiplied in an effort to raise the production volume. But the worker himself dictated the pace of his work and the number of hours his wife and children were required to assist him in producing the weekly product. The 3-day weekend, with intermittent bouts of furious labor, was a possibility during periods of high prices.[41] At other times the family worked longer hours to maintain the accepted level of subsistence. In many trades—textiles and small-metal goods, in particular—the older children were kept at home so that they could contribute to the family's income.[42] And at the critical stages in the family cycle when a surplus of infants threatened to sway the balance between mouths and hands, it was not unknown for apprentices—often orphaned paupers—to be brought into the household to restore the equilibrium.[43]

In many ways, therefore, the domestic economy of the proto-industrialists resembled that of the Russian peasantry described by Chayanov in the first part of the twentieth century.[44] Although they produced industrial products, the peasants' working life was determined by their own inner rhythms and not those of a modern economy. The notion that one worked to purchase goods was only incompletely understood, and economic modernizers complained that the preference for leisure acted as a constant brake on the expanding forces of production.[45] And like the peasantry described by Chayanov, the family budget was adapted to its members' life cycle, since family work, and not simply the work of the chief breadwinner, was the rule.

In significant ways the proto-industrial laborer was the master of his own household and was responsible for organizing his production and socializing his children. Another way in which the freedom of the proto-industrial family differed from that of agriculturalists was linked with the dispersed settlement pattern of the rural industrial communities.[46] Usually, rural domestic industries sprang up in communities that lacked strong patriarchal domination. In forest settlements, freehold villages, and urban suburbs it was possible for these households to proliferate, and the social and political implications of this lack of supervision were of real importance. It has been argued that both nonconformist religion and its Halévyian antithesis, radical politics, flourished in a seedbed of independent mechanics.[47] Such people were released from the patriarchal politics of the closed village and had their own space in which to work and think. They could interpret the world according to their own lights without the stern supervision of the old priest or the new presbyter. The radical religion of the lower classes stressed free will and individual responsibility. Not surprisingly, John Bunyan was a "mechanic preacher," and John Wesley found some of his most enthusiastic converts among the Cornish tin miners and the northeastern colliers. The opportunity for intellectual independence afforded by this proto-industrial mode of production was crucial to the emergence of a world view that was not interpreted according to the patriarchal organization of knowledge.[48] Insofar as the productive units in proto-industry had to be multiplied in order to increase production, the social structure of these communities was egalitarian.

The growth of this plebeian army of proto-industrialists was initiated through rural expropriation and was largely underwritten by its own prolific power.[49] Rural industry seemed to play a crucial role in undermining the prudential and restrictive reproductive regime of the preindustrial world. By permitting—one might even say promoting—a multiplication of productive units, each based on a separate household, the old nexus of patriarchal control over marriage was broken. Men and women could contemplate marriage knowing that their independence was not granted by supervening authority. Marriage could be undertaken with reference to a system in which they sold the products of their labor, and because there were no restrictions to entering such a marketplace, so-called beggar marriages[50] were frequent. Moreover, the average age of marriage dropped dramatically, bringing with it an increase in women's childbearing years in marriage. As the age at marriage fell, so too did the period of time between generations. There is also some evidence to suggest that marital fertility rose as well, perhaps because of the difficulty that working mothers had in breast-feeding their small children and, hence, in maintaining a long anovulatory period. It is quite clear that the combined effect of earlier and more frequent marriages and a marginally higher level of marital fertility was not counterbalanced by a drastic rise in mortality. The result was that the replacement rate of proto-industrialists far outstripped the previous levels.

An additional factor contributing to the higher population growth rates among the rural workers was illegitimacy. Paradoxically, the earlier that women married, the more likely they were to be pregnant at marriage: It does not appear that frustration with the postponement of sexual relations until marriage, some 10 years after puberty, was by itself a cause of promiscuity. The new strategy unveiled in the proto-industrial areas allowed for sexual intercourse before marriage, which unfortunately resulted in unwed mothers when economic conditions made it difficult to set up another productive unit. In a very real sense, the proto-industrialists predicated their sexual behavior on the continuation of economic growth. When the economy was sluggish, such plans were upset, and the sexual anticipation of marriage left many young women in the lurch. The planned marriage often took place when conditions improved.

SOCIAL AND INDUSTRIAL EVOLUTION IN THE "LONG" EIGHTEENTH CENTURY

The growth of a large, relatively uncontrolled proto-industrial population continued in the eighteenth-century countryside as the wealthier classes—gentry and tenant farmers alike—segregated themselves from the plebeians.[51] For example, they erected walls around their estates and parks, and the practice of boarding servants-in-husbandry waned.[52] In place of the system of household supervision, so Thompson argues, the upper classes adopted a studied style of social hegemony.[53] The law— with its bewigged judges, elaborate rituals, and powers over life itself— took the place of religion and magic as the social glue cementing the lower classes to their stations.[54] The passing of the household phase of social control left the rural laborer with a significant space, freed from patriarchal domination and supervision. The church courts never regained the powers of inquisition they had possessed before the revolution of the 1640s, and after 1689, religious toleration for all—save the papists—was a fundamental part of the English constitution. To be sure, there were agencies to maintain order and recurrent attempts to reform the manners and morals of the poor, but, overall, the tide was ebbing from the social gospel of the Reformation. What one might call the "long

eighteenth century," from 1660 to 1832, was marked by a broad tolerance of the frivolity and ignorance of the masses.[55] As long as they were
able to perform their productive tasks, their economic masters and social
superiors did not become overly exercised over their intimate behaviour.
What went on in the cottager's hovel and the laborer's shack did not
threaten a secure ruling class. Increasingly, the village poor were disciplined by the labor market, abetted by the parochial welfare system.[56]

In the course of this long eighteenth century, there were two dramatic
and fundamental changes in the reproductive patterns of the common
people. The first, the changing incidence of epidemic disease, owed almost nothing to human intervention, but the second, the growth of the
rural population after 1775, was closely connected with the local systems
of social welfare. These two changes are obviously interconnected, although it must be pointed out that in England, unlike almost every other
country in Europe, the vital revolution was not simply the result of the
declining mortality rate after 1750. Epidemic diseases became rather like
background noise: they killed off infants, who were easily replaced, but
spared adults. The enhanced life expectation of adults was a necessary
condition for the second change in reproductive patterns. For not only
were adults surviving longer, with obvious demographic repercussions,
but the actual compromise of the long eighteenth century also was built
on the foundations of a system of parochial relief in hard times.

But this parochial welfare system might have held together families
and decreased desertion. Malthus believed that the practice of supplementary relief encouraged high fertility and reduced the disincentive
for early marriage. Family reconstitution studies from a sample of English rural communities exhibit a pattern of rising fertility at later age
parities, as well as earlier ages at marriage after 1775.[57] This decline in
the age at marriage appears to have been closely connected with the
increase in the demand for agricultural labor, as rising cereal prices
meant that the farming community had an economic incentive to intensify the practices of convertible husbandry mentioned earlier. The enclosure movement (c. 1760–1820) rationalized a great deal of unfinished
business and, in the course of so doing, completed the final stages in
the expropriation of the peasantry. Parliamentary acts of enclosure did
not take away the people's land but, rather, took away their rights to
common usage. For most of these people on the margins of full-time
wage work, this abridged their claims to ownership. In return for the
use rights of real value, they were awarded a few roods or perches and
encumbered with costs and taxes. This was a catastrophically unequal
bargain that afforded an increase in agricultural efficiency at the cost of
the degradation of most of the rural proletariat.[58] For altogether dissim-

ilar reasons, then, the rural laborers developed a prolific power like that of the proto-industrialists. The phenomenon of population growth became generalized, and a high density peculiar to those regions with rural industry spread across the country during the era of the first Industrial Revolution.

The long eighteenth century witnessed the emergence of England's factory industry. In the 1830s the introduction of self-acting machinery culminated a series of technical developments that had separated the workers from ownership of the means of production and control over the pace of their labor. The evolution of steam power and the creation of factories were essential complements of this process. Although these achievements are impressive, we must not telescope the process and lose essential elements of continuity with the past.[59] It is important to remember that until the end of the nineteenth century, the workshop was the more common site than the factory, that steam power was used only in ancillary tasks in a great many trades other than textiles and hardly used at all in many industrial pursuits, and that there were important carry-overs of the family mode of production even within the factories.

The quickening pace of economic growth began in the middle of the eighteenth century when all the indicators rose concurrently: population, industrial production, aggregate demand, and so on. But if we shift from the reams of statistics to the lives of those individuals who lived through this process, we shall find it more difficult to pinpoint any definite change. Rather, what we see is a superimposition of new forms of life and work. But this compositional shift did not occur at the expense of the proto-industrial organization of family labor: the family mode of production continued, not only at home, but also in the workshops and factories that sprang up.[60] The greatest need during the initial stage of full-scale industrialization was for workers who would adapt to the regular pace of the power-driven machines. Very few adults could work hour after hour, day after day, week after week, and year after year, because the rhythms of an earlier world of work were not easily superseded. In this era of growing population, orphans and pauper children were in abundant supply, and the factories provided relief for parishes with high welfare rolls.[61] When these factory children married, they seem to have tried to recreate the family mode of production beside the power-driven machines. Master spinners preferred to employ their own children, but only for a brief time during their working lives did they have the right number of children to fill the available positions. Thus, though the master spinner might employ all his children for as long as possible, at any one time, most children were not employed by their parents, and most adults did not employ their own children. Seen from the longitudinal perspective of the individual factory-family's life cycle, however, it is possible that such statistics might not be representative. The crucial point is that the factory family was able to recreate the family work unit and that this family mode of production was the ideal against which other variants were measured. Only with the introduction of self-acting machinery in the 1830s—some 65 years after the first spinning factory opened—was the paternal role as the organizer of the work team superseded.[62] During these three generations a major industrial conurbation sprang up in southeast Lancashire, centering on Manchester, and many thousands of fathers, mothers, and children worked side by side for those stages in the life cycle when it proved feasible.

Although the residential unit was still nuclear, there is some evidence that the prevalence of early marriage, the lack of housing, and the difficulty of surviving on one wage packet were associated with an increase in coresidence for a short period after marriage when the young couple was most burdened with dependents.[63] The need to balance hands and mouths, mentioned earlier in a different context, dictated the size and composition of the household. Such needs fluctuated during the family cycle and so, too, did women's involvement in industrial labor.[64] The urban environment created new opportunities, and the working-class family used a wide variety of strategies for survival during its life together. Although migration was a significant factor in the growth of the factory proletariat, the demographic profile of the working class created a massive reservoir of potential labor power. In essence, the women marrying factory workers were young, as were the proto-industrialists' brides, and they had high fertility levels.[65] The infant and child mortality rates in the new urban agglomerations were very high, but nevertheless the high birthrates in the city center, the suburbs, the small towns, and the proto-industrial villages were able to overcome even these tragic statistics, and the industrial working class reproduced itself at a rapid pace.

INDUSTRIAL EVOLUTION
IN THE NINETEENTH CENTURY

Succeeding stages in industrial evolution in the later nineteenth century led to the increasing complexity of the class structure. The maturing industrial society was based on an increase in productivity that derived from technical change and not simply from the multiplication of the units of production. The distinguishing aspect of the industrial proletariat, as opposed to the proto-industrial one, was its internal differentiation. The demands of full-scale industrialization brought forth a new skilled working class whose culture differed in important ways from that of its predecessors. The quest for respectability on the part of the nineteenth-century workingmen was accompanied by the internalization of a sense of time thrift, frugality, and industry. There is evidence that by the middle of the nineteenth century, many British skilled workers, still dependent on wages, were able to demand something more than a pittance in return for their labor. Such "independent" workingmen imbibed the political economy of their day and held fast to a labor theory of value. They rejected the household economy of the proto- and early-industrial period, as it became a matter of masculine identity for workers to support their family and maintain their household out of their weekly wage packet.[66]

This patina of respectability was thin and fragile, as the nineteenth-century industrial economy was visited by recurrent booms and slumps. The onset of depressed conditions flung many labor aristocrats back onto a glutted labor market to compete as best they could with the reserve army of poor creatures existing on the fringes, hand to mouth. Mayhew's London and Engels's Manchester—sprawling tenements, hovels, and unspeakable filth—was the social reality from which the respectable working class sought to separate themselves. For the inhabitants of "outcast England," the vagaries of survival, the cruelty of fate, and the hardheartedness of the New Poor Law of 1834 were resonant of an earlier age when vagrants were whipped and branded and paupers were made to wear badges. For much of the English proletariat, it was as difficult to hold together their family economy in the nineteenth century as it had been one, two, or even three hundred years earlier.

Proletarianization, pauperization, and population growth advanced together, although my argument is not intended as simple demographic determinism. Far from it. I have tried to explicate the interaction between the forces of production and reproduction within the proletarian family in nascent capitalist England and have purposely selected a broad overview to explain how the changing structure of daily life led, by a variety of paths, to the formation of a proletarian army in the nineteenth century. The tenor of my presentation has been highly schematic, and I have frequently referred to stylized dichotomies between categories of life and work, even though they were by no means as distinct as I have suggested. The study of history requires us to create chronologies and structures out of a myriad of events. Social relations are worked out within structures that have their own regularities and patterns. The discovery of those averages heightens our awareness of the congruence between the social norms and social behavior of earlier formations. During the last generation we have learned a great deal about local economies and social formations in England during the transitional epoch. The ten thousand paths through the transitional thicket were unique in their own ways, but they all also were caught up in the larger process of change. My purpose has been to elucidate this larger process of change by abstracting crucial factors from their specific contexts and generalizing from them.

THE PROLETARIAN POPULATION

Let us now consider how the changing organization of production and reproduction interacted to produce a proletariat that grew more than 23-fold in 12 generations, from 600,000 in 1524–1525 to around 14 million by the middle of the nineteenth century. I propose discussing this phenomenon by creating a pair of stylized and schematic simulations in order to distinguish between the contributions of peasant expropriation and the self-sustaining demographic impetus of proletarianization.[67]

Inasmuch as population growth represented a break with the homeostatic regime ascribed to the peasantry, it may be more useful first to outline the main features of that system and then to elucidate how the various social changes led to the wide range of demographic responses. We therefore shall assume that the peasant system of family farming and restricted access to economically independent positions (niches) was inherently homeostatic.[68] There could be only very slow demographic expansion within such a framework. We also shall assume that this system of demographic equilibrium was necessarily flexible so that there would, ceteris paribus, be inverse and self-correcting responses to endogenous forces. Schofield has written a penetrating essay on this subject of how the inherently self-correcting forces contributed to long-term homeostasis in the peasant demographic regime.[69] Rises in the birthrate (i.e., higher fertility and/or earlier marriage) were usually counterbalanced by, or else called forth rises in, mortality, and vice versa. Assuming a "closed" population with almost no immigration (the situation of England during these three centuries), demographic growth could be caused by one of two factors: a rising birthrate or else a falling death rate. Either way there would be more births than deaths, and the total population would increase. Of course this simple arithmetic axiom was subject to several permutations, but we shall first establish the lineaments of the peasant demography model and then see how changes in the mixture were connected with the contemporaneous reorganization of production and reproduction among the working population. Finally, we shall assume that demographic homeostatis was a delicate balance of forces. Small shifts in the levels of the equation's components (and, in particular, the age at marriage) could lead to a massive burst of energy. Malthus's dictum that the forces of population growth, when unleashed, spark geometric increases must always be kept in mind.

The linchpin of the homeostatic peasant demographic model was relatively late and relatively infrequent marriage. We know more about the first characteristic than the second. Women in the sixteenth and seventeenth centuries married at an average age of 26.[70] The primary reason for late, deferred marriage was the need to have achieved economic independence before marriage. Though it does not appear that marriage was triggered by parental death, in a direct, mechanical fashion, there is a striking correlation between life expectation at the mean age of parenthood (i.e., in the early thirties) and the age at marriage.[71] Midway through the reproductive years, when husbands and wives were in their early thirties, life expectation was roughly 25 years. When the life expectation of the parental generation was higher, the marriage age of the next generation appears to have been later than in other communities in which adult mortality was more frequent and earlier marriage prevailed.

Clearly, each village was to a certain extent a semi-independent sphere in which local conditions influenced the application of general rules. Overall, however, the fit between what may be loosely termed *inheritance* and marriage was striking. I purposely italicized *inheritance* in the previous sentence because it is a contentious, confusing, and obfuscating concept. Although the laws and rules of inheritance are enshrined and worshiped by lawyers and desk-bound scholars, they appear to have been remarkably supple and diverse. The primary reason for this resilience is that, it was demographically impossible to adhere to the letter of the law. Wrigley explicated this conundrum with remarkable clarity.[72] He demonstrated that given prevailing demographic levels, only about three families in five would have been survived by a male heir. In light of this knowledge we have to treat inheritance carefully, since it carries with it impressive baggage. Thus we would be far better advised to see inheritance as the transmission of niches in a relatively stable economic structure.

Inheritance, then, is to be conceived of in societal and not personal terms. Since there was little economic growth in the medieval period and since the dominant mode of production remained the peasant family's subsistence farm, there was relatively little scope for continuous demographic growth. There were, of course, fluctuations, but there was in effect a ceiling imposed by the necessity of maintaining holdings that were large enough to generate a surplus that could be converted into rent for feudal landowners. In these circumstances the number of niches was usually fixed, and the social rules concerning deferred marriages were well entrenched. The natural upshot of this system was a late age of first marriage, and a corollary effect was that a proportion of the total population never married at all. There also appear to be some direct connections between the later ages at first marriage and the higher rates of permanent celibacy. The critical point is that high levels of survival and therefore excess population growth in one generation would very likely lead to increases in the number of never-married persons in the next generation, unless there were some way in which the number of niches could be expanded to permit these excess men and women to marry.

Fertility in the peasant demographic model was *natural fertility*, that is, that there were no attempts to restrict fertility after a certain number of children had been born.[73] Women continued to bear children right up to the end of their physiological fecundity period, about age 40. Colyton, the first English village to be reconstituted, provides a striking exception to this rule, although subsequent work seems to underline Colyton's peculiarity.[74] On the average, natural fertility meant that there was a span of some 14 years during which women were "at risk." The interval between births exhibited a tendency to become more prolonged as women grew older and had been married longer. Thus, first births often occurred within a year of marriage, with as many as 40% of brides in some sixteenth-century villages already pregnant at marriage and bearing their first child within 8 months.[75] Subsequent children were born at increasingly longer intervals, although there was a connection between the death of an infant and a shorter interval until the subsequent birth. This shorter interval usually occurred because the infant's death interrupted maternal lactation and the accompanying postpartum amenorrhea. The premature resumption of ovulation meant that all things being equal, the subsequent birth would occur earlier than if the preceding child had survived. In sum, there was an association between the duration of marriage and the fertility rate. So, although a woman might bear 2.25 children in the first 5 years of marriage (26–30), she would likely have, say, 1.50 births in the next 5-year period (31–35) and maybe just 1.00 in the final 4 years (36–39). In total, then, a woman who survived these years and conformed to this average fertility schedule would have borne 4.75 live children.

But since few families escaped the ravages of mortality in this period, the total fertility figures should be revised. Epidemic and famine mortality have been overrated in terms of their efficacy in halting population growth. There are two reasons for this skepticism: In the first instance, the quantitative evidence is hardly compelling, and, second, even after crisis-level mortality cut swaths through populations, the losses were made up very quickly. Plague was endemic in London during the sixteenth century and most of the following century as well. It rose to epidemic levels on a number of occasions—1563, 1603, 1625, and 1666 being the most noteworthy. But most of the population did not live in the capital or any other quasi-urban setting; they still lived in rural villages. These communities were not necessarily isolated from epidemic disease, although for the most part, they did not suffer recurrent, huge mortality. Aggregate-level surveys of 404 English villages are remarkably revealing in this context. Whereas most rural villages experienced at least 1 year (between the onset of registration in 1538 and the end of the parish register period in 1837) when the annual total of burials was four times the normal level, it was unusual to find a village so struck more than once.[76] Years of more than twice the normal level were much more frequent, but their impact was easily overcome. In Bottesford, Leicestershire, such crisis mortality (twice normal) occurred 12 times in the 160 years before 1740 and once afterwards. In one of these years, 1610, there was a plague epidemic, and about one villager in six died.[77] But in such a small village of 600, like Bottesford, the mortality rate tended to fluctuate randomly in noncrisis years. Just as there were years when more than the average number of people died; so, too, were there years when fewer died. Healthy years followed crisis years, and so they tended to cancel each other out. The parish register evidence suggests that this balancing of demographic feast and famine, as it were, it precisely what happened. Crisis years were thus naturalized and played a role in the homeostatic equation's short-run application. By killing adult men and women, plagues and epidemics relaxed the normal sanctions against marriage, and it was usual for a sharp rise in the marriage curve to follow such crises. Niches were left vacant, but not for long. By killing off children, plagues and epidemics made little impact, since children were, in effect, easily replaced. And the surge of new marriages probably depressed the age structure of the total married population, thereby leading to a short-term increase in the birthrate. Only recurrent, catastrophic mortality peaks could have a deleterious long-run effect and produce population decline. Something like this may have happened in London's seamier central parishes and working-class suburbs,[78] but otherwise the evidence that has been assembled to date does not seem to provide much comfort for those who would argue that a high death rate in normal years and a remarkably elevated one in crisis years kept the population in check.

The development of family reconstitution has provided us with an exceedingly sharp analytical scalpel for probing the anatomy of historical populations. Its great virtue is that we can now substitute reasonably accurate statistics for the often grotesquely inaccurate surmises of contemporaries. In the case of sixteenth- and seventeenth-century England, the studies seem to display a substantial degree of uniformity.[79] Infants died at the rate of about one in six, whereas of the five survivors another one was likely to die before reaching age 25. Overall, then, two-thirds of all infants survived to their mid-twenties, the average age at marriage. At age 25, life expectation was around 30 years for both sexes—women suffered excess mortality during the childbearing years but were rather better off after menopause.[80] In round figures it would appear that one marriage in three was broken by the death of a partner before the end of the wife's fecund period. Thus, allowing for the increasing likelihood of marital breakup by mortality as time progressed, approximately one-sixth of the total fertility figures given earlier would have been wiped out by taking parental mortality into account. The 4.75 total was thus reduced to 3.75 when we allow for adult mortality's lowering the married population and keeping its actual fertility below its potential.

But before discussing the effect of infant and child mortality, we must make some allowance for illegitimacy. There were a small number of illegitimate births—about 2% of the total[81]—so that the actual total fertility would have been 3.82. Of these 3.82 actual births, two-thirds, or 2.56, would have survived until their mid-twenties. If 90% of these children themselves married, then the original husband and wife would have been replaced by 2.30 married children.[82] Over a generation, a population with these demographic characteristics would have thus grown by 15%. If each generation lasted for 35 years, then over a period of five generations, for 185 years, the original population would have not quite doubled itself.

Seen by itself, the parameters of the (very nearly) homeostatic peasant demographic model seem to account for most of the population growth that occurred between 1524–1525 and 1700. However, such a deduction from the preceding account should be qualified. The deleterious effect of urbanization in general, and London in particular, was an important countervailing factor. Wrigley estimated that about one-half of the total excess of births over deaths in these years was required to underwrite London's expansion.[83] The other urban centers had mortality levels that were distinctly worse than the reconstituted results from rural villages. Density bred the conditions of high mortality: poor sanitation, contaminated water, inadequate ventilation, and a social environment in which microorganisms were easily transmitted among humans. What is striking about the demographic evidence that has so far been tabulated is that very small increases in density led to dramatic upsurges in mortality, particularly among infants, who were the most vulnerable to both transmitted diseases and a variety of enteric fevers. The market town of Gainsborough, Lincolnshire, seems to have had a level of mortality that was more than 50% greater than that of a rural settlement like Shepshed in Leicestershire, or Terling, Essex. The wealthier parishes in seventeenth-century London had infant mortality levels that were roughly double those of the rural villages, whereas the poorer parishes in the capital lost even more infants and small children.[84] Thus, the demographic toll exacted by urbanization was immense, as it cut deeply into the surplus produced by the peasant demographic model. In effect, then, the excess of births over deaths produced small generational surpluses which were largely negated by the process of stocking the urban centers.

It is generally believed that the population of England doubled between the 1520s and the end of the seventeenth century. Precise figures are bandied about, although it is hard to have much confidence in them, and it is better to approach such guesstimates skeptically. Instead, the best that we can garner from this prestatistical age is an approximate size. The same applies to the kind of demographic figures that were offered earlier, as they seem to approximate the existing state of affairs. But even approximations are valuable, since they allow us to supersede the estimates that have been used before and to play with them in constructing models that can be used to test the predictive value of competing hypotheses and explanations.

In terms of our peasant demography model, the 175 years between 1524–1525 and 1700 corresponds to a period of five generations. The peasant regime, left to itself, would have accounted for about 85% of this doubling of the population. However, as we have just argued, the need for new recruits (assuming that all such recruits were the peasants' extra children) would have substantially reduced this contribution. For the sake of concision, we shall argue that the net growth of population under the peasant demography model, after allowing for the depressive effects of urbanization, might have been from 2.4 million in the 1520s to about 3.4 million by 1700.[85] It is thus unlikely that adherence to the peasantry's demography could have generated more than a small portion of the total growth of the English population during the early modern period. We must, therefore, look elsewhere to find its main source.

It is my contention that we shall find these mainsprings of population growth by clearly explicating the disequilibrating effects of proletarianization. Moreover, the relevance of the peasant demography model declines as our period passes. The expropriation of the peasantry, a process that was in high gear after 1570, meant that by the end of the seventeenth century there were few families who still organized their demographic strategies in the ways that were common in the earlier period. In contrast with the synchronic model of family formation just outlined, we must create a variety of diachronic variations to account for the dramatic impact of proletarian family formation strategies.

The central feature of the proletarian demography model was earlier marriage. There also were three ancillary characteristics that led to a higher birthrate: more frequent marriage, higher marital fertility, and increased levels of illegitimacy. Mortality levels, by contrast, do not seem to have changed very much, except in urbanized or densely housed populations. In order to describe the demographic implications of proletarianization we should begin by comparing the main statistical contrasts between the demography of the proletariat and that of the peasantry (at this point I am not overly concerned with rural/urban or agricultural/proto-industrial subcategories).

Wage workers married earlier than peasants did, and they married younger brides who were, say, 23, on the average.[86] The proportion of permanent celibates fell from perhaps 10 to 5%. Age-specific marital fertility rose a little, by 10%, although there was no difference in the age at which childbearing ended (40), since proletarians also seem to have practiced natural fertility. And illegitimacy levels rose as economic uncertainty, largely accounted for by involvement in the marketplace rather than subsistence production, often intervened between the initiation of sexual courtship and marriage. In opposition to these "positive" forces, we may say that mortality rose a little and that this "negative" impact devolved upon infants and children. Let us now see what would have been the end result of these small changes for the demographic profile of the proletarians.

In the proletarian demography model, women married at 23 and had 17 years of childbearing. During the first 5 years they would have had 2.50 children; during the next 5 years they would have had 1.60 children; during the third 5-year period they would have had 1.40 children; and in the final 2 years they would have had 0.40 live births. In all, then, the potential total marital fertility would have been 5.90 children. Adult mortality during the childbearing years among a proletarian population was little different from that experienced by a peasant one, and so the actual marital fertility would have been five-sixths of 5.90, or 4.92 live births. In addition to these children born after marriage were the illegitimate births, say, 4% of all births, and so the final score would be 5.12 live births for each married woman. Of these illegitimate babies, fewer survived to their mid-twenties, although they had to have lived a shorter period of time to reach the now earlier age at marriage. In the peasant demography model, we estimated that two-thirds of all children survived to age 26, and in the proletarian demography model, we estimated that 65% survived to age 23. So, 3.33 children per marriage reached the average age at marriage, and of these about 95%, 3.16, eventually married. The replacement rate in the proletarian demography model was 1.58, far above that of the peasant demography model, 1.15.[87] Over a generation the proletarians' self-sustained population growth accounted for a rise of 58% over the initial base, and the peasants grew by just 15%. Moreover, earlier marriage among the proletarians meant that the length of a generation fell, too, from 35 years to 32. If during the period from 1524–1525 to 1700, the whole English population had conformed to the proletarian demography model, then it would have seen the passage of 5.5 generations. Its size would have grown from 2.4 million in 1524–1525 to 25.4 million in 1700, an increase of more than 10-fold.

Obviously, nothing of this sort happened. The proletarian demography model is clearly inapplicable to the period from 1524–1525 to 1700, but so, too, is the peasant demography model. What we are confronting is not a simple choice between ideal types but something far more difficult: the subtle blend of change and continuity that characterizes historical experience. The purpose of the foregoing exercise was not to provide an answer—the techniques, methods, and data all are far too tenuous. Instead, by highlighting the implications of these two distinct demographic regimes, I have set the stage for the one question that can now be addressed with our present understanding of past population processes: The formation and growth of the English proletariat may be said to have started in the 1520s and to have been largely completed by the middle of the nineteenth century. To what extent, then, did peasant expropriation, on the one hand, or proletarian demographic growth, on the other, contribute to this phenomenon? In answering this question, it is necessary to recognize that these two factors were interrelated and that though the first factor, peasant expropriation, was a necessary condition, it does not, by itself, explain the observable growth in the proletarian population from a generously estimated 600,000 in the 1520s to something like 14 million in the middle of the nineteenth century. And, second, we cannot have our demographic cake and eat it too—the emergence of the so-called proletarian demography model did not just happen; it had specific material causes that we must link with the changing modes of production and reproduction. Demographic factors were not only a response to economic changes; they also influenced them. Thus, the massing of labor that was generated by the proletarian demography model created the conditions that underpinned with dramatic shift in the social distribution of wealth and, particularly, income, which I described earlier. By glutting the labor market, the proletarians' own reproductive strategies created the economic conditions in which proto-industry could flourish and, by flourishing, perpetuate the process during the nascent capitalist period. Finally, the vitality of proto-industrial forms of production was critical to the capitalist relations of production. Proto-industry was a more profitable form of production than was artisanal manufacturing, in that the laborers bore many of the capital risks, such as they were, since labor and not fixed capital was the primary ingredient in most productive processes. Insofar as proto-industrialists were isolated and had little institutional leverage over the merchant capitalists, the success of proto-industry was the obverse of the decline of artisanal or guild production.

By the middle of the eighteenth century, the peasantry (i.e., the family farmers) had been superseded as the dominant productive force in the English countryside. Their place was taken by a new productive arrangement in which most of the land was worked by tenant farmers employing wage labor. Between the Reformation and the American Revolution the peasantry was expropriated, and the social mobility of most of its members fell downward into the ranks of the proletariat. The process was of greater social and economic than demographic import, however. If the peasantry of Henry VIII's reign is defined as being those country people who worked the land as family farmers, then we can assume that they accounted for about 95% of the population above the rank of wage laborers. In the early sixteenth century, then, the population could be summarily described in the following manner: 600,000 (or about 25% of the whole) were proletarians; 1.65 million (or about 70% of the total or 95% of the rest) were peasants; and the remaining 120,000 or so (5% of the total) were lords, clerics, and the bourgeoisie. Such a rough-and-ready division is meant for the purpose of argument, and though no special claims are being made for its accuracy, it does seem to approximate the elementary structures of England at the end of the medieval period. For our purposes, the most important lesson to be drawn from this exercise is that even if more than 50% of the peasants were expropriated by the time of Gregory King, at the end of the seventeenth century, this action by itself could only have had the effect of increasing the proletariat by about 1 million—from about 600,000 to something like 1.65 million. It should also be pointed out that the explanatory value of this factor (expropriation) is far less after the end of the seventeenth century mainly because there were fewer peasants left, and so later developments were mainly concerned with finishing a process that was already well under way.

Expropriation thus accounts for less than one-half of the growth of the proletariat during the Tudor–Stuart period. How, then, was the proletariat created in these years? An important component was the demographic excess of the peasantry—that is, younger sons and daughters who could not be placed in positions commensurate with their expectations at birth because they did not inherit a position, whereas the number of opportunities for relocation dwindled as more and more of the land was withdrawn from the family farming sector and given over to capitalist enterprise.

The replacement rates of the rural and urban proletariats were more sluggish in the sixteenth and seventeenth centuries than later, and it seems unlikely that the proletarian demography model, outlined earlier, can be applied to the rural agricultural laborers or the city wage earners in this period. The contribution made by expropriation was to expand the total number of proletarians rather than to make any special changes in their demographic characteristics that would have promoted population growth. The expropriated peasants swelled the ranks of a somewhat stagnant demographic section of the population and, like the water in a canal system, changed its relationship with the surrounding environment without altering its internal characteristics. The size of this group was constantly being augmented by new recruits—either peasants and their families dispossessed outright or the excess sons and daughters of those peasants who were tenaciously holding on to their family farms.

The self-generated contribution to proletarian growth before 1700 was made by those dispossessed peasants and wandering laborers who settled the proto-industrial villages and hamlets that sprang up over England. It was among this section of the proletariat—in the textile, metalworking, and mining areas—that a new demographic regime was unveiled. The linchpin of the proto-industrial strategy, as has already been described, was earlier and more frequent marriage, which had profound implications for the birthrate, even though the level of age-specific fertility rose only slightly and the rate of mortality was likewise little different. As I suggested earlier, about one-half of the total increase in the number of proletariat by the time of Gregory King was in the expansion of the proto-industrial sector, rural and urban. Thirsk has written about the tremendous impact of "policies and projects" aimed at job creation in this period.[88] Although the motivation of the politicians and projectors was initially to absorb the labor power of the expropriated peasantry, the ultimate implications were somewhat different. The policies and projects combined with indigenous forms of proto-industrial development to create material conditions for a widespread and unanticipated social phenomenon: the proletarian family economy based on proto-industrial wage labor. For a significant sector of the labor force, the ties with the land the agrarian economy were diminished. Of course, these families often had a small plot of land, common rights, and high seasonal wages from harvest work, but the crucial factors distinguishing the proto-industrialists from the farmer weaver or farmer nailer of the past was that the relative importance of industrial and agricultural incomes was being reversed. Without the emergence and development of proto-industry, a new strategy of family formation would not have been unveiled; new relations within the family would not have been engendered to cut the plebian family adrift from patriarchal controls; and the absolute growth of the proletariat would have been stunted. The expropriation of the peasantry with the perpetuation of the peasant demographic model would have meant that the proletariat would have grown far more slowly.

The dynamic role of these proto-industrial forces became fully apparent only in the period after Gregory King. Between the end of the seventeenth and the middle of the nineteenth century, the proletariat mushroomed from about 2.5 million to nearly 14 million. Both the agricultural and industrial sectors and the rural and urban areas grew. Clearly, however, the dramatic gains were in the proto-industrial, industrial, and urban spheres. Thus, although the rural agricultural proletariat probably doubled over this period, those wage workers who were finally separated from the land rose from an estimated 1 million in 1700 to something like 11 million at the time of the Crystal Palace Exhibition. It should be noted that these are not two hermetically sealed categories; there was constant intersector flow and a good deal of rural–urban movement. The crucial point is that wage work in agriculture had a limited scope for growth, whereas proto-industry and factory industry had practically insatiable appetites for new recruits.

The recruitment of this labor force was a complex procedure, although its outlines seem obvious. We can locate several sources: the last stages of peasant expropriation contributed a small portion of the total, as did the continued downward mobility of sons and daughters who were not fortunate enough to inherit a modest competence. The internally generated surplus of the proletariat was the main source of new recruits particularly when, after 1775, the combined effect of a rising birthrate and a falling death rate in the rural areas produced levels of population growth that saturated the agricultural economy and spilled over into the proto-industrial sector and, finally, when the "prolifick power" of the proto-industrial and urban industrial proletariat was unleashed. The importance of this final category is, I think, paramount. Another brief simulation follows.

I have estimated that in 1700 the nonagricultural proletariat numbered about 1 million, and in 1851 it was around 11 million. The demographic parameters of these proletarians—early and frequent marriage, high levels of marital and premarital fertility, and fairly stable rates of mortality in rural areas with rising ones in inner-city zones—could quite easily have doubled the population every 40 years in the countryside and every 80 years in the cities. Let us next assume that the 1 million nonagricultural proletarians were divided equally between rural, proto-industrial areas and urban regions. Finally, we shall assume that for heuristic reasons, the original nonagricultural populations were hermetically sealed; that is, there were no social and/or geographic movements into or out of these groups, and so they grew only through their internal demographic impetus. The 500,000 rural proto-industrialists doubled their number every 40 years, and so after 160 years, or after the original population had doubled four times, there were 8 million. The half-million urban proletarians who doubled their number at only half this rate yielded an internally generated population of 2 million after two such multiplications. Thus, the result of this admittedly simpleminded simulation would produce a 10-fold increase in the nonagricultural proletariat in the 160 years after 1700. Now, of course, this is a highly schematic kind of analysis, and yet its results reiterate the tremendous reproductive power that was unveiled when the patriarchal and economic sanctions against early marriage were undermined. In addition, this short exercise has another benefit, in that it directs attention away from the role of peasant expropriation and toward the demographic factors in the formation of the English proletariat. In a real sense, then, the English proletariat made itself.

CONCLUSIONS

In this discussion the transition from feudalism to capitalism has been treated as a protracted process. In writing social history the choice of dates and time periods is both arbitrary and ambiguous: arbitrary because no point in time can be specified with the rigor or accuracy of politics and political history, and ambiguous because the lack of rigor means that whatever dates are chosen, the integrity of the process will be subjected to a kind of rough justice. In choosing a very long time span to encapsulate the nascent capitalist period, I have created a chronology that has both limitations and contradictions. This chronology is based on the unifying conception of proletarianization in both agriculture and manufacturing.

The proliferation of consumer goods distinguished the proto-industrial manufacturing sector and provoked the sustained economic growth. But rather than seeing this proliferation as an isolated, time-specific event, it is necessary to regard the process of proto-industrialization as a long and drawn-out development. The household mode of production and the small subcontracting workshop were but two aspects of this development. They differed from the factory enterprise in which workers sold their labor time and not the products of their labor. The distinction is crucial, since on it hinges the difference between the proto-industrial mode of production and its successor which was based on high fixed-capital expenditures and the purchase of labor power to service the machinery. In the mature form of capitalist production, men and women sold their labor and their time for a wage and thus became mere adjuncts to the inanimately powered, self-acting machinery. For many who were caught up in this process, it was indeed a species of slavery. However, in the second quarter of the nineteenth century, most production was not based on this model. Most workers followed older rhythms and worked in quite different conditions. Let us, for a moment, conjure up a different England in the second quarter of the nineteenth century: one that had no factories, and so parts of the Manchester conurbation have to be expunged from our mind's eye; yet there would still be substantial manufacturing activity in the Black Country, the Potteries, East London, south Yorkshire, and older proto-industrial areas like Wiltshire, Devon, and Norfolk. Without Boulton and Watt's reciprocating steam engine and the reorganization of production that issued in its wake, England would still have possessed a substantial productive base. But the reciprocating steam engine was invented, and sectors of the industrial base were revolutionized: spinning right from the start and, with the railways, large parts of the iron and steel industries. My point is not to deny these developments but, rather, to chop them down to size.

The Industrial Revolution cannot be dated like the French Revolution because it was not an event but, rather, a process. An accretion of small technical changes, which occurred ever more rapidly, may have revolutionized production, but here the very notion of a revolution imparts a sense of dramatic and sharp change. As I have tried to argue, most of the changes that occurred during the Industrial Revolution were not brief, dramatic, or sharp. With the exception of Cottonopolis, what we see everywhere are modifications, adjustments, evolutions, and mutations.

The Mendelian model of selective breeding is appropriate here. Countless adjustments made labor time more efficient, but almost all of this tinkering activity is lost to the historians who rely on documents.

The industrial archaelogist's documents may be the most relevant, but they may also be the most misleading, as they are inevitably so incomplete and unrepresentative. Rather, we can appreciate the extent of technical changes over the period in question simply by considering the exponential rates of growth in the variety of consumer goods. Historians are forever using and then debasing their own coinage, and so we now have consumer societies and even consumer revolutions, dating from 1780, 1760, 1700, and even 1560.[89] The confusion over the dates of these revolutions and the subsequent growth of consumer societies is perversely illuminating, for it once against points to the real difficulty of finding an unambiguous chronology. None of the four historians suggesting these dates is wrong, as they all are describing the same process, but each one's specialized knowledge stands in the way of acknowledging that his or her period is overdetermined by its situation within an evolving capitalist political economy. Such overscrupulous attention to dates, which are themselves arbitrary, obscures the process. And social history is process writ very, very large. The growth of these consumer goods was not even but speeded up over time. Many more innovations and goods were evident in 1630 than in 1530; yet there were more in 1730 than in 1630 and more still in 1830 than in 1730. This is hardly surprising, since it is in the nature of historical time to speed up in the modern world. History, in a certain sense, bears witness to this intensification of our mastery of the physical world over time. Bearing this in mind, I shall end our discussion by turning back to questions of chronology and periodization.

The arbitrary and ambiguous nature of selecting any terminal date to the nascent capitalist period is obvious. Such a selection must be made in the knowledge that it can only be provisional and that its utility must be tested in practice. It is clear that the final stages of the nascent capitalist era, after 1770, also witnessed the growth of forces that broke apart the proto-industrial mode of production. But the crucial fact, it appears to me, is that over many sectors of the manufacturing economy, this proto-industrial mode continued and even flourished. These years, between 1770 and 1850, witnessed a final Indian summer for proto-industrial production. In addition, they also marked the ascendancy of the proletarian demography model as England's population lurched forward. Proletarian family formation strategies were largely predicated on the availability of work for children and the existence of a family wage economy. Ties with the land were attenuated and then irreparably severed among the inhabitants of mushrooming industrial villages, towns, and cities. It became imperative for them to purchase goods that had previously been available from common lands, tenements, and small holdings. The final stages of proto-industrialization was marked by the heightened distinction between production for exchange and production for use. The family economy was almost completely proletarianized as the family had to sell the products of its labor in order to purchase necessities. This final stage of proto-industrialization was marked by the intensification of child labor in mines, nailing communities, framework, knitting villages, and weaving hamlets, as well as in the infamous London slop trades. Many of the grievous social ills of the early Industrial Revolution were the result of involution of the proto-industrial family economy.[90] In these senses, then, the proto-industrial mode of production cannot be abridged by a chronology whose major claim is that it encapsulates the inventions of Watt, Boulton, and Arkwright or the commerical wizardry of Wedgewood. Chronology need not be self-determining and restrictive. For inasmuch as the historical process proceeds unevenly, one would expect the rise of industrial society to overlap with the final stages of the nascent capitalist period and the proto-industrial mode of production. Moreover, the rise of one was predicated on and produced the demise of the other. This diminuendo was played out at an excruciatingly slow pace as the agonies of the handloom weavers, framework knitters, nailers, and shoemakers all testify. In closing, therefore, I argue that a chronology that is relevant to social history must also be relevant to the experience of those men and women, boys and girls, who lived through this transition.

NOTES

1. In this chapter I hope to describe how microlevel demographic research, in conjunction with more usual concerns of economic historians, will lead to a reformulation of the debate over the transition from feudalism to capitalism, by stressing the transition's protracted time span, its highly uneven development, and the necessity of understanding these macroeconomic changes together with microeconomic changes in the household and family lives of those who experienced this process. The starting point for the original debate is, of course, *Capital*. The debate was regenerated after World War II with the publication of Maurice Dobb's *Studies in the Development of Capitalism*. (New York: International Publishers, 1947; rev. ed., 1963). Dobb's book sparked the transition debate that took place in the pages of *Science and Society* in the early 1950s. In 1976 New Left Books (of London) republished the original contributions and several others under the title *The Transition from Feudalism to Capitalism*, edited by Rodney Hilton. A secondary, if not so direct response to Dobb's chronology and argument emerged in the pages of *Past and Present* in the wake of E. J. Hobsbawm's two essays, "The Crisis of the 17th Century" (nos. 5 and 6, 1954). Articles on the seventeenth-century crisis appeared over the subsequent decade, and a collection of them was brought out under the title *Crisis in Europe 1560–1660*, edited by Trevor Aston (London: Routledge & Kegan Paul, 1965). During the last few years Robert

Brenner published three essays on this subject, although his concern was as much with the political implications of divergent routes to capitalism as with the emergence of the new mode of production itself: "Agrarian Class Structure and Economic Development in Pre-Industrial Europe," *Past and Present* 70 (1976): 30–75; "The Origins of Capitalist Development: A Critique of Neo-Smithian Marxism," *New Left Review* 104 (1977): 25–93. Brenner's 1976 essay provoked a flurry of comment in the pages of *Past and Present*, and he responded to his critics in a magisterial fashion: "The Agrarian Roots of European Capitalism," *Past and Present* 97 (1982): 16–113. Another line of attack on this problem was developed by those who have followed Franklin Mendels's urgings to study proto-industrialization: "Proto-Industrialization: The First Phase of Industrialization," *Journal of Economic History* 32 (1972): 241–261. Mendels was not the first scholar to study the development of cottage industry, although it might be fair to say that his article began a new phase in its historiography, which has now begun to consider merchant capitalism, domestic manufacturing, and the family economy within the broader framework of the transition. The most erudite and comprehensive overview was recently translated into English from its original German: H. Medick, J. Schlumbohm, and P. Kriedte, *Industrialization before Industrialization* (Cambridge: Cambridge University Press, 1981). For a revitalized Marxist overview of the relationship among changing modes of production, family organization, and demographic behavior, see Wally Seccombe, "Marxism and Demography," *New Left Review* 137 (1983).

2. Alan Everitt, "Farm Labourers," in J. Thirsk, ed., *The Agrarian History of England and Wales, IV, 1500–1640* (Cambridge: Cambridge University Press, 1967), 396–400. Everitt quotes subsidy assessments from various counties which range from about 20% in Leicestershire to over one-third in Devonshire. He notes that within the counties the range was very wide—in Kent, for example, there was a high of "51 per cent in the cornlands of Downhamford hundred, between Sandwich and Canterbury" and a low of "16 per cent on the thinly settled sheep pastures of Aloesbridge hundred in Romney Marsh" (p. 397). I have settled for a compromise figure of 25%, although I am fully cognizant that it is unclear if these wage workers were single or married or if wage laboring merely formed a life-cycle stage between childhood and adulthood. In a real sense the use of the term *proletarian* might by objected to as being an anachronistic license, since few of those assessed on wages would have been completely landless and wholly dependent on wages for their subsistence. Wage-work was often supplementary in that most wage workers would have had a small tenement garden, perhaps an acre or two, and also common rights to pasturage, forage, and a host of other usages. It should be pointed out that for the purposes of the present argument, exactness and accuracy are not my utmost concern, since what I am trying to establish are changing orders of magnitude. Given the lack of anything approaching certainty, we might do well to bear in mind R. H. Tawney's injunction about the relative nature of statistics in this prestatistical age: "For most sides of economic life statistical evidence is so scanty, before the day of the Political Arithmeticians that there is a temptation, when it exists, to make too much of it" In this chapter I am preferring "statistics" in the full knowledge that they are like quicksilver and slip through one's hands. They have not been supplied as fixed entities but rather as ball-park figures so that we can use them for our argument. I do not believe that the substance of the following argument would be greatly impaired if some of my "guesstimates" were revised in the light of future research.

3. R. S. Schofield and E. A. Wrigley, *The Population History of England 1541–1871* (London: Edward Arnold, 1981), app. 5 ("National Population Totals"), pp. 563–587.

4. This figure is presented in M. E. Sadler and J. W. Edwards, *Education Department,*

Special Reports on Educational Subjects, ii (London, 1898), 446–447. This reference was supplied by R. K. Webb, *The British Working Class Reader, 1790–1848* (London: Routledge, 1955), 18. Webb uses this census to arrive at a working-class population of 12.4 million in 1833. I have assumed that between 1833 and 1851 the working-class population grew to 14 million.

5. Christopher Hill has written a marvelous essay on this topic: "Pottage for Freeborn Englishmen: Attitudes to Wage-Labour in the Sixteenth and Seventeenth Centuries," in Charles Feinstein, ed., *Socialism, Capitalism and Economic Growth* (Cambridge: Cambridge University Press, 1964), 338–359. Hill's recognition of the early modern background of proletarianization and the protests against it made by those becoming proletarianized is salutary. It provides a solid counterweight to the incorrect inference that could be drawn from the work of scholars whose emphasis is on the later eighteenth and nineteenth centuries: that this process was both new to and a peculiar characteristic of their period.

6. On Gregory King and his famous analyses of the later seventeenth-century population, see D. V. Glass, "Two Papers on Gregory King," in D. V. Glass and D. E. C. Eversley, eds., *Population in History* (London: Edward Arnold, 1965), 159–200. King's figures are "guesstimates," although they have taken on an almost talismanic virtue among many historians who have been pleased to find a contemporary providing solid numbers. Peter Lindert has recently found that King's computations are largely correct, even if there are points on which the detailed emphasis might be changed: "English Occupations, 1670–1811," *Journal of Economic History* 40:4 (1980): 685–711. Lindert's sampling, based on probate inventories, found roughly the same proportion of the population that could be termed *proletarian* but more industrialists and fewer agriculturalists than King himself estimated.

7. Even those figures tend to underestimate the quantitative changes that took place in the sixteenth and seventeenth centuries. King drew up his figures to separate the poor, receiving welfare, from the rest of the population. Not all proletarians were necessarily poor, however, as there was a growing stratum of skilled workers drawing wages well above subsistence whose families also worked and so added to the household's total income. A number of commentators have suggested that it was the expansion of working-class family–household incomes that provoked the surge in domestic demand underwriting the economic growth of the nascent capitalist economy. See Joan Thirsk, *Economic Policies and Projects: The Development of a Consumer Society in Early Modern England* (Oxford, England: Oxford University Press, 1978), J. H. Plumb, *The Commercialization of Leisure in Eighteenth Century England* (Reading, England: University of Reading Press, 1973); D. E. C. Eversley, "The Home Market and Economic Growth in England, 1750–1780," in E. L. Jones and G. E. Mingay, eds., *Land, Labour and Population in the Industrial Revolution* (London: Edward Arnold, 1967). Neil McKendrick, "Home Demand and Economic Growth: A New View of the Role of Women and Children in the Industrial Revolution," in Neil McKendrick, ed., *Historical Perspectives: Studies in English Thought and Society* (London: Europa Publications, 1974). The question of poverty for wage earners was not a static one; it varied over the life cycle and was highly sensitive to change. Margaret Spufford's essay on the hard-won literacy of plebians in this period shows quite clearly how the premature death of a parent (especially a father) could send children plummeting down the social scale to a point beyond return: "First Steps in Literacy: The Reading and Writing Experiences of the Humblest Seventeenth-century Spiritual Autobiographers," *Social History* 4:3 (1979): 407–435.

8. On the public face of this debate in the 1650s, see Joyce Oldham Appleby, *Economic Thought and Ideology in Seventeenth Century England* (Princeton, N.J.: Princeton University Press, 1978), chap. 3.

9. East Worcestershire between 1550 and 1650 provides a model of this process of comparative advantage. There, as J. A. Yelling discovered, field systems and cropping patterns were completely reorganized, as the light, sandy soils became the center of convertible husbandry and arable farming, whereas the heavier clays were relegated to pasturage: "Common Land and Enclosure in East Worcestershire, 1540–1870," *Transactions of the Institute of British Geographers* 43 (1967): 157–168; "The Combination and Rotation of Crops in East Worcestershire, 1540–1660," *Agricultural History Review* 17:1 (1967): 24–43; and "Changes in Crop Production in East Worcestershire 1540–1867," *Agricultural History Review* 21:1 (1973): 18–33. For the "big picture," see Eric Kerridge, *The Agricultural Revolution* (London: Allen and Unwin, 1967).

10. Andrew Appley, "Epidemics and Famine in the Little Ice Age," *Journal of Interdisciplinary History* 10:4 (1980): 643–663. See also D. M. Palliser, "Tawney's Century: Brave New World or Malthusian Trap?" *Economic History Review*, 2nd ser., 35:3 (1982): 339–353.

11. Thorold Rogers, *Six Centuries of Work and Wages*, vol. 2, p. 479. Quoted in H. N. Brailsford, *The Levellers and the English Revolution*, edited by Christopher Hill. (London: Spokesman Books, 1976), 451.

12. W. G. Hoskins, "The Rebuilding of Rural England," *Past and Present* 4 (1953): 44–57; M. W. Barley, "Farmhouses and Cottages, 1550–1725," *Economic History Review*, 2nd ser., 7:3 (1955): 291–306. P. Machin, "The Great Rebuilding: A Reassessment," *Past and Present* 77 (1977): 33–56.

13. Peter Clark and Paul Slack, *English Towns in Transition* (Oxford, England: Oxford University Press, 1976).

14. M. J. Power, "East London Housing in the Seventeenth Century," in Peter Clark and Paul Slack, eds., *Crisis and Order in English Towns 1500–1700* (Toronto: University of Toronto Press, 1972), 237–262. Housing densities in Shadwell (in 1682) were of the order of 200 rooms per acre (p. 244). On Lime Street, in Shadwell, row houses "must have had a frontage of between 11 and 12 feet and a depth of about 15 feet" (p. 247). The 1664 Hearth Tax shows that 7,291 of 14,185 households were exempted in East London (p. 252). For comparable figures from provincial cities (43% in Leicester, 47% in Exeter, and 48% in Salisbury), see Clark and Slack, *English Towns in Transition*, 112.

15. P. Laslett and J. Harrison, "Clayworth and Cogenhoe," in H. E. Bell and R. L. Ollard, eds., *Historical Essays Presented to David Ogg* (New York: Barnes & Noble, 1963), 157–184.

16. "Vagrants and Vagrancy in England, 1598–1664," *Economic History Review*, 2nd ser., 27:2 (1974): 360–379.

17. *Religion and the Decline of Magic* (Harmondsworth, England: Penguin Books, 1978); *Witchcraft in Tudor and Stuart England* (London: Routledge, 1970).

18. W. A. Hunt, "The Godly and the Vulgar" (Ph.D. diss., Harvard University, 1974). Now revised and published as *The Puritan Moment* (Cambridge, Mass.: Harvard University Press, 1983).

19. Peter Clark, "The Alehouse and the Alternative Society," In D. Pennington and K. Thomas, eds., *Puritans and Revolutionaries* (Oxford, England: Oxford University Press, 1968), 42–72.

20. James Obelkevich, *Religion and Rural Society: South Lindsey, 1825–1875* (Oxford, England: Oxford University Press, 1976), especially chap. 6.

21. This point has been made repeatedly by Peter Laslett. For his definitive statement see his "Mean Household Size in England Since the Sixteenth Century," in Peter Laslett and Richard Wall, eds., *Household and Family in Past Times* (Cambridge: Cambridge University Press, 1972), 125–158.

22. In Terling, Essex, for instance, some 50–60% of householders were unrelated to other householders in the village, so that on a day-to-day basis it was likely that most re-

lationships would have been outside the kin group for most of the villagers. See Keith Wrightson and David Levine, *Poverty and Piety in an English Village: Terling, 1525–1700* (New York: Academic Press, 1977), 85.

23. Ann Sturm Kussmaul, "Servants in Husbandry in Early Modern England" (Ph.D. diss., University of Toronto, 1978).

24. G. Schochet, "Patriarchalism, Politics and Mass Attitudes in Stuart England," *Historical Journal* 12:3 (1969): 413–441; Howard Newby, "The Deferential Dialectic," *Comparative Studies in Society and History* 17:2 (1975): 139–164.

25. C. B. Macpherson, *The Political Theory of Possessive Individualism: Hobbes to Locke* (Oxford, England: Oxford University Press, 1962).

26. For women's health problems, see Edward Shorter, *A History of Women's Bodies* (New York: Basic Books, 1982). On the question of poverty and plague, "the preacher, William Gouge, also revealed the social limits of his sympathies in 1631, when he declared that it was lawful for those who wished to flee from the plague-stricken area, with three exceptions: the magistrates, because they had special responsibilities; the aged, because they were less vulnerable to infection; *and 'the poorer and meaner sort', because they 'are not much use, but may better be spared'* " (Thomas, *Religion and the Decline of Magic,* 790 [italics added]).

27. Brian Outhwaite, "Age at Marriage in England from the late Seventeenth Century to the Nineteenth Century," *Transactions of the Royal Historical Society,* 5th ser., 23 (1973): especially 61–62.

28. Richard Smith, "Three Centuries of Fertility, Economy and Household Formation in England," *Population and Development Review* 7:4 (1981): 595–622.

29. David Levine, *Family Formation in an Age of Nascent Capitalism* (New York: Academic Press, 1977).

30. It can be inferred from Lawrence Stone's assertation that upper-class women began to suckle their own children in the eighteenth century as a part of the growth of affect that they did not do so before. The Family, Sex and Marriage in England 1500–1800. (New York: Harper & Row, 1977), 426–432.

31. For a discussion of interclass transfer of babies from middle-class London parents to country wet nurses, see R. A. P. Finlay, "The Population of London, 1580–1640" (Ph.D. diss., Cambridge University 1977), especially 115–123.

32. On the role of breast feeding as a contraceptive measure, see Joroen Van Ginneken, "Prolonged Breastfeeding As a Birth Spacing Method" (mimeo). Subsequently published in *Studies in Family Planning* 5 (1974).

33. Although there has been little detailed research on this subject in England, Bernard Derouet has written a stimulating and original essay on the subject, concentrating on the Thimerais during the eighteenth century. "Une demographie sociale differentielle," *Annales, E. C. S.* 35:1 (1980): 3–41.

34. For a vivid example of official refusal to condone a beggar marriage, see Wrightson and Levine, *Poverty and Piety,* 80–81.

35. C. K. Harley, "British Industrialization Before 1840: Evidence of Slower Growth During the Industrial Revolution," *Journal of Economic History* 42 (1982): 267–289. Harley's article suggests that the "classic" periodization of industrialization needs to be reinterpreted, since his research demonstrates much higher levels of industrial production (i.e., proto-industry) prior to the "take-off" and, therefore, relatively lower rates of growth for the "air-borne" Industrial Revolution.

36. John U. Nef, *The Rise of the British Coal Industry,* vol. 1 (London: George Routledge and Sons, 1932), 420–421.

37. Daniel Defoe, *A Tour Through England and Wales, 1724–26,* vol. 2 (London and Toronto: Dent, Everyman Edition, 1927), 193.

38. W. G. Hoskins, "The Rise and Decline of the Serge Industry in the South-West of England, with Special Reference to the Eighteenth Century" (M. S. thesis, University of London, 1929).

39. E. P. Thompson, "Time, Work Discipline and Industrial Capitalism," *Past and Present* 38 (1967): 56–97. Thompson's view that the leisure preference declined during the heroic phase of the Industrial Revolution has been disputed by Douglas A. Read in "The Decline of St. Monday, 1776–1876," *Past and Present* 71 (1976): 77–84; and Eric Hopkins, "Working Hours and Conditions During the Industrial Revolution: A Re-Appraisal," *Economic History Review,* 2nd ser., 35:1 (1982): 52–66.

40. I am fully aware that as late as 1900 the hops harvest in Kent was largely brought in with the aid of labor from the East End of London, and my own father—born and brought up in the Salford district of Manchester—spent a few summers of his boyhood plucking flax in Lincolnshire during the First World War. My cognizance of and unease with the difficulty of applying rigid categories is obviously heightened by this knowledge. It is hard, often harmful, to stop history and examine its inner workings like those of a clock or some other machine. In stopping the historical process, stepping back from it, abstracting it, and then generalizing, there is a tendency to create dichotomies in an evolutionary development and turning points in a process of mutation. Although we may protest, sometimes we must reconstruct the chronological order of historic events. But to continue with my analogy, the emergence and development of proto-industry were the scissors that cut the plebeian family adrift and reordered its inner workings.

41. John Lyons, "Family Responses to Economic Decline: English Cotton Handloom Weavers in the Nineteenth Century" (mimeo). See also his "The Lancashire Cotton Industry and the Introduction of the Powerloom, 1815–1850" (Ph.D. diss., University of California, Berkeley, 1977).

42. The use of paupers in factory industry is well known. Their use in cottage industry is less well known, but if one looks carefully through apprenticeship indentures and connects these documents with reconstituted families, then it is possible to get a clear idea that such extra hands were brought in when the family had too many mouths.

43. A. V. Chayanov, *The Theory of the Peasant Economy,* ed. D. Thorner, R. E. F. Smith, and B. Kerblay (Homewood, Ill.: Irwin, American Economic Association, 1966).

44. D. C. Coleman, "Labour in the English Economy of the Seventeenth Century," *Economic History Review,* 2nd ser., 7:3 (1956): 280–295; Appleby, *Economic Thought and Ideology,* chap. 6. See also E. J. Hundert, "The Conception of Work and the Worker in Early Industrial England" (Ph.D. diss., University of Rochester, 1969).

45. Dennis Mills, "Landownership and Rural Population" (Ph.D. diss., University of Leicester, 1963).

46. Alan Everitt, *The Pattern of Rural Dissent.* Department of English Local History, Occasional Papers, 2nd ser., no. 4 (Leicester, England: Leicester University Press, 1972).

47. A cornerstone of this free space was the local alehouse, the site of all sorts of seditious habits in the eyes of moral reformers. Recent research into local social history provides some support for the moral reformers. Alehouses have been studied by Peter Clark, "The Alehouse and Alternative Society"; J. O. Foster, *Class Struggle and the Industrial Revolution* (London: Weidenfield & Nicolson, 1974); and David Levine and Keith Wrightson, "The Social Context of Illegitimacy in Early Modern England," in Peter Laslett, Karla Oosterveen, and Richard Smith, eds., *Bastardy and Its Comparative History* (London: Edward Arnold, 1980).

48. Much of what follows in this paragraph is based on my own earlier writings on the subject (see also my *Family Formation*).

49. The term is not English in origin but was used to explain a similar phenomenon in

the proto-industrial regions of eighteenth-century Switzerland: Rudolf Braun, "The Impact of Cottage Industry on an Agricultural Population," in D. S. Landes, ed., *The Rise of Capitalism* (New York: Macmillan, 1966); and Braun, "Early Industrialization and Demographic Change in the Canton of Zürich," in Charles Tilly, ed., *Historical Studies of Changing Fertility* (Princeton, N.J.: Princeton University Press, 1978).

50. E. P. Thompson, "Patrician Society, Plebeian Culture," *Journal of Social History* 7:4 (1974): 382–405.

51. Kussmaul, "Servants in Husbandry."

52. Randolph Trumbach, *The Rise of the Egalitarian Family* (New York: Academic Press, 1978), 141–145.

53. Thompson, "Patrician Society, Plebeian Culture."

54. Douglas Hay, "Property, Authority and the Criminal Law," in Douglas Hay and E. P. Thompson, eds., *Albion's Fatal Tree* (New York: Pantheon, 1975).

55. I am not arguing that there was no concern with public morality but, rather, that agencies like the Society for the Reformation of Manners were, in comparison with seventeenth-century practice, less formal and more tolerant. In the eighteenth century a great deal of social regulation that had previously been exercised by institutional agencies became the prerogative of the gentry. Perhaps, too, the social gospel of the Reformation had been internalized somewhat, at least to the extent of becoming public morality, and so it was less necessary to engage in the exemplary punishment of bastard bearers, fornicators, alehousehaunters, tipplers, Sabbath breakers, swearers, and the other "seditious" acts that had evoked the wrath of the Puritan pulpit and magistracy. Robert Malcolmson's study of leisure activities makes it clear that a kind of repressive tolerance replaced the earlier, more straightforward repression of both bodily and social pleasures: *Popular Recreations in English Society, 1700–1850* (Cambridge: Cambridge Univesity Press, 1973). David Rollison's discussion of the Westonbirt Groaning seems to me to lend credence to the argument advanced above, in that the actions of Sir Richard Holford were exceptional: "Property, Ideology and Popular Culture in a Gloucestershire Village 1660–1740," *Past and Present* 93 (1981): 70–97. Not only was Holford's supervision of the affairs of Westonbirt personal and meticulous, but he also saw an "independent act of plebeian culture as an act akin to rebellion, dangerous in fact and principle to the state" (p. 78). In this way his actions seem to have been as peculiar as those of the legislators who rushed the Waltham Black Acts through Parliament a couple of years later: (E. P. Thompson, *Whigs and Hunters* (New York: Pantheon, 1975). In another vein, E. A. Wrigley has also referred to a "long eighteenth century" in his most recent essay, "The Growth of Population in Eighteenth Century England: A Conundrum Resolved," *Past and Present* 98 (1983): 121–150, *passim*.

56. Wrightson and Levine, *Poverty and Piety*.

57. Levine, *Family Formation*, chap. 8.

58. Dennis Mills, "The Quality of Life in Melbourn Cambridgeshire, in the Period 1800–50," *International Review of Social History* 23 (1978): 382–404.

59. Raphael Samuel, "Workshop of the World," *History Workshop* 3 (1977): 6–72.

60. N. J. Smelser, *Social Change in the Industrial Revolution* (Chicago: University of Chicago Press, 1959). It seems to me that the key to the debate that Smelser initiated some two decades ago is to be found in Michael Anderson's discussion of the family economy of the factory family. Anderson states: "Smelser's typical picture is of a spinner recruiting his own children as piecers, and this may well have been the ideal, and *was probably indeed a usual phase in the life-cycle of almost all spinners until long after 1851.* It can never, however, have been the dominant pattern at any one time for, given the age distribution of the spinning population, rather few spinners would *ever* have had

enough children of suitable age to piece for them": "Sociological History and the Working-class Family: Smelser Revisited," *Social History* 3 (1976): 325 (italics added). Seen in this light, the objections of M. M. Edwards and R. Lloyd-Jones are almost beside the point. Of course, Smelser did overstate his case, and these two scholars have done a good job pointing out his egregious shortcomings in this regard, but they do not really come to grips with the central problem he raised as satisfactorily as Anderson did: "N. J. Smelser and the Cotton Factory Family: A Reassessment," in N. B. Harte and K. G. Ponting, eds., *Textile History and Economic History* (Manchester, England: Manchester University Press, 1973). For a later discussion of the centrality of the family economy in the cotton factories, see Patrick Joyce, *Work, Culture and Society in Victorian England* (New Brunswick, N.J.: Rutgers University Press, 1980), especially 50–64.

61. Paul Mantoux, *The Industrial Revolution in the Eighteenth Century* (London: Jonathan Cape, 1928), 421, 478, 481, n. 1.
62. Gareth Steadman-Jones, "England's First Proletariat," *New Left Review* 92 (1975): 35–70.
63. Michael Anderson, *Family Structure in Nineteenth Century Lancashire.* (Cambridge: Cambridge University Press, 1972), 29–32, 48–53.
64. Generally speaking, women worked before marriage and then for a short time thereafter. They gradually withdrew from the labor force as domestic responsibilities and the wage earning of older children transformed the family economy. Older women with adult or teenaged children went back to factory employment in relatively small numbers. For a thorough discussion of the life cycle of women's working careers, see Joan Scott and Louis Tilly, *Women, Work and Family* (New York: Basic Books, 1978).
65. Phyllis Deane and W. A. Cole, *British Economic Growth 1688–1850* (Cambridge: Cambridge University Press, 1962), 130–135.
66. For some pertinent comments on the evolution of this mentality, see Paul Willis, *Learning to Labour* (Farnborough, England: Saxon House, 1978). What Willis has to say about this distinctive point of view is worth repeating:

> Though it is difficult to obtain stature in work itself, both what work provides and the very sacrifice and strength required to do it provides the materials for an elemental self-esteem. This self-esteem derives from the achievement of a purpose which not all—particularly women—are held capable of achieving. The wage packet is the provider of freedom, and independence; the particular prize of masculinity in work. . . . A trade is judged not for itself, nor even for its general financial return, but for its ability to provide the central, domestic, masculine role for its incumbent. Clearly money is part of this—but as a measure, not the essence. . . . The wage packet as a kind of symbol of machismo dictates the domestic culture and tyrannises both men and women. (p. 150)

67. Although the point has been made repeatedly throughout the text, I would like to state clearly that the numbers I am advancing are not special or magical. Instead, they are based on my familiarity with research in English historical demography. As one who has spent a good part of the last 12 years "finessing" the statistics and coddling these numbers, I am only too well aware that they are fragile, not broken, reeds. However, I have also believed that it would be wrong to make these hard-earned statistics into a kind of shibboleth. My whole involvement with historical demography has been predicated on the belief that we need a better group of approximations so that we can begin to toss numbers about with some expectation that they will conform to past reality. In throwing around these statistics we can produce viable models of

social and demographic change. Before the advent of family reconstitution we simply could not do this. In a sense, then, what I am doing is giving exactness with one hand and more or less taking it away with the other as I boil down the descriptive statistics to their essences. Such a recipe can be tested only by tasting the product, and its success, therefore, will be integral to the validity of the whole argument put forward in this chapter.

68. Daniel Scott Smith, "A Homeostatic Demographic Regime: Patterns in West European Family Reconstitution Studies," in R. D. Lee, ed., *Population Patterns in the Past* (New York: Academic Press, 1977); and E. A. Wrigley, "Family Limitation in Pre-Industrial England," in Michael Drake, ed., *Population in Industrialization* (London: Methuen University Paperbacks, 1972).

69. "The relationship between demographic structure and environment in preindustrial western Europe," in W. Conze, ed., *Sozialgeschichte der Familie in Der Neuzeit Europas* (Stuttgart, Germany: Klett Verlag, 1977).

70. Levine and Wrightson, "The Social Context of Illegitimacy."

71. P. G. Ohlin, "Mortality, Marriage, and Growth in Pre-Industrial Populations," *Population Studies* 14:3 (1961): 190–197.

72. E. A. Wrigley, "Fertility Strategy for the Individual and the Group," in Charles Tilly, ed., *Historical Studies of Changing Fertility* (Princeton, N.J.: Princeton University Press, 1978).

73. L. Henry, "Some Data on Natural Fertility," *Eugenics Quarterly* 8 (1961): 81–91.

74. Wrigley, "Family Limitation."

75. Levine and Wrightson, "The Social Context of Illegitimacy."

76. Schofield and Wrigley, *The Population History of England*, app. 10, pp. 645–693. See also Paul Slack, "Mortality Crises and Epidemics in England, 1485–1610," in Charles Webster, ed., *Health Medicine and Mortality in the Sixteenth Century* (Cambridge: Cambridge University Press, 1979), 9–59.

77. Levine, *Family Formation*, chap. 6.

78. E. A. Wrigley, "A Simple Model of London's Importance in Changing English Society and Economy 1650–1750," *Past and Present* 37 (1967): 44–70; and Finlay, "Population of London."

79. E. A. Wrigley and R. S. Schofield, "Infant and Child Mortality in England in the Late Tudor and Early Stuart Period," in Charles Webster, ed., *Health, Medicine and Mortality in the Sixteenth Century* (Cambridge: Cambridge University Press, 1979), 75.

80. See Levine, *Family Formation*, 73–77, for an explanation of the calculation of fertility loss due to adult mortality.

81. A ratio of 2% of all births is not out of line with the figures derived by Peter Laslett and Karla Oosterveen: "Long-Term Trends in Bastardy in England," *Population Studies* 27:2 (1973): 255–286.

82. The population would have grown by 15% because we are calculating two parents reproducing 2.30 married children at the end of a generation. Unmarried children do not count because they do not reproduce themselves.

83. Wrigley, "London's Importance."

84. Finlay, "Population of London," 95–102, 124.

85. It has been assumed that more than 50% of the total surplus of the peasant demography model was "wasted" in the process of stocking London and other urban centers. Thus, the population would have grown by about 40%, and not 85%—from 2.4 million to 3.36 million.

86. Fertility was still natural and ended at 40.

87. The proletarian demography model represented a doubling of the original population every 43 years; the peasant demography model represents a doubling every 200 years.

88. Thirsk, *Economic Policies and Projects*.
89. McKendrick ("Home Demand and Economic Growth") draws attention to the expansion of the working-class demand during the classic Industrial Revolution, after 1780. Eversley ("The Home Market and Economic Growth") argues for the expansion of lower-middle-class demand between 1750 and 1780. Plumb (*Commercialization of Leisure*) situates increasing consumer demand from the beginning of the eighteenth century. Thirsk (*Policies and Projects*) suggests that the Elizabethan period saw the emergence of a consumer society.
90. In my *Family Formation*, I characterized the social and economic deterioration of living conditions among the Shepshed framework knitters as a form of "industrial involution" (pp. 33–34). The concept was, of course, borrowed from Clifford Geertz (*Agricultural Involution: The Processes of Ecological Change in Indonesia* (Berkeley and Los Angeles: University of California Press, 1968).

3

Peasant, Plebeian, and Proletarian Marriage in Britain, 1600–1900

John R. Gillis

WEDDINGS AND MARRIAGES

In truth, this is a study not of marriage but of wedding. The two are often treated as interchangeable, when, in fact, they are not at all identical. Marriage is defined by the rules of church and state; wedding is part of a larger social process, responsive to a more complex reality. Marriage is official, wedding unofficial, but this does not mean that wedding practices are without great significance or sanction. We know more about marriage because the official record is better kept, but it is well to remember the limitations of the parish register and census schedule as social documents. A considerable part of conjugal history will never be found there. On the other hand, weddings, even when illicit, are a window on the way that ordinary people think about and act on nuptiality. Wedding varies not only between but within periods. It is reflective of the particularities of class, age, and gender relations, far more responsive than marriage law to social and cultural transformation.

Among the lower orders of British society in the period between 1600

PROLETARIANIZATION
AND FAMILY HISTORY

and 1900 there existed three overlapping wedding patterns, each with its legal and illicit variants and all representing particular social formations. Predominant at the beginning of the period, particularly in the North and West, were the festive *big weddings* typical of groups ranging from marginal smallholders and tradespeople to substantial yeomen. Like the groups whose social relations it reflected, what I will call here the *peasant wedding* had already become a minority practice by the end of the seventeenth century, though it continued in attenuated form well into the industrial era, most notably in Wales, Yorkshire, and the Lake District. Its foremost competitor in the seventeenth and eighteenth centuries, which I have chosen to call the *plebeian wedding*, had been gaining ground steadily, reaching its apogee in the late eighteenth and early nineteenth centuries and reflecting the growth of the proto-industrial communities that had given it birth. By the middle of the Victorian period it, too, was giving way to a third form of popular wedding, which I have defined as the *proletarian wedding*. This was not simply an extension of the plebeian form, but an alternative to it, expressing a set of needs and values quite different from those of a population of proto-industrial producers. The proletarian wedding was the product of the capitalization of agriculture as well as urban industrialization. Thus, though both plebeian and proletarian weddings reflected Britain's protracted proletarianization process, they represented distinct, though overlapping, phases.

THE PEASANT BIG WEDDING
AND CLANDESTINE MARRIAGES

Among smallholders and artisans, nuptiality was a privileged status, and the wedding itself was an event of enormous political as well as social significance, reserved for persons in their mid- to late twenties who had acquired either the property (in the case of peasants) or the trade privileges (as with artisans) necessary to establish a separate household. The control by the married of the means of production, their rank, and especially their authority set them apart. The term *husband* conveyed a public meaning that transcended mere marital status, and a wife was automatically superior to a spinster, no matter what the latter's age or status.[1]

The most complete account of a seventeenth-century big wedding comes from the notebooks of Henry Best, a Yorkshire farmer, who recorded the marital process from courtship through wedding. He begins his description with the initial inquiries:

Usually the younge mans father, or hee himselfe, writes to the father of the maid, to knowe if he shal bee welcome to the howse, if he shall have his furtherance if hee come in such a way, or howe hee liketh of the notion; then if he [the girl's father] pretend any excuse, onely thankinge him for his good will, then that is as good as a denyall. If the notion be thought well of, and imbraced, then the younge man goeth perhapps twice, to see howe the mayd standeth affected. . . .[2]

It is clear that direct negotiations were possible only between males of equal standing; relations between patriarchs and bachelors were so unequal as to prohibit face-to-face relations. By contrast, relations with age-mates, especially fellow servants and apprentices, were open and often emotional. The years between early adolescence and marriage were normally spent away from home, and it was to companions rather than elders that young people expressed their deepest feelings.[3] Relations with members of the opposite sex were normally inhibited, in part by patriarchal restrictions, but also because the work roles were highly segregated by gender. The contacts by which young people came to know one another and assess their marriage prospects were highly ritualized. Some were religious occasions, and others were part of the traditional festivities—village wakes, hiring fairs, Valentine's and May Days— which provided regulated meetings between eligibles.[4] The festivity of the occasion was the principal guarantee against premature pairing. Country dancing, observed Baring-Gould, "allows no opportunities for conversation and consequently of flirtation, as the partners stand opposite one each other, and in figures take part with other partners quite as much as with their own proper vis-à-vis."[5]

The widespread practice of night visiting served a similar function. Peer pressure guaranteed the circulation of eligible males and prevented undue intimacy. From Roger Lowe's bachelor diary we know that the young men of seventeenth-century Lancashire rarely went courting unaccompanied. They normally took along what the Welsh of the same period called a *gwas caru*, a courtship attendant, so that when Thomas Smith wanted to know the intentions of Alice Leland, he had his friend Roger Lowe do the talking for him. Two years later, Thomas was able to return the favor by assisting Roger at a difficult point in his courtship with Em Potter. He offered to "conclude a peace" with Em, one of the many truces that eventually led to marriage.[6] In the final stages of negotiation with the woman's father, an older, more respected go-between would be employed. Ralph Josselin performed this function several times as one of the many social duties of a country parson.[7]

In so delicate and significant a matter as marriage, the parties preferred to put off face-to-face negotiations until everything was well prepared in advance. Peasant and artisan lovers therefore chose a symbolic mode of courtship that maintained the maximum degree of flexibility and secrecy. Valentine's Day was one approved occasion for cryptic messages; May Eve was another. On the latter "all the young men turned out to pay a tribute of affection to their sweethearts, or mark their disdain for girls who had jilted them."[8] Small gifts, accepted or rejected, played a major part in Best's account of courtship, in which, after the initial visits, the suitor "giveth her a ten shillinge peece of gold, or a ringe of that price. . . ."[9] At hiring fairs, affection was measured by gifts or *fairings,* accepted or rejected. When things become serious, the couple would be tested by their peers:

> The first few times a young man and a young woman appeared together at fairs, one of a group of young men was sent to "fetch" the young woman away on behalf of another member of the group. Her suitor had to buy her fairings in order to keep her, while the young man who had tried to draw her away had to buy her fairings in order to entice her.[10]

Men played the most active part in courtship, but it is clear that women enjoyed the right of rejection. To the extent that the agreement of all parties was necessary, these marriages cannot be said to have been arranged. On the other hand, young people did everything possible to secure parental agreement. They conducted their courtships out of sight of their parents in deference to their authority and feelings, the major reason that night visiting endured longest in areas of smallholding. In nineteenth-century Wales it was said that "a young man going courting was terrified lest anyone should see him in 'broad daylight.' "[11] Their relationship became public only when they had agreed between themselves and each had persuaded their parents of the value of the match:

> Soe soone as the younge folkes were agreed and contracted, then the father of the mayd carryeth her over the younge mans howse to see howe they like of all, and there doth the younge mans father meete them to treate of a dower, and likewise of a joynture or feoffment for the women; and then doe they allsoe appointe and sette downe the day of marriage, which may perhapps bee aboute a fortnight or three weekes after. . . .[12]

The couple's "contract" to one another usually consisted of an exchange of rings of two halves of a broken coin. The familial agreement constituted the public betrothal and, though conditional on both sides' delivering on their promises, was often celebrated with festivities that rivaled the wedding itself. Miles Coverdale, writing in the 1550s, reported a "great feast and superflous bancket [banquet], and even the same night are the two handfasted [betrothed] persones brought and layed together, yea certayne wekes afore they go to church.''[13] Although they abhorred this carnal license, even the Puritans conceded the need for the betrothed to get to know each other more intimately so that any obstacles to marriage might be discovered and the betrothal terminated. William Gouge insisted that ''contracted persons are in a middle degree betwixt single persons and married persons; they are neither simply single, nor actually married. . . .''[14] In concurrence with popular practice, canon law regarded betrothed couples as good as married if they had made vows in the present tense or had followed vows in the future tense by intercourse. On the other hand, church courts were also ready to dissolve betrothal obligations should any ''lets or impediments'' be discovered. In a period when divorce was discouraged by both law and public opinion, many young people appear to have taken advantage of this recognized trial period to test the relationships, not only between themselves, but also with family, peers, and the wider community. The short period between betrothal and wedding was crucial to determining whether the social, as well as the personal, dimension of their marriage was viable.[15]

Although the first stages of courtship were, by our standards, slow and awkward, the final phases seem to us indecently brief. ''Happy is the wooing that's not long in adoing,'' was the current wisdom.[16] In the three or four weeks that a couple had their banns called in church, the drama and tension increased noticeably. This highly publicized act, variously known as *askings* or *spurrings*, was the last occasion at which objections could be raised and, as such, was the focus of intense communal interest and occasional high drama. In Yorkshire the congregation became a kind of jury, shouting ''God speed 'em well'' when the banns were called for the third time without objection. Elsewhere bells were rung and guns fired in tribute, and everywhere there was a certain amount of teasing by peers, releasing the accumulated tension.[17]

The big wedding itself combined rites of both separation and inauguration. The day normally began with the age-mates of the bride and groom gathering at their respective houses to receive drink and favors. Ribbons and gloves given ''that morninge when they are allmost ready to goe to church'' were a form of symbolic compensation to former companions who would now become subordinates in the village social structure, distanced not by space but by status and authority.[18] The chosen companions of the groom, often numbering in the dozens, would then accompany him on horseback to the bride's house, overcoming along the way various symbolic obstacles, including the traditional quintain.[19]

In Wales they arrived only to find themselves "greeted by strong and sturdy men who have been appointed to prevent them from taking the girl away, and in the meantime, the girl would be guarded and the doors fastened."[20] There then ensued an oratorical battle, which ended with the appointed "seekers" entering the house and searching for the bride, who was sometimes disguised as an old woman. The drama continued even as the party was ready to leave for church: "the Girl makes great moans and Lementations, and if she can Counterfeit tears and Tearing of hair it is reckond a meritt."[21]

In Yorkshire the rites symbolizing the separation of the bride from her house and friends were less emotive, but the form was essentially the same. Best's groom enters the house and, taking his bride by the hand, asks, "Mistris, I hope you are willinge' or else kisseth her before them, and then followeth her father out of the doores." Patriarchal authority was transferred at the threshold, for in Best's account the father does not accompany the daughter to church or give her away there.[22] Instead, she is mounted behind the groom's "best man," who, with the rest of the young people, troop off to the church in a procession led by pipers and fiddlers.

The church service itself was the least important element of the big wedding. Those attending could scarcely wait until the ceremony ended when they snatched at the bride's garter or pelted the couple with hassocks, shoes, and other available missiles. In 1633 several men were charged with assulting a London groom named John Riggs, "pullinge of[f] his garters and behavinge themselves in a very irreverent and unciville manner."[23] By far the most common sequel was the barring of the church door, locking the couple in until the groom paid ransom for their release. When the clergy objected to this use of sacred property, this particular practice was moved to the church steps, where the couple were compelled to jump over a bench or stone. In the Yorkshire dales, where this practice endured into the nineteenth century, the idea was that "the twain should meet and overcome their first trouble or obstacle in life, within the precincts of the church."[24]

In later periods, obstacles were placed at the church gate or in the road itself, usually by former companions of the couple. In 1602 a West Ham man "gott a bough hanged with rope endes and besett with nettles and other weedes, and conveyed the same in the streete and churchyard before the bryde."[25] The "chaining" or "roping" of newlyweds persisted well into the Victorian era in areas of smallholders. In North Devon, couples could expect to encounter several such roadblocks, and "the bridegroom has again and again to pay his footing as a husband."[26] It was said that in the Forest of Dean the practice expressed an objection "to people, or especially brides, being taken from the parish. . . ."[27] Blakeborough's description of Yorkshire "hustlers" in the eighteenth century suggestions another kind of envy. Young men, "gaily dressed, with faces blackened," stopped the couple: "The captain of this band cried a halt, he declared that he and his merry men were in need of wives, and unless the bridegroom paid them instantly "bride guest money" his bride and every bonny bridesmaid would be kidnapped."[28]

On occasion, such emotions could spill over into more provocative forms of charivari. In 1639, Ralph Brocke, a Sussex man, was charged in church court with "wearing a great payre of hornes uppon his head in the churchyard when Henry Hall and his wife were going to be married, shewing thereby that he the said Hall was lyke to be a cuckald."[29] For the most part, however, the rough music that began at the church door and continued through the wedding night alleviated rather than exacerbated the tensions present. Charivari clarified the status changes and, even as it mocked the newlyweds, reaffirmed the superiority of the married over the unmarried. In a similar manner, the procession and ritual established the hierarchy of roles within the marriage. On leaving the church, the bride and groom proceeded for the first time as a couple, being careful at each bridge or crossing that "the husband always took precedence, for was it not right that he, as master, and still more as protector of his bride, his wife, should go first and overcome all danger."[30] The woman established her status as mistress by taking possession of the symbols of household authority—fire tongs, brooms, keys— and by relinguishing her maidenhood, symbolized by her garter. In Yorkshire, the bachelor who won the race to the wedding house was rewarded by being allowed to remove the garter as the bride stepped across the threshold for the first time.[31] Refusal by either the bride or groom to participate in this or any of the other inaugural rites—the convivial public bedding, throwing the stocking, rough music in the early morning hours—was considered a serious breach of etiquette and an indication of a bad-tempered master or mistress. In Yorkshire, a groom who did not pay his footing to the rough band could expect, at the very least, to have his chimney blocked, and a bride who refused her garter was subject to very hostile gossip and mocking songs.[32]

The final rites of inauguration often were held some days and even weeks after the marriage. When Best's groom finally took his bride to her new home, his friends were rewarded by a second large feast.[33] In Cumberland, farmers conveyed their daughters' belongings in a decorated wagon called a *bridewain*. Eighteenth-century Yorkshire brides also rode in wagons, posing in a matronly way with their spinning wheels atop the load of furnishings, whereas in Cardiganshire, a parade of female relatives carried the lighter instruments of housekeeping, and carts brought up the heavy items.[34] But it was not until the couple had taken the seats allotted to married persons in the church (sometimes reserved as the *bride seat*) that the community fully recognized their status with a round of visits.[35]

At every step the big wedding celebrated and reinforced the existing social order. All levels of the community were present. If the local gentry did not attend, they often sent gifts as a token of their patronage. The poor were invited as an appropriate act of charity. Youth and age played their ascribed roles, and the female presence emphasized subordination. Mothers were entirely off stage, and the bride's part emphasized her submission. Even the investiture of broom and tongs suggests a limited jurisdiction. The same was true of the festive consumption, which was organized and served by the men, further underscoring the degree to which the household was still a male domain.[36]

The "politics" of such affairs, as reflected in the various propitiatory rites, were enormously complicated. Parental feelings of loss were specifically recognized in the prechurch practices, which dramatized the current notion that "the bridegroom runs away with the bride without the parents' consent."[37] It was not the parents who put on the wedding; instead, the festivities were an opportunity for the new couple to demonstrate their status and generosity: It was not so much a time of receiving as of giving. To fail to invite kindred and neighbors was to risk scandal and even disruption. Accusations of witchcraft were sometimes occasioned by a lack of generosity.[38] There were numerous aspects of the big wedding specifically directed to the appeasement of envious feelings, especially those of unmarried siblings, whose nuptial chances were affected by the distribution of family property. They were compelled to dance in their stocking feet or in a hog's trough, a mild form of humiliation that was supposed to "counteract their ill luck and procure them husbands."[39] Former lovers were also treated to teasing and even made to pay "fines" symbolizing their loss. This was meant to exorcise those feelings that, if not terminated or redirected, could be disruptive to the whole social order. Love was likened to a disease, "griping griefes," which could bring ruin if not quarantined. Among the repertoire of all cunning men and wise women were the cures for lovesickness that were in such high demand throughout the seventeenth and eighteenth centuries.[40]

Some tension was present at every marriage, but there is evidence that in the course of the seventeenth century the strains that ritual was meant to mediate became more intense and less manageable. Parents attempted to strengthen their control by raising the age of consent, and parish elders were said "to hinder poor people from marrying."[41] To circumvent these restrictions, young people turned to a variety of devices. Those who could afford it purchased licenses that dispensed with the public calling of banns. Others resorted to the so-called lawless churches in which a quick, secret marriage could be bought for a very modest fee. By the early eighteenth century, perhaps as many as a half of all weddings were either by license or *clandestine*. Patriarchal and parish anxiety focused mainly on London's infamous Fleet district, but, in reality, every part of England and Wales was served by renegade parsons who offered clandestine marriage to those who, for one reason or another, found desirable a quick, private wedding. Such people included not only sailors and traveling folk who had no time for three weeks of banns but also settled rural people who had encountered some obstacle or simply could not afford the expense of a big wedding. Only a minority of even the Fleet's clientele were vagabonds or rogues. Most were respectable people like Gilbert Wright and Elizabeth Wheaton, who ran off to Formby Chapel "because of her frendes [family], that were against her, that she should not marry hym. . . ." Many found elopement a convenient way of overcoming parental opposition and, once reconciled, would marry in their home parish. Until clandestine marriage was abolished by the Hardwicke Act of 1753, it, together with license, provided a safety valve for what otherwise was a potentially explosive situation.[42]

Both big and clandestine weddings reflected a view of the world as finite. Both the material base of marriage and affection were thought to be in short supply. Among smallholders, marriage was, of necessity, a zero sum game, with winners and losers, and thus there was a need to compensate those whose envy might prove disruptive.[43] Love was seen as too unstable an element on which to base marriage. Its pathogenic qualities were transferred by means of the garter ceremony to those unmarried persons who would need it to make their own marriages. It was appropriate to youth, but not to those who had taken upon themselves the responsibilities of household. Taken as a whole, the rituals of the peasant and artisan big weddings aimed at promoting social harmony in a palpably hierarchical and unequal community. In turn, the community regarded itself as being licensed to intervene in order to restore order whenever marital discord came to its notice. In peasant Britain, charivari, which ridiculed henpecked or cuckolded husbands, expressed the acknowledged right of communal intervention.[44] That marriage was a public institution in which the privacy of the individual was secondary to a greater public good was reaffirmed by the publicity of the wedding itself.

THE EMERGENCE OF PLEBEIAN MARRIAGE

By the late eighteenth century, both the big wedding and clandestine marriage were in eclipse. The Hardwicke Act of 1753 abolished clandestine marriage in England and Wales, though it was still possible for people living close to the Scottish border to marry secretly at places like Gretna Green.[45] However, the social formations that had given form and function to the big wedding were also eroding. When marriage ceased to be based on property, the wedding itself began to change. The resultant plebeian form borrowed many rites from its predecessor but transformed them to suit the changing status, age, and gender relations of the proto-industrial communities in which it originated and developed.

Where mining, fishing, and domestic industry developed, earnings rather than property became the basis of family and marriage. There emerged a family economy dependent on the labor of wives and children as well as husbands, and instead of being sent out to service, sons and daughters were now kept home. Their earnings, so vital to the family, also affected its internal relationships. Patriarchal authority, if not displaced, was modified. In the Buckinghamshire straw-plaiting districts, the earning power of young persons was said to upset both gender and generational relations, making "parents afraid of offending their children, who thus became hardened and intractable." Proto-industrialization was blamed for "leading to very early marriage, and worse. . . ."[46] The wife's domestic employment seems also to have increased her status. At Cradley Heath, one woman ran a chain-making forge with four hearths, and her husband worked as a collier. She would not let her daughters go into service but trained them in the smithing trade. It was said of girls like hers that "the effects of early work, particularly in the forges, render these girls perfectly independent. They often enter beer shops, call for their pints and smoke their pipes like men."[47]

Proto-industrialization stabilized families and communities by eliminating the need for youthful migration and live-in service. Intermarriage fostered dense family networks, which, because they were reckoned bilaterally, were often virtually indistinguishable from the larger community. Under these conditions, the status differences typical of a peasant community diminished. Age and gender segregation, already modified within individual households, became less prominent also; young people of both sexes acquired and elaborated on their elders' habits of dress, drink, and sociability.[48] The festive calender expanded enormously, but courtship was no longer confined to holidays or late-night visiting. Instead, industrial pursuits brought young people together. When Yorkshire women gathered at "sittings" to knit, suitors joined them there, with the result that "going-a-sitting" came to have the same meaning as "a night of watching" did in a peasant community.[49] Welsh *nason weu* (knitting assemblies) and Northumberland work bees served a similar function. In the straw-plaiting districts, courtship came out of doors in good weather, and everywhere meetings between young people became more public and uninhibited, regulated less by family and more by groups of peers.[50]

The changing material base of marriage was reflected in the symbolism of courtship. Instead of giving gloves and coins to their sweethearts, suitors began to present them with sheathes for their knitting needles or carved bobbins for their lace.[51] Gifts suggest the high estimation of female work in places in which a single breadwinner was no longer sufficient. Of journeymen shoemakers, it was said that "no single-handed man can live; he must have a whole family at work . . . ," whereas among fisher folk there was the saying: "A woman suld na wed till she can win her man's bread."[52] Initiative in courtship was also shifting, as women came to use the traditional courtship devices to make their feelings known: "If a girl fancies a man and can't get to know him, she'll send him a message with her proposal or advertise."[53] In Samuel Bamford's Middleton, women took up the practice of sending their own valentines. Bamford was sitting down to a meal at his uncle's table when one such missive was shoved under the door. His aunt exploded: "It's come to summit, any any rate, 'at one canno' sit deawrn to one's meal 'it one's own heawse, but we munbi haunted we young snickets comin' after thee, an' snickin' ther letters under th' dur."[54] Middleton women were also active on May Eve and quite capable of answering male insults when the occasion arose.[55]

Young women, who were often vastly outnumbered in mining districts and industrial villages, used this to advantage.[56] The men responded by attempting to monopolize the available supply, warning off strangers, who, if they came courting, were subject to some very rough treatment. The lads of Graveley, Hertfordshire, had a ferocious reputation for exposing the backsides of interlopers to a whirling stone, but the "Grinders," as they were known, were not the only enforcers of the territorial imperative.[57] If rivals could not be frightened off, then these groups would turn their attentions to the girl in question. Sheffield women who accepted the attentions of strangers had their chastity impugned, and in the Ceiriog Valley of North Wales the local lads took any female's interest in outsiders as

an insult, which made them believe that she did not regard them as perfect
men. Her movements were closely observed, and her courtship with the
stranger was subject to gossip. She was criticized by the young men's mothers
for her arrogance and ostentation for leaving her home town to look for a lover
elsewhere, and they predicted misfortune and shame for her.[58]

That shame was inflicted by the boys themselves, who waylaid the girl
and urinated on her "until her clothes were dripping wet. In this condition she would be compelled to return home for the very shame, but
not before she had proof that they were equal in virility to lads from far
away places."[59]

The assertion of manhood through physical assault or symbolic rape
suggests the degree to which men were experiencing loss of control over
the courtship process. Manhood, like the authority of men in general,
was being reconstituted in the proto-industrial community. In the world
of the smallholder, masculinity and femininity were firmly linked to certain clearly defined roles. Now manhood and womanhood had to be
achieved partly through work and also through life-style and habits of
consumption. Full manhood and womanhood had previously been associated with marriage; now they were acquired much earlier. It was
said of young Cornish miners that their "pride and care is first a watch,
then a gun, a clock, a chest of drawers, a bed, and then last and best a
wife. . . ." In Sheffield, if girls could not afford the finery necessary to
attend a penny dance on a Saturday night, they would rent a dress.
In the course of the eighteenth century, wakes and hiring fairs became
orgies of conspicuous consumption and self-assertion.[60] Both males and
females were there to display themselves through sport and dance. For
the male, proving himself with fist or cudgel had an amorous reward:
"Tom Short behaved himself so well that most People seemed to agree
it was impossible that he should remain a Batchelor till the next Wake."[61]
Women's interest and, oftimes, participation in violent sport reflected
the premium placed on strength and prowess among working females.[62]
In "The Colliers' Pay Week" it is evident that plebeian dancing had also
broken free from the traditional country forms and become a demonstration of the new standards of masculinity and femininity:

> The damsel displays all her graces,
> The collier exerts all his power;
> they caper in circling paces
> And set at each end of the floor.
> He jumps, and his heels knack and rattle,
> At turns of the music so sweet
> He makes such a thundering battle
> the floor seems afraid of his feet[63]

In the same ballad the violent exertions of the dance floor are followed by a brawl between the dancer's companions and a rival village youth group, which ends when one of the combatants is shorn of his breeches and, by implication, his virility.

Young people paired off much earlier and, as the dances suggest, no longer felt the need for go-betweens at any stage in their courtship. The peasant practice of betrothal agreements between families lapsed whenever young people had their own earnings and thus were able to accumulate their own marriage portions. There was no evidence of parental consultation when one young straw plaiter suddenly declared that she was ready to draw her money from the bank. "So am I, too," declared her young man, "We're both a goin' to draw out, and we're goin' to be married on the plait money. Ain't we, Mary."[64] This pair would continue their common work after marriage. Such occupational endogamy was common among London garment workers, as well as in northern weaving and nailing villages, and, even in places where the men worked separately, there was a tendency to marry within the same occupational group:

> Collier lads get gold and silver
> Factory lads get nobbut brass
> who'ed get married to a two-loom weaver
> when there's plenty of collier lads?[65]

Plebeian lovers might still exchange rings or break coins as a symbol of their personal commitment, but this was done privately or in the company of a few friends rather than at an elaborate family occasion. Nor did they wait for formal betrothal to become intimate. The eroticization of relationships began even before serious courtship. In the Ceiriog Valley it was said that "as regards sexual matters boys and girls mature young. Girls on the whole [are] more rapid in development than boys. Boys and girls consider that taking liberties is natural."[66] Familiarities once reserved for married adults were no longer shameful. Ceiriog lads exposed themselves to their sweethearts, and on the Isle of Portland, another quarrying community, "proving" meant actual intercourse. No Portland man would consider marrying a woman until she had shown signs of pregnancy, a precaution common in other parts of Devon and elsewhere.[67]

This precocious mating did not always run smoothly, however. If parents no longer controlled courtship in the old ways, they nevertheless had something to say about marriage. The importance of young persons' labor to the family economy meant that couples often had to contend with parental possessiveness. In Northumberland, miners still courted "under hidlings," keeping things secret as long as possible, and often crossing over the border for a hasty Scots wedding when either parental or peer pressure necessitated this form of elopement.[68] The strong preference in both the North and West for marriage by license reflected similar complications.[69] At Ceiriog, frustrated lovers would elope "over the mountain" and then return to the bride's home, where there would be an episode of "weeping, scolding, and forgiving."[70]

On Portland, parents were not informed until the pregnancy was confirmed. When a woman knew she was with child, "she tells her mother; the mother tells her father; her father tells his father, and he tells his son that it is then proper time to be married," a chain of authority that virtually reversed the generational and gender order of the peasant community. In the Ceiriog, it was also the bride's mother who presided over courtship, and in Edward Chicken's "Collier's Wedding," it is she who is asked to give consent, a practice that suggests a radical change in power relations both within and between families.[71] In proto-industrial areas, marriage had ceased to be a matter negotiated exclusively by patriarchs. Mothers were consulted not just in the absence of fathers, but because the children, especially the girls but also the boys employed in domestic industry, were more apt to be under maternal authority. In the smithing, weaving, and knitting communities, children were essential to the family economy, and it was with great reluctance that they were allowed to establish a separate household that would also be a competing enterprise. At Cradley Heath a form of compromise was worked out in which marriage was permitted, but the young people would "continue to work, living in the home of their respective parents. . . . This tendency has been sufficiently strong to overcome the usual practice of making a home first."[72] In the Lancashire weaving community of Culcheth, young women who became pregnant remained home without formal marriage. The illegitimacy rate there shot up to more than 30% during the period of home industry.[73] In the Ceiriog, where the men mined and the women prepared wool, the situation was much the same. There young couples went through a form of common law marriage known as a *besom wedding*. By jumping over a broom in the presence of witnesses, they established a relationship that could either be transformed into legal marriage at some future point or terminated by jumping back over the broom. There too the tendency of women to remain with their families was evident. Children of besom weddings took their mother's name and were considered her property, though the father was also responsible for their support.[74] Instead of losing a daughter, the family gained another potential earner. Mothering took on a collective meaning whenever grandparents accepted the children as their own. The previously sharp division between legitimate and illegitimate blurred when all became part of one large family.

The practice of delaying formal marriage was also evident in agricultural areas. Especially when a woman was in service and the man was employed elsewhere, the couple would live together when they could "and are thus relieved at least of the responsibilities and the duties of housekeeping, living better on their separate earnings than they could do in a house of their own. This practice of cohabitation before marriage is almost universal. . . ."[75] The extraordinarily high mobility of miners, navvies, and sailors contributed to their fondness for various forms of "little weddings," sometimes a prelude to but often now a substitute for regular marriage. Ceremonies popular in the rapidly expanding South Wales coalfields emphasized the flexibility of conjugal arrangements.

> Some Couples (especially among the miners) either having no friends, or seeing this kind of public marriage [marriage by banns] too troublesome and Impracticable, procure a man to wed them privately which will not cost about two or 3 mugs of ale. Sometimes half a dozen Couples will agree to a merry meeting, and are thus wedded and bedded together. They call this *Priodas vach* (i.e., the Little Wedding) and is frequently made use of among miners and others to make sure of a woman. . . . The little wedding doth not bind them to Effectually, but that after a months trial, they may part by Consent, When a Miner leaves his Mistress, and removes to a Minework in some distant Country, and the Girl is not worse look'd upon among the miners that if she had been an unspotted Virgin, so Prevalent and Arbitrary is Custom.[76]

Yorkshire miners were also said to "exchange" wives. The agreement to part and remarry would be made and witnessed at a public house; there would be a feast and the men would make token gifts to their new brides, "whom they now maintain together with the 'childers' of the union. . . ."[77] In Southhampton many women established temporary unions with sailors, drawing their half-pay while they were at sea and then looking after them while they were in port. As late as the 1870s this was said to be "looked upon as nearly as good as marriage among that class."[78] At Woodhead in Cheshire, where a thousand railway navvies were camped in 1845, a proletarianized version of the besom wedding was reported: "the couple jumped over a broomstick in the presence of a roomful of men assembled to drink on the occasion, and were put to bed at once, in the same room."[79]

When men were constantly on the move, these little weddings permitted flexible arrangements that provided at least some support for the parties involved. They were clearly an adaptation to a more mobile society, in which conditions of employment and residence were very uncertain and family rarely close at hand. Whereas the besom wedding had been a family and communal event, often presided over by women, the urban industrial variant, called *jumping brush and steel*, was usually witnessed by work mates, most of them male. In time even this publicity fell away, and by the end of the nineteenth century, the favored form of both common-law marriage and divorce was the putting on or removing of rings, an act usually performed in private.[80]

Little weddings were meant to be conditional contracts, not very different from the other kinds of wage, rent, and mutual aid agreements that workers would normally enter into. Common-law unions were often called *tally bargains*, and when a partner was separated in order to marry another person, he or she was said to be *leased*.[81] Although urban variants of divorce did not require the publicity characteristic of the small-town practice of wife sale, couples continued to make and break marriages according to certain well-understood rules that incorporated the notion of equity and mutuality. Sometime around 1850 Elizabeth and William Capras parted, and he thought himself "leased" to take up with Emily Hickson. To put their common-law union on a firm footing, the new couple consulted a Birmingham lawyer, who drew up for them the following agreement:

> It is hereby mutually agreed upon, by and between said William Charles Capras and Emily Hickson, that they the said shall live and reside together during the remainder of their lives, and that they shall mutually exert themselves by work and labour, and by following all their business pursuits, to the best of their abilities, skill, and understanding, and by advising and assisting each other, for their mutual benefit and advantage, and also to provide for themselves and each other the best supports and comforts of life which their means and income can afford.[82]

"Little weddings" were characteristic of a particular phase in the history of those proto-industrial people who were still struggling to maintain their economic and social status as independent petty producers against the increasingly devastating competition of industrial capitalism. In early nineteenth-century London, tailors, shoemakers, weavers, and other young aspiring tradesmen put off marrying the women they were living with in the belief that they would still establish themselves as masters in their own right and then have a proper big wedding. Whereas the traditional craftsman had made economic independence the condition of conjugality, those involved in the piecework labor of London's vast putting-out system reversed the priorities. Living with a woman now became their hope of gaining autonomy. The combined earnings of the couple were the only way such men could now achieve the kind of standing that the traditional craftsman gained through inheritance or guild privilege. And it was on the promise of future marriage that women agreed to live and work in such an arrangement. Even as the goal of independence and big wedding became more remote, many of these common-law couples still regarded their cohabitation as only temporary and thus quite legitimate. Like the cohabiting tailor who told Mayhew that "he could not go to be married in his shirt sleeves," there were many who were too proud and too poor to be wed in a formal manner.[83]

We can only guess at the extent of common-law marriage in the nineteenth century. One recent study of a rural Kent parish between 1750 and 1834 found it to be about 15%.[84] Hidden behind the high illegitimacy rates of many northern and western districts was an even higher incidence.[85] Colquhoun wrote of the "prodigious number among the lower classes who cohabit together without marriage" in the London of the 1790s, and when the London City Missionaries visited poor neighborhoods in the 1840s they found whole streets of "infidels" refusing to marry according to church rites.[86] At about the same time, McQueen estimated that if those living in common law were added to those who had married by license, the two combined would outnumber those married with the publicity of banns.[87]

THE PLEBEIAN BIG WEDDING

Among the plebeian population, rites such as the besom wedding were resorted to when the formation of a separate household was delayed or permanently obstructed. But because the family was the functional unit of domestic industry, the wedding, when it did occur, was normally a big one, often surpassing in scale the peasant festivities. Though more flexible in the making of marriages, plebeians were no less strict when it came to their maintenance. They carried forward the tradition of the charivari, altering it, however, so as to punish wife beaters rather than cuckolded husbands and termagant wives. Plebeian rough music was also directed against flagrant adulterers and false-hearted lovers, especially those aristocratic rakes featured so prominently in popular song and story. They lost no opportunity, through ballad and popular satire, to remind their betters of these delinquencies.[88]

In plebeian communities, marriage delayed did not mean wedding abandoned. In regard to the rites themselves, the plebeians outdid the peasants in both scale and publicity. Northumberland colliers normally made a holiday of their mates' weddings, trooping in parties of hundreds to Newcastle to celebrate.[89] To one unsympathetic observer of Cornish miners, "the wedding was then little better than a drunken spree for the bridegroom and his companions, continuing their orgies for three or four days, or until their little savings were expended."[90] No one seemed much concerned about calling the banns, especially when the relationship had been announced by the pregnancy of the bride or the existence of one or more natural children. Furthermore, there was considerable resentment against marriage fees, even in those communities that insisted on church weddings. Chicken's boisterous colliers made of these an occasion for the demonstration of popular anticlericalism:

> Some shout the bride and some the groom,
> Till just as mad to church they come;
> Knock, swear and rattle at the gate,
> And vow to break the beadle's pate,
> And call his wife a bitch and whore;
> They will be in or break the door!
> The gates fly open, all rush in;
> The church is full with folks and din,
> And all the crew, both great and small,
> Behave as in a common hall;
> For some perhaps that were three score
> were never in a church before.[91]

Plebeian anticlericalism was frequently accompanied by class antagonism. This was sometimes expressed in hostility to outsiders but could also take the form of rough music for local couples of superior wealth or pretension.[92] Plebeian weddings were less likely to express tensions within or between families. The patriarchal household no longer held center stage, and brides were not fetched from home but made their own way to church. Once they were ready to let sons and daughters go, proto-industrial parents required no symbolic compensation. Rites aimed at siblings fell away for the same reason. The highlighted tensions were now those between the sexes. Brides were known to refuse the vow of obedience, and bridesmaids now challenged the groom's men in the race for the garter.[93] Chaining and roping still expressed the envy of peers, but the old inauguration rites tended to disappear entirely. Postchurch festivities shifted from the household to the nearest tavern or village green. In "The Collier's Wedding" it is the bride's mother who presides at the feast, but a more common plebeian rite was the so-called *public bridal,* in which an even broader spectrum of the community participated.[94]

Among smallholders it had been family property that determined the scale of the wedding. The couple symbolized their status by providing festivities appropriate to their wealth and authority. Among proto-industrial populations, the situation was reversed. Because the couple had no property of their own, either kinsfolk and friends staged a public bridal for their benefit, or the young people used their own entrepreneurial talents to put on a big wedding for themselves. Both types can be traced to the long-standing tradition of the *bride ale*, which before the Reformation was sponsored by the church and in the seventeenth century was still popular among the propertied as well as the poor. Ralph Josselin officiated at a friend's wedding in 1647 at which "friends offered freely and he took above 56 pound."[95] It was apparently common in seventeenth-century Essex for the bride to collect money from the guests and also to auction off a pair of gloves: "And he who gives the most, and he whose lot it is for to have them, shall withal have a kiss of the bride."[96]

Although the propertied classes had abandoned the bride ale by the eighteenth century, the institution was seized on and elaborated by people of "respectability and slender means." In South and West Wales there emerged a particularly elaborate form of *bidding wedding*, which involved hiring a local bard, known as the bidder, to go around the countryside announcing the wedding. The more who knew of the event, the more who would attend, "so it was the advantage of the bride and bride-groom elect to make their wedding as public as possible, as the greater number of guests, the greater the donation. . . ."[97] To entice attendance, the bidder promised a great feast, "good beef and cabbage, mutton and turnips, por and pork and potatoes. . . . a quarter of drink for fourpence, a cake for a penny, clean chairs to sit down upon, clean pipes and tobacco." In return, each guest was asked to bring a gift, each according to his or her means: "Pigs, cocks, hens, geese, goslings, ducks, turkeys, a saddle or bridle, or a child's cradle, or what the house can afford. A great many can help one, but one cannot help a great many. . . ."[98]

Gifts were normally delivered the night before the wedding, and in those parts of Wales in which the bidding took its most elaborate form, careful note was taken of each, so that the donation could be repaid either by the couple or their kinfolk at future weddings. In effect, the bidding wedding was a form of mutual aid.[99] Although the gifts were small, multiplied by a hundred or two hundred they could amount to a tidy sum. According to Lewis Morris, a quite ordinary bidding in the 1760s brought in "a round sum of money, sometimes £30 or £40 is Collected in this way in Money, cheese and butter, to the great benefit of a Young Couple who had not otherwise scarce a penny to begin the world with."[100] In Cumberland, the local form of public bridal was called a *bridewain*, recalling the wagon that transferred the bride's property to her new home, but now an institution serving the propertyless. It now meant the collection taken at the wedding feast by the bride, "holding a pewter dish on her knee, half covered with a napkin. Into this dish every person present makes it a point to put something.''[101] Similar affairs, appropriately called *penny weddings*, were reported in parts of Northumberland in the 1820s and in Durham villages in the 1830s and 1840s.[102]

Bidding weddings were most common where domestic industry was mixed with smallholding. A certain density of family relationships was necessary to sustain the practice, for when an individual could not make a contribution, his or her relations would do so. If there was no family obligation, the plebeian population proved ingenious in making money from their weddings in a more overtly commercial fashion.[103] When John Jones and Mary Evans invited people by newspaper advertisement to gather at a local inn in 1827 to celebrate their wedding, they offered ''bread, cheese, and kisses,'' the latter auctioned off to the highest bidder. A special point was made of the fact that John and Mary had ''the privilege (by paying the duty) of selling ale to the persons assembled.'' So successful were their joint efforts that they raised between 50 and 100 pounds.[104] At other public bridals, saddles and hunting horns were the prizes offered to the winners of races. In addition to sport, Joseph Rawlings and Mary Dixon announced that their wedding would feature a ''Pantomine Exhibition,'' and George and Ann Collins offered as enticement ''a girdle (*centure de Venus*) possessing qualities not to be described, and many other articles, sports, and pastimes, too numerous to mention. . . . ''[105] The magic of the garter, by this time losing its original magical meaning, was thus converted into cash value.

In addition to their material contributions, guests were often expected to help in erecting so-called one-night houses, squatters' cottages made of wood or sod, which, if they could be built undetected on waste or commons, gave the new couple the right to a house and some small land. In Cumberland, Cornwall, Lancashire, and North Wales, the plebeian wedding between 1790 and 1840 often featured what was called a *clay daubing* or *clay biggin,* the work of young people who, ''always ready to help one another . . . would assemble about dawn at the appointed spot, and labouring with good will, each at an allotted task, would erect, long ere sunset, the clay walls of a dwelling for some young couple who would rely on the bridewain for means to finish and furnish it.''[106] In many places a settler could still establish claim to the land by paying a ''fine'' for entry at the local manor court, thereafter paying rent like any other copyholder. In North Wales, where squatters' settlements were very common, the right of the *Ty un nos* was jealously guarded:

> The customer in modern time presumed the right of any newly married resi-
> dent to a cottage which he had himself, with the help of friends, built upon

waste land in the township in a single night (smoke seen issuing from the chimney in the morning being claimed to be sufficient evidence of completion), and also a certain area of land round the cottage.[107]

Some of the bedding and rough music traditions persisted in proto-industrial areas, though those inauguration rites that established hierarchy within and between families did not survive as well. Couples no longer bothered to take their seats in church. For women, adult status came to be associated more with being a worker or a mother than a wife. It was said that in Ceiriog both boys and girls were emotionally attached to their mothers and that females aspired at an early age to having their own child.[108] Childbirth was elaborately celebrated, and the "churching" of a new mother, whether married or unmarried, was an event in the female life cycle rivaling, if not overshadowing, the wedding itself.[109] As for the man, fatherhood was sometimes experienced as *couvade*, but his status was more likely to be expressed through and at his work. Miners delighted in exacting a footing from new husbands, perhaps because in their occupation, marriage often meant additional benefits, including free coal and subsidized housing.[110] When any number of a pit gang was wed, he was therefore expected to "pay aff" or "stand his hand," treating his mates in a manner similar to the footings expected of peasant grooms.[111] In Northumbeland the new husband was mounted on a pole (stang) and carried to a public house, where he treated his mates to a *blaw out*.[112] On the Isle of Portland the rite of passage was peformed at the work site, where the new groom was "jumped" across an iron bar while he recited the lines: "Young men and bachelors, I bid you all adieu/Old men and married men, I' coming on to you."[113]

Most other plebeian occupations did not keep such compensatory customs, however. Among weavers, smiths, and petty tradespeople, marriage did not create social and economic distinctions of the kind that invited envy and required some form of symbolic recognition. Taken as a whole, the plebeian wedding emphasized horizontal rather than hierarchical relationships, thus underlining the interdependence of families and of work mates (often but not always segregated by sex) and of the kind of mutuality expressed by the bidder's phrase "a great many can help one, but one cannot help a great many." The privileged character of the peasant wedding had given way to a form of nuptiality that was less socially divisive. Rites like the besom wedding allowed children and parents to reconcile potentially explosive differences, and the public bridal established a network of obligations vital to the establishment of new households. At the same time, the disappearance from plebeian rites of peasant inauguration rituals suggests a degree of equality in plebeian marriage. Community pressure, expressed through charivari, no longer reinforced a rigid subordination of wives but now served to moderate domestic violence and restore the desired degree of reciprocity. Plebeian communities were no more tolerant of adultery than the peasantry was but they did permit divorce, not only under conditions of a "little wedding," but even when a formal marriage had broken down completely. Plebeian divorce rites, such as the wife sale and the *lease*, suggest that collective approval was generally sought before couples made their separation final.[114]

The plebeian variant of the big wedding reflected both changed material circumstances and a distinctive world view. Unlike the smallholder, whose work did not necessarily expand his property, inheritance, or marriage chances, the male and female domestic worker could perceive a positive relationship between labor and resources. The plebeian population no longer regarded the social and material world as finite. Neither wealth nor affection was in such limited supply that each heterosexual relationship needed to be viewed as a zero sum game in which the winners must compensate the losers.[115] On the contrary, both plebeian courtship and wedding suggest a notion of wealth, power, and affection as extendable and therefore capable of being shared both between the marriage partners and with the community at large. Love ceased to be viewed as a dangerous, disruptive force and was now seen as a desirable element not just of courtship but of marriage itself.

The possibilities of a conjugality based on mutual affection was explored by radical and Owenite movements during the early nineteenth century. Their advocacy of a nuptiality responsive to human needs and terminable when these were not fulfilled appealed precisely to those rural and urban plebeian elements already engaged in flexible marriage and mothering practices. This was not simply a matter of adopting the "affective individualism" by then typical of the upper classes. That was associated closely with conventional marriage and the nuclear family arrangements that the plebeians had already rejected. Robert Owen spoke contemptuously of church marriage and "single family arrangements," and when the Owenites experimented with collective living arrangements and advocated the freedom to divorce, they were not building on elite values but on well-established plebeian practice.[116]

The weddings of patricians and plebeians in the late eighteenth and early nineteenth centuries reflected two contrasting cultures. Upper-class marriage, emphasizing the privilege and exclusivity, was mainly by license. Patricians were careful to avoid any embarrassing publicity. Plebeians, on the other hand, used the big wedding as an occasion to display anticlericalism and class hostility. The envy that had divided

peasant communities was less apparent among the proto-industrial population. Their resentments were more likely to be directed at outsiders,
including the clergy and patricians, than toward their own kind, and
they could make it very uncomfortable for those who contravened their
customs. In turn, the elites came to regard the popular big wedding with
considerable suspicion. Its festivities promoted spending rather than
saving, encouraged idleness, and threatened a social order based on rigid
sumptuary distinctions. Efforts to repress public bridals can be traced
back to at least the sixteenth century, when the gentry began to withdraw their patronage from bride ales, but the eighteenth-century attack
on plebeian big weddings was part of a sustained campaign against all
those popular consumption patterns that the rural and urban capitalist
class regarded as both immoral and inefficient. What rankled both evangelicals and utilitarians was that public bridals permitted so many to
marry who otherwise would not have been able to do so. This hostility,
already evident when the Hardwicke Act was passed in 1753, took on
a more overtly class character in the population and birth control controversies of the early nineteenth century. Malthusianism found expression in local efforts to curb big weddings, punish illegitimacy, and root
out common-law practices.[117] This repression provoked in turn a wave
of popular anticlericalism and class hostility that found a voice in the
radicalism and Owenism of the 1830s and 1840s.

NINETEENTH-CENTURY PROLETARIAN WEDDINGS

By 1850, however, the struggle was largely over. Magistrates were
refusing to license the private sale of ale, and there was no place for a
pantomine or a "clay daubin" in the crowded cities where factory industrialization was now concentrating the population. The closest thing
to an urban public bridal was the wedding breakfast in the neighborhood beer shop, where it was customary to take up a collection to assist
the new couple in furnishing their rented room. The marriages of the
urban proletariat were likely to be hurried, truncated affairs, scheduled
for Christmas, Easter, Whitsun and, later in the nineteenth century, August Bank Holiday, times when the laboring poor had a little time and
money to spend. Manchester Cathedral's low fees attracted hundreds
at Christmas and Whitsun, causing couples to be married in batches.[118]
The same was true of London's "marrying churches," located mainly
in the East End, where the fees were reduced at Easter and people lined
up to be wed. A London cabinet maker, who married in 1904, remembered standing with five other couples:

And the old padre come along you know—wilt thou—and you know, the usual
marriage ceremony, individually. Oh yes. Then we filed into the vestry and
signed our names you know and—one after the other and then—out—out we
came. Had to rush because of the morning service you see, Christmas morning,
about half-past ten.[119]

It was rare that urban couples processed to church. Many preferred
to arrive separately and leave through side doors in order to avoid
friends and thus unnecessary expenses. The only extravagance that East
Londoners of the 1850s allowed themselves was white gloves, which
were regarded as a necessity, even though they might have to rent them
for the occasion.[120] Brides dressed in their Sunday best; few could afford
the white that had recently become fashionable among the upper classes,
though sometimes "the poor seamstress flaunts in an old white satin
and dirty veil of the West End, or rather, of the sold-off wardrobe of
some minor theatre." The postnuptial festivities were equally diminished, "for these are generally industrious folks, who have no time for
idle amusement, and do not make a holiday even of their marriage
morning."[121]

Rural weddings in the regions of highly capitalized agriculture were
equally quiet. Edward Grey described the cottage weddings of the 1870s
as "simple homely affairs. . . ."[122] The party that walked to church was
small, "maybe the best man was a relative, but, however, he would give
the bride away, for very very rarely did the father conduct his daughter
to church, in many cases he would have to be at work on the farm, for
he could ill afford any reduction of his small wage owing to loss of time.
. . ." Celebrations were postponed until the evening "so that any members of either family who have been at work on the farm would have
by this time arrived home, and having washed and spruced up a bit,
would now be able to be present at this pleasant tea-time meal." There
would be wedding cake and gifts, "but they would be, as a rule, from
their own respective families, near neighbours, and more intimate
friends, and mainly in the form of food or useful household items."[123]
Later the furniture would be pushed aside for dancing, and although
there was ordinarily some drinking, it lasted only "until 10 or 11 o'clock,
at which time the young couple repair to their new abode. The bride-
maids and guests are seen home by their 'young men;' each with a bit
of wedding cake, to dream of their own wedding day."[124] Rough bands
no longer broke the evening silence, for "the young man would have
to be out and about his work on the farm the next morning at the usual
early hour. . . ."[125]

The illicit side of proletarian marriage was also unobtrusive, subdued
by the powers of the clergy and the magistrates and by changes that

privatized every aspect of the marriage process. Courtship became less public when it was disassociated from work. Factories were not a favorable setting, and now matchmaking was confined to the workers' free time and located in those commercialized places—first the pub, later the music hall, and finally the cinema—that became the locus of urban working-class culture. Some of the traditional holidays retained their special meaning, but there was a tendency for courtship to become an everyday affair, determined by, rather than dictating to, the rhythms of work and leisure. By the end of the century, the weekend was beginning to take on a special importance, and in northern industrial towns there developed a ritualized form of promenading, known locally as the *monkey rank*, which gave to adolescent flirtation a particular form and locale.[126] But for those closer to the marriage age, mating went on mainly in commercial venues. Couples no longer met at fairs, family gatherings, or in church or chapel, but in more anonymous settings. They were more likely to be strangers to each other, from different places, and employed in different kinds of work.[127] The occupational endogamy typical of proto-industrial communities broke down everywhere, and domestic service became the prime female employment.[128] In the cities the "No Followers" rule kept domestic servants from their suitors. With so many single females living away from home, parental possessiveness was no longer as important as it once had been.[129]

Young male workers were also more likely to live away from their families, on the tramp in search of work, residing in lodgings and socializing with strangers. Their courtships were unregulated by either family or peer group, and their relations with women were much more direct and personal, beginning with a casual acquaintance, developing from "walking out" to "keeping company," and sometimes evolving into some kind of cohabitation, but now much more likely to lead to a church or (after 1837) civil marriage. Peasant forms of public betrothal were wholly obsolescent, though it was still common for men to make an oral promise of marriage and to give the woman a ring or other token. Working-class women continued to insist on a promise of marriage before intercourse, but with the disappearance of public rites like the besom wedding, these engagements were only rarely witnessed and therefore difficult to enforce. The advantages that women had had in the highly publicized world of the proto-industrial community were receding, with the result that their role in courtship became more passive and defensive as time passed.[130]

When a church or civil marriage was held, it was now more likely to be a private affair. Even when the bride or groom lived at home, the parental role was recessive. Under the conditions of advanced capitalist agriculture and industry, the family was less likely to be an economic unit threatened by the loss of a son or daughter. Many young people married away from home, and even those who remained felt a persistent parental pressure to get out on their own, either through migration or marriage. Under these circumstances, parents encouraged early courtship. In the proletarianized fenlands of Cambridgeshire, suitors were invited to a hot meal before being left alone for the night. It seems that bundling practices were relatively new to the fens, having been introduced by migrant Irish laborers, but parents seized on them as a way of encouraging intimacy. Through their connivance, "many a Fen youth must have been forced to marry."[131] Similar pressures were generated by the parish authorities. In the South and East, young people had little choice but to marry or migrate. "Go away and work, you foolish boy," one bachelor was told by the parish overseers. "Ah, but sir," he replied, "I married yesterday, and I expect the parish to find me a place to live."[132] Everywhere that capitalist agriculture developed, married men were given priority in housing and employment. Parishes became intolerant of the old arrangements for the maintenance of bastard children that had been made in the proto-industrial areas, especially in the North and West. In the regions of capitalist agriculture, there were many more forced marriages, with the magistrates using their powers under the old poor law to bring reluctant couples (sometimes in chains) to the altar.[133]

A forced marriage was not likely to be an occasion for rejoicing, but even when necessity was not a factor, the rural and urban proletariat preferred to keep neighbors and workmates at arm's length, knowing that their presence would be an expense rather than a benefit. When the bonds of family and community had been dissolved by high rates of mobility, the bidding wedding was no longer practicable.[134] Bethnal Green people went to other parishes to be married because they "have very strong objection to be married in their own Church, desiring to avoid their neighbours." In Spitalfields "they try to escape the risk of jeering and rude banter."[135] Once it had become an excuse for begging, the old tradition of sharing, whether symbolic or real, experienced a rapid demise.

It is not surprising that there was little celebration of an event that meant no addition to wealth, status, or power. To the proletarianized male breadwinner, marriage portended additional mouths to feed; to his mate it involved motherhood but did not bring her the appurtenances of domesticity that Victorian society associated with proper womanhood. To Lucy Bettesworth, who was born to field work, marriage made virtually no social difference. She continued to do stoop labor, and although she had two children, both died. Her house was too mean for her even to aspire to the title of "mistress," and so her marriage constituted a "kind of dogged comradship . . . what commonly unites the labouring man and his wife; they are partners and equals running their impecunious affairs by mutual help."[136]

In nineteenth-century mining and factory towns, marriage and the establishment of the status of householders were disassociated. It was not uncommon for newlyweds to move in with parents, usually the bride's.[137] This represented a saving, but at the expense of the status that went with a home of one's own. Especially when women continued to work after marriage, the meaning of the event, and thus the desire for ceremony and festivity, was much diminished.

The privatization of working-class weddings in the second half of the nineteenth century reveals the degree to which the idea of collective responsibility had waned. Marriage ceased to be an occasion for communal solidarity and became, in those cases in which the pair lived near or at home, strictly a family affair. Expressions of anticlericalism and class antagonism became exceptional when people ceased to confront the marriage law and simply ignored it. The ethic of equality and mutuality also disappeared from the marriage itself, replaced by a highly segmented form of nuptiality in which the worlds of husbands and wives barely overlapped. Husbands worked outside the home and derived their status and authority from their role as the principal breadwinner. Wives controlled the domestic sphere, including the children, and obtained a measure of power from this function. But although this may suggest a certain complementarity similar to that in peasant marriages, the fact that the arrangement was based on earnings rather than property made it far more vulnerable to discord and disruption. The violence with which workingmen reacted to their wives' complaints about money reflected a deep-seated insecurity about their ability to uphold the prescribed masculine role of breadwinner.[138] Women, on the other hand, expressed great anxiety about maintaining themselves and their children and being able to remain respectable. Without the support of a tradition of collective mothering, women, especially the unwed, were now experiencing reproduction as a much greater burden.[139]

The quality of "dogged comradship" that characterized proletarian marriages did not protect them from conflict and fissure. The new notion of mutuality lacked both the clear definition that had given such stability to peasant marriage and the communal support enjoyed by plebeian practice. As the privacy of their weddings suggests, proletarian couples were on their own in coping with the emerging sexual division of labor that assigned to men the role of breadwinner and to women the place of homemaker and supplementary wage earner. The conflicts in nineteenth-century working-class marriages revolved mainly around the definition and performance of these duties.[140] A woman's slovenly housekeeping or a man's irregular earnings were often the cause of domestic violence in both legal and common-law marriage, though it was sometimes said that "tally" couples enjoyed a greater degree of marital harmony.[141]

The kinds of domestic disputes that came before the courts in the mid-nineteenth century suggest just how much the material and social basis of marriage had contracted, how dependent wives had become, and how much husbands relied on and demanded of their spouses. These narrowly nuclear arrangements could not be expected to stand the strain of low and uncertain earnings. It appeared that marriage itself had once again become a zero sum game, with envy and jealousy major causes of domestic violence and marital breakdown. Marriage no longer held the privileged status it had had among the smallholders, nor did it have the support it had enjoyed among the proto-industrial community. Proletarian couples no longer had to contend with possessive parents or envious siblings; their marriages were no longer a class issue. But although they were free to marry when and whom they wished, they were wholly on their own and subject to new strains for which there was little relief, especially for women.[142]

It is not surprising that some proletarian men still avoided legal marriage, because it meant obligations they could not sustain. Some women also believed they were better off single because their earnings, children, and person were better protected as spinsters than as wives. When asked why she never married the man she had lived with, one woman explained she "didn't choose to be knocked about, nor her children treated bad, neither."[143] Yet, the frequency of common-law marriage seems to have diminished greatly over the course of the nineteenth century. Illegitimacy was already decreasing by mid-century, reflecting the difficulty of sustaining motherhood outside marriage. Although the depressed decades of the 1870s and 1880s seem to have erected certain barriers to matrimony, the popularity of legal marriage had recovered fully by 1900. By then working people were not only marrying more and at younger ages, but also more conventionally. Common-law marriage was in eclipse, and there were signs of a revival of big weddings, first among the elites, who during the Victorian period had elaborated most of the features of what we now call the *white wedding*. It was some time before the working classes adopted this patently patriarchal ritual, but when in the first decades of this century, working-class fathers began to "give away" their veiled daughters in elaborate church ceremonies, another turning point in the complex history of popular marriage had clearly been reached.[144]

NOTES

1. It should be noted that this chapter is concerned with first marriages in England and Wales. For an excellent parallel study of Scotland, see T. C. Smout, "Scottish Marriage, Regular and Irregular, 1500–1940," in R. B. Outhwaite, ed., *Marriage and Society: Studies in the Social History of Marriage* (New York: St. Martin's 1981), pp. 204–236. The percentage of never-married reached almost 30% in the late sixteenth century and again in the late seventeenth century. See E. A. Wrigley and R. S. Schofield, *The Population History of England, 1541–1871* (Cambridge, Mass.: Harvard University Press, 1981), pp. 256–265. For peasant marriage, consult Keith Wrightson, *English Society, 1580–1680* (New Brunswick, N.J.: Rutgers University Press, 1982), chaps. 3–5; and David Jenkins, *The Agricultural Community in South-West Wales at the Turn of the Twentieth Century* (Cardiff, Wales: University of Wales, 1971), chap. 5.
2. Henry Best, *Rural Economy in Yorkshire in 1641* (Durham, England, 1857), p. 116.
3. See *The Diary of Roger Lowe* (New Haven, Conn.: Yale University Press, 1938), *passim*; J. R. Gillis, *Youth and History: Tradition and Change in European Age Relations, 1770–Present* (New York: Academic Press, 1974), chap. 1.
4. The subject of courtship will be treated more fully in my forthcoming *For Better, for Worse: A Political and Social History of British Marriage, 1600–Present*, chap. 1.
5. Sabine Baring-Gould, *Old Country-Life* (London, 1890), p. 192; Jollie, *Sketch of Cumberland Manners and Customs* (Carlisle, England, 1811), p. 40.
6. *Diary of Roger Lowe*, pp. 20, 91.
7. A. MacFarlane, *The Family Life of Ralph Josselin* (Cambridge, 1970): pp. 30–31.
8. Christina Hole, *A Dictionary of British Folk Customs* (London: Granada, 1976), pp. 191–192; U. B. Chisenhale-Marsh, "Folk Lore in Essex and Herts," *Essex Review* 5 (1896): 147.
9. Best, p. 116.
10. Jenkins, p. 127.
11. Trefor Owen, "West Glamorgan Customs," *Folk Life* 3 (1965): 47.
12. Best, pp. 116–117.
13. Quoted in George C. Homans, *English Villagers of the Thirteenth Century* (New York: Norton, 1975), p. 164.
14. R. H. Helmholtz, *Marriage Litigation in Medieval England* (Cambridge: Cambridge University Press, 1974), p. 28.
15. This is dealt with more thoroughly in Gillis, *For Better, for Worse*, chap. 1.
16. Evan Jones Notebooks, Welsh Folk Museum, St. Fagans.
17. J. Vaux, *Church Folklore* (London, 1894), pp. 91–93; E. Radford and M. A. Radford, *Encylopaedia of Superstition* (London: Hutchinson, 1961), p. 27.
18. Best, p. 117.
19. John Aubrey, *Remaines of Gentilisme and Judaism* (London, 1881), pp. 171–172.
20. Owen, p. 52; Dafydd Ifan, "Lewis Morris ac Afrerion Priodi yng Ngheredigion," *Ceredigion* 8 (1972): 194.
21. Ifan, pp. 199–200.
22. Best, p. 117.
23. William H. Hale, *A Series of Precedents and Proceedings in Criminal Causes, 1475–1640, from the Act-Books of the Ecclesiastical Courts of Diocese of London* (London, 1847), p. 258.

24. R. Blakeborough, "A Country Wedding a Century Age" (manuscript, Blakeborough MSS, Sheffield University); W. Crooke, "Lifting the Bride," *Folk Lore* 13 (1902): 227.

25. Hale, p. 226. On this form of compensation, see Arnold van Gennep, *The Rites of Passage* (Chicago: University of Chicago Press, 1969), pp. 119, 124.

26. Sarah Hewitt, *Nummits and Crummits: Devonshire Customs, Characteristics and Folklore* (London, 1900), p. 101.

27. Noted in *Folk Lore* 22 (1911): 237.

28. Sods were thrown at Pudsey couples in the early nineteenth century. See Joseph Lawson, *Letters to the Young on Progress in Pudsey During the Last Sixty Years* (Stanninglen, 1887), p. 20; also S. O. Addy, *Household Tales with Other Traditional Remains* (London, 1895), p. 122; Crooke, p. 232.

29. Walter C. Renshaw, "Notes from the Act Book of the Archdeaconry Court of Lewes," *Sussex Archaeological Collection* 49 (1906): 64.

30. Blakeborough, p. 12.

31. *Ibid*; also Richard Blakeborough, *Wit, Character, Folklife and Customs of the North Riding of Yorkshire* (Salburn by-the-Sea, 1911), p. 92; Margaret Baker, *The Folklore and Customs of Love and Marriage* (Aylesbury, David and Charles: 1974), p. 38.

32. From *Notes & Queries*, 2d ser., vol. 8, September 17, 1859, p. 239.

33. Best, p. 117.

34. Baker, pp. 47, 49; Ifan, p. 194.

35. D. D. Dixon and Whittingham Vale, *Northumberland: Its History, Traditions and Folklore* (Newcastle, 1895), p. 290; *Notes and Queries*, 1st ser., vol. 6, September 11, 1852, p. 246, and October 30, 1852, p. 424.

36. John Brand, *Observations on Popular Antiquities* (London, 1877), p. 375; Best, p. 117.

37. Vaux, p. 103. The nature of rites used to ward off discord is discussed by G. M. Foster, "Anatomy of Envy: A Study of Symbolic Behavior." *Current Anthropology* 8 (April 1972): 165–202.

38. Keith Thomas, *Religion and the Decline of Magic* (New York: Scribner's, 1971), p. 556.

39. Francis Grose, *A Provincial Glossary* (London, 1811), p. 293; *Cymru Fu*, June 2, 1882, p. 192; Thomas, pp. 233–234; T. Gwynn Jones, *Welsh Folklore and Folk Custom* (London: Metheun, 1930), p. 131.

40. Lawrence Babb, "The Physiological Conception of Love in the Elizabethan and Early Stuart Drama," *PMLA* 56 (December 1941): 1024.

41. Keith Wrightson and David Levine, *Poverty and Piety in an English Village: Terling, 1525–1700* (New York: Academic Press, 1979), pp. 80, 133; C. Reynel, *The True English Intent* (1674), reprinted in Joan Thirsk and J. P. Cooper, eds., *Seventeenth Century Economic Documents*. (Oxford: Oxford University Press, 1972), p. 759.

42. This occurred in 1563. See F. J. Furnivall, *Child-Marriages, Divorces, and Ratifications and in the Diocese of Chester* (London, 1897), p. 88; R. Tudor Jones, "Religion in Post-Restoration Brecknockshire, 1660–68," *Brycheiniog* 8 (1962): 37; for further evidence on clandestine marriage, see Roger Brown, "The Rise and Fall of the Fleet Marriage," in R. B. Outhwaite, ed., *Marriage and Society* (New York: St. Martin's, 1981); J. Gillis, "Conjugal Settlements: Resort to Clandestine Common Law Marriage in English and Wales, 1650–1850," in J. Bossy, ed., *Disputes and Settlements* (Cambridge: Cambridge University Press, 1983). Also Consistory Court Records, Archdeaconry of Brecon, SD/CCB (G), 268, 268a, National Library of Wales.

43. On this point, see G. M. Foster, "Anatomy of Envy: A Study of Symbolic Behavior," *Current Anthropology* 13 (April 1972): 165–202; G. M. Foster, "Peasant Society and the Image of the Limited Good," *American Anthropologist* 67 (April 1965): 156–202.

44. The literature on this is too voluminous to cite. See E. P. Thompson, " 'Rough Music;' le charivari angalais," *Annales E.S.C.* 27 (March-April 1972): 295–312.

45. Gillis, "Conjugal Settlements."
46. David Levine, *Family Formation in an Age of Nascent Capitalism* (New York: Academic Press, 1977), passim; Hans Medick, "The Proto-Industrial Family Economy: The Structural Function of Household and Family During the Transition from Peasant Society to Industrial Capitalism," *Social History* 3 (1976): 291–315; Peter Kriedte, Hans Medick, and Jürgen Schlumbohm, *Industrialization before Industrialization: Rural Industry in the Genesis of Capitalism* (Cambridge: Cambridge University Press, 1981); Pamela Horn, "The Bucks Straw Plait Trade in Victorian England," *Records of Buckinghamshire* 19 (1971–1974): 48–49.
47. Ivy Pinchbeck, *Women Workers and the Industrial Revolution*, (London: Routledge, 1930), p. 273.
48. Medick, "The Proto-Industrial Family Economy," pp. 310–314.
49. W. Howitt, *The Rural Life of England* (London, 1862), p. 238.
50. S. M. Tibbutt, "Knitting Stockings in Wales—A Domestic Craft," *Folk Life* 16 (1978): 66; Edwin Grey, *Cottage Life in a Hertfordshire Village* (Harpenden: Harpenden and District Local History Society, 1977), p. 147.
51. Information from an exhibition of love tokens, Birmingham Museum, February 1980.
52. Medick, p. 305; Peter Anson, *Fisher Folk Lore* (London, 1965), p. 27.
53. Gordon Rattray Taylor, *The Angel Makers* (New York: Dutton, 1974), p. 4.
54. Samuel Bamford, *Passages in the Life of a Radical and Early Days* (London, 1853), p. 128.
55. Pinchbeck, p. 273; Bamford, p. 128.
56. John Benson, *British Coalminers in the Nineteenth Century: A Social History* (New York: Holmes and Meier, 1980), p. 122.
57. Doris Jones-Baker, *The Folklore of Hertfordshire* (London: Nelson, 1977), p. 65.
58. William Rhys Jones, "Lore of Courtship and Marriage," trans. from the William Rhys Jones papers, National Library of Wales, fol. 85.
59. William Rhys Jones Papers 2593/63, Welsh Folk Museum.
60. George Henwood, *Cornwall's Mines and Miners* (Truro, 1972), p. 68; J. H. Plumb, "The New World of Children." in N. McKendrick, J. Brewer, and J. H. Plumb, eds., *The Birth of a Consumer Society: The Commercialization of Eighteenth Century England* (Bloomington: Indiana University Press, 1982), p. 311.
61. Robert Malcolmson, *Popular Recreations in English Society, 1700–1850* (Cambridge: Cambridge University Press, 1973), pp. 54–55.
62. For evidence of participation of women in boxing, wrestling, and other violent sports, see John Latimer, *The Annals of Bristol in the 18th Century*, n.p., 1893, pp. 168–169, 279; Taylor, pp. 11–12.
63. "The Colliers' Pay Week," in A. L. Lloyd, ed., *Come All Ye Bold Miners, Ballads and Songs of the Coalfields* (London: Lawrence, 1952), p. 33.
64. Jennie Kitteringham, "Country Work Girls in Nineteenth-Century England," in Raphael Samuel, ed., *Village Life and Labour* (London: Routledge, 1975), p. 127.
65. Benson, p. 79.
66. William Rhys Jones, "Folk Lore of the Ceiriog Valley," trans. from the William Rhys Jones papers, National Library of Wales, fol. 85.
67. John Hutchins, *The History and Antiquities of the County of Dorset*, vol. 2 (London, 1863), pp. 808, 820–821; J. H. Bettey, *The Island and Royal Manor of Portland* (Weymouth, 1970), pp. 25–32; Robert Douch, "Customs and Traditions of the Isle of Portland, Dorset," *Antiquity* 23 (1949): 140–152. For a fictionalized account of this tradition, see Thomas Hardy's *Two on a Tower*.
68. N. Neville, *A Corner of the North* (Newcastle, 1909), p. 98.
69. R. B. Outhwaite, "Age at Marriage in England from the Late Seventeenth to

the Nineteenth Centuries," *Transactions of the Royal Historical Society*, 5th ser., 23 (1973): 62.

70. Jones, "Lore of Courtship and Marriage," fols. 83, 97.
71. "The Collier's Wedding," *Come All Ye Bold Miners*, p. 54.
72. E. Orme, "Conditions of Work in the Nail, Chain, and Bolt Making Industries in the Black Country, "Royal Commission on Labour," *Parliamentary Papers* 36 (1892):573.
73. G. N. Gandy, "Illegitimacy in a Handloom Weaving Community: Fertility Patterns in Culcheth, Lancashire, 1781–1860" (Ph.D. diss., Oxford University, 1978).
74. Gillis, "Conjugal Settlements."
75. Kitteringham, p. 130.
76. Ifan, p. 201; Leonard T. Davies and A. Edwards, *Welsh Life in the Eighteenth Century* (London: Country Life Ltd., 1939), p. 231.
77. *Notes and Queries*, 10th ser., vol. 9, March 14, 1908, p. 201, and May 23, 1908, p. 416.
78. Judith Walkowitz, *Prostitution and Victorian Society: Women, Class, and the State* (Cambridge: Cambridge University Press, 1980), pp. 203–205.
79. Terry Coleman, *The Railway Navvies* (London: Hutchinson, 1965), p. 22.
80. The term is used in the song "Navvy on the Line," in Roy Palmer, ed., *A Touch on the Times* (Harmondsworth: Penguin 1974), pp. 40–41; further details in Gillis, "Conjugal Settlements."
81. Gillis, *For Better, for Worse*, chap. 5.
82. Clippings relating to "leasing" in Box 12, Folklore Society Archives, University of London.
83. Eileen Yeo and E. P. Thompson, eds., *The Unknown Mayhew* (New York: Schocken, 1972), p. 120.
84. Anthea Newman, "An Evaluation of Bastardy Recordings in an East Kent Parish," in P. Laslett, K. Oosterveen, and Richard M. Smith, eds., *Bastardy and its Comparative History*, (Cambridge, Mass.: Harvard University Press, 1980), pp. 141–157.
85. On the relationship between common-law arrangements and high illegitimacy rates, see Gandy, pp. 379–389.
86. *London City Mission Magazine* 16(January 1851):16, 18(June 1853):83. I am indebted to Barbara Taylor for this reference. For the connection between radicalism and common-law practices, see Barbara Taylor *Eve and the New Jerusalem: Socialism and Feminism in the Nineteenth Century* (New York: Pantheon, 1983), chap. 5; and Eileen Yeo, "Robert Owen and Radical Culture," in S. Pollard and J. Salt, eds., *Robert Owen: Prophet of the Poor* (London: Macmillan, 1971), pp. 100–103.
87. D. Steel, *National Index of Parish Registers*, vol. 1 (London, 1968), pp. 62–63.
88. This theme of popular radicalism is explored by Anna K. Clark, "The Myth of Seduction: Class and Gender Politics in England, 1748–1848" (Paper delivered at Rutgers Women's History Seminar, 1982). Thompson, "Rough Music."
89. Lydia Fish, *The Folklore of the Coal Mines of the Northeast of England* (Norwood, Pa.: Norwood Editions, 1975), p. 45.
90. Henwood, p. 68.
91. *Come All Ye Bold Miners*, p. 56.
92. Tensions in Yorkshire Dales described in Gillis, *For Better, for Worse*, chap. 4.
93. *Dalesman* (January 1976): 774; *Cupid's Pupils: From Courtship to Honeymoon, Being the Recollections of a Parish Clerk* (London, 1899), pp. 232–233; Brand, pp. 384, 390.
94. *Come All Ye Bold Miners*, p. 57.
95. A. Macfarlane, ed., *The Diary of Ralph Josselin* (London: Oxford Univeristy Press, 1976), p. 98.
96. George Monger, "A Note on the Similarities Between Some Wedding Customs of England and France," *Lore and Language* 2 (July 1974): 35–37; *Essex Review* 5 (1896).

97. C. C. Davies, *The Folklore of West and Mid-Wales* (Aberystwyth, 1911), p. 18.
98. Trefor Owen, *Welsh Folk Customs* (Cardiff, University of Wales Press, 1978), pp. 161–162; for another such *rammas*, see David Thomas Collection, B 75, National Library of Wales.
99. Jenkins, pp. 131–134; T. Owen, "Some Aspects of Bidding in Cardiganshire," *Ceredigion* 4 (1960): 37–46.
100. *Gentleman's Magazine* (1791): 1103; Peter Roberts, *The Cambrian Popular Antiquities* (Norwood, Pa.: Norwood Editions, 1973), p. 160.
101. A. C. Atkinson, *A Glossary of Cleveland Dialect* (London, 1868), pp. 71–72.
102. *Notes and Queries* 168 (May 25, 1935): 376.
103. For Scotland, see Smout, pp. 218, 235.
104. W. Howells, *Cambrian Superstitions* (London, 1831), p. 169.
105. W. Rollinson, *Life and Tradition in the Lake District* (London: Dent, 1974), p. 58; W. T. McIntire, *Lakeland and the Borders* (Carlisle, 1948), p. 212.
106. A. Craig Gibson, "Ancient Custom and Superstitions in Cumberland," *Transactions of the Historic Society of Lancashire and Cheshire* 10 (1857–1858): 103.
107. R. U. Sayce, "Popular Enclosures and the One-Night House," *Montgomerryshire Collections* 47, pt. 2 (1942): 109–117.
108. Translation of Gwenith Gwyn, "Lore of Courtship," Welsh Folk Museum, MS 236, p. 82.
109. On churching see Brand, pp. 333–338.
110. Benson, p. 73. At Corfe Castle, another quarry community, the newest husband had to provide a football for the annual game, which also served to keep open the quarrymen's right of way. See J. H. Betty, *Rural Life in Wessex, 1500–1900* (Bradford-on-Avon: Moonraker Press, 1977), p. 102. On the custom of *couvade*, see *Folklore* 29 (1918): 320; *Folklore* 42 (1931): 293; *Folklore* 45 (1934): 158.
111. David Rovie, "Mining Folk of Fife," *County Folklore* 8 (1914): 393; John Raven, *The Folklore of Staffordshire* (London, private printing, 1978), p. 61.
112. M. C. Balfour and N. W. Thomas, *Examples of Printed Folklore Concerning Northumberland* (London, 1904), pp. 98–99.
113. Douch, pp. 149–150.
114. E. P. Thompson, "Rough Music," pp. 302–303. On the plebeian ritual of the wife sale and other divorce rites, see Samuel Pyeatt Menefee, *Wives for Sale: An Ethnographic Study of British Popular Divorce* (New York: St. Martins, 1981).
115. Gillis, *For Better, for Worse*, chap. 4; and Foster, "Anatomy of Envy," pp. 180ff.
116. The connection between plebeian practice and Owenite socialist-feminist thought is explored in Barbara Taylor, *Eve and the New Jerusalem*, chap. 6. For the contrasting ideology of "affective individualism," see Lawrence Stone, *The Family, Sex and Marriage in England, 1500–1800* (New York: Harper & Row, 1977), chaps. 6 and 7.
117. Gillis, *For Better, for Worse*, chap. 4.
118. *Byegones*, 2d ser., vol. 8, May 25, 1904, p. 348; Manchester Scrap Book, F924.7389 M 122, pp. 47–49, Manchester Central Library.
119. Transcript 225, Family Life and Work Oral History Archive, Essex University.
120. "Marriage in Low Life," *Chambers Journal* 12 (July–December, 1859): 399.
121. *Ibid.*
122. Grey, pp. 152–153.
123. *Ibid.*, pp. 155–157.
124. Henwood, p. 70.
125. Grey, p. 158.
126. Derek Thompson, "Courtship and Marriage in Preston Between the Wars," *Oral History* 3 (1975): 39–43.

127. This was particularly true in London after 1850. (Information from a study of 1,200 couples whose case histories are in the record of London Foundling Hospital.)

128. For suggestive late nineteenth-century evidence, see Hugh McLeod, *Class and Religion in the Late Victorian City* (London: Croom Helm, 1974), especially pp. 3, 7, 8.

129. See J. R. Gillis, "Servants, Sexual Relations, and the Risks of Illegitimacy in London, 1801–1900," *Feminist Studies* 5 (Spring 1979): 142–167.

130. Gillis, "Changing Balances of Sexual Power in Nineteenth Century England" (Paper given at International Conference in Women's History, University of Maryland, 1977).

131. This interesting adaptation of custom is described in Enid Porter, *Cambridgeshire Customs and Folklore* (London: Routledge, 1969), pp. 3–4.

132. Report of His Majesty's Commission to Inquire into the Poor Laws, app. A, pt. 2, p. 29.

133. John Skinner, *Diary of a Somerset Rector 1803–34: John Skinner*, ed. H. Coombs and P. Coombs (Bath: Kingsmead, 1971), pp. 63–64.

134. Jenkins, p. 135.

135. Visitation to St. Thomas, Bethnal Green, 1858, Fulham Papers 461, Lambeth Palace Library; 1883 Middlesex Visitation, Fulham Papers 508.

136. George Bourne, *Lucy Bettesworth* (London, 1913), *passim*.

137. Michael Anderson, *Family Structure in Nineteenth Century Lancashire* (Cambridge: Cambridge University Press, 1971), pp. 43–67.

138. Nancy Tomes, "A 'Torrent of Abuse:' Crimes of Violence Between Working Class Men and Women in London, 1840–1875," *Journal of Social History* 11 (Spring 1978): 338.

139. Ellen Ross, " 'Fierce Questions and Taunts:' Married Life in Working Class London, 1870–1914," *Feminist Studies* 8 (Fall 1982): 575–602.

140. *Ibid.*

141. I do not wish to romanticize common-law marriage, which was not without its strains and violence. My point is that during this period legal marriage structured family violence in a particular way.

142. This change is the subject of Chapters 6 and 7 of Gillis, *For Better, for Worse.*

143. Iris Minor, "Working-Class Women and Matrimonial Law Reform, 1890–1914," in D. Martin and D. Rubenstein, eds., *Ideology and the Labour Movement* (London: Croom Helm, 1979), p. 113.

144. This chapter cannot encompass subsequent shifts in proletarian marriage. For a full discussion, see Gillis, "Conventional Marriage and the Common People; from Resistance to Compliance" (Plenary paper, Anglo-American Historians Conference, London, July 1982).

4

Policing the Early Modern Proletariat, 1450–1850

Catharina Lis
Hugo Soly

INTRODUCTION

The emergence and subsequent transformation of social policy in various parts of Europe during the early modern period cannot be explained apart from the newly evolving structures of surplus extraction and class power, which critically conditioned patterns of overall economic and demographic development. The rise of novel class relations to the basic means of production and subsistence not only divorced swelling numbers of peasants from the land; it also generated distinctive family formations and fertility patterns among the rural masses. The aggregate sociodemographic result was a massive expansion of the proletariat.[1] Presuming, as does Charles Tilly, that Europe outside Russia resembled Saxony, then the numbers wholly or partly dependent on wage work for their survival increased more than eightfold between the mid-sixteenth and mid-nineteenth centuries, whereas the total population merely trebled over the same period; in other words, the pro-

163

portion of proletarians rose dramatically, from something like 24% in 1550 to almost 71% in 1843.[2] The magnitude of this change forced the ruling classes to seek new solutions to control, discipline, and stabilize the base of the social pyramid: the more so as proletarianization was accompanied by pauperization and rebelliousness.[3] The landlords of northeastern Europe were able to develop new forms of the feudal state, enserfing both the peasants and the nearly landless and thereby establishing forceful political domination over the direct producers. This option was foreclosed, however, to their seigneurial counterparts in the West: There the peasantry succeeded in erasing the stigma of personal servility so that they were "free" to leave home and live elsewhere. As a result, the upper classes and their subalterns among the "middling sort" in western Europe were confronted with a true "social problem."

This chapter is an investigation of the ways in which secular governments, ecclesiastical authorities, and private entrepreneurs throughout western Europe reacted to the mushrooming growth of the proletariat. All of them had an obvious interest in policing the laboring poor. The problem was that they could not foresee the aggregate effects of proletarianization, and so their perceptions of the opportunities and dangers inherent in this long-term process did not always coincide. The fact that proletarianization was not an end in itself for capitalists (but rather the outcome of actions to control the means of production) meant that a social problem was generated that contemporaries could not see as a whole. Since the numbers and the reproductive capacities of the landless and nearly landless generally exceeded the demand for their labor, the agents of the State regarded the relative surplus population as a threat. For public authorities it was of paramount importance, consequently, to control the idlers and to discipline or punish the recalcitrant in order to maintain social stability. The agents of capitalism, on the other hand, were primarily concerned with profit and the recruitment of a cheap and docile labor force. Hence the quest of the ruling classes for an ordered hierarchy needs to be considered alongside the demands of capitalists for a free labor market. Attention must also be paid to ideologies and the institutions that helped to transmit them, especially in the light of attempts by religious reformers to repress certain features of popular belief and popular culture. Fear of increasing godlessness and moral disorder inclined the clergy to cooperate with secular governments on the issue of discipline, but this does not mean that both groups had the same ends in view. To what extent, then, were the objectives of State, Church, and employers mutually exclusive or compatible? Did economic, political, and ideological motives play equally important roles? What means did they actually use to keep the laboring poor under control, impose ecclesiastical discipline on them, and regulate the labor market?

To answer these questions it is necessary to focus on the unevenness of capitalism, of proletarianization, and of national experiences. Although western Europe as a whole witnessed proletarianization throughout the early modern period, both the chronology and the geography of this process varied greatly. Given the importance of capitalism to the pattern of proletarian natural increase, it is arguable that the periods characterized by the accelerated development of capitalism were also periods in which the pace of proletarianization quickened. In any case, the social problems generated by the economic and demographic changes of the "long sixteenth century" and the century after 1750 were balanced by a relaxation of tension during the intervening period, when there was a distinctly different conjuncture—slower rates of population growth, lethargic demand for commodities, rising real wages, and so on. The combination of different rates and degrees of proletarianization and different patterns of overall economic and demographic development clearly played a role in determining social policies within a given historical period.

The uneven emergence of capitalism involved regional divergences as well as temporal variations. In England, the evolution toward agrarian capitalism and the strengthening of Parliament signified that the landed classes found it increasingly necessary and possible to focus on the regulation of the labor market. In many Continental countries, in contrast, the rise of absolutist tax states (which intervened to support peasant ownership) entailed punitive controls and penal policies. Obviously, the experiences of each of the countries of western Europe cannot be analyzed and compared within the scope of this chapter; without denying the importance of other areas, special attention will be paid to England and France, because the divergent paths followed by these two countries clearly show the inherent possibilities and limitations of specific forms of policing.

Finally, did the measures taken by states, churches, and employers achieve the results desired; did they "domesticate" the proletariat? This crucial question points to the need for a close look at the various ways in which different social groups responded to new calls for more disciplined standards of individual behavior, and this requires a discussion of the political and ideological trade-offs, both within the elite and between the upper classes and the middling sort. Hence it is necessary to examine to what extent the logic of paternalism clashed with the logic of control; whether the new forms of restraint imposed from above fulfilled the interests of the lower-middle strata; and how far the operation of capitalism itself limited the proletariat's freedom of action or weakened their resistance to policing. At this point, of course, the question arises of whether the laboring poor were accomplices in their own oppression.

RESTORING ORDER AND ENFORCING
LOW-WAGE WORK

The "long sixteenth century" was not the first period in the history of western Europe characterized by laws that resulted in making the lower classes pay the costs of economic and demographic change.[4] In contrast with the Middle Ages, however, systematic forms of policing emerged during the early modern period, when the interrelated, mutually reinforcing effects of capitalist development and demographic growth led to a massive expansion of the proletariat. Worsening living conditions in many rural areas obliged landless laborers to find subsistence elsewhere. In effect, from the mid-fifteenth century on, migratory movements assumed alarming proportions, as evinced by contemporaries' innumerable complaints of hordes of "masterless men" and also by the accelerated pace of urban growth. Between 1500 and 1600, the number of persons living in cities of 5,000 or more rose by 47%, although the total population of Europe increased by only 28%.[5] Naturally, not every rural resident who abandoned his or her place of birth was a subsistence migrant, but it seems incontrovertible that the attractive power of urban centers during this period played only a subordinate role in the movement to the towns. On the one hand, the mass of wandering poor came to be viewed by central and local governments as a threat to public order, especially in periods of political turmoil. In towns with important export industries, on the other hand, entrepreneurs could use the uprooted inhabitants of the countryside as a "reserve army" to put pressure on urban workers regarding wages and labor discipline. The necessity to take care of vagrants (to preserve the traditional hierarchy of society) was combined with the desire to set the poor to work (to increase the supply of cheap labor in the towns), spurring the authorities to develop new modes of discipline.

From the second half of the fifteenth century, central and local governments throughout western Europe took measures against "antisocial elements": the transient poor were forbidden to beg, were threatened with corporal punishment, and were sent to the galleys. Poverty, whether voluntary or not, was no longer glorified, and even more significantly, mendicancy was increasingly identified with vagabondage. This inversion of traditional values was expressed in a stream of books concerned with the evil practices and shameless customs of the "deceitful" tramp: the *Narrenschiff* of Sebastian Brant (1494), *Le droit chemin de l'hôpital* of Robert de Balsac (1502), and the *Liber Vagatorum*, of which no fewer than 32 different editions appeared between 1510 and 1529, one of them prefaced by Martin Luther.[6] In the following decades, hundreds of pamphlets gruesomely pictured the "monstrous world" of the transient poor. Though retaining many of the elements present in the *Liber Vagatorum*, later writers built them into a closed system: Beggars and vagabonds were members of a kingdom apart, a dangerous caricature of "civilized" society, a real "underworld."[7] This new stereotype of a large body of idle disorderly persons justified the disciplining of any individual belonging to the lower strata of the population, whether settled or not. Indeed, the equation of the "social problem" and the "problem of crime"[8] implied that idleness was the parent of vice or, in other words, that forced labor was the remedy for all evils.

Although humanists regarded begging as symptomatic of a defectively functioning society and conceded that many of the transient poor were unemployed through no fault of their own, the practical remedy they recommended was compulsory labor. To Edmund Dudley, writing in 1509–1510, idleness was "the mother of all vice . . . , and lineal grandame of poverty and misery, and the deadly enemy of this tree of common-wealth." In Utopia, declared Thomas More in 1516, begging would be forbidden and work obligatory for all inhabitants. In 1524, Desiderius Erasmus proposed that municipalities take strong measures against beggars and put them to work. A year later, Juan Luis Vives in his famous book *De subventione pauperum* admonished the authorities to extirpate idleness wherever they could find it. Nobody, Vives argued, was really unable to work; even the blind could gain their livelihood by spinning or making baskets. In 1532–1533 Thomas Starkey attributed the increasing number of beggars to "much idleness and ill policy; for it is their own cause and negligence that they so beg."[9]

Religious reformers were equally preoccupied with the discipline of work. Luther, Zwingli, and Calvin held different views on many points, but they agreed that work was a social duty, that it contributed to order in society and to moral worth in the individual, and that in short it was a cure-all. Calvin went even further: Work was not only a necessity, but first and foremost it was a positive good, something to be done for the glory of God; it was saintly. The pragmatic approach of the three reformers, however, followed the same general lines: prohibition of begging, forced labor, and centralization of poor relief. Luther even considered that support had to be strictly limited to the subsistence minimum.[10]

In sum, then, during the late fifteenth and early sixteenth centuries the criticism of idleness and its counterpart, the exaltation of work, became major themes in the writings of both prominent men and middling people, laity and clergy, and Catholics and Protestants throughout western Europe. Their reaction was not limited to mere words. In the Netherlands (1531), France (1534), England (1531 and especially 1536), Scotland (1535), and Spain (1541), the central authorities proclaimed ordinances concerning begging and/or poor-relief; detailed regulations were, however, relegated to the local governments. Between 1522 and 1545 some 62 towns created a coordinated system of public assistance: at least 30 in Germany, 15 or 16 in the Low Countries, 8 in France, 6 in Switzerland, and 2 in northern Italy.[11] In nearly all towns two principles dominated: strict prohibition of begging for the able-bodied poor, regardless of age and sex, in order to compel them to accept work at any wage, and centralization of the existing funds into a "common box" to enable the selection and control of the "true needy."[12] This social policy, which signified a radical break with the highly indiscriminate, discontinuous, and private alms giving of medieval poor-relief, could simultaneously serve as a means of disciplining the proletariat and a mechanism for regulating the labor market.

It is no accident that 45 of the 62 municipal authorities that carried out a radical reformation of poor-relief between 1522 and 1545 did so before 1536. Until the third decade of the sixteenth century, cereals had been relatively abundant, but during the dearth year of 1521–1522 the writing on the wall could clearly be seen. Demographic growth without problems proved incompatible with the structure of agragrian production. Between 1527 and 1534 a series of harvest failures led to catastrophic famines and epidemics. Furthermore, wars and financial crises depressed international commerce and, consequently, industrial production. The dwindling demand for manufactured goods caused underemployment, reducing yet again real income.[13] It comes as no surprise, then, that central governments and municipalities alike faced strikes and uprisings, often of dangerous proportions, during the 1520s and 1530s.[14] This wave of revolts filled the members of the upper classes, whether laymen or clerics, Catholic or Protestant, with fear.[15] The lower classes in general and the poor in particular were looked upon as the source of civil and moral disorder. Discipline became the new code word. In most places, the practical application of the new poor-relief schemes resulted in the registration of the name, address, profession, age, civil status, physical condition, and wage of every person seeking public assistance. Special supervisors were empowered to investigate all aspects of the daily life and conduct of the needy. They refused support to anyone who was not industrious, orderly, honest, and sober. Protest against disciplinary measures was ruled out, for as one contemporary writer declared bluntly, the fear of punishment "is the end and virtue of all law."[16]

The war waged by local authorities against begging and vagabondage would have been hopeless but for the judicial system created by the State to arrest and punish "idle" persons. From the early sixteenth century on, central governments began to proclaim vagrancy acts to augment their poor laws, the better to deal with the masterless men. The term *vagabond* was more widely defined to include anyone refusing to work for "reasonable" wages, and eventually it included all potentially dangerous persons, such as wandering or unlicensed pedlars, players, minstrels, fortune tellers, jugglers, and scholars.[17] Henceforth, in the words of Michael Weisser, "Crime and the criminal would be defined on a class basis, and in terms of the conflict between classes."[18] The objective was not simply to inflict punishment on actual criminals but, rather, to criminalize the transient poor.

Rebellion itself, however, was not a sufficient precondition to generate new forms of policing.[19] A number of factors indicate that the regulation of the urban labor market was generally the ulterior motive for the creation of a coordinated system of public assistance. First, nearly all ordinances concerned with the reorganization of poor-relief were proclaimed in that part of Europe where commercial capitalism made its greatest advances, and nearly all of the towns involved had export industries that were in difficulty during the 1520s and 1530s. Second, there is abundant evidence that municipalities did take concrete steps to enforce low-wage work: The unemployed were obliged to go into the service of merchant entrepreneurs or artisans and were forbidden to object to their working conditions or to desert their masters on pain of being stricken from the poor list; pauper children were placed with craftsmen and punished if they "idled."[20] Third, the new system of poor-relief was generally maintained only as long as it served economic interests, that is, as long as employers needed a "reserve army." Moreover, it should be noted that it was precisely those countries where this social policy made its deepest inroads—England, France, Germany, the Netherlands—that witnessed a veritable explosion of legislative activity regarding wages, labor relations, and terms of employment.

Given that the welfare recipients comprised only a portion of the urban proletariat (albeit a large portion), a coordinated system of public support could not be expected to regulate adequately the labor market by itself. It was of the greatest importance for employers that the level of wages, conditions of work, and mobility of labor be controlled closely. Sporadic attempts at wage fixing and related matters in many countries dated back to the Black Death, but the growing prevalence of wage labor in the western European economy spurred the upper classes to pursue a more consistent policy. From the end of the fifteenth century onward, urban oligarchies in England, France, Germany, and the Netherlands began systematically to subject workers to maximum-wage legislation. English judges even resolved that an "insurrection" to obtain higher wages should be regarded as levying war against the king and therefore would be treason.

The working day became more strictly regulated. With the support of local governments, many guilds succeeded in lengthening it substantially. The number of holidays was constantly under attack. In the Netherlands, Charles V, as early as 1531, ordered that henceforth yearly fairs be consolidated into single-day events in the interest of saving time and money. The writer of a 1549 treatise on policies designed to increase the wealth of England included a large reduction in the number of annual holidays as one of his proposals for a more vigorous economy; the Act of 1552 sought to reduce their number.

Journeymen were prohibited from joining in confraternities, even those with purely religious or humanitarian aims, for such organizations could be turned against employers. If public authorities did approve the foundation of pious confraternities or associations for mutual assistance, they took care that the guild masters were in control. The ordinance of Villers-Coterêts, promulgated by Francis I in 1539, forbade unions of journeymen in any craft and ordered that the funds of existing confraternities be handed over to the local magistracy on pain of imprisonment and heavy fines. This repressive policy was considered all the more necessary because the guild masters, often supported by the public authorities, made it increasingly difficult for workers to obtain the status of master. They limited the number of free journeymen and compensated for this reduction by hiring more apprentices or unfree laborers. Above all, the entrance fee was gradually raised until it reached a formidable sum: by the middle of the sixteenth century, Antwerp's carpenters, joiners, and cloth dressers had to pay the equivalent of, respectively, 75, 112, and 150 days' wages to attain mastership. As a result of these measures, the majority of journeymen in every craft had no other choice but to remain wage laborers all their lives.[21]

These and other measures designed to keep the urban proletariat in their place served the interests of the merchant entrepreneurs, who

could see quite clearly the great advantages that centralized public assistance provided, both as a mean of disciplining the reserve army and
as a mechanism for enforcing low-wage work.[22] The most active sup-
porters of the new poor laws and labor codes, however, were the lower-
middle strata. For lesser master craftsmen—who found it more and more
difficult to keep their heads above water during this period of increasing
competition—it was indeed important to hold the wages of their employees as low as possible. Where the merchants had succeeded in
organizing putting-out systems, the ruthless exploitation of journeymen
and apprentices was the only means by which those master craftsmen
who had become dependent on capitalist entrepreneurs could turn any
profit at all. Since the downward pressure on wages generated strikes
and disturbances,[23] smaller commodity producers naturally favored new
modes of discipline that conformed to their interests.

It must be emphasized that nowhere in western Europe was there
established a more efficient machinery to regulate the labor market than
in England. Although the main ideas of the Statute of Artificers, passed
in 1563, had been applied for centuries to particular trades and localities,
the famous act "made a new departure by dealing in one comprehensive measure with all the principal relationships surrounding the contract between employer and employed," to cite Tawney. This elaborate
code, which created the legal framework for English labor for over two
centuries, did not impose a uniform, national rate but provided for the
annual assessment of maximum wages by the justices of the peace in
the counties and the chief officers in the cities, taking into account "the
plenty or scarcity of the time."[24] With good reason, Fisher considered
the Statute of Artificers as a product of a demographic crisis during 1557
and 1558, reducing the labor force and inducing an upward pressure on
wages and greater mobility.[25] This reasoning, however, does not elucidate why the rulers in other western European lands failed to establish
a similar machinery, though they too confronted a temporary shortage
of labor following the high mortality of the late 1550s.[26] What is the
explanation of this divergence? In Tudor England (in the course of its
evolution toward agrarian capitalism), laborers and their dependents
made up a significantly higher proportion of the rural population than
elsewhere in Europe. Therefore the Statute of Artificers served a critical
function: it attempted to secure a cheap labor force for agriculture and
to prevent excessive social mobility. In contrast, the central and local
governments on the Continent merely sought to control the urban proletariat.

Neither in England nor in the other countries of western Europe,
however, could the ruling class depend on the operation of "imper-

sonal," "economic" processes to control and discipline the base of the social pyramid. Nor did legal compulsion and public assistance suffice to ensure the docility of the lower orders; instead, the repression of the body had to be conjoined to the repression of the soul, that is, the internalization of new forms of restraint. The Church, in both its Catholic and Protestant manifestations, played an important role in this regard. It is not that ecclesiastical authorities sought to support the social policies of secular governments—Church and State had interests that were often conflicting; nonetheless, they were equally concerned with disorderly life.

The clergy had good reason to cooperate with secular authorities on the issue of discipline. The uprooted people could not be integrated into the parish community and, consequently, lacked instruction in Christian virtues. In 1517 the aldermen of Bruges complained of "the great multitude of able-bodied poor, both young and old who are begging for alms in and around the city without having any knowledge of the articles of faith and the commandments of God our creator." They did not exaggerate: many of the vagabonds sentenced by the *schepenbank* at Gouda in the 1520s confessed to not having taken communion for several years.[27] Both Catholics and Protestants in this period noted that many of the *vulgus nostrum* did not attend the service on Sundays, did not confess, and ignored the most elementary principles of the Christian doctrine. Hence, the lower orders were increasingly equated with the ungodly.[28] Since the call for religious discipline coincided with a call for social control, Church and State had an interest in joining hands. As the French preacher Charles-Louis Frossard explained: "Ecclesiastical discipline does not diminish the authority of the Magistrate at all, but, on the contrary, is the Magistrate's organ in disposing man's heart and will with the aim to make him more obedient."[29] The new poor relief schemes were often used as mechanisms to enforce religious conformity. That was the case not only in Protestant regions, where reformers themselves drafted municipal poor relief ordinances, but also in Catholic countries. Nearly all the local governments in the Netherlands and France that developed a new system of poor relief stipulated that anyone seeking public assistance had to know or to learn the Paternoster, the Ave Maria, and the Ten Commandments, and everywhere an unChristian way of life was a sufficient reason to be stricken from the poor list.[30]

Humanists as well as religious reformers were convinced that the tendency of the propertyless masses toward "idleness, disobedience, and godlessness" could be corrected through the education of the young. Since a child's mind was very malleable, the community should act *in loco parentis* in order to counter the evil influence of the impoverished home. "Schools are needed more than ever now," Philip Melanchton wrote in 1525, "so that young people may be raised to be peaceful and decent," and Martin Bucer felt that "learning to read makes the common people more polite, peaceful, and disposed to a civic life." Similar views were expressed by Vives: Pauper children should be put into public schools at an early age to receive education and training, together with support; only in this way would they grow into industrious and virtuous citizens. However, with the exception of Germany (where many governments embraced "Luther's House of Learning"), the official urban programs for disciplining and indoctrinating poor children, dating from the first half of the sixteenth century, were not so much influenced by the ideas of educational reformers as dictated by social and economic realities. In 1524 the magistrates of Bruges declared that large numbers of boys and girls, compelled by their parents or simply left to their fate, wandered in the streets asking for alms. Some 20 years later, the same complaint was raised at Antwerp, where the relief officers registered no fewer than 1,500 foundlings and abandoned children, in a city of 70,000 to 80,000 inhabitants.

In large towns, in particular, the presence of young people lacking family ties and without means of assistance posed serious problems. According to contemporaries, poor children often banded together for protection and common profit: they formed gangs that extorted alms and committed petty thefts. Whether or not such gangs really existed is rather irrelevant here. The point is that municipal authorities did draw a close connection between juvenile poverty and crime and that this in no small measure motivated them to care for the children of the poor. In many places, hospitals for foundlings and separate orphanages for boys and girls were established. These institutions were not exactly new, but in the late fifteenth and sixteenth centuries they sprang up everywhere. Also, local governments began to pay special attention to the education of pauper children. At Bruges as early as 1517, a school was opened for poor boys aged 8–13, and around 1550 it cared for some 230 children. By this time, at least a dozen towns in Flanders and Brabant had undertaken similar initiatives. Since these efforts entailed financial "sacrifices," the authorities tried to combine charity and education with their own economic interests. As the citizens of London argued in 1552: the upbringing of a poor child had to be "profitable to the commonweal." Identical principles clearly guided the overwhelming majority of local governments in western Europe. Nearly everywhere pauper children were put to work or apprenticed when they had reached the appropriate age, and in many cases without pay.[31]

The call for discipline also implied an attack on various aspects of "popular culture." Certainly, churchmen had condemned popular customs from the early days of Christianity onward, but attempts at reform remained sporadic until the end of the Middle Ages. In the first half of the sixteenth century, on the contrary, efforts to purge religious practice of its "paganism" and to repress "excesses" in popular festive life became more frequent and systematic. Both Catholic and Protestant reformers insisted on the separation between the sacred and the profane, and secular authorities tried to impose obedience and order. Although the influence exercised by an educated clerical elite should not be underestimated, attacks on traditional popular recreations in this period seemed to be launched primarily by local governments. Numerous municipalities throughout western Europe abolished the Feast of Fools, forbade the wearing of masks during Carnival and eventually the festival itself, took control of processions, subjected players in popular dramas to stringent rules, prohibited all sorts of games, and licensed and even tried to suppress alehouses. Their objections were twofold. On the one hand, the magistrates denounced many popular recreations as invitations to moral and political disorder: large gatherings of people and the heavy consumption of alcohol all too easily led the "worser sort" to express hostility toward their superiors, and violence, verbal as well as physical, could trigger revolt. On the other hand, feasting and its attendant excesses, especially drinking, were condemned for keeping people from their work and, consequently, causing employers to suffer losses. Alehouses, in the words of a prominent contemporary, were "places of waste" and "harbors for such men as live in idleness."[32]

Thus, by the end of the sixteenth century a new attitude toward poverty and charity was everywhere in evidence. In contrast with their medieval predecessors, Catholic and Protestant secular and ecclesiastical authorities throughout western Europe agreed that it was important to regulate all aspects of private and public life in order to preserve society's traditional hierarchical structure. The interconnected economic and demographic pressures of the sixteenth century had polarized wealth and poverty to a degree unknown previously. Everywhere growing numbers of people lived below subsistence levels, many of them wholly or partly dependent on wage labor. The upper classes again and again pointed to the negative symptoms of the process of change: a greater incidence of crime, revolt, illegitimacy, and infanticide.[33] Poverty, in consequence, was clearly identified with disorder and godlessness. The political and religious upheavals had taught the ruling elites a lesson they did not soon forget: only tight organization and solidarity among propertied laymen and learned clerics could keep the "many-headed multitude" under control. Hence the State endorsed the Church's policy to establish a watertight system of parochial conformity, whereas the Church lent a moral sanction to secular policy—it was the duty of the clergy to inculcate notions of hierarchy and authority, the foundations of political submission, into the minds of the common people. In other words, social control and ecclesiastical discipline overlapped.[34]

Both the Catholic and Protestant churches expended enormous energies during the late sixteenth and early seventeenth centuries to instill uniform habits of religious observance. They sought to improve the quality of the clergy and to emphasize even more their pastoral duties. Although there were considerable regional differences, these activities did indeed bear fruit. By the mid-seventeenth century, most parishes in western Europe were served by their own pastors, and it proved possible to raise to a remarkable degree the level of instruction and the morality of the clergy. At the same time, the churches applied a whole series of measures to introduce a new form of belief among the populace, a belief more individually oriented and more exigent than in the past. Toward that end, schools were founded to initiate children in Christian teachings; catechism classes were organized for the children of the poor; baptisms and marriages were recorded; and attendance at Sunday service was regulated. These efforts were backed by a reinvigorated apparatus of ecclesiastical discipline. Church courts crusaded against "heathenish" ways. Sexual "deviances" such as cohabitation, premarital sex, adultery, and incest were more intensely prosecuted and more severely punished than before. The churches, moreover, strove to repress or at least to control traditional popular amusements; not only mystery plays and ritual festivities of questionable origins, but also fairs, dances, drinking bouts, masquerades, and many other "invitations to sin."[35]

Secular authorities fully supported this "silent revolution," as can be seen from the ordinances proclaimed by Archdukes Albert and Isabella, corulers of the Spanish Netherlands. In 1601, they subjected all dramatic performances to the prior approval of the local clergy; in 1606, they initiated a merciless suppression of witchcraft; in 1607, they forbade frequenting taverns, dancing, or attending plays during church services; in 1608, they gave the force of law to the dispositions of the third provincial synod in Mechelen, which affected the laity; in 1613, they determined that henceforth no more than 40 guests could be invited to a marriage feast; and in 1616, they ordered the local authorities to limit drastically the number of taverns.[36] The situation was no different in the Protestant countries. The English Parliament, for example, enacted numerous statutes for the punishment of drunkenness, swearing, alehouse disorders, and profanation of the Sabbath.[37] Nor did the matter end there: secular courts throughout western Europe proved to be active in prosecuting alehousekeepers and their disorderly customers, persons who failed to attend church, and other offenders against the penal law.[38]

Yet pressure from above could elicit a response only when those who mediated between the courts and the local community were prepared to accept that authority. In the absence of a professional police force, the implementation of ecclesiastical and social discipline depended not so much on coercion as on assent. There is abundant evidence to show that the middling sort of people in western Europe did indeed move closer to the elites in terms of both interests and values and, consequently, distanced themselves from their poorer neighbors. Economic transformation not only led to proletarianization but also offered new and greater opportunities for upward social mobility to certain groups. Although the latter phenomenon presumably was most pronounced in England and the United Provinces, there is no doubt that a minority of villagers and urbanites in other western European countries bettered their positions. To these economically independent men, collectively designated the "industrious sort of people," the call for ecclesiastical and social discipline had an appeal insofar as it conformed to their interests. They were in favor of new codes prohibiting clandestine marriages and premarital sex, for as property-holding parents they had a vital interest in the selection of suitable partners for their children at the appropriate age. Thus they also supported the clergy in their struggle against dances and popular festivals, occasions that young people used to meet one another. They were inclined to accept political authority in terms of the patriarchal theory of obligation, because this patriarchalism justified the duty of both children and employees to "be in subjection and obedience." They wholeheartedly sympathized with preachers who portrayed work as the foundation of morality, the key to order, and the elementary form of social discipline. In short, social change widened the gap between the values of the industrious sort of people and those of the poor, and this cultural divide was reinforced by the expansion of educational facilities.[39] Consequently, the lower classes in general and the poor in particular came to represent all that the more substantial villagers and townsmen despised: ignorance, profanity, idleness, and disorder. No wonder that the latter began to consider many popular beliefs, attitudes, and values as typical of a culture of poverty from which respectable persons should distance themselves.

Needless to say, the convergence of social polarization and cultural differentiation generated tensions within local communities. In the early

seventeenth century, however, the system of law enforcement and social control functioned better because the middling sort were motivated
to make it work. Their increasing adherence to the values of their superiors, both laity and clergy, brought them to appeal more frequently
to the machinery of control. They showed a greater willingness to accuse
their poorer neighbors of witchcraft and to testify against them, to bring
petty thieves into court, to prosecute those guilty of disorderly behavior,
to extend closer control over alehouses, and to suppress traditional recreations. Moreover, they systematically controlled petty malefactors
through the allocation of poor-relief. Aid was denied to the mothers of
bastards and to persons who indulged in social drinking, who did not
attend church, or who otherwise caused "scandal." As Keith Wrightson
remarked, the middling sort were "attempting to mould their communities into conformity with standards of behavior which accorded
with their interests and reflected their prejudices as ratepayers, masters,
employers and pillars of the Church."[40]

Viewing separately each component of the social policy adopted during this long sixteenth century, we might question its modernity. If,
however, one considers that the central governments and many of the
municipalities of western Europe roughly simultaneously took comparable measures to control the reserve army of the poor and to enforce
low-wage work, then one clearly discerns a turning point. Never before
had such a systematic effort been made to combine economic gain with
social discipline. The connection between the development of capitalism
and the emergence of social policy appears undeniable. In all regions
where capital forced its way into the sphere of production at an accelerated pace—and only there—a machinery was pieced together with the
aim of turning the poor into industrious and orderly wage laborers.

How successful were those measures? England, the only country to
see the breakthrough of agrarian capitalism, was also the only state that
continued and completed the poor-relief schemes begun tentatively in
the 1530s.[41] In contrast, the Continent saw no extension of the role of
the State with respect to public assistance in the late sixteenth and early
seventeenth centuries. In France and the Netherlands, central governments did not even attempt to enforce the poor laws promulgated in
the 1530s. The reasons are obvious: in France, there was civil war between 1562 and 1598, and in the Netherlands a revolutionary movement
emerged in 1566 and eventually led to the independence of the United
Provinces. In both countries, decisions regarding poor-relief were left to
the municipalities, which often saw no particular reason to continue a
coordinated social policy. Many towns experienced growing economic
problems, aggravated by war, and so the poor-relief schemes introduced

in the 1520s and 1530s lost their labor-regulating function. In Germany, too, the urban *Armenordnungen* underwent a shift in their concern: Whereas at their inception they had focused on those refusing to labor, after mid-century their emphasis was on preventing the immigration of propertyless transients.[42]

If, with the exception of England, sixteenth-century attempts to employ poor-relief as a mechanism to regulate the labor market generally provided merely temporary results, then it follows that campaigns to impose more disciplined standards of personal behavior on paupers completely miscarried. That conclusion can be inferred from the fact that prohibitions against certain forms of popular recreation had to be promulgated again and again. A more radical approach, however, was not long in coming.

THE DISCIPLINE OF WORK

By the early seventeenth century, in both rural areas and urban centers, a large and permanent proletariat had emerged, collectively designated the "laboring poor." The crystallization of this class of workers, deprived of the basic means of production, wholly or partly dependent on wage labor, and living in constant danger of destitution, was a new phenomenon in history. The upper classes did not fail to notice that the problem of poverty and its control had changed from an occasional, epiphenomenal disorder to an endemic disease of the body politic. After first establishing the ideological resolve to grapple with the impoverishment, rootlessness, and insubordination accompanying the mushroom growth of the proletariat, they felt that novel solutions were required to control and stabilize the base of the social pyramid. Reams of statutes were promulgated against the poor, and at the same time as this punitive imperative was being developed, new modes of discipline were created. In order to convey the essential principles of this discipline, the elites decided to separate the "rough" and the "deserving" members of the proletariat from one another.

We have already detailed the ways that secular and ecclesiastical authorities sought to co-opt the respectable and the unfortunate, and so let us now turn to the other side of this process. How was the stigma of poverty and its associated character faults to be identified? How were the "sturdy beggars" to be separated from the respectable masses? And, finally, how were they to reform themselves—that is, how were "the transient, marginal, and deviant" to be domesticated?

The new solution was simplicity itself: after the recalcitrant were identified, they were not only whipped, branded, and badged—they were also locked up and put to work.[43] According to Michel Foucault, *enfermement* protected the public from potentially dangerous idlers whose debauchery might infect the healthy elements of the social body.[44] Foucault, however, does not explain why some countries emphasized the educational value of prison work, whereas others stressed the gains to be drawn from the workhouses. In effect, the new institutions fulfilled widely diverging functions from one time and place to another, and these variations are mostly attributable to the unevenness of capitalist development.

During the seventeenth and early eighteenth centuries, as Robert Brenner has stated, past social and political formations critically conditioned the dramatic regional divergences that characterized this epoch of general crisis.[45] The Dutch and English ruling classes no longer needed direct, extraeconomic compulsion to extract a surplus, because they could depend largely on the operation of contractually based economic processes. They only required the State to perform roles intrinsic to the new system of social relations: protecting private property, facilitating the accumulation of capital, and legitimating a social policy that would mold laborers to the requirements of the market. In France and Germany, in contrast, the long-term expansion of the absolutist State and the taxes it levied proved to be disastrous for economic development. The intensification of political accumulation in all its forms led to protracted, systemic crisis, aggravated by devastating wars. Certainly, the rulers of these countries introduced mercantilist measures intended to promote agriculture and industry, but the concerns of the State's agents for ordered hierarchy continued to prevail over the demands of capitalist entrepreneurs for disciplined labor. Clearly, economic as well as political factors could bring about the movement to "lock up the poor."

The connections among capitalism, poverty, and incarceration can be clearly delineated in the province of Holland, the commercial and industrial heartland of the Dutch Republic, which was the main site of early workhouses, *tuchthuizen*. In 1595 the Amsterdam magistracy set up a rasphouse for male delinquents, and in 1596 a spinning house for women. During the first half of the seventeeth century similar institutions were located in some 20 other towns with flourishing capitalist sectors. The major ideological impulse behind this policy was not simply to isolate idlers from civilized society but also to turn them into docile and profitable workers. In this way the actions of the Dutch elites forbidding begging and limiting assistance to the aged, ill, and infirm can be understood in terms of their patriarchal responsibility just as easily as the disciplining of the recalcitrant by a strict work regime can be understood in terms of the logic of entrepreneurial capitalism. The aims of these early institutions were thus threefold: to encourage the lower classes to fulfill their duties to society for fear of landing in a place ruled by an iron hand, to reeducate the inmates through compulsory labor, and to make some profit or at least to ensure self-sufficiency by means of centralized handicraft production.[46]

In England the social policy of confinement and exemplary punishment was just as closely linked with the imperatives of a nascent industrial political economy. One may note the earliest evidence of this incarcerationist mentality in London in 1552–1553 when the city fathers decided to shut away vagrants and shiftless members of the proletariat in the Bridewell prison with the aim of reforming them through compulsory labor. Though one may remark upon early examples such as this one, it was after the Restoration that the policy of confinement became a national practice. In England, in contrast with its Continental neighbors, economic development continued from 1650 to 1750. The transformation of agricultural production, based on the landlord/capitalist tenant/wage laborer system, favored the expansion of the home market, which in turn stimulated rapid industrial and overall economic growth. English entrepreneurs had an extensive work force at their disposal: the total population doubled between the 1520s and the end of the seventeenth century; moreover, the proletariat more than quadrupled over this period, and among the 2.5 million wage workers of 1700, about 1 million had been separated from the land.[47] The capitalists faced two major problems, however. First, the pace at which the poor were uprooted and then absorbed into industry varied considerably from region to region, and so migrations had to be conducted along the desired channels. Second, it was very important to be cost-competitive on the international market during this time of sluggish demand. Hence most entrepreneurs tried to put pressure on their workers regarding wages and labor discipline. In their opinion, such a policy was both necessary and attainable—real wages were rising as a result of the downward drift of grain prices.

In 1662 Parliament enacted the Law of Settlement and Removal to deal with the rising numbers of uprooted men and women. The justices of the peace were empowered to eject all newcomers to a parish who had no means of subsistence and send them back to their last legal residence.[48] It was not sufficient, however, to regulate only the mobility of labor; the growing proletariat also had to be employed profitably—the more so, because the simultaneous perception of economic expansion and greater ''idleness'' brought the upper classes to consider the poor as the secret but untapped weapon in the nation's struggle to augment its productive capacity. As Joyce Appleby remarked: "The unwelcome hordes of masterless men at the beginning of the century appeared to the most concerned of their betters seventy years later as a pool of badly managed labor." From the 1660s on, innumerable schemes were proposed to combine poor-relief with economic progress. Most protagonists of a constructive social policy paid special attention to three topics that in their opinion were interlocked: wages, work discipline, and child labor. William Carter, John Houghton, Thomas Manley, Sir William Petty, and many other writers stated that high wages were equivalent to low production. Houghton, for example, declared that whenever "the framework knitters or masters of silk stockings had a great price for their work, they have been observed seldom to work on Mondays and Tuesdays, but to spend most of their time at the ale-house or nine-pins." Hence actions should be taken for "reducing the wages of servants, labourers and workmen of all sorts." The overwhelming majority of commentators did not disapprove of the poor laws, which they saw as an indispensable machinery to secure order, but they sharply criticized the magistrates who failed to enforce statutes against begging and to provide work. As one pamphleteer claimed: The "mischief" of high wages "is occasioned by reason of the idleness of so vast a number of people . . . so that those who are industrious . . . make men pay what they please for their wages: but set the poor at work and then these men will be forced to lower their rates." Even if the poor could not be employed profitably, they had to be put to work. "It is better," the merchant Thomas Firmin wrote, "to lose something in a way that will make our poor people better and skillful, than to suffer them to live in idleness." Sir William Petty went so far as to suggest that it would be "better to burn a thousand men's labours for a time, than to let those thousand men by non-employment lose their faculty of labouring." The discipline of work had to be inculcated, of course, at as early an age as possible. Sir Francis Brewster recommended working schools for poor children in order to "Manure and Improve the first Sprouts as they come into the world," and the philosopher John Locke saw workhouses as the means of educating children aged from 3 to 14.[49]

But how should the profitable employment of the poor be realized? John Cary, a rich merchant, gave the answer. Under his impulse the Corporation of the Poor was created at Bristol, which opened two workhouses in 1696, one for women and the other for young children and the aged. Similar institutions were set up in other towns at the end of the seventeenth century, but the main impetus came from the act of 1723, which soon led to the construction of 100 to 200 workhousefactories. These enterprises were not only found in London and the old textile areas, such as Suffolk, Norfolk, and the West Country, but also, more significantly, in new textile centers like Manchester, Liverpool, and Nottingham.[50] From the businessman's point of view, the establishment of a workhouse was highly desirable, even if the institution was in no condition to pay its own way, for it was built and maintained at the community's expense. Its advantages were threefold: the supply of cheap yarn could be augmented rapidly; the large-scale employment of paupers exerted pressure on free laborers; and the workhouse's disciplinary regime prepared poor children for a life of hard work.

In France, by contrast, mercantilist concerns with the price and subordination of labor were submerged by the nervous anxiety of a ruling class whose political edict was fiercely contested. Although Cardinal Richelieu had, in 1625, drafted a paper urging local governments to create hospitals in which "the able-bodied poor could be employed on public works," with the exception of Lyons, municipal patriarchs turned a deaf ear to his call. The wave of rebellious movements, often of dangerous proportions, that swept over France during the second quarter of the seventeenth century pressed authorities to act on sociopolitical problems. The lower classes had to be taught that the distinction between masters and servants was part of a divine order. In addition, the forceful religious revival between 1600 and 1640–1650, the "time of the saints," brought with it a growing interest not only in disciplined ascetic piety but also in the submission of souls. Since the poor were deemed crude and ignorant, they had to be helped toward salvation. The prerequisite to attain this end was work, for idleness bred vice. Those who did not understand that a life of labor was God's commandment had to be shown the light. That the two objectives could easily be combined is apparent from the ruthless crusade against the "evils of the age" carried out by the Company of the Holy Sacrament.

This secret organization of devout laity and clergy, founded in Paris between 1627 and 1630, elaborated numerous schemes for political and religious repression that were based on the idea that a proper society could be sustained only by removing and reeducating its antisocial elements. By the middle of the century, the company had established a strictly controlled network of some sixty provincial branches. Many prominent aristocrats and *officiers*, including Chancellor Pierre Séguier, notorious for his merciless action against rebels, joined the Cabale des Dévots. Through wealth, influence, and intense propaganda they quickly succeeded in putting into practice their ideas regarding order and godliness. At their urging, the theological faculty of the Sorbonne in 1645 solemnly declared that journeymen who became members of *compagnonnages* committed a mortal sin. In 1656 the company managed to convert the *parlement* of Paris to its views that confinement was the only proper way "to save the souls of the poor, who cohabitate without being married, who are completely ignorant of religion, who spurn the Holy Sacraments, and who indulge in all sorts of vices." A year later, *enfermement* was accomplished in the capital: 4,000 to 5,000 paupers of both sexes were locked up in the Hôpital Général de la Charité and put to work. Meanwhile the *dévots* had created the Committee of Spiritual Police to keep an eye on the needy in receipt of out-relief. Their homes were visited and their neighbors were questioned to make sure that they were living as good Christians. The company's crowning achievement was the royal edict of June 1662, which ordered that "in all cities . . . where a *hôpital général* has not yet been established, the foundation of such a hospital be undertaken immediately . . . in order to intern beggars . . . and to instruct them in piety and Christian religion." Although the Company of the Holy Sacrament had to dissolve itself in the mid-1660s (Louis XIV looked askance at its constant interference in the affairs of state), the *dévots* had secured their principal object: The *enfermement* was well under way. By the second quarter of the eighteenth century, all centers of more than 5,000 inhabitants had an *hôpital général*.[51]

Colbert stressed the potential gains to be drawn from the general hospitals. In his opinion, they ought to become "factories" in which the poor would not merely be disciplined but also employed profitably. The projects of the untiring minister went much further indeed than perfecting the existing system of social control. He was convinced that it sufficed to give French industry systematic public support and provide an extensive, cheap, and docile work force for the nation's wealth to be increased. Hence his attempts to prevent the emigration of laborers, to fix maximum wage rates, to annihilate the *compagnonnages*, to bind apprentices to their masters, and to set idlers to work. Purely artificial means could not, however, aid French industry very much: structural obstacles limited in advance the economic effect of such attempts. Some exceptions aside, the *hôpitaux généraux* soon turned into asylums, which admitted large numbers of widows and orphans along with social undesirables. Although in most of these institutions the importance of work was strongly emphasized, they had little significance as factories or even as training centers.[52]

In Germany, the mercantilist reeducation of labor was likewise compromised by the historical necessity of controlling vagrants and co-opting political dissent by segregating into confined places those most likely to rebel. Certainly, the promoters of the *Zuchthäusern* were concerned with profit, but after a while most of these institutions fulfilled several functions simultaneously: workshop, prison, hospital; this multiplicity of roles hindered the rational division of labor. It is equally true that in the late seventeenth and early eighteenth centuries, many German rulers took measures with an eye toward the regulation of the labor market. Within the anachronistic framework of the Holy Roman Empire, however, there was no room for the optimal application of economic and social policies. The empire contained no fewer than 294 states and 2,303 territorial entities, each of them having the right to control its own domestic affairs. In some principalities, the upper classes had an interest in developing manufacturing activities and, consequently, enforced the *Reichshandwerksordung* (imperial craftwork decree) of 1731, but in many other regions this was not the case. In the superstates of the Hapsburgs and the Hohenzollerns, moreover, the central governments were pursuing two largely contradictory objects, namely, the maintenance of the feudal relations of production and the creation of a proper industrial organization. In such circumstances a coordinated social policy was out of the question. On the one hand measures were necessary to prevent serfs from moving about or embracing a trade without their lord's permission, but on the other hand schemes had to be developed through which urban entrepreneurs could dispose of an extensive labor force.[53]

The great confinement, then, was not a complete success. Its application was deeply influenced by the ebbs and flows of capitalist development and the struggles for local political mastery that are so much a part of the history of the absolutist state. Although the lineaments of a new system of discipline, control, and rigorous supervision were emerging, its implementation was more problematic. Indeed, one might well ask how much was achieved by all these attempts at policing the proletariat. At first, one would be inclined to suppose that the elites, in association with the middling sort of people, had succeeded, at the end of the seventeenth century, in imposing more disciplined standards of behavior on the poor. Illegitimate births and premarital conceptions by then had become infrequent throughout western Europe, compared with their incidence between 1580 and 1620, but this phenomenon can largely be explained by changes in the social environment. As David Levine and Keith Wrightson explained; from the 1620s, the disequilibrium between customary expectations and sexual behavior on one hand and socioeconomic opportunities on the other slowly began to be resolved, and the lower classes developed new and different patterns of courtship and marital strategies.[54] It is true that the poor, in both Catholic and Protestant regions, were expected to marry in church, usually brought their children for baptism shortly after birth, often took communion at least once a year, and attended the services on Sundays more regularly than in the past. More uniform parochial observance, however, is not a "submission of souls." At the end of the seventeenth century, Catholic priests as well as Lutheran and Calvinist ministers still expressed dismay at the apathy of the lower classes toward sermons and catechism lessons, their ignorance or misunderstanding of the rudiments of Christian doctrine, and above all their physical excesses: drinking, dancing, and gambling. Notwithstanding the unflagging crusade of legislators and administrators to restrict the numbers of alehouses and to control the activities of alehouse keepers and their customers, numerous houses continued to spring up unlicensed, and disorders could not be eradicated. Although ecclesiastical and secular authorities left no stone unturned to enforce strict observance of the Sabbath in order to educate, discipline, and control the ungodly, the anti-Sabbatarianism of the poor remained a constant source of scandal.[55]

The very campaign led by central and local governments in the late seventeenth and early eighteenth centuries to transform the poor into industrious wage laborers attests to the extraordinary tenacity of popular resistance to values and norms imposed from above. The lower classes were open only to those ideas that coincided with their own demands or that they considered useful to their struggle for survival. E. P. Thompson's statement about the English laboring poor also holds for their Continental counterparts: they "imposed upon the rich some of the duties and functions of paternalism just as much as deference was in turn imposed upon them. Both parties to the equation were constrained within a common field-of-force." Certainly, the lives of the proletariat were inescapably affected by the realities of class power, implying an exchange of essentially unequal obligations, but the acceptance of authority by the propertyless masses was very conditional. They continued to define social and political relationships in terms of respect for customary standards and rights, which established the limits beyond which the rulers and employers could not go.[56]

DIVERGING ECONOMIC STRUCTURES
AND SOCIAL POLICIES

The century after 1750 must be considered essentially a phase of acceleration in the development of capitalism, entailing decisive changes in the size and the nature of the proletariat. Wage labor was not new, of course, but the extent, rate, and degree of proletarianization now reached levels previously unknown.

Broad segments of the population were finally reduced to mere objects, formally as exchangeable commodities and in reality as means of production in the labor process. On the one hand, the tightening grip of capital on both agriculture and the industrial sector quickened the "commodification" of labor power. Peasants and artisans alike found it increasingly difficult to maintain subsistence activities, petty commodity production, and noncapitalist distribution networks, so that more households and more members of individual households relied on money wages for their income. On the other hand, the definitive break-through of the capitalist mode of production meant that fewer workers could control the labor process in its entirety. The introduction of the factory system greatly accelerated this movement from the formal to the real subjection of labor to capital.

The emergence of industrial capitalism also brought about both a re-shaping of the international division of labor, thereby creating or rein-forcing regional disparities, and a recomposition of the labor force in particular areas, by rendering certain groups of workers redundant while at the same time inadequately ensuring the supply of the needed kinds of workers. In effect, the imperfections in the labor market signified that labor shortages in some regions or industries did not cancel out sur-pluses in others. Large sections of the proletariat, therefore, not only saw their skills being eroded; they also were turned into a relative sur-plus population and, consequently, were impoverished.

Finally, the demographic component of proletarianization must be taken into account. The transformation of peasants and artisans into ag-ricultural and industrial proletarians led to important changes in strat-egies of family formation. New household structures came into being, their formation and their size determined by the weakening of custom-ary restraints on early marriage and (above all) by the development of exploitative regimes demanding more labor for less and less reward.[57] The resulting spiral of self-exploitation (which was not connected to some supposedly autonomous family economy) in turn further stimu-lated the growth of the proletariat. Although this demographic dynamic had its limits, it brought into being a pool of landless laborers wholly dependent on wage work for their survival, vulnerable whenever the supply of labor exceeded the number of available jobs.

The combined effects of natural increase, social mobility, and migra-tion generated massive proletarianization. Tilly estimated that the in-crease in the proletariat from 1750 to 1843 was on the order of 71 million, nearly equivalent to the total increase in Europe's population. The num-ber of wage laborers doubled during this period, though the population as a whole rose by a mere 52%.[58] The "social problem" had not only assumed greater proportions, however; it also became more complex and manifested itself in very different ways according to time and place.

Nowhere else in Europe did the proportion of landless laborers reach levels comparable to those in England. Independent peasants, already rare in the corn counties by the end of the seventeenth century, had virtually disappeared by the 1850s. The explanation must be sought in the triumph of agrarian capitalism. Disastrous as it was for the peasantry, the development of large-scale farming, with labor performed by wage earners, led to greater agricultural productivity, which in turn favored rapid demographic growth and urbanization. It was the combination of massive proletarianization—through expropriation and, above all, natural increase (as a result of changes in nuptiality)—with the rising agricultural output in the eighteenth century that brought about the expansion of the home market. Growing domestic demand for cheap manufactured goods in turn greatly stimulated the process of industrialization, the more so because entrepreneurs were supplied with an extensive and mobile work force reproducing itself quickly and without cost.[59]

In rural France, in contrast with England, the small family-run peasant farm retained a clear numerical predominance far past the middle of the nineteenth century. Most cottars lived in structural poverty and depended on an extensive economy to stay alive, and their wages accounted for only a part, albeit an ever-increasing part, of the family income. Subsistence peasants, not propertyless laborers, made up the overwhelming majority of the working population engaged in agriculture, which still totaled 54% in 1856, as against merely 22% in Great Britain. One result of the comparatively smaller size of its proletariat was that France experienced a slower demographic growth than did England. The French population expanded at about 0.4% per year between 1750 and 1780, lost momentum in the next 15 years, and thereafter recovered to increase by 0.5% per year on the average until 1840. In contrast, the English annual growth rate rose from about 0.55% between 1751 and 1771 to almost 1% during the next three decades, whereas in the early nineteenth century it rose further to reach a maximum of 1.55% between 1821 and 1826. Not surprisingly, French urbanization proceeded slowly: People living in centers with more than 10,000 inhabitants in 1851 still accounted for only 14% of the entire population, as opposed to some 40% in England and Wales. Also, the low rate of proletarianization set severe limits on the market for mass-produced goods. The fact that the bulk of the population were enmeshed in an "economy of makeshifts" precluded French industry from embarking on the path of development followed by England. Unlike their English counterparts, French entrepreneurs were confronted with the slow growth of both internal demand and mobile labor power. The only palliative was a con-

tinued expansion of rural industries based on the putting-out system
and of urban high-quality manufacture, which took place in the households of highly skilled artisans or in small workshops.[60]

Evidently, divergent paths of development entailed different social
problems and these, in turn, necessitated specific forms of policing. The
ways in which the English and the French sought to discipline the proletariat in the period from 1650 to 1750 (when there was a totally different conjuncture of economic and social forces on either side of the
channel) have already been described. How did the agents of capitalism
and the agents of the State in these two countries react to the growth
and impoverishment of the proletariat between 1750 and 1850, during
the Great Transformation?

THE DISCIPLINE OF WAGES: ENGLAND, 1750–1850

Massive proletarianization in conjunction with rapid economic growth
meant that English capitalists had every reason to focus on the regulation of the labor market. They disposed of a large reservoir of labor,
which reproduced itself quickly, and they could use this reserve army
quite profitably in both agriculture and industry.

The rise in food prices after 1750 pushed the landed classes to seize
even greater control of labor power. The age-old processes of expropriation accelerated, and many rural workers were deprived of the last ves-
tiges of nonmonetary income. Enclosure undoubtedly can be seen as
contributing to improved farming, but the elimination of the "right of
commonage" offered many cottagers only a choice between becoming
free laborers on the land or abandoning agriculture. Although the importance of this movement should not be overestimated, it is important
to appreciate that it reinforced the notion of absolute private ownership
of land. Hence claims of custom and usage could be criminalized. Enclosure had other advantages: it kept the working population from
wasting their time, for commons, complained a board of agriculture report of 1794, only gave laborers "the means of subsisting in idleness."
The purposeful destruction of cottages and the ban on domestic industry in some "close" parishes must be viewed from the same perspective.
Moreover, in the regions of newly enclosed larger farms, mainly the
South and East, domestics were gradually replaced by day laborers, and
the remaining servants had to accept ever-shorter terms of service. In
these areas of large-scale grain cultivation, the elimination of the commons, reduced demand for servants, and rapid population growth combined to create a mass of able-bodied paupers lacking alternative outlets

for agricultural day labor and yet unable to work all the year round.[61] In short, a latent relative surplus population was created that could function as a reserve army.

Consequently, the overwhelming majority of rural parishes in southeastern England favored legislation restricting the mobility of labor and a system of poor-relief enforcing work at very low wages. Although Pitt's Act of 1795 somewhat weakened the grip of parish settlement, the law continued to discourage the rural unemployed from seeking work elsewhere. Moreover, the Speenhamland system (and especially its variants, the "Roundsmen" and the "Labor-rate"), introduced in the same year, supplied capitalist farmers with an extensive and very cheap work force. The new poor-relief scheme had the advantage that wage increases were superfluous (or could at least be kept to a minimum), whereas the recipients became more dependent than ever on the authorities, who determined payments on a case-by-case basis. Speenhamland, however, served not only the interests of capitalist farmers. As Raymond Williams stated: "There was always a contradiction in English agrarian capitalism: its economics were those of a market order; its politics were those of a self-styled aristocracy and squirearchy, exerting quite different and 'traditional' disciplines and controls." Only as a last resort did the landed elites use naked power to inculcate notions of hierarchy and authority, because this would have endangered the stability of the social system. Instead, they legitimated their position through a deferential dialectic, a set of reciprocal rights and duties that encouraged popular belief in the reality of paternal benevolence. Poor-relief was one of the most important elements in reconciling the rural proletariat to the subordination of the landlords, who profited fully from the capitalist transformation of agriculture, though they nonetheless were hardly viewed as economic agents. The poor saw the large proprietors primarily in the guise of magistrates, who could virtually dictate the local relief policy and to whom they could appeal against the decisions of the overseers.[62] Thus, Speenhamland was both an instrument for the regulation of the rural labor market and a method of social control largely reliant on personal interaction between the "obedient" poor and a "benevolent" magistracy.

The development of cottage industries posed different problems. The continuing expansion of both home and overseas demand for manufactured goods spurred entrepreneurs to strengthen their grip on the mass of domestic workers. They left no stone unturned in making direct producers dependent on money wages, obliging them to spend more time on industrial activities and reducing the price of their labor. First, the old custom of the workers keeping for themselves some scraps left over from the labor process was made criminal. Numerous embezzlement statutes were passed, most of them subject to the justices of the peace's summary justice, and the severity of these statutes increased steadily. The Act of 1703 relating to the wool, linen, fustian, cotton, and iron industries ordered that a worker found guilty of theft of property entrusted to him be fined twice its value, and in 1746 the costs of prosecution were added to this penalty. Nine years later, it was stipulated that matters previously considered "breaches of contract in husbandry"—a broad category that comprised any possible form of disobedience by the rural work force against their employers, including the embezzlement of tools or materials—would henceforth be considered a criminal offense, punishable by 2 weeks of imprisonment, and by 1777 this term had risen to 3 months. The employers themselves saw to it that the laws were enforced. They set up committees that raised funds to hire inspectors and proceed against offenders. In Gloucestershire, with its extensive rural industry, no less than 70% of all commitments to the county institutions between 1792 and 1809 fell in the category of summary offenses, and of these the most frequent were "breaches of contract in husbandry."[63]

Employers put up a vigorous fight against "leisure preference." According to most contemporary observers, domestic workers were inclined to chose free time instead of extra money income in times of plenty, leading to a "backward-sloping supply-of-labor curve."[64] How can this be reconciled with another complaint raised by eighteenth-century commentators, that the poor were "aping their betters" in pleasures and luxuries? Clearly, if the propensity to produce less when offered more pay was as widespread as most observers claimed, there would have been little purchasing power at all to spend on "extravagancies." "Leisure preference," an "ethic of laziness," or "economic irrationality" all were false, subjective representations of the functioning of the rural labor market; rather, rural spinners, weavers, and colliers still had diametrically opposed ideas to industrial entrepreneurs as to making the most of work time. As long as the process of proletarianization had not yet been completed, the annual labor cycle of many rural workers continued to contain a multiplicity of subsistence activities and strategies, and during the harvest, manufacturing was simply abandoned. The resulting discontinuity in industrial employment naturally clashed with the desires of putting-out merchants and manufacturers to have a large, cheap, and dependable labor force always at hand. Complaints about leisure preference in fact relate to those activities that did not yield a profit for industrial entrepreneurs, and as a result, they were deemed a waste of time.

During the eighteenth century, a series of measures was taken to remedy that evil. "Common custom has established so many Holy-Days," declared John Clayton in his *Friendly Advice to the Poor* (1755), "that few of our Manufacturing Work-Folks are closely and regularly employed above two third Parts of their Time." From the 1760s on, there was a steady growth of standing orders against carnivals from quarter sessions. The game laws, which turned poaching into a summary crime in the eighteenth century, also were used to enforce work discipline in the countryside. According to William Blackstone, writing in 1769, the purpose behind penalizing the taking of rabbits was primarily to prevent "low and indigent persons" from being lured away by the hunt from "their proper employments and callings."[65]

Attacks on leisure preference could produce only tangible effects, however, when incomes were reduced to the level of subsistence. Since most capitalists and economists focused their attention on the export markets, they regarded laborers only as producers and, consequently, felt that low wages were a necessary condition both for gaining a competitive advantage and enforcing work discipline. This last point was strongly emphasized by one commentator in 1786: "It seems to be a law of nature," wrote Joseph Townshend, "that there may always be some to fulfill the most servile, the most wretched and the most ignoble offices in the community. . . . When hunger is either felt or feared the desire of obtaining bread will quickly dispose the mind to undergo the greatest hardships and will sweeten the severest labours." Poor workers were thus highly valued on the condition that their poverty could be converted into profitable employment. Patrick Colquhoun was not alone in distinguishing between poverty and indigence. "Poverty," he wrote, "is the source of wealth, since without poverty there would be no labour and without labour there could be no riches, no refinement, no comfort, and no benefit to those who may be possessed of wealth." Indigence, on the contrary, he considered "one of the greatest calamities which can afflict civil society, since, with certain exceptions of physical inabilities, it generates every thing that is noxious, criminal and vicious in the body politic."[66] The public interest, in other words, required that workers be driven by a discipline of low wages, hard work, and permanent poverty.

New laws against begging and vagabondage demonstrated the upper classes' refusal to tolerate laziness. The Act of 1744 not only consolidated the numerous measures taken over the preceding century but also considerably widened the scope of offenses. Besides empowering magistrates to whip or imprison beggars and "rogues" of both sexes and to place their children with anyone willing to employ them, it authorized justices to send the "idle and disorderly" to a house of correction, with hard labor, for up to a month. The idle and disorderly were a very broad class, "whose basic offence might almost be seen as passive pauperism," to quote Radzinowicz. Indeed, they included, among others, all persons who refused to work for the usual wages. The number of offenses punishable under the vagrancy laws was systematically extended: the Act of 1755 stipulated that anyone might be detained in prison for six days on the mere suspicion of being idle. An act passed in 1783 classed as a rogue anyone found near a warehouse with the intent to steal, and in 1787 those who allowed their families to become chargeable to rates by "neglecting" their work or "squandering" their wages were added to the long list of idle and disorderly.[67]

Although methods of personal control and supervision were gradually superseded by impersonal, market-oriented policing during the second half of the eighteenth century, many workhouses continued to be used as manufactories or as training centers for unskilled workers, particularly in textile areas. The pioneering entrepreneurs of the industrial revolution had difficulty not only in recruiting laborers but also in imprinting new standards of discipline and regularity. The majority of the old established industrial workers, both urban and rural, were utterly averse to moving to the factories. As long as there were still chances for employment in "honorable trades," even if steadily more poorly paid, they did not enter the "dark, Satanic mills," for these were places where they had to submit themselves to an iron discipline. "I found the utmost distaste," one hosier reported as late as 1806,

> on the part of the men to any regular hours or regular habits. . . . The men themselves were considerably dissatisfied, because they could not go in and out as they pleased, and have what holidays they pleased, and go on just as they had been used to do, and were subject during after-hours to the ill-natured observations of other workmen, to such an extent as completely to disgust them with the whole system, and I was obliged to break it up.[68]

Given that they sought to hold production costs as low as possible, it comes as no surprise that many manufacturers first turned to unfree labor. The landlords and clothiers of East Suffolk, for example, erected between 1753 and 1771 nine huge workhouses, called Houses of Industry, to exploit the labor of the poor who were made to pick and prepare wool. Similar initiatives were undertaken in other textile areas during the 1770s and 1780s. At the end of the eighteenth century, Jeremy Bentham even proposed building 250 workhouses, on the principle of the Panopticon, each able to accommodate 2,000 paupers. He had no doubt that his scheme would be profitable, for

What hold can another manufacturer have upon his workmen, equal to what my manufacturer would have upon his? What other master is there that can reduce his workmen, if idle, to a situation next to starving, without suffering them to go elsewhere? What other master is there whose men can never get drunk unless he chooses they should do so? And who, so far from being able to raise their wages by combinations are obliged to take whatever pittance he thinks it most in his interest to allow?[69]

Yet it came to nothing. Entrepreneurs approved of policies designed to mold laborers to the requirements of the market, but they were no longer inclined to use systematic, extraeconomic compulsion to attain this goal. On the one hand, they had learned from past experiences that adult men with no other incentive than punishment were virtually immune to work discipline. On the other hand, they were now in a position to employ women and children who had not been able to make a living since spinning had been mechanized.

Children, in particular, were in great demand by factory owners. They could be employed on a large scale because most operations in the cotton mills required little training and little muscular strength, and so they were an extremely good bargain. Entrepreneurs besieged orphanages and poorhouses in order to gather the "cheapest raw material in the market." The youthful work force found in such institutions offered a further advantage: They could be returned during periods of economic regression.

That women and children comprised the bulk of the labor force in the cotton mills (often up to 75%) did not signify that employers at last had available animate mechanisms who reacted automatically to the stimuli provided. Factory owners complained about the unwillingness and irregularity of child laborers. Although their overseers kept a steady eye on them and did not hesitate to punish them for any mistake at all, the youthful laboring force was still beset with difficulties. Employers thus heartily welcomed workers who brought along their own offspring or those of their kinfolk, and so parental control was extended to the factory. From the point of view of the employers, widows with numerous children were ideal workers. The owners of cotton mills in New Lanark and Catrine in Scotland recruited dozens of such households, and they were not the only ones who openly announced how gladly they would welcome more. Not surprisingly, interest in the schooling of paupers' children diminished rapidly. The founders of charity schools in eighteenth-century England did not so much have the intention of instructing these children as keeping them off the street, keeping them busy, and giving them some industrial training. The factory met all these expectations and more, which explains why the owners saw themselves not only as employers but also as moral crusaders. In any case, the education of poor children in this period mainly consisted of instruction in work discipline. One of its results was that the level of literacy among industrial workers dropped.[70]

The early factory owners, moreover, were constantly harassed by the mobility of their adult laborers. Any means, therefore, that tied the worker to the factory met with their approval. Although tending a spinning machine required not much more than a month's training, many cotton manufacturers, both in England and on the Continent, hired only workers who bound themselves to work for several months for an apprentice's wages. Also, employers lent their workers such large advances on their wages that they could seldom redeem their debts and were consequently tied hand and foot to the factory. Some paternalistic entrepreneurs provided homes, schools, and chapels for their workers in "model villages," but the main purpose behind these humanitarian initiatives was to prevent the labor force from leaving its "patron."[71] In short, capitalism had created a free labor market, but the early factory owners considered variants of unfree labor to be necessary to the smooth functioning of the new industrial apparatus. No wonder that the proletariat equated factories with prisons.

The rise of industrial capitalism also meant the breakdown of former restrictions on the freedom of economic action. The major entrepreneurs needed a labor force whose supply and price were determined by the "natural" laws of a free market. During the eighteenth and early nineteenth centuries, the old paternalistic policy of industrial regulation, implying the maintenance of certain standards and rights, was gradually jettisoned. Numerous measures were taken to deprive skilled workers of what they considered to be a "just and honourable means of subsistence," to make them dependent on money wages, to prevent them from combining against their employers, and to subject them to a strict work discipline—in short to reduce them to commodities. Workers repeatedly and strongly protested against these assaults on their rights—the right to just rewards, the right to have their skills and competence considered, and the right to resist the arbitrary will of employers. The unlimited and uncontrolled introduction of new techniques, conjoined to recruitment on the grand scale of untrained labor, however, increasingly undermined their bargaining position. The abolition of older laws barring machinery and regulating wages and finally in 1814 the repeal of the apprenticeship clauses of the 1563 statute were decisive steps in the triumph of laissez-faire capitalism. Luddism and other labor protests have to be seen in the perspective of this progressive loss of control over the production process, whereby skills were usurped by capitalist entrepreneurs. No doubt the Manchester weavers voiced the feelings of the majority of artisans in 1823 with their criticism of the new industrial policy: "The weaver's qualifications may be considered as his property and support. It is as real property to him as buildings and lands are to others. Like them his qualifications cost time, application and money. There is no point of view (except visible and tangible) wherein they differ."[72]

The cornerstone of the new disciplinary edifice, ensuring capitalist domination over labor, rested on the abrogation of the old poor law. Arguments against outdoor relief abounded by the 1820s. Alongside the excessive cost, the critics reasoned, this system allowed uncontrolled population growth and gave the needy the impression that they had a right to assistance. Nor did the distribution of allowances fit the conception that work was plentiful—even Adam Smith assumed that full employment was the normal state of affairs. Certainly, political economists took note of the many able-bodied workers who were living in destitution or who were regularly out of work, but these phenomena were written off as the fruits of laziness and obstinance.[73] Moreover, the provision of outdoor relief to able-bodied paupers became an obstacle to the growth of a free labor market after the Napoleonic Wars. Both the drastic fall in grain prices and the continuing rationalization of the primary sector meant that capitalist farmers no longer needed an extensive work force. They thus advocated measures that would reduce relief payments and create a "push" from the agricultural counties. The Poor Law Amendment Act of 1834, which established the machinery of Victorian public assistance, did meet their wishes.

The foremost result of the new poor law was that the mobility of the rural reserve army increased. Most of the restrictions laid down by the Act of Settlement and Removal were abolished, and the workhouses were turned into instruments of terror in order to expel redundant wage laborers from the countryside. This policy was deemed all the more necessary because of the difficulties of bringing together capital and labor. Contemporaries were confronted with the paradox of the existence of a reserve army whose means of subsistence were wholly inadequate, whereas entrepreneurs found it difficult to recruit workers. The transition to industrial capitalism did indeed cause a considerable gap in time and space between the formation of a relative surplus population and the eventual redeployment of that population to new economic activities, although for reasons totally different from those advanced at the time. In any case, the authorities employed every means at their disposal to force workers to accept any job in any place for any wage.

The New Poor Law, which rested on the principle of less eligibility, ensured that relief was granted only to those in utter destitution. It institutionalized the vital minimum. Some exceptions aside, henceforth no support would be given to an able-bodied indigent unless he was prepared to enter a "well-regulated" workhouse. Such a step was considered to "be a self-acting test of the claim of the applicant. . . . If the claimant does not comply with the terms on which relief is given to the destitute, he gets nothing; and if he does comply, the compliance proves the truth of the claim—namely, his destitution." In contrast with earlier workhouses, the promotors of which focused on the profitable employment of unfree labor, the new deterrent houses were used as indirect means of increasing the supply of free (but cheap) labor. Or at least, that was the intent. It became clear quite soon, however, that large numbers of paupers, including able-bodied adults, voluntarily entered the workhouses, because even an iron discipline is preferable to starvation, which led some commentators to complain about the leniency of the new regime.[74]

Thus, the breakthrough of the capitalist mode of production obviated the need for legal compulsion to turn idlers into docile and profitable workers. Henceforth, the poor were free to work or not, as there was no direct force applied. But able-bodied paupers had to provide for themselves and for their families without help from the parish so that actually they were given the choice between subjecting themselves to capital and entering a well-regulated workhouse. That capitalism, by imposing the discipline of wages, became the coordinating force in policing the proletariat does not signify, however, that the poor-law reformers of 1834 primarily intended to favor industrial (and overall) economic growth. The new deterrent attitude toward public assistance reflected the anxieties and fears of the gentry and the middling sort of people rather than the profit-maximizing impulses of capitalists.

Although during the late eighteenth and early nineteenth centuries, the landed elites continued to take seriously their social responsibilities, the widening gulf between rich and poor undermined the ideal of an organic community. As gentlemen, the rich still wanted to uphold the illusion of paternalism, but as large estate-owners they felt that property ought to be protected in a period of massive pauperization. Whether or not crime and disorder were really on the increase is rather irrelevant here. The point is that men of property in rural areas encouraged the creation of voluntary associations for the prosecution of felons, giving expression to their fears of a breakdown of society. Yet the gentry were not readily inclined to abandon a personalized administration of relief that maintained the chain of connection linking the ranks of rural society and, consequently, that reinforced their legitimacy. The troubled years of the early nineteenth century even saw an increased need for methods of control based on deference and face-to-face relations. Hence, land-lords continued to form a barrier between the poor and the rate-paying occupiers, mostly tenant farmers, who insisted on curtailing relief. The widespread rural disturbances of 1830–1831 provided a decisive discon-tinuity. As Peter Dunkley pointed out, "The fact of riot on such a vast scale . . . seemed proof enough that the resources of the old order, in-cluding popular patronage and paternal discipline, were no longer suf-ficient to ensure the content and obedience that were essential for the maintenance of stability in the strongholds of landed power." For the gentry, further identification with a system of support that no longer functioned properly had become a threat. They were won over to a new poor law: faceless, distant, professional, and uniform.[75] Growing social unrest, moreover, led many county magistrates to abandon whatever reservations they may have had toward the use of police forces for im-posing order. They remained as opposed to the creation of a profes-sional body based on French centralized practice as their counterparts in the eighteenth century were, but they did assent to the Rural Con-stabulary Act of 1839, which gave them the opportunity to establish po-lice forces if they wished.[76]

This does not mean that the ideal of reciprocity in social relations no longer influenced aristocratic and gentry behavior. For decades to come, the landed elites attempted to preserve the deferential dialectic through the institution of charities for the "deserving" poor. They founded coal and blanket clubs, subscribed to soup kitchens, provided Christmas din-ners, granted allotment gardens, and so on.[77] The argument that such initiatives were nothing but the residue of an obsolescent paternalism is unsound. Assistances dispensed on a personal and localized basis played an important role, albeit a diminishing one, in moralizing and controlling the rural proletariat during this period of fundamental change.

The attitudes of the middling sort of people toward the paupers were much harsher than those of the traditional elites. For this amorphous group (comprising various urban strata, including small capitalists, professionals, and artisans) aristocratic paternalism was totally point-less—it neither helped regulate city life nor made sense of the newly evolving class structure. On the one hand, the lower middle class did not have the power or the financial means to exercise a fatherly au-thority over the rapidly multiplying poor of the towns. On the other hand, they confronted, daily and directly, the devastating effects of in-dustrial and urban growth: pauperism, crime, prostitution, drunken-ness, and other "diseases." The fears induced by these social problems led the petty bourgeoisie to distance themselves more than ever from the proletariat, criminalizing what they took to be bad morals and advocating the strict application of the vagrancy laws and the disciplining of prisoners by hard work; in short, they called for an efficient system of preventive policing. It is not that every campaign against "vicious, debauched and profane people" was prompted by partisan interest; but, in any event, the radical efforts of the reform movement to impose a new morality on the rest of society were perfectly compatible with the defense of property and the subordination of the urban proletariat.

Idlers in general and vagrants in particular were the select targets of the "Evangelical policemen." The Philanthropic Society, founded in London in 1788, described such people as "a class which belongs to no rank of the civil community, they are excommunicates in police, extra-social, extra-civil, extra-legal; they are links which have fallen off the chain of society, and which are going to decay, injure and obstruct the movements of the whole *machine*." The social crisis of the late eighteenth and early nineteenth centuries gave a further impetus to the creation of societies preaching the gospel of contentment and subordination. The new apostles disclaimed any intention other than philanthropy, but most of their leaders were members of the Clapham Sect, uniting businessmen and politicians. It was not for nothing that William Wilberforce in 1801 founded the Society for the Suppression of Vice and the Encouragement of Religion and Virtue under the motto "When bad men combine, the Good must Associate" or that he advocated low wages, denied the workers the right to strike, and was in favor of the Combination Laws of 1799–1800.[78]

During the early nineteenth century, many Christian philanthropists came to accept Malthus's conclusions that the growth of population was the real cause of poverty and that the poor law actually aggravated the evil it was supposed to remedy. John Bird Sumner, bishop of Chester, even published a treatise in which he zealously defended Malthus. Also, he followed Colquhoun in distinguishing poverty, "both honourable and comfortable," from indigence, "commonly the state into which intemperence and want of prudent foresight push poverty." Working people themselves, consequently, were responsible for their condition. They had to exercise control over their own numbers, put into operation preventive checks, avoid imprudent marriages; for, as one commentator explained in 1824, what their social superiors could do for them was "as dust of the balance compared with what they can do for themselves." The doctrine of individual self-restraint implied that alms giving and provision for the poor were fundamentally wrong. Thus David Ricardo objected to proposals for sending pauper children to schools of industry, because "if parents felt assured that any asylum would be provided for their children, in which they would be treated with humanity and tenderness, there would be then no check to that increase of population which was so apt to take place among the labouring classes." Harriet Martineau, a most devoted disciple of Malthus, went as far as to denounce the custom of giving coals and blankets to the poor at Christmas, since this encouraged them "to multiply beyond their means."[79]

The medical profession in no small measure contributed to the stigmatization of the proletariat. More and more physicians ascribed the diseases contracted by the laboring poor to their immorality and lack of self-discipline. John Mason Good, physician of Cold Bath Fields prison, bluntly declared in 1795 that the poor were liable to disease, because "they feel not, from want of education, the same happy exertion of delicacy, honour and moral sentiment which everywhere else is to be met with." Thomas Percival, the first doctor who investigated labor conditions in factories, similarly mixed medical and class categories. Although he admitted that workers in large cotton mills were particularly susceptible to contagious fevers, he insisted that the poor could not be cured in their homes: they needed moral therapy as well, and this medicine could be administered only in institutions that promoted hygienic asceticism.[80]

Attempts by evangelicals and other reformers (such as the Dissenters and the Benthamites) to impress their moral standards on the urban proletariat had little effect. However, they did undermine paternalist orthodoxies and reinforce "the entrepreneurial ideal of the self-made man, the capitalist version of the puritan pilgrim," to quote Perkin.[81] In effect, the belief of the middling sort in the moral value of work—God helps those who help themselves—and their emphasis on self-discipline as the prerequisite of upward social mobility led to the conclusion that destitution was the reward of idleness and, consequently, justified deterrent attitudes toward poor-relief. Furthermore they played an important role in bringing members of Parliament to cast aside their deep-rooted prejudices against a uniformed, preventive police. It was apprehension for the security of property rather than fear of disorder that was the necessary condition for the creation of the Metropolitan Police in 1829 and the establishment of police forces in provincial towns after 1839. The police, however, had the task of preventing crime (especially theft), and since the middling sort closely associated popular leisure and illegal behavior, the key institutions of proletarian neighborhood and recreation were put under constant surveillance. A policeman, in short, was expected to serve as a sort of "domestic missionary," an instrument of moral reform and urban discipline.[82] Although campaigns against public-house gambling, Sunday drinking, and other proletarian passtimes were motivated primarily by fear that such activities would spark crime and disorder, the advocates of this style of policing unwittingly served the interests of capitalist entrepreneurs, for whom the war on popular leisure was just another means of gaining control over their labor force.

ORDER AND AUTHORITY: FRANCE, 1750–1850

The social problem manifested itself in a wholly different fashion in France than in England. In both countries, poverty grew during the century after 1750, but in France this process was not accompanied by massive proletarianization. French authorities were therefore less interested in regulating the labor market than in maintaining control over the paupers.

In the second half of the eighteenth century, the combination of land fragmentation with increasing surplus extraction by the absolutist State and the nobility left innumerable peasants on holdings too small to provide subsistence. For these *manouvriers*, an "economy of makeshifts" became their sole means of retaining their parcel of land and thus avoiding complete expropriation: They needed supplementary income from industry, seasonal migration, or begging. It was certainly no accident that in 1762 the government proclaimed an edict that emancipated rural textile production from guild supervision. The displacement of industry to the countryside was already perceptible in the seventeenth century, particularly in the North and Northeast, but from 1700 on, the movement accelerated and extended to other regions. There can be little doubt that the government primarily intended to break down restrictions on the national economy, including the monopolies of urban corporations, but it cherished the hope that in rurual industrialization lay the remedy for poverty. This was also the view of Turgot, who clearly understood that the precarious situation of the small proprietor was the core of the social problem. The *ateliers de charité* that sprouted in the 1770s offered cottars needed ancillary income during those months when there was neither local work nor opportunity for seasonal labor. However, the monarchy did not have sufficient funds at its disposal, and the provincial elites were often unwilling to contribute financially, and so it was impossible to establish a nationwide network of workshops. The meager significance of this form of relief can be seen, in that all the *ateliers de charité* together provided work for only 31,000 men, women, and children during the hard winter of 1788–1789.[83]

During the eighteenth century, many small proprietors turned to seasonal labor to feed their families. A certain degree of mobility was inherent in the economies of many regions. However, the problem was that the departments with opportunities for casual laborers also attracted those who had had to abandon their homes altogether, so that patterns of vagrancy necessarily coincided with patterns of labor migration. Fear of the *mauvais pauvres* mirrored itself in legislation. The Edict of 1764 provided stiff punishments for vagabonds and encouraged the provincial assemblies to create *dépôts de mendicité* in order to discipline sturdy beggars through a regime of regular work. When those instructions proved fruitless, a general ordinance was published in 1767 that required the construction of *dépôts* in every province of the kingdom. A few years later, most *généralités* had three or four *dépôts*, holding between 100 and 200 offenders. Theoretically these institutions were houses of correction for "social renegades," but in practice it was impossible to distinguish clearly between seasonal migrants and beggars or vagrants, because many migrants depended on alms to stay alive on their long journeys.[84] Some enlightened persons, notably Turgot, argued that repression was inadequate to exterminate mendicity and that the real remedy lay in economic reforms,[85] but such considerations did not convince a ruling class that needed extraeconomic compulsion to extract a surplus and, consequently, was primarily interested in maintaining order.

It was left to the Revolution to proclaim the fundamental right of subsistence for the laboring poor. The Convention tried to solve social problems by uniform, legislative methods: nationalization of poor relief, confiscation and sale of the property of the old charitable institutions and the monastic orders, abolition of ecclesiastical tithes and feudal dues, division of the commons, and so on. However, since the government could not raise enough money to replace abolished revenues, while having to divert ever more resources to military uses, the revolutionary ideal of *bienfaisance* (as opposed to the charity of the old regime) was but cold comfort for the poor who now had to rely exclusively on state intervention. Not surprisingly, the Thermidorians were willing enough to resume the policies of the *ancien régime*, albeit in a more systematic way. The laws of 1796 established public assistance on a local basis. In each *commune*, two secular institutions were created, one for the administration of all charities and the other for the distribution of outdoor relief. Although the direction of these institutions was in the hands of municipal authorities, the central government soon exercised iron control through the prefect.[86] In France, in contrast with England, the system was not abolished during the nineteenth century, and outdoor relief constituted part of a wider and larger effort by the State's agents to settle the relative surplus population.

The fact that public assistance in France fulfilled functions that were essentially those of control does not mean that there was no interest in the profitable employment of the poor. Both before and after the Revolution many municipalities tried to make the *ateliers de charité* into factories. These attempts to stimulate the economy generally miscarried, however, because the competitive advantages enjoyed by French industry rested in large measure on highly specialized handicrafts. Consequently, employment of the poor on a large scale had nothing to contribute to France's industrial growth. Most paupers were unschooled laborers who produced work of inferior quality for which no market could be found. Even if the authorities resolved to give them training in order to manufacture quality goods in the *ateliers,* these efforts nearly always ran up against the opposition of local entrepreneurs. Most *manufactures des pauvres* thus sooner or later turned into asylums for unemployed paupers who did not satisfy the formal requirements for outdoor relief; they had to remain in the institution from morning to night, and they were subjected to an iron discipline in return for a free meal and (sometimes) a little cash. Even in cities where the factory system developed, mainly in the North, the *ateliers de charité* served only as temporary reception centers, keeping the unemployed off the streets.[87] In short, the French poor-relief system continued to function as an instrument of social control rather than as a means for regulating the labor market.

The historical necessity of subjecting the surplus population to supervision and management explains why public assistance committees in nineteenth-century France categorized the needy in such fine detail. Individuals who depended on bureaucratized forms of support because of some physical or mental infirmity were sent to institutions separate from those for individuals with irregular lives outside the framework of the family: the sick and the unhealthy, the blind and the deaf, the insane, the aged, the orphaned, abandoned children, and beggars. Outdoor relief was reserved for those who followed the rules: a "normal" family pattern and a moral character without blemish. *Ne pas défaire les liens de la famille,* "familial bonds are not to be broken," ran the motto. This approach to outdoor relief implied that the overseers of the poor exercised regulatory and repressive functions. In the large towns in particular, control was deemed to be an absolute necessity because the growing tendency toward spatial segregation meant that the elites knew less and less about how the lower classes actually lived. They belonged, as it were, to another world, the world of the ghetto, in which the "right sort" of people never set foot. It was an urban jungle in need of systematic exploration and constant supervision.

The overseers of the poor did do their jobs: They regularly visited and then revisited needy people on relief, setting up files case by case and noting down the characters of the families at hand. Protest against these disciplinary methods was ruled out, for as the poor-law administration stipulated: "Workers who apply for relief put themselves into the position of minors, of necessity forsaking their rights as citizens, and as fathers." Unexpected visits, interrogation of neighbors, consultation with doctors and parish priests all went into a comprehensive program of inspection, based on the principle that the laboring poor must at the same time be both supervised and reformed. They had to be taught how to subsist at the least expense. Exposing their "irrational" spending patterns individualized misery and reduced it to a matter of morals, the obvious result of personal failings.[88]

The physician became indispensible, as the one who studied scientifically the living conditions of the lower classes: their sexuality, their diet, their dwellings, and their clothes. And no one was more competent to regulate these aspects than a physician, for he paid attention not only to the physical man but also to the moral man. Many members of the medical profession aided public authorities by conducting large-scale surveys and devising means of "lancing the social boil." Certainly, not every program of "biomanagement" was intended to fulfill sociopolitical functions, but they did serve as theoretical justifications for the social engineering of the State. As Foucault explained, "A politico-medical grasp upon the population came about, pigeonholing them with prescriptions not only for their illnesses but also for the general contours of their way of life."[89]

Control of the population in general and of the laboring poor in particular remained the overriding concern of the authorities. The role of the police in French society can hardly be exaggerated. Many police regulations dated from the seventeenth century and even from the time of Francis I, but from the late eighteenth century on, they grew increasingly more comprehensive and detailed. Hundreds of instructions and even a half dozen *traités de police* and *dictionnaires de la police* were composed in order to make clear to the *commissaires* whom and what they had to keep under surveillance. And these directives were followed, especially in Paris and the larger provincial towns. The police patrolled the wards with large concentrations of workers. Lists were drawn up of lodging houses and pubs and were regularly revised, noting what sorts of people frequented which establishments. Street musicians and other potential firebrands received special attention, with personal police dossiers. For the same reasons, popular festivities were closely supervised: How many participants? How did they behave? In short, the police put under surveillance anyone belonging to the "dangerous classes."[90]

At first glance, it would seem that the French and English police performed similar tasks during this period. Nonetheless, the differences were clearly pronounced. In England, it was primarily concern about crime that won propertied men to the idea of professional policing; proposals to manage and deploy the new forces from the center were never implemented, however. By contrast, the *raison d'être* of the French police was the security of the State. Hence, their major task, both before and after the Revolution, was not to prevent petty crime but to repress political opposition. The police in general and secret agents in particular were the eyes and ears of a ruling class fearful of plots and political upheavals.[91]

Although the lower classes were viewed as potential troublemakers who had to be controlled at all costs, many members of the enlightened community advocated measures that would benefit the physical health and procreative powers of the rural masses. They thought that France was menaced by a declining birthrate, and their anxieties were all the greater because of their conviction that population was an index of national well-being and, consequently, played an important role in determining the power of the State. Although demographic growth quickened somewhat after the turn of the nineteenth century, the possibility of a diminishing population concerned the ruling class for several decades to come. The greatest attention was devoted to the countryside, the prime basket of a healthy people—in contrast with the urban graveyard, the *ville-tombeau*. This fixation on a rising population led to the sharp condemnation of celibacy, family planning, and masturbation and to investigations into fluctuations in mortality, in particular, infant mortality and its relationship to wet nursing.[92]

While English moralists and scientists developed "destructive" ideas regarding the growth of the proletariat and fulminated against so-called inconsiderate marriages, their French counterparts took initiatives directed toward the "improvement" of census figures. These divergent approaches were undoubtedly determined in part by the demand for soldiers for France's many wars. Nothing generated so much concern as the health of the soldier, for official inquiries showed that the height of recruits was dropping, a phenomenon that was not interpreted by contemporaries as the result of a declining living standard but as a clear sign of the degeneration of the "race," a threat to the French nation.[93]

These "hygienist" considerations were absent in England. The philanthropist Jonas Hanway alone made proposals, during the 1750s and 1760s, in a similar vein: to save lives in the interest of the State and to turn prostitutes into mothers, domestic servants into parents, and poor boys into sailors and soldiers on whom the security of the State depended. He also argued that the population was inadequate to meet the needs of the State and that marriage was a civil duty.[94] Hanway's "Christian mercantilism," however, was obsolete by the end of the eighteenth century. Populationist concepts gave way to Malthusian rhetoric, which matched more closely the current reality, the rapid growth of the proletariat.

The predominance of small units of production based on the household, in association with the fear of a mobile labor force and the belief that the power of the State depended on its population, assigned to the family a central place in French political and intellectual thought. The family and, consequently, marriage were not only the ideal nurseries of population growth; they also, if well regulated, were the foundation of a strong state. Order in the family signified order in the State, for authority within the family and authority within society at large were inextricably bound together. For Auguste Comte, Louis de Bonald, and many others, any erosion of the structure of authority within the family threatened the State. The family endured only through the authority of the father, and if he failed, the established order was endangered.[95] The central government thus had to carry out a policy that strengthened the pyramid of familial subordinations. Hence almost every article in the *code civil* relating to the family reinforced the power of the husband over his wife and of parents over their children. It was no mere coincidence that French authors writing on patriotism frequently described the *patrie* as a family. Such ideas answered to perfection the aspirations of political authorities for stability, which, after the revolutionary period, was deemed more essential than ever.

Marriage came to be seen as the preeminent instrument for the "sedentarizing" and pacification of the laboring poor. Numerous charitable societies were founded with the sole aim of regularizing free unions. The foremost task of the members of St. Jean-François Régis, actively supported by the government, was to enable proletarian couples to obtain the documents and to pay the fees required for a civil marriage. The explanation was

> A man and a woman living in sin feel right only in those places where vice and criminality prosper. They do not save. Hunger and sickness seize them. They commonly do not care for their children, yet if they do have contact with them, they pervert them. In contrast, if a man and a woman who live together outside of the law do marry, then they leave their sullied lodgings and set up properly. Their first concern becomes removing their children from the foster homes where they had placed them. Married fathers and mothers form *families*.[96]

In other words, stabilization of the household maintained order and eliminated poverty. Of necessity, solutions had to be found for the unavoidable waste, the *déchêts de famille,* and hence the universalization of the *tour* for foundlings in the late eighteenth and early nineteenth centuries. This ingenious mechanism, which guaranteed anonymity, allowed the babies of "unfit" mothers to be saved for the nation, without causing scandal.[97]

School constituted the necessary complement of the family. Poor-relief was refused to parents who failed to educate their children. School instilled obedience, orderliness, and morality in poor children, values that the children would then, like missionaries, pass on to their parents and even their social milieu. Children in school were expected to be "the antidote, the vaccine injected into the sick and deficient family." Through the interaction of school and family, the sons and daughters of the laboring poor in France were themselves given the role of educators.[98] However, the instruction that these children received could not be exemplary in its thoroughness, as La Chalotais, the procureur-général of the parlement of Rennes and a correspondent of Voltaire, declared in 1763: "The well-being of society requires that the knowledge of the people stretch no further than that necessary for their employment." Some notable exceptions aside, the *philosophes* felt that the main objectives of popular education were to offer poor children physical training, to prepare them for the rigors of life, to teach them some skills suited to their *état,* and to inculcate social and civic values, especially warm patriotic feelings.[99] The Frères des Écoles Chrétiennes, who had established a nationwide network of elementary schools by the end of the eighteenth century, agreed. Their program was to take poor children from the streets, to catechize them, to reform their manners, and to prepare them for regular work.[100] The bias in eighteenth-century England was against popular education as such and toward industrial training; in contrast, considerable efforts were made in France to use schools as socializing agencies for the lower classes. It is impossible to assess the ideological impact of the eighteenth-century schools on the French poor, but in any event they greatly helped to reduce illiteracy. Demands for state control and centralization of education, associated with patriotism, were formulated and attained at an early date in France. The reasons for this were exposed by François Guizot in 1833, when he passed his law requiring every village to have a primary school: "We have tried to create in every commune a moral force which the government can use as needed." And the inspection machinery did see to it that teachers preached submission, respect for the law, and love of order.[101]

The fact that maintenance of order was the central objective of French social policy did not mean that the agents of the State turned a deaf ear to the demands of capitalist entrepreneurs for the "liberty of labor."

Certainly, the small workshop remained the predominant unit of production until far into the nineteenth century, but from the 1720s on, changes in the legal framework of industry gradually narrowed the workers' room for maneuver. The edicts of 1723 and 1729 only reinforced the measures taken in 1670 by Colbert for the purpose of restricting the rights of journeymen and apprentices, but in 1749 the government went much further: All industrial workers were prohibited from leaving their employers unless they had received a *billet de congé*. A quarter-century later, Turgot stipulated that wage laborers henceforth were subject to the same statutes as servants were, which meant that their masters listed their names, which were open to the inspection of the police. This new regulation was closely connected to the abolition of trade corporations, which hitherto had functioned as a means of surveillance. Although Turgot's edicts were soon repealed in 1776, there actually was no way back. Within the next four years, new legislation broke down many corporate restrictions, and in 1791 the Law d'Allarde finally and definitively suppressed all guilds. The "abolition of privilege," however, did not mean that the workers were free to do as they pleased. The Law d'Allarde banned the secret societies of journeymen, and the Le Chapelier Law, which was passed in the same year, forbade workers from forming coalitions under penalty of heavy fines and imprisonment.[102]

Yet, unlike their English counterparts, the French ruling classes were not inclined to suppress all obstacles to the growth of a free labor market. They actively favored industrialization and commercialization, but they continued to subordinate economic questions to political concerns—quite understandably, for France experienced three revolutions and 10 constitutional changes between the end of the old regime and 1848. Taking into account that this turbulent period was also an age of pauperism, it comes as no surprise that French governments were so concerned with the stability of the State. Not the workers per se but the impoverished and unruly mass as a whole constituted the "social problem." Consequently the family, school, medical profession, police, and poor-relief were the privileged channels through which the State attempted to sedentarize, control, and pacify its subjects.

THE LIMITS OF SOCIAL CONTROL

The most important question of all remains: did the ruling classes and their subalterns among the middling sort succeed in domesticating the proletariat? Taking into account our present state of knowledge, it is risky to generalize. Nevertheless, it seems clear that three interrelated factors limited the effectiveness of the new modes of discipline created during the early modern period: the continuing presence of many transitional forms between the relatively independent small producer and the fully proletarianized worker; the lack of unanimity among the major constellations of power, each of which had its own programs reflecting its own interests; and proletarian resistance to policing, both collectively and individually.

Although numerous cottagers and artisans came to rely on wage work for their survival, most proletarians continued to be members of part-time labor households drawing on multiple sources of income. The agents of the State in many countries on the Continent frequently intervened to protect small peasant proprietors in order to levy their own taxes on them. Economic factors too played a role in retarding the "commodification" of labor power, on the Continent as well as in England. So long as they concentrated on the external market and (as a result) regarded the lower orders essentially as producers, the capitalists sought to hire persons living in households that obtained a substantial proportion of their income from subsistence activities or petty commodity production. Indeed, the ability of such households to meet their material needs in part through their own productive activities allowed employers to pay wages that were below the biological minimum wage. At the same time, however, the predominance of "income-pooling" households among proletarian households prevented the capitalists from exercising complete control over their workers. Certainly, numerous efforts were made to render direct producers more dependent on money wages, but such a policy had its limits: if the majority of proletarian households were deprived of all sources of income outside the context of capitalist production, they had to be paid wages that covered most of the costs of their reproduction. Thus pressures to maintain part-time proletarian household patterns were found alongside counterpressures to increase the commodification of labor power, although the latter assumed ever-growing importance.[103]

As long as proletarianization was incomplete, capitalists required other power groups to develop and implement the social policies that would enforce work discipline and regulate the labor market. In effect, the periods and regions in which capital most rapidly forced its way into the productive sphere were also those that saw the greatest activity by the public authorities to reeducate the laboring poor. During the second quarter of the sixteenth century, the triumph of commercial capitalism led many western European towns, in particular in south Germany and in the southern Netherlands, to create a system of poor-relief that provided employers with sufficiently cheap labor. The Dutch Republic, the economic giant of Europe during the first half of the seventeenth century, pioneered in penology by erecting workhouses that accentuated the profitable employment of the "idle" poor. Nowhere else in early modern Europe was there established a more efficient machinery to regulate the labor market than in England, the first country to see the rise of agrarian capitalism and the breakthrough of industrial capitalism: the Statute of Artificers (1563), the Elizabethan Poor Law, the Act of Settlement and Removal (1662), and eventually the New Poor Law (1834). The clergy, for their part, both in Catholic and Protestant countries, played an important role throughout the early modern period, enforcing the work ethic and changing the attitudes and values of the lower orders regarding family life, leisure, and recreation. In short, political and ecclesiastical authorities devised new modes of discipline that met the interests of capitalist entrepreneurs. This does not signify, however, that they deliberately intended to mold the propertyless masses to the requirements of the market or to condition them into accepting and practicing moral standards that would sustain the reproduction of the capital–labor relationship.

In discussing the issue of social control, attention must be paid to the main preoccupations of the various power groups. Although the lurching growth of the proletariat put rural and urban entrepreneurs in a position to apply downward pressure on wages and impose work discipline on their employees, that process confronted State and Church with problems of control. Central and local governments had a goal of their own, the maintenance of order, which was an outgrowth of their primarily political objectives, and so they were inclined to develop punitive controls and penal policies to deter potentially dangerous idlers. This intervention served the interests of employers insofar as it entailed a psychological war for access to men's and women's labor: badging, whipping, branding, and confinement not only had physical implications; they also helped segregate people with "given" behavioral characteristics, particularly idleness, by identifying the bearer and labeling that person as a deviant. If the governing classes were carried away by their anxieties and fears, however, they completely subordinated demands for disciplined labor to their concerns for an ordered hierarchy, thereby slowing down capitalist development. Protestant and Catholic reformers defended the new principles of secular regulation and punishment, but only to achieve their own ends: destroying vestigial paganism and imposing uniform standards of belief. Political authorities in turn supported the crusade of the clergy against profanity, idleness, drunkenness, licentiousness, and other "disorders of the poor" because they hoped that ecclesiastical discipline would help keep the proper-tyless masses under control. The "reformation of manners" was not to be imposed on the political nation, however. Just as the Puritan desire for a holy commonwealth, based on local self-government by godly lay-men, was unacceptable to the English ruling class, so the constant in-terference of the *dévôts* in public affairs was incompatible with French absolutism. In sum, then, the objectives of State and Church did not always coincide, nor were they necessarily consonant with those of pri-vate entrepreneurs. This relative autonomy meant that there was no co-ordinated social policy supported by every group within the constellation of power, designed exclusively to underpin the growth of capitalism.

England was the only European country in which efforts toward pol-icing came to be embedded primarily within the workings of the econ-omy itself. In effect, the iron discipline of wages is the supreme in-strument of social control. As Karl Marx wrote:

> The organization of the capitalist process of production, once fully developed, breaks down all resistance. The constant generation of a relative surplus-population keeps the law of supply and demand of labour, and therefore keeps wages, in a rut that corresponds with the wants of capital. The dull compulsion of economic relations completes the subjection of the labourer to the capitalist. Direct force, outside economic conditions, is of course still used, but only ex-ceptionally. In the ordinary run of things, the labourer can be left to the "nat-ural laws of production" i.e. to his dependence on capital.[104]

Yet the modes of appropriating surplus value in the labor process were necessary but by no means sufficient conditions to reproduce the sub-jection of labor to capital. This domination requires, as Lazonick has argued, the development of the capitalist system, tending to ensure the appropriate reproduction of labor, not only in the labor process, but also through a variety of institutions that are not under the direct control of capital.[105] A number of historians have recently focused on this issue, drawing explicit links between social policies and the economic, politi-cal, and cultural characteristics of capitalist societies. It is apparent from their studies that social policies are not purely humanitarian enterprises. But there is a tendency in some of these studies to explain all political and cultural developments in terms of the needs of the capitalist sys-tem.[106] Although an analysis of theories regarding social control in the later nineteenth and twentieth centuries falls outside the scope of this chapter, it is essential to ask whether or not the different groups in the constellation of power in England pursued similar objects with regard to policing between 1750 and 1850.

All the available evidence points in the same (not unexpected) direc-tion: social control meant different things to different men during the

Great Transformation. Reforms in social administration were riddled with class attitudes, but they cannot be interpreted as the result of some grand design. The mechanisms of control created by the agents of the State and the organizers of various social agencies were inspired by very mixed motives. The fears and anxieties induced by the rapidly growing numbers and discontents of the lower orders played as important a role as did the demands for labor regulation. In effect, none among the landed aristocracy, industrial capitalists, or incipient petty bourgeoisie in the towns could perceive the social problem as a whole. It follows that the proletariat as such did not constitute a relevant category for those who had property, power, authority, and influence. Rather, different manifestations of the proletariat were subjected to control by different social agencies for widely divergent reasons. Many members of the upper classes and the middling sort were concerned with the "natural" inclination of the laboring poor toward crime and sedition; others labeled them the ungodly who had to be rescued for religion; and still others were worried about their ignorance, dirtiness, and viciousness, fearing degeneration of the race. Industrial capitalists alone regarded the proletariat first and foremost as labor power, but by themselves they did not dispose of the means of control. There is no doubt that most reforms in social administration contributed to the subjection of labor to capital, but that was often an unintended consequence. It must be emphasized, moreover, that there was no unanimity among factory owners on important issues such as child labor and the education of the poor. Conservative measures directed toward maximum short-term exploitation and repression frequently clashed with more "enlightened" approaches that focused on the reproduction of the work force and on long-term class relations.[107] In short, policing was not a linear, continuous, purposeful, and unidimensional process wherein different yet like-minded elites developed mechanisms to control those target groups upon whose position they could agree.

The laboring poor were not passive recipients of outside forces and influences. There is abundant evidence that the proletariat stubbornly resisted all forms of policing that limited its freedom of action. Because work is the central experience of the proletariat, it comes as no surprise that most struggles were fought around the formal and real subjection of labor to capital. Employers attempted to cut daily wages or piece rates, impose new forms of disputes procedures, intensify the rhythm of work, increase the subdivision of labor, and introduce new machinery. Each of the steps taken by capital at one time or another to reduce the price of labor and increase its subordination encountered vigorous opposition. Wage contests, "bargaining by riot," strikes, and other collective actions, along with individual resistance—embezzlement, weaving more loosely, reeling false, and so on—did not halt the development of capitalism, but they prevented employers from destroying every semblance of worker autonomy. Capitalist control of the labor process was never fully realized; it always remained problematic. Time and time again, new means of labor regulation and discipline had to be devised, and these newer constraints in turn became points of conflict and struggle.[108]

Resistance to policing manifested itself not only in the sphere of production. Struggles over political and cultural norms and practices were as central an aspect of proletarian self-assertion as were struggles over the labor process. Certainly, the propertyless masses found it increasingly difficult to generate and defend their own values and attitudes. The wide range of variations (chronological, geographical, and social) presented by early-modern policing should not obscure the fact that all nonproletarian groups in one way or another, whether consciously or not, participated in the development of institutions through which the hegemony of the ruling class was transmitted. Yet the elites and their subalterns among the middling sort did not succeed in producing a docile proletariat. Neither political and cultural repression nor psychological manipulation accomplished this goal. Many examples demonstrate that the laboring poor rejected, evaded, distorted, adapted, or accepted the dictates of the upper classes according to their own interests. The values and attitudes of the proletariat around 1850 undoubtedly differed from those of their counterparts at the turn of the sixteenth century, but the changes cannot be explained simply in terms of successful policies of social control. Rather, cultural transformation was a part of a continually shifting dynamic between resistance and subordination whereby the common people adjusted their survival strategies to the new forces and relations of production that were shaping their daily lives.

There were areas on which neither the State nor the Church and neither the employer nor the philanthropist had any real hold, because these areas were essential elements of sociability patterns and relational networks, the maintenance of which was of crucial importance in the struggle for survival. For instance, the public drinking house was simultaneously a place of domesticity, refreshment, and entertainment, a house of call, a shop, a newsroom, and so on. Going to the pub was the most rational means of satisfying in the cheapest possible way a host of essential needs. Hence the numerous attempts by secular governments, ecclesiastical authorities, and middle-class reformers to subject the pub to social control never achieved the results desired. The laboring poor not only found devious and effective ways to bypass legal constraints, but they also turned the moral denunciations of their supposed antisocial sociability into positive values: their drinking culture strengthened just that solidarity that was a fundamental part of their own life-style.[109]

Nor was the importance or the function of a discipline-wielding institution determined in advance; in many cases, it was transformed by the active involvement of the proletariat. English Sunday schools, for example, were intended to be instruments of social control, but the proletariat was also able to realize their own interests via these institutions.[110] One could argue that educators imposed on working-class children habits of thrift, diligence, orderliness, cleanliness, and punctuality, thereby playing the game of the upper classes and the lower-middle strata. Though this may be true, one must bear in mind that the laboring poor, precisely because of their precarious position and permanent insecurity, aspired to respectability and self-improvement. This explains why "in both ideological and institutional terms, thrift was . . . an outgrowth of working-class attitudes towards moral and social independence and stability, and not merely a habit thrust on them by other social groups."[111] Capitalist relations of production meant that securing some autonomy required practicing certain values that were preached by the bourgeoisie. The leaders of the labor movement therefore frequently developed strategies that—unintentionally—subjected body and soul to controls resembling those desired by the dominant classes. It does not follow that their purposes were parallel. Thus, the authorities in England and the leaders of the labor movement railed against street soccer, both of them using terms such as *barbarous recklessness* and *supreme folly*. Delves, however, has shown that the similarities were only in appearance, "for the objections and objectives of the working class critics of popular recreation were antithetical to those of the middle classes."[112]

The proletariat disciplined themselves in more than one respect. Current research indicates that in the eighteenth and early nineteenth centuries the lower orders turned more frequently than before to the apparatus of repression. It would be a mistake to attribute this change in attitude to the efforts toward social control of the policymakers or middle-class reformers. Rather, proletarianization and pauperization raised the levels of intolerance prevalent among the laboring poor toward the unruly lives of their own families, while undermining the effectiveness of infrajudicial solutions. Husbands who were unwilling to work or who squandered their wages were hauled into court by their wives, and parents had their idle children shut away in houses of correction.[113] Diminished tolerance, especially in the larger cities with their growing anonymity, is also evident in the numerous presentments for theft lodged by one worker against another.[114] Thus, certain forms of restraint were internalized, and in some circumstances the laboring poor on their own initiative—that is, forced by material problems—turned to the authorities to have some of their own disciplined: a rational form of behavior, given that the margin of survival was slim indeed. However, the result was the further strengthening of the apparatus of repression and its legitimation.

In sum, then, the manifestations of what may be called a proletarian culture were neither simple nor invariant. They may seem at first to be contradictory, at one moment giving the impression of submission, and at another moment the appearance of independence. But during this period, neither was the case; rather, they all were strategies that derived their coherence from the struggle just to survive proletarianization and pauperization.

NOTES

1. On the origins of the different property systems that emerged in different regions of Europe during the early modern period, see the brilliant essay by R. Brenner, "The Agrarian Roots of European Capitalism," Past and Present 97 (1982): 16–113. On the demographic dimension of the early proletariat's growth from the ranks of the rural landless, see the contributions of David Levine and Charles Tilly to this volume. Also see G. Derouet, "Une démographie différentielle: les populations rurales d'Ancien Régime," Annales. E. S. C. 35 (1980): 3–41; and W. Seccombe, "Marxism and Demography," New Left Review 137, (1983): 22–47.
2. See his contribution to this volume (Chapter 1).
3. On the overall decline in the standard of living of the lower classes in the period between the late Middle Ages and the early nineteenth century, see C. Lis and H. Soly, Poverty and Capitalism in Pre-Industrial Europe (Atlantic Highlands, N.J.: Humanities Press, 1979); F. Braudel, Civilisation matérielle, économie et capitalisme, XVe–XVIIIe siècle, 3 vols. (Paris: Armand Colin, 1979): vol. 1, pp.107–109, 136–143, 164–167, and vol. 3, pp. 69–70; W. Abel, Stufen der Ernährung. Eine historische Skizze (Göttingen: Vandenhoeck & Ruprecht, 1981).
4. To cope with the structural shortage of labor caused by the Black Death, many rulers had published ordinances around 1350 establishing the duty of all able-bodied men to work and curtailing the mobility of rural labor. The resolute resistance of village communities against seigneurial reaction in western Europe made the enforcement of such laws impossible within a few decades, however (Lis and Soly, Poverty and Capitalism, pp. 48–51).
5. Calculated from J. de Vries, "Patterns of Urbanization in Pre-Industrial Europe, 1500–1800," in H. Schmal, ed., Patterns of European Urbanization Since 1500 (London: Croom Helm, 1980), p. 88.
6. Sebastian Brant, Das Narrenschiff, H. A. Junghaus, trans., (Stuttgart, 1966), especially p. 221 ff.; Robert de Balsac, Le droit chemin de l'hôpital, ed. P. Allut, Etude biographique et bibliographique sur Symphorien Champier (Lyons, 1859), pp. 119–26; an English trans-

lation of the *Liber Vagatorum* has been edited by D. B. Thomas, *The Book of Vagabonds and Beggars* (London, 1931). The best survey of this literature is B. Geremek, *Truands et misérables dans l'Europe moderne, 1350–1600* (Paris: Gallimard/Julliard, 1980), pp. 179–212. For the Low Countries, see H. Pleij, *Het gilde van de Blauwe Schuit. Literatuur, volksfeest en burgermoraal in de late middeleeuwen* (Amsterdam: Meulenhoff, 1979).

7. Among collections of such pamphlets, the following should be noted: A. V. Judges, ed., *The Elizabethan Underworld* (London: Routledge, 1930, reprinted 1965); G. Salgado, ed., *Cony-Catchers and Bawdy Baskets* (Harmondsworth, England: Penguin, 1972); F. C. B. Avé-Lallemant, ed., *Das Deutsche Gaunerthum*, vol. 1 (Leipzig, 1858, reprinted Wiesbaden: Verlag Ralph Suchier, 1979); F. Kluge, ed., *Rotwelsch. Quellen und Wortschatz der Gaunersprache und der verwandten Geheimsprachen*, vol. 1, *Rotwelsches Quellenbuch* (Strasbourg, 1901). There is a mass of modern work on the "literature of roguery." Useful introductions are R. Chartier, "Les élites et les gueux. Quelques représentations, XVIe–XVIIe siècles," *Revue d'Histoire moderne et contemporaine* 21 (1974): 376–388; M. Jones-Davies, ed., *Misère et gueuserie au temps de la Renaissance. Colloque sur les gueux et gueuserie* (Paris: Centre de Recherches sur la Renaissance, 1976); B. Geremek, "Gergo," in *Enciclopedia Einaudi*, vol. 6 (Turin: Einaudi, 1979), pp. 724–746. Current research indicates that most "vagrants" were simply displaced people who often claimed to have an occupation and who had never been engaged in crimes other than wandering, whereas the records of theft make clear that the vast majority of those arrested consisted of first-time offenders. All in all, there is little evidence of the existence of an alternative society of professional criminals as portrayed in the contemporary rogue literature. See P. Clark, "The Migrant in Kentish Towns, 1580–1640," in P. Clark and P. Slack, eds., *Crisis and Order in English Towns, 1500–1700: Essays in Urban History* (London: Routledge, 1972), pp. 134–138; P. A. Slack, "Vagrants and Vagrancy in England, 1598–1664," *Economic History Review*, 2d ser., 27 (1974): 360–379; A. L. Beier, "Vagrants and the Social Order in Elizabethan England," *Past and Present* 44 (1974): 3–29.

8. See the perceptive remarks of T. C. Curtis and F. M. Hale, "English Thinking About Crime, 1530–1620," in L. A. Knafla, ed., *Crime and Criminal Justice* (Ontario: Wilfried Laurier University Press, 1982), pp. 123–124. Also F. Graus, "Randgruppen der städtischen Gesellschaft im Spätmittelalter," *Zeitschrift für historische Forschung* 8 (1981): 421–422, 427, 433.

9. Edmund Dudley, *The Tree of Common Wealth*, ed. D. M. Brodie (Cambridge: Cambridge University Press, 1948), p. 40; Erasmus's colloquy "Beggar Talk" in C. R. Thompson, trans., *The Colloquies of Erasmus* (Chicago: University of Chicago Press, 1965); Vives's editions given by R. A. Casanova and L. Caby, eds., *De l'assistance aux pauvres* (Brussels: Valero & Fils, 1943), pp. 265–288; Thomas Starkey quoted in W. R. D. Jones, *The Tudor Commonwealth, 1519–1559* (London: Athlone Press, 1970), p. 125. See also M. Bataillon, "J. L. Vives, réformateur de la bienfaisance," *Bibliothèque d'Humanisme et Renaissance* 19 (1952): 140–159; and N. Z. Davis, *Society and Culture in Early Modern France* (Palo Alto, Calif: Stanford University Press, 1975), pp. 17–34.

10. H. J. Grimm, "Luther's Contributions to Sixteenth-Century Organization of Poor Relief," *Archiv für Reformationsgeschichte* 61 (1970): 222–234; R. M. Kingdon, "Social Welfare in Calvin's Geneva," *American Historical Review* 76 (1971): 50–69; C. Lindberg, "There Should Be No Beggars Among Christians: Karlstadt, Luther, and the Origins of Protestant Poor Relief," *Church History* 46 (1977): 313–334.

11. H. Soly, "Economische ontwikkeling en sociale politiek in Europa tijdens de overgang van middeleeuwen naar nieuwe tijden," *Tijdschrift voor Geschiedenis* 88 (1975): 591–592. The following towns should be added to the list compiled by this author for Germany, Königsberg (1524), Danzig (1525), Esslingen (1528), Lübeck (1531),

Göttingen (1531), Bremen (1534), and Hannover (1536), for the Low Countries, Ni-
euwpoort (1529) and perhaps Bruges (before 1530?). See A. L. Richter, *Die evange-
lischen Kirchenordnungen des sechszehnten Jahrhundert*, vol. 1 (Weimar: Landes-
Industriecomptoir, 1846); F. Lampaert, *Heksenvervolging en hekserij in de kasselrij Veurne,
1580–1660* (Licentiate thesis, State University of Ghent, 1982), p. 16; J. Denolf, *Brugge,
1748* (Licentiated thesis, State University of Ghent, 1981), pp. 192–193.

12. Lis and Soly, *Poverty and Capitalism*, 88–92. An excellent survey of sixteenth-century
poor-relief that has appeared since the publication of our book is R. Jütte, ''Poor
Relief and Social Discipline in Sixteenth-Century Europe,'' *European Studies Review*
11 (1981): 25–52. On developments in individual countries, valuable recent works are
for England, A. L. Beier, *The Problem of the Poor in Tudor and Early Stuart England*
(London and New York: Methuen, 1983); for Germany, T. Fischer, *Städtische Armut
und Armenfürsorge im 15. und 16. Jahrhundert* (Göttingen: Schwartz, 1979); and C.
Sachsse and F. Tennstedt, *Geschichte der Armenfürsorge in Deutschland. Vom Spätmittelalter bis zum Ersten Weltkrieg* (Stuttgart: Kohlhammer, 1980), pp. 23–84.

13. At Antwerp, the summer's daily wages of mason's laborers tumbled from an average
of 21 liters of rye in the years 1501–1510 to scarcely 15 liters between 1521 and 1540;
that is, a diminution of 30%. See E. Scholliers, ''De lagere klassen. Een kwantitatieve
benadering van levensstandaard en levenswijze,'' in *Antweren in de XVIde eeuw* (Antwerp: Mercurius, 1975), pp. 161–180. For the international context, see W. Abel,
Massenarmut und Hungerkrisen im vorindustriellen Europa. Versuch einer Synopsis (Hamburg and Berlin: Paul Parley, 1974), pp. 47–54; P. Abrams and E. A. Wrigley, eds.,
Towns in Societies (Cambridge: Cambridge University Press, 1978), pp. 163–183; C. V.
Phytian-Adams, *Desolation of a City: Coventry and the Urban Crisis of the Late Middle
Ages* (Cambridge: Cambridge University Press, 1979), pp. 281ff.

14. For England, see A. Fletcher, *Tudor Rebellions* (London: Longmans, 1979); P. Williams, *The Tudor Regime* (Oxford: Clarendon Press, 1979), chap. 10. For France, see
E. Coornaert, *Les corporations en France avant 1789* (Paris: Editions Ouvrières, 1968),
pp. 114–117; R. Gascon, ''La France du mouvement: les commerces et les villes,'' in
F. Braudel and E. Labrousse, eds., *Histoire économique et sociale de la France*, vol. 1, *De
1450 à 1660* (Paris: Presses Universitaires de France, 1977), pp. 447–458. For Germany, see E. Maschke, ''Deutsche Städte am Ausgang des Mittelalters,'' in W.
Rausch, ed., *Die Stadt am Ausgang des Mittelalters* (Linz: Wimmer, 1974), pp. 75–78,
especially n. 206; O. Rammstedt, ''Stadtunruhen 1525,'' in H. Wehler, ed., *Der
deutsche Bauernkrieg, 1524–26* (Göttingen: Vandenhoeck & Ruprecht, 1975), pp. 239–
276. For the Low Countries, see A. Henne, *Histoire du règne de Charles-Quint en Belgique*, 10 vols. (Brussels and Leipzig: Emil Flatau, 1858–1860), *passim*.

15. In 1525 Martin Luther urged the German princes to crush the rebels in his famous
treatise *Against the Robbing and Murdering Peasants*, which appeared in no less than
21 editions. A year later, Nicholas Bolcyr gave a hair-raising description of the Peasant War in Alsace. In 1527 Sir Thomas More painted a horrifying picture of the dangers incarnated in all those who acted ''with contempt of God and all good men, and
obstinate rebellious mind against all laws, rule, and governance.'' In 1529 Lyon's
earliest humanist, the physician and former consul Symphorien Champier, wrote a
book on the *Grande Rebeyne*. The Pilgrimage of Grace in 1536 brought Sir Richard
Morison to analyze the forces threatening the bases of society: not only poverty and
its roots (lack of education and, above all, idleness), but also the deep-seated jealousy
of the ''worser sort'' of their superiors. In 1549 the *Homily Against Disobedience and
Wilful Rebellion*, published after the rising in Norfolk and reprinted many times, identified rebelliousness as the source of all other sins. See H. Claus, *Der deutsche Bauernkrieg im Druckschaffen der Jahre 1524–1526. Verzeichnis der Flugschriften und Dichtungen*

(Gotha: Forschungsbibliothek, 1975), pp. 44-59; N. Z. Davis, *Society and Culture in Early Modern France* (Palo Alto, Calif: Stanford University Press, 1975), p. 28; Jones, *Tudor Commonwealth*, pp. 56-57; Williams, *Tudor Regime*, p. 352.

16. See, for example, Fischer, *Städtische Armut*, pp. 247-248.

17. For England, see W. J. Chambliss, "A Sociological Analysis of the Law of Vagrancy," *Social Problems* 12 (1964): 67-77. For France, see J. P. Gutton, *La société et les pauvres. L'exemple de la généralité de Lyon, 1534-1789* (Paris: Les Belles Lettres, 1971), pp. 251-255; J. Richard, "Les errants au XVIe siècle: une rafle au baillage d'Auxois en 1556," *Annales de Bourgogne* 45 (1973): 96-108. For Germany, see G. K. Schmelzeisen, *Polizeiordnungen und Privatrecht* (Münster and Cologne: Böhlau-Verlag, 1955), pp. 316-317. For the Low Countries, see *Recueil des Ordonnances des Pays-Bas*, 2d ser., 7 vols. (Brussels: J. Goemaere, 1893-1957), *passim*.

18. M. Weisser, *Crime and Punishment in Early Modern Europe* (Atlantic Highlands, N.J.: Humanities Press, 1979), p. 105.

19. Although Spain witnessed major revolts during the 1520s, the central government limited itself to the regulation of begging; not one town on the Iberian Peninsula took stronger measures. J. Soubeyroux, "Organisation de la bienfaisance en Espagne au XVIe siècle," *Bulletin Hispanique* 74 (1972): 118ff.; J. Vilar, "Le picarisme espagnol: De l'interférence des marginalités à leur sublimation esthétique," in *Les marginaux et les exclus dans l'histoire. Cahiers Jussieu n° 5* (Paris: Union Générale d'Editions, 1979), pp. 29-77.

20. Lis and Soly, *Poverty and Capitalism*, pp. 93-94. See also Geremek, *Truands et misérables*, pp. 83, 93, 95, 162ff; and Fischer, *Städtische Armut*, pp. 301ff.

21. For England, see G. Unwin, *Industrial Organization in the Sixteenth and Seventeenth Centuries* (London, 1963), pp. 47-49; W. G. Hoskins, *The Age of Plunder: King Henry's England, 1500-1547* (London and New York: Frank Cass, 1976), pp. 108-111. For France, see H. Hauser, *Ouvriers du temps passé, XVe-XVIe siècles* (Paris: Félix Alcan, 1927), pp. 62-63, 67-68, 121-126, 166-167, 174-175, 246-249; B. Chevalier, *Les bonnes villes de France, du XIVe au XVIe siècle* (Paris: Aubier, 1982), pp. 165-170. For Germany, see Schmelzeisen, *Polizeiordnungen*, chap. 8. For the Low Countries, see E. Scholliers, "Vrije en onvrije arbeiders, voornamelijk te Antwerpen in de XVIe eeuw," *Bijdragen voor de Geschiedenis der Nederlanden* 11 (1956): 285-322.

22. See, for example, Davis, *Society and Culture*, pp. 34, 40, 43.

23. E. Scholliers, *Loonarbeid en Honger. De levensstandaard te Antwerpen in de XVe en XVIe eeuw* (Antwerp: De Sikkel, 1960), pp. 127-128, 130, 133, 137-139; Coornaert, *Corporations*, 114-115.

24. W. E. Minchinton, ed., *Wage Regulation in Pre-Industrial England* (Newton Abbot: David & Charles, 1972), *passim* (Tawney on p. 47); D. Woodward, "The Background to the Statute of Artificers: the Genesis of Labour Policy, 1558-63," *Economic History Review*, 2d ser., vol. 33 (1980): 32-34.

25. F. J. Fisher, "Influenza and Inflation in Tudor England," *Economic History Review*, 2d ser., vol. 15 (1965): 120-129.

26. In the Netherlands, for example, wages had risen to such an extent as a result of famine and epidemics that some provincial estates in 1561 made proposals to lower wages substantially and to subject them to a ceiling. The central government scorned the idea of a uniform rate, but it approved of a coordinated plan to fix new maximum wages locally. Yet it came to nothing. Ch. Verlinden and J. Craeybeckx, *Prijzen- en lonenpolitiek in de Nederlanden in 1561 en 1588-1589. Onuitgegeven adviezen, ontwerpen en ordonnanties* (Brussels: Paleis der Academiën, 1962).

27. A. Duke, "The Face of Popular Religious Dissent in the Low Countries, 1520-1530," *Journal of Ecclesiastical History* 26 (1975): 50, n. 1. The quotation comes from J. De-

cavele, *De dageraad van de Reformatie in Vlaanderen, 1520–1565* (Brussels: Paleis der Academiën, 1975), p. 118, n. 3.

28. J. Delumeau, *Le catholicisme entre Luther et Voltaire* (Paris: Presses Universitaires de France, 1979), pp. 237–253; St. Ozment, *The Age of Reform, 1250–1550: An Intellectual and Religious History of Late Medieval and Reformation Europe* (New Haven, Conn.: Yale University Press, 1980), pp. 204–222.

29. Jütte, "Poor Relief," pp. 28–30, 45, n. 33.

30. See J. Cuvelier, "Documents concernant la réforme de la bienfaisance à Louvain au XVIe siècle," *Bulletin de la Commission royale d'Histoire de Belgique* 105 (1940): 41–42, 68; A. N. Galpern, *The Religions of the People in Sixteenth-Century Campagne* (Cambridge, Mass.: Harvard University Press, 1976), pp. 100–101; Fischer, *Städtische Armut*, p. 245.

31. For England, see I. Pinchbeck and M. Hewitt, *Children in English Society*, vol. 1, *From Tudor Times to the Eighteenth Century* (London and Toronto: Routledge & Kegan Paul, 1969), pp. 94–98, 127–135; R. O'Day, *Education and Society, 1500–1800* (London: Longman, 1982), pp. 238–247. For France, see Davis, *Culture and Society*, pp. 42–49. For Germany, see G. Strauss, *Luther's House of Learning: Indoctrination of the Young in the German Reformation* (Baltimore and London: Johns Hopkins Press, 1978); Fischer, *Städtische Armut*, pp. 309–311. For the Low Countries, see P. Bonenfant, *Le problème du paupérisme en Belgique à la fin de l'Ancien Régime* (Brussels: Marcel Hayez, 1934), pp. 86–87; Decavele, *Dageraad van de Reformatie*, pp. 137–139.

32. P. Burke, *Popular Culture in Early Modern Europe* (London: Temple Smith, 1978), pp. 207–214. For England, see Williams, *Tudor Regime*, pp. 305–307. For France, see R. Muchembled, *Culture populaire et culture des élites dans la France moderne, XVe–XVIIIe siècles* (Paris: Flammarion, 1978), pp. 189–215; R. Chartier, "Dominants et dominés: Du partage à l'exclusion," in G. Duby, ed., *Histoire de la France urbaine*, vol. 3, *La ville classique, de la Renaissance aux Révolutions*, ed. E. Le Roy Ladurie (Paris: Seuil, 1981), pp. 180–198. For Germany, see Sachsse and Tennstedt, *Geschichte der Armenfürsorge*, pp. 34–35, 37–38; R. W. Scribner, *For the Sake of Simple Folk: Popular Propaganda for the German Reformation* (Cambridge: Cambridge University Press, 1981), pp. 67–75. For the Low Countries, see H. Soly, "Openbare feesten in Brabantse en Vlaamse steden, 16e–18e eeuw," in *Het openbaar initiatief van de gemeenten in België. Historische grondslagen, Ancien Régime* (forthcoming).

33. The available evidence suggests that the overall crime rate did indeed rise markedly in Elizabethan and early Stuart England, especially between 1590 and 1620: J. Samaha, *Law and Order in Historical Perspective. The Case of Elizabethan Essex* (New York and London: Academic Press, 1974), pp. 19–22, 27; J. S. Cockburn, "The Nature and Incidence of Crime in England, 1559–1625," in J. S. Cockburn, ed., *Crime in England, 1550–1800* (London: Methuen, 1977), pp. 52–53; K. Wrightson and D. Levine, *Poverty and Piety in an English Village: Terling, 1525–1700* (New York and London: Academic Press, 1979), pp. 113–119. For the Spanish Netherlands, see H. Deneweth, *Criminaliteit als bron voor de sociale geschiedenis te Brugge gedurende de eerste helft van de 17de eeuw* (Licentiate thesis, State University of Ghent, 1983), pp. 238–240; M. De Soete, *De criminaliteit in het Brugse Vrije tijdens de eerste helft van de 17de eeuw* (Licentiate thesis, State University of Ghent, 1983), pp. 52ff. On the incidence of popular revolts, see H. Kamen, *The Iron Century: Social Change in Europe, 1550–1660* (London: Weidenfeld and Nicolson, 1971), chaps. 9, 10. Demographic research has revealed that the illegitimacy ratio reached a peak at the turn of the seventeenth century. For England, see P. Laslett, *Family Life and Illicit Love in Earlier Generations* (Cambridge: Cambridge University Press, 1977), pp. 113, 115–117, 125; G. R. Quaife, *Wanton Wenches and*

Wayward Wives: Peasants and Illicit Sex in Early Seventeenth-Century England (London: Croom Helm, 1979), pp. 56-57; D. Levine and K. Wrightson, "The Social Context of Illegitimacy in Early Modern England," in P. Laslett, K. Oosterveen, and R. M. Smith, eds., *Bastardy and its Comparative History* (London: Edward Arnold, 1980), pp. 158-175. For France, see A. Croix, *Nantes et le pays nantais au XVIe siècle. Etude démographique* (Paris: SEVPEN, 1974), pp. 94-97. For the Southern Netherlands, see C. Vandenbroeke, "Het seksueel gedrag der jongeren in Vlaanderen sinds de late 16e eeuw," *Bijdragen tot de Geschiedenis* 62 (1979): 202, 208-210.

34. See Jütte, "Poor Relief," pp. 29-30; and Muchembled, *Culture populaire*, pp. 225-285.

35. On Reformation and Counter-Reformation attempts to subject the lives of Christians to more careful pastoral supervision, see J. Bossy, "The Counter-Reformation and the People of Catholic Europe," *Past and Present* 47 (1970): 51-70; Delumeau, *Catholicisme*, pp. 266-302; B. Scribner, "Religion, Society and Culture: Reorientating the Reformation," *History Workshop* 14 (1982): 11-15; J. Estèbe and B. Vogler, "La genèse d'une société protestante: Étude comparée de quelques registres consistoriaux languedociens et palatins vers 1600," *Annales, E. S. C.* 31 (1976): 362-388. For an excellent survey of the reformation of popular culture, see Burke, *Popular Culture*, chap. 8; Y. M. Bercé, *Fête et révolte. Des mentalités populaires du XVIe au XVIIIe siècle* (Paris: Hachett, 1976), chap. 4. Among recent studies on the "repression of body and soul" in individual countries, see, for England, K. Wrightson, *English Society, 1580-1680* (London: Hutchinson, 1972), pp. 199-220. For France, see R. Taveneaux, *Le catholicisme dans la France classique, 1610-1715* (Paris: S.E.D.E.S., 1980), chaps. 5, 6, 11, 12; Muchembled, *Culture populaire*, chaps. 4, 5; R. Chartier, "Discipline et invention. Les fêtes en France, XVe-XVIIIe siècle," *Diogène* (1982): 51-71. For Germany, see G. Strauss, "Success and Failure in the German Reformation," *Past and Present* 67 (1975), 30-63. For the Spanish Netherlands, see M. Cloet, "Het gelovige volk in de 17de eeuw," in *Algemene Geschiedenis der Nederlanden* 8 (Haarlem: Fibula–Van Dishoeck, 1979), pp. 393-417; and A. Lottin, "Contre-Réforme et religion populaire: Un mariage difficile mais réussi aux XVIe et XVIIIe siècles en Flandre et en Hainaut?" in *La religion populaire* (Paris: C.N.R.S., 1979), pp. 53-63. For the United Provinces, see A. van Deursen, *Het kopergeld van de Gouden Eeuw*, vol. 4, *Hel en hemel* (Assen: Van Gorcum, 1980). For Switzerland, see R. M. Kingdon, "The Control of Morals in Calvin's Geneva," in L. Buck and J. Zophy, eds., *The Social History of the Reformation* (Columbus, Ohio: Ohio State University Press, 1972), pp. 1-14; and T. M. Safley, "To Preserve the Marital State: The Basler Ehegericht, 1550-1592," *Journal of Family History* 7 (1982): 162-179.

36. H. Soly, "Le grand essor du capitalisme commercial: Villes et campagnes, XVIe–XVIIIe siècles," in E. Witte, ed., *Histoire de Flandre* (Brussels: La Renaissance du Livre, 1983), pp. 142-143.

37. On these themes, see C. Hill, *Society and Puritanism in Pre-Revolutionary England* (London: Secker & Warburg, 1964), chap. 5; P. Clark, "The Alehouse and the Alternative Society," in D. Pennington and K. Thomas, eds., *Puritans and Revolutionaries. Essays Presented to Christopher Hill* (Oxford: Clarendon Press, 1978), pp. 49-61; S. K. Roberts, "Alehouses, Brewing, and Government Under the Early Stuarts," *Southern History* 2 (1980): 45-71; K. Wrightson, "Alehouses, Order and Reformation in Rural England, 1590-1660," in E. Yeo and S. Yeo, eds., *Popular Culture and Class Conflict, 1590-1914* (Brighton: Harvester Press, 1981), pp. 1-27; J. A. Sharpe, *Crime in Seventeenth-Century England: A County Study* (Cambridge: Cambridge University Press, 1983), Ch. 4.

38. See, for example, Wrightson and Levine, *Poverty and Piety*, pp. 63ff; K. Wrightson, "Two Concepts of Order: Justices, Constables and Jurymen in Seventeenth-Century

England,'' in J. Brewer and J. Styles, eds., *An Ungovernable People: The English and Their Law in the Seventeenth and Eighteenth Centuries* (London: Hutchinson, 1980), pp. 39–44.

39. On these themes, see G. J. Schochet, "Patriarchalism, Politics and Mass Attitudes in Stuart England," *Historical Journal* 12 (1969): 413–441; Muchembled, *Culture populaire*, pp. 243–247; Wrightson and Levine, *Poverty and Piety*, pp. 115–116; T. Robisheaux, "Peasants and Pastors: Rural Youth Control and the Reformation in Hohenlohe, 1540–1680," *Social History* 6 (1981): 292–294; Scribner, "Religion, Society and Culture," pp. 9–10.

40. Wrightson, *English Society*, pp. 222–228 (on p. 227). For examples of the local conflicts underlying witchcraft accusations, see K. Thomas, *Religion and the Decline of Magic* (London: Weidenfeld & Nicolson, 1971), chaps. 16, 17; A. Macfarlane, *Witchcraft in Tudor and Stuart England: A Regional and Comparative Study* (London: Routledge, 1970); R. Muchembled, "Sorcières du Cambrésis. L'acculturation du monde rural aux XVIe et XVIIe siècles," in M. S. Dupont-Bouchat, W. Frijhoff, and R. Muchembled, *Prophètes et sorcières dans les Pays-Bas, XVIe–XVIIe siècles* (Paris: Hachett, 1978), with English version in J. Obelkevish, ed., *Religion and the People, 800–1700* (Chapel Hill, N.C.: University of North Carolina Press, 1979), pp. 221–276.

41. In 1563, contribution to the poor box was made compulsory; in 1572, local authorities were pressed to levy a poor tax in order to eliminate fluctuations in the receipts of the centralized relief fund, and the Act of 1576 ordered the provision of raw materials on which the able-bodied poor could be set to work. The two major statutes of 1597 and 1601 did not add any new principles; rather, they synthesized earlier measures concerning public assistance, and they greatly facilitated the practical implementation of the law. Williams, *Tudor Regime*, pp. 196–215; Beier, *Problems of the Poor*, pp. 24, 40–41.

42. Gascon, "La France du mouvement," p. 458; Bonenfant, *Problème du paupérisme*, p. 88; Sachsse and Tennstedt, *Geschichte der Armenfürsorge*, pp. 39–40.

43. For a comprehensive bibliography, see P. Spierenburg "The Sociogenesis and Development of Houses of Correction in Europe" (paper, Rotterdam, 1980). A useful introduction is D. Melossi and M. Pavarini, *The Prison and the Factory. Origins of the Penitentiary System* (London: Macmillan, 1981), especially pp. 11–32. For England: E. M. Leonard, *The Early History of English Poor Relief* (Cambridge: Cambridge University Press, 1900; reprinted New York: Frank Cass, 1965), pp. 25–46, 112–115; A. van der Slice, "Elizabethan Houses of Correction," *Journal of the American Institute of Criminal Law and Criminology* 27 (1936–1937): 45–67. For France: Gutton, *La société et les pauvres*, pp. 295–303. For the German lands: H. von Weber, "Die Entwicklung des Zuchthauswesens in Deutschland im 17. und 18. Jahrhundert," in *Festschrift Adolf Zycha* (Weimar: Verlag Hermann Böhlaus Nachfolger, 1941), pp. 427–468; H. Eichler, "Zucht- und Arbeitshäuser in den mittleren und östichen Provinzen Brandenburg-Preussens," *Jahrbuch für Wirtschaftsgeschichte* (1970), pp. 127–147; H. Stekl, *Oesterreichs Zucht- und Arbeitshäuser, 1671–1920* (Vienna: Verlag für Geschichte und Politik, 1978). For the Spanish Netherlands: Bonenfant, *Problème du paupérisme*, pp. 89–91. For the United Provinces: Th. Sellin, *Pioneering in Penology. The Amsterdam Houses of Correction in the Sixteenth and Seventeenth Centuries* (Philadelphia and London: University of Pennsylvania Press, 1944); A. Hallema, *Geschiedenis van het gevangeniswezen, hoofdzakelijk in Nederland* (The Hague: Staatsdrukkerij, 1958).

44. M. Foucault, *Folie et déraison. Histoire de la folie à l'âge classique* (Paris: Plon, 1961), pp. 54–81.

45. Brenner, "Agrarian Roots," pp. 80–89.

46. By the early eighteenth century, many of the Dutch *tuchthuizen* had become recep-

tacles for all sorts of disorderly persons: beggars and vagabonds as well as alcoholics and prostitutes; even the "bad" children and "miscreant" relatives of good burghers were accepted if their families paid for maintenance. This reversal is not surprising: From around 1670 appeared the first signs of economic stagnation and even decline.

47. See the contribution of David Levine to this volume.
48. S. Webb and B. Webb, *English Poor Law History*, pt. I, *The Old Poor Law* (London: Longmans, 1927), chap. 5; Ph. Styles, "The Evolution of the Law of Settlement," *University of Birmingham Historical Journal* 9 (1963–1964), pp. 33–63; James St. Taylor, "The Impact of Pauper Settlement, 1691–1834," *Past and Present* 73 (1976): 47–53; P. Clark, "Migration in England During the Late Seventeenth and Early Eighteenth Centuries," *Past and Present* 83 (1979): 81–89.
49. J. O. Appleby, *Economic Thought and Ideology in Seventeenth-Century England* (Princeton, N.J.: Princeton University Press, 1978), chap. 6 (on p. 152). See also E. S. Furniss, *The Position of the Laborer in a System of Nationalism: A Study in the Labor Theories of the Later English Mercantilists* (Boston: Houghton Mifflin, 1920); G. V. R. Rimlinger, *Welfare Politics and Industrialization in Europe, America and Russia* (New York: John Wiley 1971), pp. 16–22; A. W. Coats, "The Relief of Poverty: Attitudes to Labour and Economic Change in England, 1660–1782," *International Review of Social History* 21 (1976): 98–115; J. A. Garraty, *Unemployment in History. Economic Thought and Public Policy* (New York: Harper & Row, 1978), pp. 37–40, 42. On the enforcement of labor discipline through the assizes, see Sharpe, *Crime*, pp. 197–198.
50. K. De Schweinitz, *England's Road to Social Security* (Philadelphia: University of Pennsylvania Press, 1943), chap. 6; S. Pollard, *The Genesis of Modern Management: A Study of the Industrial Revolution in Great Britain* (London: Arnold, 1965), pp. 163–164.
51. R. Allier, *La cabale des dévots, 1627–1666* (Paris: Colin, 1902; reprinted Geneva: Slatkine Reprints, 1970; E. Chill, "Religion and Mendicity in Seventeenth-Century France," *International Review of Social History* 7 (1962): 400–425; Orest A. Ranum, *Paris in the Age of Absolutism: An Essay* (New York: John Wiley, 1968), pp. 109–131; Cissie C. Fairchilds, *Poverty and Charity in Aix-en-Provence, 1640–1789* (Baltimore and London: Johns Hopkins Press, 1976), pp. 33–35; P. J. Edwards, "An Aspect of the French Counter-Reform Movement: La Compagnie du Saint-Sacrement," *Dalhousie Review* 56 (1976): 479–492; M. Jeorger, "La structure hospitalière de la France sous l'Ancien Régime," *Annales. E.S.C.* 32 (1977): 1025–1051.
52. C. W. Cole, *Colbert and a Century of French Mercantilism*, 2 vols. (New York: Columbia University Press, 1939), vol. 1, pp. 464ff.; P. Goubert, *Louis XIV et vingt millions de Français* (Paris: Fayard, 1966), pp. 85–95; P. Deyon, *Le mercantilisme* (Paris: Flammarion, 1969), pp. 23–30.
53. See the perceptive remarks of R. Schulze, *Die Polizeigesetzgebung zur Wirtschafts- und Arbeitsordnung der Mark Brandenburg in der frühen Neuzeit* (Aalen: Scientia, 1978), pp. 91–92, 183–185, and *passim*. Also Schmelzeisen, *Polizeiordnungen*, pp. 319–323, 352–353, 367–369; H. Mottek, *Wirtschaftsgeschichte Deutschlands*, vol. 1, *Von den Anfängen bis zur Zeit der Französischen Revolution* (Berlin: VEB Deutscher Verlag der Wissenschaften, 1968), pp. 294ff, 313ff.; P. Kriedte, H. Medick, and J. Schlumbohm, *Industrialization Before Industrialization. Rural Industry in the Genesis of Capitalism* (Paris and Cambridge: Maison des Sciences de l'Homme/Cambridge University Press, 1981), chap. 6 (Kriedte).
54. Levine and Wrightson, "Social Context of Illegitimacy," pp. 174–175.
55. For England: M. Walzer, *The Revolution of the Saints. A Study in the Origins of Radical Politics* (New York: Atheneum, 1968), pp. 229–231; D. Brailsford, *Sport and Society: Elizabeth to Anne* (London and Toronto: Routledge/University of Toronto Press, 1969), pp. 139, 154–156; Thomas, *Religion and the Decline of Magic*, chaps. 18 and 22; Wright-

son, *English Society*, pp. 212–213, 215–216, 220–221. For France: P. Goubert, "Family and Province: A Contribution to the Knowledge of Family Structures in Early Modern France," *Journal of Family History* 2 (1977): 191–193; Chartier, "Discipline," pp. 55, 66–67. For Germany: Robisheaux, "Peasants and Pastors," pp. 290–291; Scribner, "Religion, Society and Culture," p. 15. For the United Provinces: A. Th. van Deursen, *Het kopergeld van de Gouden Eeuw*, vol. 2, *Volkskultuur* (Assen: Van Gorcum, 1978), chap. 2.

56. E. P. Thompson, "Eighteenth-Century English Society: Class Struggle Without Class?" *Social History* 3 (1978): 133–165 (on p. 163). See also Wrightson, *English Society*, pp. 172–173; R. W. Malcolmson, *Life and Labour in England, 1700–1780* (London: Hutchinson, 1981), pp. 102–107; B. Bushaway, *By Rite: Custom, Ceremony and Community in England, 1700–1800* (London: Junction Books, 1982). For France: E. Le Roy Ladurie, "Révoltes et contestations rurales en France de 1675 à 1788," *Annales. E.S.C.* 29 (1974): 6–22; J. P. Gutton, *La sociabilité villageoise dans l'ancienne France* (Paris: Hachette, 1979), pp. 141–151; H. Luxardo, *Les paysans. Les républiques villageoises, 10e–19e siècles* (Paris: Aubier, 1981), pp. 168–175. For the United Provinces: A. Th. van Deursen, *Het kopergeld van de Gouden Eeuw*, vol. 3, *Volk en overheid* (Assen: Van Gorcum, 1979), pp. 53–64; R. Dekker, *Holland in beroering. Oproeren in de 17de en 18de eeuw* (Baarn: Ambo, 1982), pp. 79–82, 122–129.

57. D. Levine, *Family Formation in an Age of Nascent Capitalism* (New York: Academic Press, 1977), *passim* (especially pp. 178 and 191). But see F. Perlin, "Proto-Industrialization and Pre-Colonial South Asia," *Past and Present* 98 (1983): 48–50, for a more consistent emphasis on labor demand theory.

58. See his contribution to this volume (Chapter 1).

59. On these themes, see Brenner, "Agrarian Roots," pp. 89–106, 110–113; E. A. Wrigley, "The Growth of Population in Eighteenth-Century England: A Conundrum Resolved," *Past and Present* 98 (1983): 121–150; Seccombe, "Marxism and Demography," pp. 33–38, 41–44, 47; and the contribution of David Levine to this volume. On the importance of exports and the domestic market, see F. Crouzet, "Toward an Export Economy: British Exports During the Industrial Revolution," *Explorations in Economic History* 17 (1980): 77–78, 81–82, 87–92; and W. A. Cole, "Factors in Demand, 1700–80," in R. Floud and D. McCloskey, eds., *The Economic History of Britain Since 1700*, vol. 1, *1700–1860* (Cambridge: Cambridge University Press, 1981), pp. 36–65.

60. L. A. Tilly and J. W. Scott, *Women, Work, and Family* (New York: Holt, Rinehart, and Winston, 1978), pp. 13–14, 63–79; W. H. Sewell, *Work and Revolution in France. The Language of Labor from the Old Regime to 1848* (Cambridge: Cambridge University Press, 1980), pp. 146–161. On demographic developments, see E. A. Wrigley and R. S. Schofield, *The Population History of England, 1541–1871. A Reconstruction* (London: Edward Arnold, 1981), pp. 212–215.

61. See the general surveys by Malcolmson, *Life and Labour*, chap. 6; and P. Horn, *The Rural World, 1780–1850* (London: Hutchinson, 1980). Also B. A. Holderness, " 'Open' and 'Close' Parishes in England in the Eighteenth and Nineteenth Centuries," *Agricultural History Review* 22 (1972): 126–138; K. D. M. Snell, "Agricultural Seasonal Unemployment: The Standard of Living and Women's Work in the South and East, 1690–1800," *Economic History Review*, 2d ser., vol. 34 (1981), pp. 407–437; A. Kussmaul, *Servants in Husbandry in Early Modern England* (Cambridge: Cambridge University Press, 1981).

62. R. Williams, *The Country and the City* (London: Chatto and Windus, 1973), p. 182; H. Newby, "The Deferential Dialectic," *Comparative Studies in Society and Culture* 17 (1975): 139–164; P. Dunkley, "Paternalism, the Magistracy and Poor Relief in England, 1795–1834," *International Review of Social History* 24 (1979): 371–397.

63. T. S. Ashton, *An Economic History of England: The Eighteenth Century* (London: Methuen, 1955), pp. 102, 210; D. S. Landes, *The Unbound Prometheus: Technological Change and Industrial Development in Western Europe from 1750 to the Present* (Cambridge: Cambridge University Press, 1969), pp. 44, 54–56, 71, 82, 118–119; M. Ignatieff, *A Just Measure of Pain: The Penitentiary in the Industrial Revolution, 1750–1850* (London: Macmillan, 1978), pp. 26–28.

64. Furniss, *Position of the Laborer*, chap. 6; P. Mathias, *The Transformation of England. Essays in the Economic and Social History of England in the Eighteenth Century* (London: Methuen, 1979), pp. 148–167.

65. E. P. Thompson, "Time, Work-Discipline, and Industrial Capitalism," *Past and Present* 38 (1967): 76–77; R. W. Malcolmson, *Popular Recreations in English Society, 1700–1850* (Cambridge: Cambridge University Press, 1973), pp. 93–99 (Clayton on p. 94); Ignatieff, *Just Measure of Pain*, p. 26 (Blackstone); P. B. Munsche, *Gentlemen and Poachers: The English Game Laws, 1671–1831* (Cambridge: Cambridge University Press, 1982), chap. 2.

66. Townshend quoted in J. R. Poynter, *Society and Pauperism* (London: Routledge, 1969), pp. xvi–xvii. On Colquhoun, see L. Radzinowicz, *A History of English Criminal Law and its Administration from 1750*, vol. 3, *Cross-Currents in the Movement for the Reform of the Police* (London: Stevens, 1956), pp. 211–251 (on pp. 232–233); and J. Roach, *Social Reform in England, 1780–1880* (London: Batsford, 1978), pp. 67–70.

67. Radzinowicz, *History of English Criminal Law*, vol. 4, *Grappling for Control* (London: Stevens, 1968), pp. 17–21.

68. Pollard, *Genesis of Modern Management*, chaps. 2 and 5 (on p. 162).

69. Ignatieff, *Just Measure of Pain*, pp. 31–32, 110 (Bentham); R. G. Cowherd, *Political Economists and the English Poor Laws. A Historical Study of the Influence of Classical Economics on the Formation of Social Welfare Policy* (Athens, Ohio: Ohio University Press, 1977), pp. 82–101; A. Digby, *Pauper Palaces* (London: Routledge, 1978), pp. 101–104; M. E. DeLacy, "Grinding Men Good? Lancashire's Prisons at Mid-Century," in V. Bailey, ed., *Policing and Punishment in Nineteenth-Century Britain* (London: Croom Helm, 1981), p. 200. At Ghent, the premier industrial center of Flanders, cotton manufacturers even had to put prisoners to work in the absence of free laborers. J. Dhondt, "Note sur les ouvriers industriels gantois à l'époque française," *Revue du Nord* 36 (1954): 309–324.

70. J. L. Hammond and B. Hammond, *The Town Labourer*, edited by John Lovell (London and New York: Longmans, 1978), chap. 8; Pollard, *Genesis of Modern Management*, pp. 161, 185–186, 188–189; T. C. Smout, *A History of the Scottish People, 1560–1830* (London: Fontana, 1972), pp. 381–383. On education and literacy, see M. G. Jones, *The Charity School Movement. A Study of Eighteenth-Century Puritanism in Action* (Cambridge: Cambridge University Press, 1938), pp. 85–87, 160–161; D. Owen, *English Philanthropy, 1660–1960* (Cambridge, Mass.: Harvard University Press, 1964), pp. 20–27; R. S. Schofield, "Dimensions of Illiteracy, 1750–1850," *Explorations in Economic History* 10 (1973): 452–453; M. Sanderson, "Literacy and Social Mobility in the Industrial Revolution in England," *Past and Present* 56 (1972): 75–104; W. B. Stephens, "Illiteracy and Schooling in the Provincial Towns, 1640–1870: A Comparative Approach," in D. A. Reeder, ed., *Urban Education in the Nineteenth Century* (London: Taylor & Francis, 1977), pp. 27–48; O'Day, *Education and Society*, pp. 252–255.

71. Pollard, *Genesis of Modern Management*, pp. 181–184, 187, 189–192; D. Roberts, *Paternalism in Early Victorian England* (London: Croom Helm, 1979), pp. 179–181. See also N. McKendrick, "Josiah Wedgewood and Factory Discipline," *Historical Journal* 4 (1961): 30–55. For some Continental examples, see Dhondt, "Note sur les ouvriers industriels gantois," *passim*; S. Chassagne, "Familie und Industrialisierung im Spie-

gel der Standesamtregister," in N. Bulst, J. Goy, and J. Hoock, eds., *Familie zwischen Tradition und Moderne* (Göttingen: Vandenhoeck & Ruprecht, 1981), p. 249; W. Kula, "Recherches comparatives sur la formation de la classe ouvrière," in *Second International Conference of Economic History* (Paris and The Hague: Mouton, 1960), p. 519.

72. J. Rule, *The Experience of Labour in Eighteenth-Century Industry* (London: Croom Helm, 1981), *passim* (especially chaps. 5–6); Malcolmson, *Life and Labour*, pp. 123–126; P. Linebaugh, "Labour History Without the Labour Process: A Note on John Gast and His Time," *Social History* 7 (1982): 319–328. On the incidence of industrial disputes, see C. R. Dobson, *Masters and Journeymen: A Pre-History of Industrial Relations, 1717–1800* (London: Croom Helm, 1980), pp. 22–26, 154–160. The quotation comes from the Hammonds, *Town Labourer*, p. 205.

73. Cowherd, *Political Economists*, pp. 138–146; Garraty, *Unemployment*, pp. 64–66.

74. S. G. Checkland and E. O. A. Checkland, eds., *The Poor Law Report of 1834* (Harmondsworth: Penquin, 1974), *passim* (on pp. 67, 335, 378). The best overall discussion of the new poor law is U. R. Q. Henriques, *Before the Welfare State. Social Administration in Early Industrial Britain* (London and New York: Longmans, 1979), pp. 26–34, 39–59. See also the pertinent remarks of H. Perkin, *The Origins of Modern English Society, 1780–1880* (London: Routledge, 1969), pp. 224–225; R. A. Nisbet, *Tradition and Revolt: Historical and Sociological Essays* (New York: Random House, 1970), pp. 63–65; Rimlinger, *Welfare Politics*, pp. 51–54; P. Dunkley, *The Crisis of the Old Poor Law in England, 1795–1834. An Interpretive Essay* (New York and London: Garland Publishing, 1980), pp. 144–181.

75. A. Shubert, "Private Initiative in Law Enforcement: Associations for the Prosecution of Felons, 1744–1856," in Bailey, ed., *Policing*, pp. 25–41; Dunkley, *Crisis of the Old Poor Law*, chaps. 3–4 (on p. 106). See also E. P. Thompson, "Patrician Society, Plebeian Culture," *Journal of Social History* 7 (1974): 382–405.

76. Cl. Emsley, *Policing and Its Context, 1750–1870* (London: Macmillan, 1983), pp. 70–71.

77. Roberts, *Paternalism*, pp. 270–276; Horn, *Rural World*, pp. 140–144.

78. Radzinowicz, *History of English Criminal Law*, vol. 3, *Cross-Currents*, chaps. 6–8, vol. 4, *Grappling for Control*, pp. 43–55; Perkin, *Origins of Modern English Society*, pp. 282–285. The quotation comes from D. George, *London Life in the Eighteenth Century* (London: Kegan Paul, 1925), p. 223.

79. Cowherd, *Political Economists*, pp. 29–46 (Sumner on pp. 39–40), 117 (Ricardo), 148 (McCulloch). See also J. Huzel, "Malthus, the Poor Law, and Population in Early Nineteenth-Century England," *Economic History Review*, 2d ser., vol. 20 (1969): 433–437; N. Longmate, *The Workhouse* (London: Temple Smith, 1974), p. 54 (Martineau); Roach, *Social Reform*, pp. 55–59.

80. Ignatieff, *Just Measure of Pain*, pp. 60–68. See also K. Figlio, "Chlorosis and Chronic Disease in Nineteenth-Century Britain: The Social Constitution of Somatic Illness in a Capitalist Society," *Social History* 3 (1978): 188–191.

81. Perkin, *Origins of Modern English Society*, p. 290.

82. R. D. Storch, "The Policeman as Domestic Missionary: Urban Discipline and Popular Culture in Northern England, 1850–1880," *Journal of Social History* 9 (1976): 481–509.

83. O. Hufton, *The Poor of Eighteenth-Century France, 1750–1789* (Oxford: Clarendon Press, 1974), pp. 182–193.

84. *Ibid.*, chap. 3. Recent research has shown that the majority of the inmates of the dépôts were in fact legitimately in search of a job and had committed no other offense than asking for alms. Few inmates fit the standard government conception of the beggar, as can be seen from Cissie Fairchilds's sample: only 27% of the people arrested on the roads and imprisoned in the dépôt of Aix-en-Provence had been trav-

eling in a group, and of these the vast majority were in groups of two, mostly relatives. Fairchilds, *Poverty and Charity*, pp. 103–109. See also C. Engrand, "Paupérisme et condition ouvrière dans la seconde moitié du XVIIIe siècle: l'exemple amiénois," *Revue d'Histoire moderne et contemporaine* 29 (1982): 407; and C. Romon, "Le monde des pauvres à Paris au XVIIIe siècle," *Annales E.S.C.* 37 (1982): 729–763.

85. Ira O. Wade, "Poverty in the Enlightenment," in *Europäische Aufklärung. Herbert Dieckmann zum 60. Geburtstag* (Munich, 1967), pp. 321–322.

86. A. Forrest, *The French Revolution and the Poor* (Oxford: Blackwell, 1981); C. Jones, *Charity and 'Bienfaisance': The Treatment of the Poor in the Montpellier Region, 1740–1815* (Cambridge: Cambridge University Press, 1982).

87. Hufton, *Poor of Eighteenth-Century France*, pp. 156, 169, 183–184, 192–193, 233–234; R. Vanberkel, "Les ateliers de charité dans le département du Nord," *Revue d'Histoire économique et sociale* 47 (1969): 77–91; Cl. Quetel, "En maison de force au Siècle des Lumières," in *Cahiers des Annales de Normandie* 13 (Caen, 1981): 57–58.

88. L. Chevalier, *Classes laborieuses, classes dangereuses à Paris pendant la première moitié du XIXe siècle* (Paris: Plon, 1958), p. 1; I. Joseph and Ph. Fritsch, *Disciplines à domicile. Recherches n° 28* (Fontenay-sous-Bois: Recherches, 1977), pp. 27, 87–97, 257; G. Leclerc, *L'observation de l'homme. Une histoire des enquêtes sociales* (Paris: Seuil, 1979), pp. 83–85, 164–169; M. N. Bourquet, "Topographie des häuslichen Raums und soziales Ritual. Das Bild der Familie in der Departementsstatistik Frankreichs während der napoleontischen Zeit," in Bulst, Goy, and Hoock, eds., *Familie*, pp. 89–98.

89. J. P. Peter, "Le grand rêve de l'ordre médical, en 1770 et aujourd'hui," *Autrement* 4 (1975–1976): 183–192; B.-P. Lecuyer, "La médicalisation de la société française dans la deuxième moitié du XVIIIe siècle en France: aux origines des premiers traités de médecine légale," *Annales de Bretagne et des Pays de l'Ouest* 86 (1979): 231–250; M. Foucault, "La politique de la santé au XVIIIe siècle," in *idem*, ed., *Les machines à guérir* (Brussels: Pierre Mardaga, 1979), pp. 9, 13–14; J. Léonard, *La médecine entre les pouvoirs et les savoirs. Histoire intellectuelle et politique de la médecine française au XIXe siècle* (Paris: Aubier, 1981), W. R. Albury, "Heart of Darkness: J. N. Corvisart and the Medicalization of Life," in J.-P. Goubert, ed., *La médicalisation de la société française, 1770–1830* (Waterloo, Ontario: Historical Reflections Press, 1982), pp. 17–31.

90. R. Cobb, *The Police and the People. French Popular Protest, 1789–1820* (Oxford: 1970), pp. 17–37; Steven L. Kaplan, "Réflexions sur la police du monde du travail, 1700–1815," *Revue Historique* 529 (1979): 65–68; A. Williams, *The Police of Paris, 1718–1789* (Baton Rouge, La.: Louisiana State University Press, 1979); J. Aubert, ed., *L'Etat et sa police en France, 1789–1914* (Geneva: Droz, 1979).

91. Emsley, *Policing*, pp. 86–87, 138–139.

92. J. Spengler, *French Predecessors of Malthus. A Study in Eighteenth-Century Wage and Population Theory* (Durham: Duke University Press, 1942); A. McLaren, "Some Secular Attitudes Toward Sexual Behavior," *French Historical Studies* 8 (1974): 619; J. Donzelot, *La police des familles* (Paris: Editions de Minuit, 1977), pp. 15–16, 36; Joseph and Fritsch, *Disciplines à domicile*, pp. 59–69; M.-F. Morel, "Ville et campagne dans le discours médical sur la petite enfance au XVIIIe siècle," *Annales, E.S.C.* 32 (1977): 1010–1011.

93. G. Vigarello, *Le corps redressé. Histoire d'un pouvoir pédagogique* (Paris: Jean Pierre Delarge, 1978), pp. 164–181.

94. J. S. Taylor, "Philanthropy and Empire: Jonas Hanway and the Infant Poor of London," *Eighteenth-Century Studies* 12 (1979): 285–305.

95. Donzelot, *Police des familles*, pp. 27–29; Joseph and Fritsch, *Disciplines à domicile*, pp. 230 n. 37, 231ff.; J. F. Traer, *Marriage and the Family in Eighteenth-Century France* (Ithaca, N.Y.: Cornell University Press, 1980), pp. 137–191.

96. H. Chisick, *The Limits of Reform in the Enlightenment. Attitudes toward the Education of the Lower Classes in Eighteenth-Century France* (Princeton, N.J.: Princeton University Press, 1981), pp. 224–225; R. Deniel, *Une image de la famille et de la société sous la Restauration, 1815–1830* (Paris: Editions Ouvrières, 1965), pp. 133, 276; Donzelot, *Police des familles*, pp. 34–38 (on p. 35).

97. Donzelot, *Police des familles*, pp. 30, 50–51; A. Corbin, *Alexandre Parent-Duchâtelet. La prostitution à Paris au XIXe siècle* (Paris: Seuil, 1981), p. 38.

98. Joseph and Fritsch, *Disciplines à domicile*, pp. 118–120.

99. J. Leith, "The Hope for Moral Regeneration in French Educational Thought, 1750–1789," in P. Fritz and D. Williams, eds., *City and Society in the 18th Century* (Toronto: Hakkert, 1973), pp. 215–230; J. Defrance, "Esquisse d'une histoire sociale de la gymnastique, 1760–1870," *Actes de la Recherche en Sciences sociales* 6 (1976): 37; Joseph and Fritsch, *Disciplines à domicile*, pp. 41–46 (La Chalotais on p. 42); Chisick, *Limits of Reform*, pp. 177–178, 203, 238–243, 279–280.

100. A. Petitat, *Production de l'école, production de la société. Analyse socio-historique de quelques moments décisifs de l'évolution scolaire en Occident* (Geneva and Paris: Droz, 1982), pp. 174–175, 180–181.

101. F. Furet and J. Ozouf, *Lire et écrire. L'alphabétisation des Français de Calvin à Jules Ferry*, 2 vols. (Paris: Presses Universitaires de France, 1977). Guizot quoted by Th. Zeldin, *France, 1848–1945*, vol. 2, *Intellect, Taste and Anxiety* (Oxford: Clarendon Press, 1977), p. 150.

102. P. Deyon, *Le temps des prisons* (Paris: Editions Universitaires, 1975), pp. 54–61; Kaplan, "Réflexions sur la police," pp. 27–30, 48–49, 56–57, 76–77; Sewell, *Work and Revolution*, pp. 72–91.

103. The fullest and the most thoughtful discussion of these matters is to be found in I. Wallerstein, W. G. Martin, and T. Dickinson, "Household Structures and Production Processes: Preliminary Theses and Findings," *Review* 5 (1982): 437–458. On the importance of nonmonetary transactions that endowed the world of workshop production during the early modern period, see P. Léon, "Morcellement et émergence du monde ouvrier," in F. Braudel and E. Labrousse, eds., *Histoire économique et sociale de la France*, vol. 2, *Des derniers temps de l'âge seigneurial aux préludes de l'âge industriel, 1660–1789* (Paris: Presses Universitaires de France, 1970), pp. 666–668; E. Scholliers, "Remuneratiemodaliteiten bij loontrekkenden," in H. Coppejans-Desmedt, ed., *Economische geschiedenis van België. Behandeling van de bronnen en problematiek. Handelingen van het Colloquium te Brussel, 17–19 Nov. 1971, Ve en VIe secties* (Brussels: Archief- en Bibliotheekwezen in België, 1973), pp. 50–51; D. Woodward, "Wage Rates and Living Standards in Pre-Industrial England," *Past and Present* 91 (1981): 28–46; M. Sonenscher, "Work and Wages in Paris in the Eighteenth Century," in M. Berg, P. Hudson, and M. Sonenscher, eds., *Manufacture in Town and Country Before the Factory* (Cambridge: Cambridge University Press, 1983), pp. 147–172. R. S. DuPlessis and M. C. Howell, "Reconsidering the Early Modern Urban Economy: The Cases of Leiden and Lille," *Past and Present* 94 (1982): 49–84, have demonstrated that small commodity production sometimes resolved a range of needs within both the ruling class and the larger society. See also C. R. Friedrichs, *Urban Society in an Age of War: Nördlingen, 1580–1720* (Princeton, N.J.: Princeton University Press, 1979), pp. 204–206, 258–287, 294–297.

104. K. Marx, *Capital*, vol. I (London: Lawrence and Wishart, 1977), p. 694. In 1827, Thomas Batty Addison, summarizing John Clay's ideas with regard to prison reform, wrote that because factory labor provided its own discipline, few factory workers committed property crimes. It was the pieceworkers "who are under no restraint as to the Regularity of their Employment, or the Hours of Labour" who filled the pris-

ons. DeLacy, "Grinding Men Good," p. 206. See also Ignatieff, *Just Measure of Pain*, p. 175; and Melossi and Pavarini, *The Prison and the Factory*, pp. 46–47. The physicians Mareska and Heyman, who during the 1840s investigated working conditions in the cotton factories of Ghent, came to the conclusion that factory workers had become far more compliant and that the downward pressure on wages had played a crucial role in that development. They reported that "punishment is much less frequent these days than in the beginnings of the cotton industry because diminutions of wages reduced drunkenness and frivolity and made the loss of any money at all keenly felt." J. Mareska and J. Heyman, *Enquête sur le travail et la condition physique et morale des ouvriers employés dans les manufactures de coton à Gand* (Ghent, 1845), p. 84.

105. W. Lazonick, "The Subjection of Labour to Capital: The Rise of the Capitalist System," *Review of Radical Political Economy* 10 (1978): 1–31.

106. A good sense of the weakness of social control theories of social policy is conveyed in the articles by Gareth Stedman Jones, "Class Expression Versus Social Control? A Critique of Recent Trends in the Social History of Leisure," *History Workshop* 4 (1977): 162–170; J. Higgins, "Social Control Theories of Social Policy," *Journal of Social Policy* 9 (1980): 1–23; F. M. L. Thompson, "Social Control in Victorian Britain," *Economic History Review*, 2d ser., vol. 34 (1981): 189–208.

107. See Henriques, *Before the Welfare State, passim* (especially chaps. 4–5, 10–11).

108. See the perceptive remarks of R. Price, "The Labour Process and Labour History," *Social History* 8 (1983): 57–75.

109. B. Trinder, "Drink and Sobriety in an Early-Victorian Country Town: Banbury, 1830–1860," *English Historical Review*, Suppl. 4 (1969): 5–9; B. Harrison, *Drink and the Victorians* (London: Faber, 1971), pp. 37–63; E. J. Hobsbawm, "Les classes ouvrières anglaises et la culture depuis les débuts de la révolution industrielle," in *Niveaux de culture et groupes sociaux* (Paris and The Hague: Mouton, 1971), p. 195; A. Delves, "Popular Recreation and Social Conflict in Derby, 1800–1850," in Yeo, ed., *Popular Culture*, pp. 98–100; M. A. Smith, "Social Usages of the Public Drinking House: Changing Aspects of Class and Leisure," *British Journal of Sociology* 34 (1983): 367–385. For the Continent: J. S. Roberts, "Der Alkoholkonsum deutscher Arbeiter im 19. Jahrhundert," *Geschichte und Gesellschaft* 6 (1980): 220–242, and debate in vol. 8 (1982): 141–144, 427–433; H. Soly, "Kroeglopen in Brabant en Vlaanderen," *Spiegel Historiael* 18 (1983): 569–577.

110. Th. W. Laqueur, *Religion and Respectability: Sunday Schools and Working Class Culture, 1790–1850* (New Haven and London: Yale University Press, 1976), pp. 94, 155, 172–175, 214–227, 230, 237–239. See also R. Johnson, " 'Really Useful Knowledge': Radical Education and Working-Class Culture, 1790–1848," in J. Clarke, C. Critcher, and R. Johnson, eds., *Working Class Culture. Studies in History and Theory* (London: Hutchinson, 1979), pp. 75–102.

111. B. Supple, "Legislation and Virtue: An Essay on Working Class Self Help and the State in the Early Nineteenth Century," in N. McKendrick, ed., *Historical Perspectives. Studies in English Thought and Society* (London: Europa Publications, 1974), pp. 211–225 (on p. 215). See also C. Reid, "Middle Class Values and Working Class Culture in Nineteenth-Century Sheffield. The Pursuit of Respectability," in S. Pollard and C. Holmes, eds., *Essays in the Economic and Social History of South Yorkshire* (Sheffield: South Yorkshire County Council, 1976), pp. 282–283; F. Hearn, *Domination, Legitimation, and Resistance. The Incorporation of the Nineteenth-Century Working Class* (Westport and London: Greenwood Press, 1978), p. 129; P. Bailey, " 'Will the Real Bill Banks Please Stand Up?' Towards a Role Analysis of Mid-Victorian Working Class Respectability," *Journal of Social History* (1979): 336–353; R. D. Storch, "Introduction:

Persistence and Change in Nineteenth-Century Popular Culture," in *idem*, ed., *Popular Culture and Custom in Nineteenth-Century England* (London and New York: Croom Helm, 1982), p. 5.

112. Delves, "Popular Recreation," pp. 89–98, 103–108, 115–116. See also J. K. Walton and R. Poole, "The Lancashire Wakes in the Nineteenth-Century," in Storch, ed., *Popular Culture*, p. 117; and R. Storch, "The Problem of Working-Class Leisure. Some Roots of Middle-Class Reform in the Industrial North, 1825–50," in A. P. Donajgrodzki, ed., *Social Control in Nineteenth-Century Britain* (London: Croom Helm, 1977), p. 151.

113. See, for example, A. Farge and M. Foucault, *Le désordre des familles. Lettres de cachet des Archives de la Bastille au XVIIIe siècle* (Paris: Gallimard/Julliard, 1982), pp. 15–19, 345–350; B. Schotte, "Bestrijding van "Quaet gedragh" te Brugge in de 18e eeuw, 1724–1774" (Licentiate thesis, State University of Ghent, 1982), pp. 146–147, 161, 367–369; F. Mahy, *De Brugse tuchthuizen in de 17de en 18de eeuw. Een onderzoek naar hun maatschappelijke functie* (Licentiate thesis, State University of Ghent, 1982), pp. 93ff.; A.-M. Roets, *De sociale aspecten van de misdadigheid te Gent in de achttiende eeuw* (Licentiate thesis, State University of Ghent, 1981), pp. 92, 223–226, 256, 269.

114. See, for example, D. Philips, *Crime and Authority in Victorian England: The Black Country, 1835–1860* (London: Croom Helm, 1977), p. 128; A. Soman, "Deviance and Criminal Justice in Western Europe, 1300–1800: An Essay in Structure," *Criminal Justice History* 1 (1980): 1–28; J. M. Beattie, "Judicial Records and the Measurement of Crime in Eighteenth-Century England," in Knafla, ed., *Crime*, pp. 135–136; O. Hufton, "Crime in Pre-Industrial Europe," *Newsletter of the International Association for the History of Crime and Criminal Justice* 4 (1981): 19–24, 26, 29–31; A. Wills, *Crime and Punishment in Revolutionary Paris* (Westport and London: Greenwood Press, 1981), pp. 125, 139.

ACKNOWLEDGMENTS

This chapter was translated by James C. Coonan. John Gillis kindly offered us the opportunity to present an earlier draft to a conference on "Proletarianization: Past and Present" at Rutgers University in May 1983. We wish to thank all of the participants for their helpful comments and especially to acknowledge Robert S. DuPlessis's friendly and firm pressure to be more specific about the role of the State and the concept of social control. We also benefited from stimulating discussions with Franklin F. Mendels. Above all, we are deeply indebted to David Levine for the substantial time and effort he gave in criticizing and suggesting improvements on our contribution. None, of course, can be held responsible for its shortcomings.

5

Social Formation and Class Formation in North America, 1800–1900

Bryan D. Palmer

CONCEIVING LABOR AND CAPITAL IN PAST TIMES

> The positing of the individual as a *worker*, in this nakedness, is itself a product of *history*.
>
> Marx, *Grundrisse* (1857–1858)

The process of proletarianization in the New World commenced in the late fifteenth century. It was premised not on demographic growth but on demograhic destruction. In the words of C. L. R. James:

> Christopher Columbus landed first in the New World at the Island of San Salvador, and after praising God enquired urgently for gold. The natives, Red Indians, were peaceable and friendly and directed him to Haiti. . . .
> . . . The Spaniards, the most advanced Europeans of their day, annexed the island, called it Hispaniola, and took the backward natives under their protection. They introduced Christianity, forced labour in the mines, murder, rape, bloodhounds, strange diseases, and artificial famine (by the destruction of cultivation to starve the rebellious). These and other requirements of the higher civilization reduced the native population from an estimated half-a-million, perhaps a million, to 60,000 in 15 years.[1]

For Marx, this original accumulation was the outcome of economic

229

power, of that brutish midwife, sheer force, cast in new, internationalist dress:

> The discovery of gold and silver in America, the extirpation, enslavement and entombment in the mines of the aboriginal population, the beginning of the conquest and looting of the East Indies, the turning of Africa into a warren for the commercial hunting of black skins, signalised the rosy dawn of the era of capitalist production. These idyllic proceedings are the chief momenta of primitive accumulation.[2]

By the early eighteenth century, the historical consciousness of the stages of these developments noted by James and Marx was sufficiently rooted to find expression in popular fiction, *Robinson Crusoe* being, among other things, an allegorical depiction of the origins of the rising bourgeoisie:

> My island was now peopled, and I thought myself very rich in subjects; and it was a merry reflection which I frequently made, how like a king I looked. First of all, the whole country was my own property, so that I had undoubted right of dominion. Secondly, my people were perfectly subjected. I was absolute lord and lawgiver; they all owed their lives to me, and were ready to lay down their lives, if there had been occasion of it for me. It was remarkable, too, we had but three subjects, and they were of three different religions. My man Friday was a Protestant, his father was a pagan and a cannibal, and the Spaniard was a Papist. However, I allowed liberty of conscience throughout my dominions.[3]

Crusoe's self-satisfied assessment introduces us to themes of relevance in the history of class formation. We are immediately confronted with a series of relationships: population and property, subordination and superordination, and hegemony and segmentation. But this complacent and controlled caricature of class formation is ahistorical. As Hymer suggests, we also need "the story of Friday's grandchildren."[4] And we need to recognize, as well, that no society, let alone one as vast and complex as that of North America, is an island as simple as Crusoe's domain.

Capitalism in North America was premised on an initial expropriation of aboriginal peoples. The diversity of paths to this end ran the gamut from the genocidal assault on Newfoundland's Beothuks[5] to the less overt, but massively brutal, clearances of Andrew Jackson's southern "campaigns" (1814–1824).[6] Equally traumatic were the superficially more benign disruptions associated with the range of European interventions—cultural, religious, physiological, social, and economic—in the ecosystems of the tribes of the coasts and woodlots, in which the universal aim was the appropriation of profit from a commerce in luxury commodities harvested through the native people's skills, knowledge, and proximity to the fur-bearing animal world.[7] This was not an unmediated process of Indian acquiescence and subjugation.[8] As studies of Indian women and the fur trade have shown, it did not always leave the white population in firm and settled control of the land. The production of furs was, on occasion, inseparable from the reproduction of a mixed-blood population that would prove a thorn in the side of capitalist development in the Canadian West well into the 1880s.[9] Despite all the complexities, the paths of appropriation and expropriation converged, by the 1880s, in a hegemony that merged class and racial interests.[10]

Seldom has this history received its due, and rare are the attempts to tie together the processes of expropriation, accumulation, and racial authority in the early history of American capital. It was this initial development, however, that established the preconditions for much of the march of economic and social differentiation in North America. Jackson was perhaps understating the importance of this historical process in a curt line on Indian–white relations in his message to Congress (1829): "Our conduct toward these people is deeply interesting to our national character."[11] But he was nevertheless aware of its continuity. His program of Indian removal had precedents in the Northeast and could unite plantation slaveholder, independent yeoman, merchant trader, manufacturer, and the waged plebeian masses in often unattainable agreement. Where the "Indian question" was settled first and most decisively, the economic, social, and political separation of labor and capital proceeded to consolidate quickly. In the cities of the eastern seaboard, well before 1800, essential inequalities were a recognizable part of the social order[12] and as early as the 1760s had solidified sufficiently to manifest explicit cultural and political expression.[13]

At the risk of leaving many of the essential interpretive and empirical knots unraveled, this chapter aims to present a view of social and class formation in ninteenth-century North America. It seeks to explore the material contexts of a changing series of social formations, establishing the boundaries within which a working class was formed. To be sure, Canada and the United States were never entirely collapsible into a single social unit; indeed, within each large geographic entity, regional peculiarities readily separated themselves out from the political economy as a whole, as the processes of combined and uneven development ran their course. But there were, nevertheless, general patterns and parallels of striking similarity. It is these that are thrown into relief in the pages that follow.

To address the relation of social and class formation in nineteenth-century North America, it is necessary, first, to conceptualize a periodization of capitalist development and, second, to root that process in the concrete context of a particularly cluttered and ever-changing social formation. It is striking how little of this basic kind of rethinking of the nineteenth-century experience has been done. The so-called new social history, in spite of the advances it has made, generally neglects this kind of analysis.[14] For all the flaws in the older Commons literature, it at least never abandoned so readily the *longue durée* for a substitutionist immersion in the particular.[15] An older set of reifications—the market and the union—has been replaced with a newer, more fashionable and formidable fetishization of method and discrete subject.[16] We in North America are dangerously close to "a historical practice, which, however far removed from traditional canons, confines itself to specialist areas, partial problems, and tentative technical innovations, and thereby remains loyal in fact to the least creative kind of empiricism." In the words of Pierre Vilar, " 'Real' Marxist history, by contrast, must be ambitious in order to advance."[17]

My ambitions here are threefold. First, I want to introduce some essential Marxist notions regarding the stages of capitalist development into the discourse on North American class formation. To do so, of course, is to generalize broadly and to select, across the span of a century, chunks of historical time that bear some resemblance to one another. (I have further simplified the complexities by taking the century as my chosen field and the decades as my rough points of division. As will be apparent, any exact dating of various moments of historical transition within a geographic and socioeconomic entity as cumbersome and unwieldly as North America is will prove contentious, but it is the larger patterns of development I am concerned with here).[18] Second, if it is essential to return to Marxist categories, it is also my aim to suggest some possible ways of rethinking these analytic premises. It should be clear that Marx's analytic categories, derived from the "classical" case of English proletarianization, may well require some "groping" through if they are to stand the test of the American experience. And that, the testing of a Marxist sense of periodization against the class formations and struggles of a set of North American social formations, is my third and final aim.

Marx, writing before the advent of monopoly capital, posited three stages in capitalist development: the so-called primitive accumulation, the period of manufacture proper, and the culmination of capitalism's protracted development, modern industry. In the period of primitive accumulation, the preconditions necessary for the realization of capitalist accumulation were established, giving rise to forms of production and discrete social formations favorable to the future accumulation of capital at the same time that they were, internally, inhibited in their capacity to generate development along purely capitalistic lines. With the creation of a wage-labor force, the commodification of labor power, and the concentration of capital, the process of primitive accumulation precipitated a crisis in the social order. Out of this restructuring emerged the period of manufacture proper. Its defining characteristic was the subordination of productive and property forms to the generalized hegemony of industrial capital, which in turn was marked by the cooperative employment of labor and the emergence of a rudimentary division of labor in handicraft production. Productive life, though turning on the cooperative employment of labor, retained its reliance on human beings and the "subjection of labour was only a formal result of the fact that the labourer, instead of working for himself, works for and consequently under the capitalist."[19] With the division of labor, upon which manufacture rested, arose a refinement of the instruments of labor. This refinement, in turn, transformed the tool into the machine, and with the development of machinery there occurred a fundamental change in the historical development of the productive process: the breakthrough into modern industry. Technical change and the pulse of mechanization, according to Marx, precipitated the productive process into the final stages of capitalist development.[20]

As far as this goes, it is a significant conceptual formulation providing the essential ground on which a Marxist historiography of the transition from feudalism to capitalism has come to rest.[21] But some silences, ambiguities, and ambivalences intrude. First, Marx and subsequent Marxists have, as Seccombe stresses, reduced the field of production to the goods, instruments, and site of waged labor. Production has been divorced from the complex range of socioeconomic activities—gestation and generation of the species, domestic socialization, and a range of productions associated with use, as opposed to exchange, values—that have come to be associated with the reproductive realm. Yet these productions are, in fact, historically central to the creation and continuity of specific social formations.[22] Second, Marx's stages of capitalist development, conceived at the apparent zenith of one mode of production, convey too easily an impression of stasis, in which one stage supersedes another, restructuring the social order with a decisiveness and finality that much recent historical investigation calls into question.[23] Third, as Lebowitz suggests, Marx's oeuvre, and necessarily his stages of capitalist development, were one-sided: concentrating on capital, his analysis "overdetermined" his argument away from concerns with the multifarious agencies of class experience.[24] Class formation was both structured necessity and active self-creation.[25]

Let us turn to the stages of North American capitalist development, exploring the complexity of specific social formations in the discrete periods suggested by Marx's own periodization. But let us as well extend the argument in those lines originally suggested by Robinson Crusoe. The reductionist, static, and one-sided analysis of capitalist development (and consequently of class formation) over time can be avoided by bearing in mind those very relationships that Crusoe called attention to: population and property, subordination and superordination, and hegemony and segmentation.

To do this, however, presupposes a rejection of the stress, in much Marxist literature, on mode(s) of production. And here, though not in many other analytic realms, it is possible to reach agreement with Hindess and Hirst, who argue:

> At most the concept of determinate social formation specifies the structure of an "economy" (forms of production and distribution, forms of trade, conditions and reproduction of these forms), forms of state and politics and forms of culture and ideology and their relation to that economy, economic classes and their relations, and the conditions for transformation of certain of these forms.[26]

Thus, the movement away from the mode of production as a conceptual core of interpreting class formation is an attempt to supersede "the unjustifiable reduction of analysis to an extremely limited range of economic class relations in which there is one category of possessing agent and one of non-possessing agent and the consequent neglect of . . . more complex forms of class relations." Refocusing our attention on the social formation promises to liberate Marxist analysis from "a false narrowing of the field of the socio-economic," overcoming almost a century of "failure to conceptualize adequately the integration of the socio-economic with politico-legal relations of state and the cultural formation of groups and classes."[27]

THE SOCIAL FORMATION, 1800–1850

The Hegemony of Merchant Capital

> Especially during the rise and expansion of capitalism, merchant capital displayed a particular ability to organize various, and even competing forms of labour; to centralize the profits from disparate economic activities and even economic systems; to coexist with a wide range of political institutions, ideologies, and regimes; to link different economic systems through the manipulation of their respective surpluses; to promote economic growth and yet to freeze it within a particular set of social relations of production; and, in short, to act as an agent of economic and social change within narrow limits and as an agent of political stability and *status quo* outside those limits.
>
> Fox-Genovese and Genovese,
> "The Janus Face of Merchant Capital" (1983), pp. 5–6

Merchant capital, as the Genoveses have recently reminded us and as Dobb, following Marx, long ago argued, is neither a mode of production nor a stage in economic development.[28] It is, rather, an intermediary, always prone to parasitism and political compromise, quick to assert the primacy of an economism of commercial exchange over the more substantive transformation of the social relations of production.[29]

A merchant in Defoe's *The Compleat English Gentleman*, when confronted with a squire's dismissal that he was no gentleman, reached into the very substance of his class position to reply: "No sir, but I can buy a gentleman." Historical destiny, however, cannot be purchased. The merchants, ever dependent on the allies they aimed to subordinate to their commercial ends, could never dispense with these other social groups. As a class, the merchants "nowhere turn up on their own: here we find merchants plus planters, there, merchants plus the representatives of the state." To see merchant capital in this way is not to minimize its importance or to dismiss its historical impact:

> The fruits of merchant capital included the primitive accumulation of capital that proved indispensable to the flowering of the capitalist mode of production; organized and far-reaching markets with extensive dealing not only in luxuries but increasingly in the staples that would lay the basis for a mass world market; systems of law and procedures of accounting appropriate to the rational conduct of business; territorial enclaves of bourgeois social relations is still fundamentally precapitalist societies; and the gruesome resurrection of such ancient forms of business and labour as the slave trade and chattel slavery.[30]

In an epoch of late primitive accumulation, in which a market system was in place, but a market society, rooted in the impersonality of productive relations, was not yet consolidated, merchant capital looked always to the past while the movement of socioeconomic life twisted its head in the direction of the future.

Across the length and breadth of the pre-1850 North American social formation, merchant capital was hegemonic: in the South a planter ruling class embedded in the slave relations of production was nevertheless structured into dependency on the world market and its bourgeois relations; in much of the manufacturing Northeast, commercial capital orchestrated sweatshop labor and craft forms of production; and among the many farms of British North America and the free states, subsistence was supplemented by mercantile credit and staples production. Merchant capital restructured the social order at the same time that it sought to solidify tried and true modes of accumulation. Ever attentive to the movement of goods, it created a transportation infrastructure to facilitate exchange. Such projects necessarily called into being a wage-labor force, altered relations of town and country, and demanded stark self-examinations on the part of promoters, politicians, and planters. All of this took place, moreover, against any conscious attempt to revamp the nature of the political economy. But the consequences of such consequences were anything but a preservative of the status quo. A home market was in the making, and its rise signaled the emergence of a social order bent toward commodity production. Trade had created the preconditions eroding its own hegemony as the movement of staples came to be overshadowed by the output of goods.[31]

Merchant capital, its face turned to the past, had brought such relationships into being, at the same time that it knew little of what their impact would be in the future. Bargains were struck between contending factors but were structured along lines determined by merchant capital's hegemony. Jeffersonian agrarians and Hamiltonian commercialists reached the ultimate compromise, reflective of merchant capital's capacity to conciliate seemingly competitive economies, political institutions, ideologies, and forms of extraction of labor surplus. Bowden's *Industrial History of the United States* offers a cogent description of this process:

> To the Jeffersonians the propertied classes most worthy of power were the landed classes. To them the moneyed classes cherished by Hamiltonian policy were at first anathema. But . . . the Jeffersonian party came to terms with men of money property. There was a reconciliation of the business men with the agrarian government on the basis of their acquiescence in "the reformed order of things"—which meant not a whole loaf as under Hamilton but a goodly portion.[32]

This metaphor of "not a whole loaf . . . but a goodly portion" captures the character of social relations in an epoch of primitive accumulation and the hegemony of merchant capital. The preconditions of capitalist accumulation were everywhere being established and forcing merchant capital against its conservative grain in the direction of a truly revolutionary role.

The Momenta of Primitive Accumulation: Reaching toward the Crisis of Mid-Century

> The specific economic form in which unpaid surplus—labour is pumped out of direct producers, determines the relationship of rulers and ruled, as it grows directly out of production itself and, in turn, reacts upon it as a determining element. Upon this, however, is founded the entire formation of the economic community which grows up out of productive relations themselves, thereby simultaneously its specific political form. It is always the direct relationship of the owners of the conditions of production to the direct producers—a relation always naturally corresponding to a definite stage in the development of the methods of labour and thereby its social productivity—which reveals the in-

nermost secret, the hidden basis of the entire social structure, and with it the political form of the relation of sovereignty and dependence in short, the corresponding specific form of the state.

Marx, *Capital*, vol. 3 (1894)

A hegemonic merchant capital served as broker for at least three distinct economic forms of appropriating surplus in the social formation of the pre-1850 years: plantation slavery; agrarian petty capital rooted in the productive household; and early, if inhibited, manufacturing.[33] As Brenner has stressed, in the case of European development, town and country, though divorced from one another in our arbitrary classifications and empirical inquiries, were in fact caught up in similar processes of large-scale transformation.[34] What proves decisive in the North American case is the extent to which each of these specific economic forms gave rise to internal contradictions that by mid-century demanded resolution. Out of the dissolution of these momenta of primitive accumulation came the transition to industrial capitalism.

Plantation Slavery and the South

Slavery was neither peculiar to the South nor numerically predominant in the slave states. It existed for two centuries in the Canadas but eventually lapsed as a form of labor organization, although other types of bound labor prevailed there, as in other regions of early America.[35] Nearly three-quarters of all free southerners owned no slaves, nor were they connected with slavery in any direct sense. In 1860, 385,000 southern slave owners, 72% of whom owned less than 10 slaves, were dwarfed by the well over 1 million nonslaveholding free families. Slaves themselves, though expanding in numbers from 1,538,022 in 1820 to 3,953,760 in 1860 (a reproductive capacity that surpassed all other Western slave economies), made up less than one-third of the population of the South.[36] Yet slavery was absolutely fundamental in "supplying the dominant propertied classes with their surplus," because "slavery provided the foundation on which the South rose and grew. . . . The hegemony of slaveholders, presupposing the social and economic preponderance of great slave plantations, determined the character of the South. . . . They imparted to Southern life a special social, economic, political, ideological, and psychological content."[37]

A long and distinguished line of analysts of the slave South, stretching from Gray and Hacker to Fogel and Engerman, details the economics of slavery and, despite many disagreements, posits slavery as a planter capitalism.[38] Yet detailed criticism, directed most frontally at *Time on the Cross*, has now made this position untenable. It is apparent that the slave South, though at times exhibiting capitalist tendencies, was profoundly uncapitalistic.[39] The social relations of production, the extraction of surplus, and the organization of the labor process under slavery were consistently determined and structured by the master-slave relation in ways that defied capitalism's capacity to restructure the mode of accumulation by rationalizing a diversity of ways in which labor power could be orchestrated and appropriated. When the laborer was owned outright with direct and unmediated claims to his or her body, such a range of potential did not present itself. To look at the slave South between 1800 and 1850 is to see a rigidly limited mode of extracting surplus caught in the vice of crisis.

Alone in sustaining the slave South was the region's domination of the world market for raw cotton. Southern cotton production, stimulated by both soaring demand and technological innovations, rose from 150,000 bales in 1815 to 2.25 million bales in 1849 (doubling, as well, between 1849 and 1859). Cotton comprised between 22 and 27% of all American exports between 1810 and 1860. Prices, however, moved downward from 1802, bottoming out in 1844 and recovering modestly throughout the late 1840s and 1850s. As long as productivity soared, this deflation proved no great catastrophe to the masters, and the 1850s were years of escalating profit for the planters.[40]

But the weak link in this chain of slavery's development was its continuity and potential for expansion, a potential that had to be met if the slave South as an economic, political, and sociocultural entity was to survive. The slaveholders were dependent on a form of economic extraction of surplus that allowed few options. Gang labor and the absolute appropriation of surplus dictated the necessity of simple instruments of production[41] and restricted the possibility of driving labor to expanded production. The initial costs of securing slave labor were sufficiently prohibitive to constrict the possibility of intensifying labor through increasing the numbers of slaves working a particular acreage, especially for the smaller slaveholders who comprised the bulk of farming producers in the South. According to Phillips, slave prices rose dramatically between 1812 and 1819, 1830 and 1837, and 1845 and 1860. In New Orleans, the ratio of cents of cotton per pound to hundreds of dollars for the average slave dropped from 5 to 1 in 1805 to 0.6 to 1 in 1860, indicating that the price of slaves after 1845 was outstripping the returns of cotton production, giving rise to the "fire-eaters" agitation to reopen the slave trade.[42] Taken in conjunction with soil exhaustion, slavery's tendency to retard economic diversification and to stifle wage labor, mounting marketing costs, and the post-1845 threat to reverse the Missouri Compromise of 1820, the slaveholding planters of the South and their many advocates saw clearly the imperative of the hour. In this context (1) the price of labor had to be reduced, preferably by reviving the African trade; (2) free trade had to be secured to lessen southern dependency on the North and open the market to preferable English goods; (3) the hegemony of the northern mercantile and banking interests over shipping, brokerage, insurance, and credit had to be broken; (4) obstacles needed to be erected against the emerging alliance of northeastern capital and western enterprise, including resistance to the northwestern railways, homesteading, and immigration; and (5) movement into western lands had to be checked to curb the consolidation and expansion of political power in the free states.[43]

Throughout the 1850s, merchant capital balanced the strategic interests of its various productive forms, one against the other, producing here a decision of one camp, there a judgment for another, and yet again another compromise. This was the history of the years stretching from Clay's Compromise of 1850 through the Kansas–Nebraska Act of 1854 to the Dred Scott decision of 1857. This strategy of conciliation had served merchant capital well for over a century. But by the 1850s its time had passed, for other economic forms of appropriation were also maturing to the point that their coexistence in a social formation characterized by competing and contradictory modes of accumulation, however mediated by merchant capital, proved increasingly difficult and contentious.[44]

One measure of this development and a telling indication of the obvious symbiosis of production and reproduction under slavery was the extent to which a slave South caught in the vice of crisis responded with "slave breeding." Though Fogel and Engerman dismiss such "breeding" as mere myth, Sutch has presented conclusive empirical evidence establishing that those slave states of the border and Atlantic coast, where soils were poor and more depleted, were providing the newer slave plantations of Texas, Arkansas, Florida, Mississippi, and Louisiana with a labor force.[45] In the "breeding" states of slavery's productive demise, the reproduction of labor power essential to the slave order as a whole was proceeding apace: slave women in these states exhibited higher fertility than did those of the importing Southwest, and sex ratios saw inordinate surpluses of women.[46] Small wonder that the slave family, so central to the plantation's capacity to produce profit and reproduce itself—an agent of organization, socialization, and discipline—became the locus of class struggle in the slave South.[47]

Agrarian Petty Capital and the Productive Household

Beyond slavery, production and reproduction also meshed in the many households of agrarian America. For a time these households coexisted with slavery, content to subsist and market a minimal portion of their product. But by the 1840s and 1850s, household economies had been largely structured into commodity relations, deepening the North American social division of labor and extending the home market. As Aglietta argues[48] for the United States and as McCallum contends for Upper Canada/Ontario (which lagged a decade or more behind developments to the south), agrarian petty capital stimulated the emergence of farm implements industries, processing plants, and urban expansion.[49] In the process, agrarian petty capital was both subordinated to industrial capital and pitted against slavery, which, if allowed to expand, promised to smother the emerging social formation of manufacture and stifle its politics of growth.

Slavery, of course, was regionally based. Indeed, it had to be if it was not to overtake other productive forms and subjugate merchant capital itself. Agrarian petty capital, on the other hand, was pervasive. Some have seen it as an independent mode of production, bounded by patriarchal authority: a brake on capitalist development governed by the logic of subsistence.[50] In the seventeenth-century world of "New England peasants," in which the importance of land, patrilineage, and the stem family outweighed the incursions of market and merchant, this may have been the case.[51] But in seventeenth-century French Canada, ironically, where one would have expected traditional social relations to consolidate on the legal bedrock of seigneurialism, the *menu peuple* of the land exhibited an irksome individualism and valued their independence.[52]

The *habitants'* refusal to accommodate placidly to a "natural economy" hinted at the degree to which merchant capital and the market mediated the social relations of a patriarchal landed society. To be sure, on the frontier of agrarian production where farms and families marched hand in hand, such forces were far from pervasive as late as the 1820s. Work was arranged along familial lines, and cash was not a universal equivalent but only one of many useful products. Authority was vested not in wealth but in legal control over land, an age- and gender-bound process of social differentiation.[53] Ryan's study of the family in Oneida County, New York, suggests, moreover, that between 1790 and 1820 the household was the principal, if not the solitary, place of both production and social reproduction. Parents conceived children as their flesh and blood at the same time that they conceived of their offspring as labor power, owing them time. In such a context, large families were a sign of the "prosperous farmer." Family loyalty was an economic calculation resting on the expectation of compensation in the single most valued commodity of productive life: land.[54]

Petty capital in the household economy of the agrarian milieu, like

slavery, was thus premised on expansion. It managed, with the movement of farmers to the West, to stave off its ultimate reckoning for a
time, but this postponement of its own demise was secured by the disintegration of the household economy and the rise of a commercialized
agriculture, centered in the West, that was subordinate to merchant capital. Indeed, through land policy, speculation, and internal improvements, the latter fostered a climate of technical innovation and rising
productivity on the newly established farms of the 1840s and 1850s, raising the costs of farming and striking the decisive and final blow against
whatever autonomy and subsistence character the household economy
had once possessed.[55]

Even before this process had run its course, petty capital was trau-
matized by the demographic and sociocultural realities of a disintegrating rural milieu. Across rural North America fertility plummeted, access
to the land tightened considerably, a generalized crisis introduced aged
landholders to insecurity and inability to provide for their offspring, and
the young were forced to migrate or become proletarians. In discrete
rural cultures, the paths to this end took different twists and turns. The
ultimate consequences were not, however, dissimilar.

Old Quebec experienced the most severe dislocations. Hardly redu-
cible to agrarian petty capital, the seigneurial system of Lower Canada
nevertheless illuminated the tendency toward the disintegration of the
rurally rooted productive household. Precisely because seigneurialism
was a long-standing, if juridically archaic, social organization of landed
relations, it brings into relief the process of rural decay in the pre-1850
social formation. Rural prosperity, increasing marriage and birth rates,
and the declining mortality of French Canada in the years of seigneurial
revival (1792-1802) gave way to a widespread malaise. Declining prices
and yields were exacerbated by crop failures, the devastating impact of
the wheat fly epidemics of 1836 and 1837, soil exhaustion, overpopulation, and a system of perfectly partible inheritance among the *habitants*. The internal market constricted; the size of individual farms
shrank; and in older parishes, fertility declined, many of them recording
an absolute loss of population after 1822. The landless laborers proliferated: thousands were forced off the land and some to outright rebellion in 1837-1838. The crisis of French Canadian society began to
resolve itself in the settling of accounts with an emerging industrial capital in the 1840s and 1850s. Seigneurialism was abolished in 1853-1854.
Over 500,000 *canadiens* migrated to the mill towns and woodlots of New
England and Michigan, as countless others ventured into the urban centers of Montreal and Quebec or trekked to the northern shield. Not until
a second agricultural revolution and concentration on commodity pro-

duction for the dairy industry tipped the rural scales in the direction of agribusiness in the 1880s, did the Quebec countryside exhibit any semblence of even the most modest recovery.[56]

On the Upper Canadian frontier, a crisis on the land did not develop until well after 1840, but early speculators held much of the best land, and church and state each took one-seventh of the province's acreage. Free land grants, originally designed to attract settlers, were turned back in 1826, replaced by sale through public auctions that were exploited by large land companies and unscrupulous colonizing agents. Assisted emigration efforts were curtailed, and prospective landowners now had to pay for their passages and purchase their lots. Small freeholders, who had gained a foothold before and during the 1820s, found the going rather rough in later decades. Even large families could not insure their prosperity, and prior to 1840 only 2 to 5% of all rural producers in Upper Canada had over 100 acres in cultivation. Although a distinct minority could afford to hire labor for the initial land clearance, few new arrivals in Upper Canada were willing to work for wages. As Lord Goderich, the colonial secretary, explained in 1831: "Without some division of labour, without a class of persons willing to work for wages, how can society be prevented from falling into a state of almost primitive rudeness, and how are the comforts and refinements of civilized life to be procured?"[57]

By the mid-1830s, land policy, speculative endeavors and hoarding, and the penetration of the market and social differentiation in town and country were lending considerable force to Goderich's insistence that "there should be in every society a class of labourers as well as a class of Capitalists or Landowners" (presaging Edward Gibbon Wakefield's later enunciation, in 1833, of his theory of "systematic colonization").[58] An irate Kingston mechanic complained in the midst of the severe depression of the late 1830s that "country mechanics, like birds of passage, this summer are pouring into undertakers, working late and early for *twelve dollars a month* subject to be hired out again like slaves, to others at advanced wages—a degradation that the meanest bushwacker swaying an axe, who neither spent years nor months in practice or study of his calling seldom submits to." By 1851, in the rural areas of the Home District to the east of Toronto, some 10,172 out of 14,994 laboring-age males (67.8%) were landless, and wage rates had plummeted across the Canadas.[59]

The demographic dimensions of the mid-century crisis in Canadian rural life have been explored recently by Gagan in a study of Peel County. His research confirms the early alienation of land in the 1830s, the place of speculation and land policy in the creation of early fortunes, and the privileges and economic stability accruing to those present at the outset of Peel's settlement. In the ensuing years, families devised new inheritance strategies that attempted to offset the more debilitating consequences of the wheat boom in the 1840s and 1850s when land prices soared. But the depression of 1857 burst this bubble, and by the 1860s rural society had collapsed. Its fall was secured by the historical drift into overspecialization in a commodity that could no longer reap an economic bonanza. As wheat production declined markedly between 1860 and 1870 (by approximately 60%), the uncertainties of a hopeful generation were confirmed in their worst possible light. Indeed, over time, farm families had been adapting to the structural collapse of the household economy. They grew smaller and more persistently simple (signifying the disappearance of relatives, visitors, boarders, and hired help), at the same time that the birthrate dropped and marriage was delayed until later ages. These were the demographic contours of a society of constricting opportunity and deteriorating potential, the reproductive reflection of productive disorder. They were one moment in the historical development of these forces pushing people into wage labor and closing the door on the independent household economy. The expansion and contraction of the wheat monoculture thus provided the agricultural surplus that stimulated economic growth and set the stage for rising land prices that moved the newly arrived into the labor market. Finally, it forced the "surplus" offspring of petty producers in the same direction as the promise of rural Canadian life faded in the face of pressures it could not absorb and had to deflect.[60]

Elsewhere, too, merchant capital fostered reliance on staples that stifled economic diversification and conditioned particular forms of proletarianization and specific modes of social reproduction. This process had vast ramifications in the interconnected productive and reproductive spheres. The subversion of the household economy revamped social structure and may well have had far-reaching cultural consequences. In the timber colony of New Brunswick this could give rise to a derogatory mythology of the lumber workers' demoralization,[61] while in the Newfoundland outport family fishery, it might be reflected in a uniquely ritualistic reorganization of the social relations of working life during the Christmas/New Year's festive mumming.[62] And in the farming communities of the northeastern United States, where the emergence of urban markets and a transportation system capable of reaching them engendered commercialized agriculture after 1820, declining fertility signaled the end of the patriarchal household. With this came the recognition that economic considerations based on the limited availability of land now overrode customary inheritance practices and the primacy of family preservation.[63] In Oneida County, for instance, an "undulating wave of evangelical fervor" in the pre-1840 years expressed "a more decidedly privatized and feminized form of religious and social reproduction."[64] Coupled with the increasing penetration of commercial specialization, this development challenged the patriarchal household and proclaimed the arrival of a more differentiated social order, leaning noticeably toward acquisitive individualism.[65]

In its capacity to transform its very substance, the productive household of agrarian petty capital was able, unlike slavery, to subordinate itself to commodity relations and the voracious demands of merchant capital. It paid the price that slavery never could, relinquishing its particular form of accumulation, ideology, and culture, privatizing the family, and ultimately subjecting itself to a revolutionary economic rationality. Movement west was thus a striving for independence and a rejection of the familial restrictions of past productive life in the household.[66] In this "leveling spirit" of expansion, however, merchant capital remained hegemonic. A transplanted and commercialized agrarian capital adapted to, rather than challenged, its dominance.[67] Early manufacturing, for a time, followed a similar course, as yet another momentum of primitive accumulation could be expected to do. But unlike slavery and the rural household, it was destined to do more than mark time while waiting for another economic form to swamp it in its wake.

Early Manufacturing

In 1794 Tench Coxe described American manufacturers as "farmer craftsmen". By 1825 Zachariah Allen had characterized them as "village artificers." On the eve of the Civil War James M. Williams's *An American Town* viewed such manufacturers as "city operatives."[68] These evolving perceptions capture the drift from household production to mill town to the factory system. But at any given time, textile production could take place in the homespun manufactures of New England villages, the declining putting-out system of New York, or the mechanized mills of Pennsylvania's Rockdale.[69] Cotton manufacturing outpaced all other production, employing 33,150 males and 59,136 females by mid-century, with over 1,000 establishments scattered across 24 of the 31 states turning out goods valued at more than $43 million.[70] The diversity, volume, and geographic distribution of early manufacturing was remarkable. Competitive shoe manufacturers were found in Lynn (Massachusetts), Montreal, and Toronto,[71] rural iron works early located in St. Maurice, Lower Canada, Marmora and Potter's Creek, Upper Canada, Pennsylvania, and the slave states of Georgia and South Carolina,[72] whereas the metal manufactures gravitated toward the large cities.[73] Specific products, both luxury specialities and essentials to an age of merchant capital, were associated with particular locales: Danbury (Connecticut) with hat making, Waterbury (Connecticut) with cutlery, and shipbuilding with Quebec City.[74] By the late 1840s, paced by Jerome I. Chase and Cyrus McCormick, the agricultural implements industry had consolidated in the Midwest and gave indications of its future centrality in the capitalist transformation of the third quarter of the century, when it would comprise one-quarter of all machine production.[75] Dwarfed by agriculture, manufacturing employed roughly 1.26 million in mid-nineteenth century North America, a bare 5% of the population of approximately 25.5 million.[76]

Although manufacturing was concentrated in both town and country, the former locale was the most visible. Indeed, town and country divisions were increasingly broken down, the two productive sites being linked by the port cities of the eastern seaboard and the Great Lakes. It was here, in the commercial entrepôts of merchant capital, that "metropolitan industrialization" developed most unambiguously, a process capturing Toronto, Montreal, New York, Philadelphia, and a host of other North American cities between 1820 and 1850.[77]

Laurie has delineated the diversity of the structural contexts of work settings in this metropolitan industrialization. In Philadelphia no less than five "discrete but overlapping" laboring milieus existed, "distinguished by scale and mechanization as the first order of differentiation and market orientation as the second."[78] Factories powered by steam or water were concentrated in iron and textile production, which lacked traditional craft organization and averaged significantly larger work forces, 35.7 as opposed to 12.9. Manufactories lacked the power sources to drive mechanized processes but employed more than 25 workers per site. Such enterprises, displacing small shops and the putting-out system, were bound by handicraft organization. They were common to printing, saddle and harness making, hatting, and cabinet or clothing production. Beneath factory and manufactory was the sweatshop, a vehicle for capital-starved journeymen to make the leap to employer status. Hiring cheap, rushed in season, devastated during dull times, trimming costs at every opportunity, and toiling among their workers (who numbered between 6 and 25 per shop), such garret capitalists dominated the tobacco trades. They were also a significant force in furniture, hat and cap, and boot and shoe output. Butchers, blacksmiths, and bakers often toiled in a fourth type of establishment, the ubiquitous small artisan neighborhood shop, in which fewer than 6 workers produced for an immediate market. An absolute majority of Philadelphia's employers as late as 1850, such master craftsmen purchased only a minor, and declining, share of the city's labor power (12.8% of the work force). The lowliest of all producers, many of them women, were hired by manufacturers or merchant capitalists as outworkers, whose weaving, tailoring, or shoemaking could be done in the home, for wages that could not "decently support life."[79]

Such a range of labor process organization suggests why early manufacturing cannot be considered the establishment or the consolidation of accumulation on unambiguously capitalist grounds. Rather, like slavery and petty capital in agrarian production, it was yet another moment in primitive accumulation, establishing the preconditions for capital's ultimate seizure of the social formation. Unlike slavery and the household economy of rural production, however, manufacturing was the beneficiary of the epoch of primitive accumulation. But this was a post-1850 phenomenon, and at least five factors contributed to early manufacturing's limits.

First, even at the very center of metropolitan industrialization, the factory system was never more than a harbinger of what, in the future, could develop. In the advanced city of Philadelphia, for instance, factories employed only marginally more than one-quarter of all workers as late as 1850 and comprised less than 5% of all firms. The pervasive segmentation of the local labor markets meant that mechanization was not an immediate imperative. Tradesmen could exploit the advantages of skill, access to credit, and a generation of stability to advance up a few rungs of the social ladder. Continued reliance on artisanal forms of production and the commercial city's demand for luxury goods simply exacerbated the basic inhibitions to a generalized proliferation of factory conditions.[80] At mid-century, 60% of all New York City clothing workers may have been outworkers or sweated labor.

In the less developed economic context of the Canadas, similar developments unfolded. Hamilton boasted a mere 53 machinists in 1851, and less than one-quarter of the labor force worked in establishments with 10 or more employees. In Toronto in the late 1840s almost 50 shoemaking shops coexisted with two factories. Across southcentral Canada West only the foundries averaged more than 10 workers in 1851 (14.6), and the average productive concern employed only 3.3 workers.[81] As Wilentz argues, such limitations cannot be conceived only as stasis, for changes in work, marketing, and social differentiation had revamped the very nature of craft production: "The shell of the old artisan system remained; within that shell, the system disintegrated, creating new social tensions between large groups of masters and employees."[82]

Such limitations on the organization of production led to a second confinement: manufacturing was restricted for much of the early nineteenth century by the relative scarcity of labor.[83] Labor recruitment necessitated specific concessions. In the textile industry New England employers adopted one of two methods to secure labor power: the Waltham-Lowell system of hiring single women, housing them in dormitories, and substituting an industrial paternalism for the disintegrating patriarchy of the family farm; or the Rhode Island option, in which patriarchy's form was preserved in the face of its economic nullification by acquiring whole families to labor in the mills.[84] And where the factory system was less developed, as in the Canadas, labor scarcity induced employers to practice a pervasive paternalism.[85] The social relations of impersonality, in which nothing but the wage stood between capital and labor, had not yet arrived. This provided the ideological and material foundation on which craft workers labored for a "price," battled to secure a "competency," and "United to support—not combined to Injure."[86] It circumscribed their struggles, as we shall see, but it also confined capital, which was often forced to toast its respectable coproducers or sit down among them to a dinner of cabbage and goose.[87]

The labor shortages that necessitated such class compromises were not overcome until the massive waves of immigration of the 1840s and 1850s, the need for which indicated a third, related limitation of early manufactures. Although substantial in the 1820s (128,502) and 1830s (538,381), immigration to the United States transformed the social structure in the 1840s, particularly in the five years from 1846 to 1850, when 1,282,915 new Americans flooded into the urban labor markets and formed "nomadic armies" of canal and railway navvies. Almost half of these were Irish (593,700), many of them adherents of the Church of Rome, and between 1840 and 1860 the number of American Catholics soared from 663,000 to over 3 million. To the North, the famine-induced migrations of the Irish to British North America were no less phenomenal, totaling approximately 230,000 (or 12.5% of the 1851 population of Ontario-Quebec) in the same half-decade. Sheer numbers of this order helped in the creation of a capitalistic labor market.[88]

It was the very hegemony of merchant capital, a fourth curb on manufacturing, that facilitated such massive demographic inputs into the social formation of the 1840s and 1850s. Between 1843 and 1856, merchant capital experienced its years of "last hurrah." Mechanized consumer-goods industries in New England, the colonization of the Pacific Slope and the Southwest, and the wildly fluctuating returns of King Cotton filled its coffers. These years saw the completion of the North American canal system and the expansion of railway mileage from 4,185 to almost 24,000 miles. Merchants stood directly behind such expansion.

As Porter and Livesay have revealed, they marketed the wares of early manufactures and financed the production of both consumer goods and the heavy needs of the railway supply industry. Their control was as pervasive as it was problematic.[89] Along with land policy and the chaos of early banking, which both "settled" new territories and structured recently arrived immigrants in specific, eventually class, directions,[90] immigration provided the labor force so essential to merchant capital's transportation revolution.

A fifth and final brake on capital accumulation lay in the realm of policy. Merchant capital dictated, in its erratic and fluctuating quest to balance off the particular needs of specific forms of appropriation with the dictates of exchange, the economic program of the state. This was most evident in the wide-ranging debate over tariff protection, a central political issue in the realm of economic policy. In the United States a protective tariff of 1832 was immediately succeeded by the classic compromise, as merchant capital bowed to the demands of Calhoun's slaveocracy in 1833. Future tariff acts offered manufactures only the most modest protections, and not until the Civil War years were duties revised significantly upward. In 1850 Phillips could write that "the income of capital, that is, the advantage annually accruing to every man, rich, or of ever so small possessions, in land, tools, or industrial materials or means of whatever description" was depressed by the curtailment of employment resulting from the neglect of protection, "a wicked, calamitous, and ruinous" aspect of state legislation.[91] Running through the history of the evolution of Canadian "national policy," from the debates of the 1840s through the writings of Robert Baldwin Sullivan, Isaac Buchanan, and William Weir, into the agitation of the Association for the Promotion of Canadian Industry, and culminating in the Galt–Cayley tariff of 1858, Confederation (1867), and the beefing up of protection in 1879, was the same refrain.[92] Not until merchant capital had been nudged to a compliant background was state policy turned to capital's ends.

By 1850, then, in various and different ways, the momenta of primitive accumulation had run their respective courses. Competing forms of appropriation had either reached their limits or were perched on the edge of an historical ledge separating them from their future potential. Through its own contradictory complex of inertia, dynamism, and class compromise, merchant capital brought North America to the brink of an economic transformation that would have far-reaching social and political ramifications, not the least of which would be the nature of the emerging working class.

CLASS FORMATION, 1800–1850

Does not the true character of each epoch come alive in the nature of its children?

Marx, *Grundrisse* (1857–1858)

Labor was the child of the pre-1850 social formation and, like its parentage, was both complex and limited. Historical demographers have paid far too little attention to this reproduction of labor power in North America. Rising from just over 4 million in 1790 to approximately 25.5 million by mid-century, population growth was clearly one component of economic development and specialization.[93]

Little, however, has been done to address the class component of this demographic explosion, reducing much of what little work exists to what Marx dismissed as "an abstraction . . . a chaotic conception of the whole."[94] Moreover, historical demographers have been far too inattentive to the property structures and forms of appropriation within which demographic change took place and which most have conditioned particular reproductive strategies.[95] At the very same moment of historical crisis—the 1840s and 1850s—within merchant capital's epoch of primitive accumulation, slave fertility in sections of the South was rising, farm family fertility was declining, and whole communities were being created out of people displaced from the Old World to the New.

All such demographic developments were conditioned by the limits of particular forms of appropriation, and all led toward increasing social differentiation. About one of six working Americans in 1800 was engaged in nonagricultural labor; by 1850 the proportion had more than doubled to over one-third. The numbers gainfully employed in nonagricultural pursuits rose from 812,000 in 1820 to 2,795,000 in 1850, and those working on the land climbed from 2,069,000 to 4,902,000, the rate of increase in nonfarm labor exceeding that of agricultural work by a ratio of almost 3 to 2. Whereas the general population grew 2.4 times in these three decades, the numbers working in nonagricultural labor expanded 3.4 times. In the four mainland colonies of the Canadas, the work force was more difficult to categorize but may have been even less tilted toward the land, with 276,000 laboring in nonagricultural realms, 215,000 in agriculture, and 159,000 in unclassifiable settings.[96]

Numbers such as these, situated in the schematically outlined contexts of laboring life presented above, are a part of the process of class formation. To see the 1800–1850 social formation as a hybrid of forms of appropriation presided over by merchant capital is to comprehend the essential complexity of class formation in these years. Concerned principally with exchange and only secondarily with production, merchant capital was incapacitated in its ability to effect a revolutionary and universal transformation in the social relations of production. In its fixation on the short term and on the movement of goods through trade, it was willing to coexist peaceably with various productive modes, adapting to them and reconciling their interests as long as its own hegemony remained unchanged. The result was that a segmented working class was recruited and structured into an emerging home market. In such societies, in which capital has not yet usurped the right to rule, class struggle is both a central component of the class's own contribution to its making and a broad process extending past collective acts of resistance into the very substance of the everyday relations of exploitation. This was what Marx and Engels meant when they wrote, "The history of all hitherto existing society *is* the history of class struggles."[97] That such struggles unfold outside any explicit awareness of class, behind the back of a direct political consciousness of common class grievance or program, has been argued forcefully by E.P. Thompson and G.E.M. de Ste. Croix. The confrontations of class experience were therefore exceedingly complex and unfolded in obscure realms, including the patterns and pace of reproduction itself. "In the period of its formation, before the Industrial Revolution," Seccombe concludes, "the working class evidently 'made itself' in more ways than one."[98]

Much of the class struggle of the epoch of primitive accumulation, for instance, is intelligible as resistance to proletarianization. Such resistance, however, took various forms rooted in the specific contexts of appropriation prevailing under the patriarchal agrarian household, slavery, or the manufactories of town and country. It colored the social relations of families and the politics of the age.

Class struggles on the land, for instance, took place predominantly within families. Those driven to landlessness, hiring themselves out to a patriarchal head, proved a troublesome lot. Moodie saw them as an abusive, insulting, and independent contingent, likely to reply to a stern rebuke with hostile dismissal of their "place" and a curt reminder that "they are as good as you; that they can get twenty better places by the morrow, and that they don't care a snap for your anger."[99] More problematic were the traumas associated with the easing of one's own kin into proletarianization. Sons whose access to the land was blocked and lacked alternatives to farming, found their lives of labor stressful in the extreme. One such disgruntled 25-year-old reported in 1834: "I take no peace when at my labor. My father and elder brother are scolding me everytime they come into my presence. Everything I do is all wrong. It is impossible to please them and I get nothing for my labor scarcely at all."[100] Daughters fared even worse and, until they were able to establish their own households, suffered through years of dependency. Those mill women of New England "liberated" from such forms of patriarchal domination, however, found little to their liking in the new regime of waged labor. For some, a few days at the machines cured their "mill fever" forever, and according to Ware, turnover was extensive. To stave off this stark confrontation with proletarianization, many families modified inheritance and devised adaptive "strategies of heirship." Cash began to replace land as fathers struggled both to settle their offspring and to leave customary man–land ratios intact. When parents rocked the fragile social order with rash acts of an "unnatural" second marriage, threatening the interests of the children of the first bed, a charivari might result.[101]

The pervasive unease of potential proletarianization even seeped into the political arena defining much of the ferment associated with discontented Upper Canadian yeomen attracted to Mackenzie or the exotic range of ideological energies associated with the Age of Jackson (Skidmoreite agrarianism, Owenite perfectionism, antibankism, Mormonism, revivalism).[102] For Luther the crisis of proletarianization was the disintegration of the household economy and of "name":

> Where shall we bury our shame?
> Where in that desolate place,
> Hide the last wreck of a name,
> Thus broken and stained by disgrace?

A debased patriarchy threw down the gauntlet of challenge to inequality and the emerging "American System": "But if you want to improve your minds, take care of your families, and educate your children, you are called 'Disturbers of the peace,' 'Agitators,' 'An unholy alliance,' Disorganizers, a 'Dangerous Comination' against the *higher* ORDERS."[103] Class struggle on the land, at the shared point of reproduction and production, oozed out of the family into the very fabric of the social formation.[104]

For slaves the process of resistance was both more subtle and, on rare occasions, more bloodily explicit. This was as it had to be in a system of absolute appropriation of labor power and direct brutalizing ownership. Notable slave revolts—Prosser's Virginia plot (1800), the St. John Parish, Louisiana, uprising (1811), Vesey's Charleston conspiracy (1822), and the Nat Turner rebellion (1831)—were but the visible tip of a veritable iceberg of discontent.[105] In a society so pervasively patriarchal, the family was an agent of class oppression and exploitation at one level and an essential force in the defense of a humanity undercut daily, on another.[106] Family ties sustained Afro-Americans through their enslavement, building bridges to their future freedom, republicanism, and difficult entry into the working class. "White folks," testified one ex-slave in the 1930s, "do as they please, and the darkies do as they can."[107] With the nature of choice severely limited under slavery, the class struggle assumed forms familiar to all, encompassing efforts less dramatic than open revolt, nurtured in "quarters which produced a collective spiritual life."[108]

At the classic point of production, the class struggle assumed more easily recognizable forms, although much of the best recent work in social history underscores the need to see past the work site into the evangelical fervor, pleasurable recalcitrance, street festivals, and attachments to raucous, respectable, or republican behavior that themselves colored so much conflict in the cultural, political, and ideological realms.[109] By the 1830s, especially in the commercial cities of metropolitan industrialization, craft workers were cognizant of the exploitation and invasion of their "dearest rights" following in the wake of a social differentiation that was

> Rigid, unequal, and unjust
> That monster ground us to the dust,—
> And rolled us in the gutter.

The formation of unions, labor parties, benevolent associations, and a general trades assembly that marched through Philadelphia's streets under the banner "We Are All Day Laborers" attested to the skilled workers' emerging challenge. For the first time, moreover, the trades, as indicated in verse from the port city of Saint John, New Brunswick, were reaching toward an unprecedented solidarity of labor:

> And more of old Jack's Kin
> Would flock to our banners;
> We do not mean Merchants, Priests,
> Doctors, or Lawyers,
> But Founders and Fishermen
> Hewers and Sawyers,
> With Sad'lers, Sailmakers, and
> Coopers and Barbers,
> And pondmen and others who
> work round our harbours,
> You may guess we have still a
> vast host left behind,
> And to show you still more of
> the public mind,
> Zoby Zog signs for scores who
> go on barefoot or hobnail,
> Buck-sawyers and rabble and
> rag-tag and bob tail[110]

But for all the promise of collectivity, the early workingmen's movement was not an expression of the unified class front that it strove to present.[111]

If the working women of the New England mills succeeded in integrating their struggle for the 10-hour day in the 1840s with craftsmen's demands, the cohesion of these years was fragile at best and about to wither as the mill women were replaced by incoming Irish and French-Canadian labor.[112] Among the women domestics and sweated toilers of home "industry," however, few were the ties to labor as an organized entity. They were outside such developments, just as they remained inside the isolation of work ecologies walled in by the kitchen or the attic.[113] Equally outside were the timber workers of the Ottawa Valley, whose Shiners' wars of the 1830s defied incorporation in anything resembling a labor movement, or the rough canalers who, if not isolated from one another, lived in worlds apart from the printers, building tradesmen, shoemakers, stone masons, and shipwrights of the urban trades.[114] Segmented labor markets differentiated by gender, level of skill, ethnicity, region, and organization of production, fostered divisions and tensions that coexisted uneasily with developing forms of protest.[115]

These were the reflection of the many fragmentations conditioned by merchant capital's hegemony and the nature of an epoch of primitive accumulation. At the level of the state, such limitations were incorporated in a range of barriers erected against the freedoms and impersonalities of market relations. Certain tradesmen—butchers, cartmen, porters, and coachmen—were licensed by authority, but others were confined by the legal conception of conspiracy, defined by English criminal law and the Combination Acts of 1799–1800, to which, ironically, both revolutionary Americans and loyalist Canadian colonists looked.[116] As this class struggle in the legal arena was fought out between 1806 and 1842, it threatened to stifle more visible forms of collective action. Yet it was never entirely successful in muffling the voice of labor. In British North America in the first 50 years of the nineteenth century, at least 45 local unions were formed, and 60 or more strikes were waged. As the legal assault on early unionism peaked in the mid-1830s, 173 strikes were waged in Jacksonian America (1833–1837), and at least 26,250 were enrolled in the ranks of trade unions.[117] To fully comprehend class struggle and collective resistance, however, it is necessary to supplement our meager knowledge of strikes with an appreciation of the riot as an expression of class grievance in both the economic and ethnocultural-sociopolitical realms. Over 400 such riots have been identified in the Canadas prior to 1855, and they occurred in equal numbers in the states to the south.[118]

Class formation, then, both structurally and as an active process of self-making, was a fitful process. It proceeded outside any conscious collectivity or commonality among diverse segments of the producing poor. The forms of struggle engendered were unique to particular forms of appropriation. Strategies of resistance were dramatically divergent. Even within a generalized context, such as wage labor, the range of possibilities was striking. An epoch of primitive accumulation had produced a social formation in which the preconditions for capital accumulation were, by 1850, finally established. The development of class was similarly circumscribed, and the years prior to mid-century saw workers' expanding numbers, rudimentary organization, and acts of resistance reveal the potential of class formation. Yet a child, labor would grow to adolescence and eventual adulthood in the future social formations of late nineteenth-century North America.

THE SOCIAL FORMATION, 1850–1880

In the United States of America every independent movement of the workers was paralysed so long as slavery disfigured a part of the Republic. Labour cannot emancipate itself in the white skin where in the black it is branded.

Marx, *Capital*, vol. 1 (1867)

Marx's assessment of the limitations of class formation in the United States has often, quite rightly, been taken as a statement on the ways in which slavery and racism inhibited class consciousness and class struggle. Yet it could equally stand as an evaluation of the social formation, for slavery's persistence attested to the coexistence of various and competing forms of the appropriation of labor power. Merchant capital thrived on such coexistence, even though the social relations of production were consequently crippled. In many spheres of production, then, the revolutionary rupture of the various shackles on the "free" disposal of labor power was postponed until slavery was vanquished, agrarian petty capital sufficiently rooted to expand capital's growing home market (a development slavery's expansionism thwarted), and state policies conducive to capital accumulation on a large scale implemented.[119] Then and only then could labor realize—in both senses of the word—its freedom, comprising the right to sell its power to a "vampire [that would] not lose its hold . . . so long as there [was] a muscle, a nerve, a drop of blood to be exploited."[120]

"I know, as you know," declared William H. Seward, an expansionist Republican and future secretary of state, in 1858, "that a revolution has begun. I know, and all the world knows, that revolutions never go backward."[121] In the same year, in language more cautiously Canadian, the lieutenant governor of New Brunswick warned the colonial office: "All British North America is fermenting."[122] What began as a pervasive set of socioeconomic changes in the 1850s gathered momentum over the course of the next two decades, sweeping aside entrenched social relations of production and restructuring the balance of class forces in North America.

Between 1854 and 1877 the American industrial bourgeoisie triumphed, forged a party to pilot it through the perils of policy formation, seized the reins of state, militarily defended that federal government against an armed secession, consolidated regional support in the West and neutralized the border states, and finally and reluctantly cut the visible chains of chattel slavery.[123] The Canadas had no confrontation with slavery, but the railway promoters who conceived the union of the provinces and engineered the process of state formation, culminating in Confederation in 1867, were not unlike their counterparts south of the 49th parallel. They, too, were moved by fears of incursions upon their terrain, especially of the free soil American expansion into Rupert's Land and the Pacific Northwest, where a bellicose Americanism had reared its head in the Oregon movement. George Brown, the voice of capitalistically inclined agrarianism, articulated the comingling of national and class aspirations:

> The opening up of the country belongs not to Great Britain, but to those who will benefit by it, to Canada. . . . It is an empire we have in view, and its whole export and import trade will be concentrated in the hands of canadian merchants and manufacturers if we strike for it now. . . . If we let the west go to the United States, if the rest of the continent outside Canada and the Atlantic provinces acknowledges the sway of the Republic, we should be unable to contend with her. Our ultimate absorption would be inevitable.

Nor were propertied interests unaware of the economic returns to be reaped from integrating a home market. In the Confederation debates, Alexander Galt voiced this promoter's perspective:

> One of the greatest . . . benefits to be derived from the union (of the province) will spring up from the breaking down of these barriers, and the opening up of the markets of all provinces to the different industries of each. In this manner we may hope to supply Newfoundland and the great fishing districts of the Gulf with agricultural production of western Canada, we may hope to obtain from Nova Scotia our supply of coal; and the manufacturing industry of Lower Canada may hope to find more extensive outlets in supplying many of these articles which are now purchased in foreign markets.[124]

If such class forces did not have to address a regional identity defined by slavery, their compromise would nevertheless unite class factions by discarding the historical and democratic rights of such "national" minorities (which were, of course, effective majorities in meaningful locales) as Quebeçois and Metis.[125]

If the freedmen, francophones, and mixed bloods of North America came up short in this bargaining away of their needs and values, merchant capital was also overtaken. The severe depressions of the late 1850s and 1873–1879 not only proletarianized masses of producers; they also dealt a series of harsh blows to those who found their mercantile houses resting on foundations of shifting sand.[126] Overextension of credit to failed handicraftsmen and the vicissitudes of unpredictable markets undermined precarious empires.[127] At the same time, industrial capital was securing its own long-term interests. As depression drove the weakest to the wall, concentration resulted. The failure rate among U.S. businesses nearly doubled between 1870 and 1878, climbing from 83 to 158 per 10,000 establishments, but the average number of workers per concern increased by 24%. In the industrial heartland of the Dominion of Canada, the depression of the 1870s consolidated capital: over the course of the decade, the number of agricultural implements works decreased by 32, but the hands engaged increased by over 1,000; 100 fewer sawmills employed 3,000 more mill hands; and 6 more factories turned out railway cars and locomotives, but their labor force had increased 30-fold.[128] Especially during the period from the Civil War into the depression of 1873–1878, capital utilized such crises to extract concessions from the state, most visible in favorable tariff schedules secured in the United States in 1864 and in Canada in 1878 and 1879.[129]

If a servile state did not fall easily into line, capital intervened with that most effective persuader: cash. The railway scandals of 1872, around Credit Mobilier and the Canadian Pacific line, were but the public revelations of what Friedrich Sorge dubbed "a true witches' sabbath of corruption . . . in official, business, and financial circles in all bourgeois enterprises."[130] An Ohio spokesman described the House of Representatives in 1873 as "an auction room where more valuable considerations were disposed of under the speaker's hammer than in any other place on earth."[131] He apparently had not been to Parliament Hill in Ottawa. After more than two decades of scandal, bribery, and blatant theft of public lands and resources, the *Saturday Review* could declare that Canada could "modestly challenge comparison" with the United States. Although "her opportunities and means are not so great as those wielded by the lobbyists and log-rollers of Washington, or the bosses and wire-pullers of New York, . . . the most has been made of them."[132]

These actions, legal as well as illicit, fed into industrial capital's emerging hegemony. That hegemony grew out of the developments of the 1850s and 1860s as railway mania and the proliferation of banks and rationalization of currency allowed industrial capital to liquidate debts and break the financial hold that merchant capital exercised over it. Wartime "profit" inflation, most directly in the United States but also in Canada, gave a decisive push to the modest beginnings of such developments that were present in the 1850s. The 1860s, then, as Toronto's *People's Journal* announced, was a decade that "set a going an industrial revolution."[133]

That industrial revolution was unfolding because the old limitations of an age of primitive accumulation were in the process of being displaced. With slavery replaced by sharecropping, the cotton South no longer posed, through its imperialistic designs on free soil, a threat to western farming. Liberalized immigration laws, land acts, and tariff policies all attested to both the state's pliancy in industrial capital's hands and the subordination of mercantile interests. In the realm of manufacturing, Marx's "really revolutionary" path to capitalist production was being followed by many North American direct producers. In 1869 the *New York Times* reported that small manufacturers were being swallowed up by "the greater establishments, whose larger purses, labor-saving machines, *etc.*, refused to allow the small manufacturers a separate existence."[134] By 1872 industry could now be regarded as hegemonic, a product of historical and political, as well as economic advance:

> In the study of our industry, and of its effects upon the growth of civilization, and also of the effects produced upon industry by political and other causes, the United States offer a most important and suggestive field. In the first place our history is complete; the beginning of the nation dates from a definite historical period, and the foundation of its industry is not lost in the obscuring mists of tradition. Then, again, the political constitution of the country, its social equality, and the necessities of the new conditions of its settlement, all conspired to make more evident the fact that productive industry is of necessity the foundation of progress of civilization.[135]

Certainly there were signs of industrial capital's vitality. Canadian cities like Hamilton, Toronto, and Montreal boasted significant industrial populations by 1870. Between 50 and 60% of such work forces, moreover, worked in factorylike settings employing 50 or more workers, a dramatic shift away from the character of work organization at midcentury. By 1880, as Laurie and Schmitz have shown, Philadelphia's factory production expanded markedly, encompassing 90% of the workers in textiles, 75% in printing, and 45% in food processing—rates of distribution that had almost doubled since 1850. Across the United States the percentage of the total labor force engaged in nonagricultural production increased from 41 to 47% during the 1860s. Technological change, accelerating in the post-1850 years with the introduction of the McKay stitcher and a range of specialized machine tools, lent force to such developments. So, too, did the adaptation of the well over 2 million immigrants, largely German and Irish, who came to North America between 1846 and 1857. They and their offspring were the cannon fodder of industrial battle, confined to the lowliest, most poorly paid jobs. Social forces such as these lay behind the rising productivity in the pivotal industrial sections of iron, coal, and railway lines, as well as in the sweated trades of the metropolitan centers. Manufacturing output increased substantially in the depression-ridden decade between 1869 and 1879, outpacing both the 1850s and 1860s. North American capitalism had apparently arrived.[136]

In fact, it had not, although the vast changes of three brief decades convinced most contemporaries that something was afoot. But just what to call it was never precisely defined, and Americans referred to their particular political economy not as *capitalism* but as the *free labor system*. Real producers saw their interests as manufacturers or mechanics in reciprocal rather than antagonistic terms.[137] Although technology had diluted skills in shoemaking and tailoring and was about to debase cigar making and coopering, there were a vast array of trades not yet subordinated to capital. Even where significant specialization had developed, as in hatting or the building trades, an element of workmanship and considerable pride remained in the work-place lives of the skilled. Especially among some crucially placed and thoroughly industrial sectors, such as iron working (molders, rollers, and puddlers), control mechanisms were consolidated in early union legislation. In the perhaps overstated words of Montgomery, "all the boss did was . . . buy the equipment and raw materials and sell the finished product."[138]

Capital itself rarely revolutionized the social relations of production. Instead, it adhered to traditional guidelines and practices and saw production as a quantitative problem reduced to "so many hands, so many dollars." It concentrated on producing more rather than rationalizing the work process or the market. Not until the later 1870s, when the debilitating consequences of the resulting crisis of overproduction, falling rate of profit, deflation, and business disorder revealed themselves in the catastrophic collapse of economic life, did capital turn away from the competitive anarchy of entrepreneurial capitalism and the limitations of the patriarchal firm to embrace combinations, pools, and trusts. Before this, however, throughout much of the period between 1850 and 1880, capital strove relentlessly to reduce rather than reform its labor costs, holding stubbornly to the entrenched if archaic methods of wage cuts, script payment, fines, and month-long pay periods that were the peculiar privilege of an atavistic industrial paternalism straddling both town and country.[139]

Industrial capital's march to hegemony thus commenced in this period of manufacture, from 1850 to 1880, but it was not completed. Capital subordinated other productive forms to its dictates and consolidated a capitalistic labor market. But its pace was slowed by its internal incapacities, and it was locked into the limitations of a social formation bounded by the productive relations of an age of manufacture. Much industrial activity remained concentrated in the country, and nearly 60% of Canadian manufacturing as late as 1880 was located in communities of less than 10,000 population; scarcely one-quarter of the American population lived in settings of 2,500 or more inhabitants. Between 1860 and 1870 U.S. manufacturing employment in the three largest cities increased by 53%, but in those smaller enclaves, ranked twenty-first through fiftieth in population, the increase was almost 80%. Although the conquest of the country by the town, so essential to capitalist transformation, was thus under way, it had not yet proceeded to the point that it had "ruralized" the country, curbing proto-industrialization and reducing the agrarian economy to an adjunct of industry, agriculture. Nor had manufacture's expansion of productivity subordinated labor to capital in other than formal ways.[140]

In fact, it was reproduction rather than production that was crucially responsible for rising output. Gallman argued that the increased supply of labor between 1839 and 1899 accounted for two-thirds of the growth in commodity production. It was not until the 1880s that the output per worker increased significantly (it had stagnated over the 1860s and risen marginally in the 1870s).[141] In this context of limitation and the relatively high social cost of appropriating surplus, the real subjection of labor to capital awaited another epoch. Class formation bore the contradictory marks of this protracted moment of transition.

CLASS FORMATION, 1850–1880

It is not what is done for the people, but what people do for themselves, that acts upon their character and condition.

William H. Sylvis, "Speech to the Iron Molders International Union" (1865)

Between 1867 and 1880 the population of the United States and Canada increased by roughly 26%, from 40,839,000 to 54,517,000. Immigration provided much of this growth, with almost 4,500,000 largely British, Irish, and German newcomers moving into North American cities and counties. They and their second generation offspring became, in many urban enclaves, the American working class. In 1880, more than 70 of every 100 persons in San Francisco, St. Louis, Cleveland, New York, Detroit, Milwaukee, and Chicago were immigrants or the sons and daughters of the foreign-born. As Gutman has demonstrated, it was the second generation that was pivotal in reconstituting the demographic contours of the working class. Aggregate data indicating that immigrants constituted only one-third of the nation's industrial workers mask the numbers of second-generation ethnic laborers in the more than 3.3 million nonfarm wage earners who were classified as native-born Americans. Thus, between 1848 and 1881, the percentage of Toronto's population born in Canada rose from 35 to 60, but the census figures hide the extent to which the majority must have come from immigrant stock. In some locales, like New York, the immigrant workers' significance could not be understated, with 12 of every 13 common laborers coming from their ranks. Among miners, cigar makers, bakers, and stonecutters, the foreign-born and their offspring were highly visible. "Not every workingman is a foreigner," noticed one clergyman, "but in the cities, at least, it may almost be said that every foreigner is a workingman."[142]

Class formation was thus deeply affected by the movement of European peoples into the North American social formation. It was also transformed by the aftermath of slavery, which saw Afro-Americans become acclimatized to wage labor and new forms of dependency. Although this process would not run its course until well after Reconstruction, indeed not until the great migrations of the early twentieth-century war years, its origins lay in this period. As Dubois and Leon Litwack have shown, ex-slaves tasted the first exhilarating breath of freedom in this period, joined the restless movement that a whole series of mobility studies have confirmed was central to white labor, and then found themselves the class losers in a "counterrevolution of property."[143] This was a process encompassing continuity and change, degradation and delight. One part was articulated in a white reverend's Louisville, Kentucky advice to Afro-American Episcopalians:

> You know it is better to work for Mr. Cash than Mr. Lash. A black man looks better now to the white than he used to do. He looks taller, brighter, and more like a man. The more money you make, the lighter your skin will be. The more land and houses you get, the straighter your hair will be.

A black preacher, however, saw the options and possibilities as more open-ended, urging his peers in Florida: "you mus' move clar away from de ole places what you knows, ter de ne places what you don't know, whey you kin raise up yore head douten no fear o' Marse dis un

Marse Tudder.'' Like the freedman's song he saw freedom as leaving behind the oppressions of racial inequality associated with place and one people's power over another: "Bye, bye, don't grieve arter me,/ 'Cause you be here an' I'll gone.''[144]

Many lacked the ex-slaves' compulsion to move and were apt to explore other avenues of seizing the new potentials of a social formation given over to manufacture. The quantitative expansion of the means of production, coupled with the leveling of skills attendant upon the limited use of machines, opened corners of the labor market to women and children. With the introduction of the cigar mold in the 1860s, the number of women cigar makers in the United States soared from 731 to 21,409 in a brief ten years. Seventy percent of all women in U.S. manufacturing in 1870 labored in the needle trades, boots and shoe production, and the textile industry in which, with children, they supplied between 50 and 67% of the work force. Some sectors, such as iron making, flour milling, the building trades, and furniture construction, employed males almost exclusively, leading some historians to minimize the vital place of female–child labor in these years. Yet were we to have looked to Toronto in 1871, we would have noted that 74.6% of all employees in the clothing industry were female or under the age of 16. In printing, tobacco, and even furniture production, between 1 and 5 workers in 10 were women or children. American cities like Chicago, New York, and Cincinnati were known as hives of female and child labor. In Montreal, women and the young were pivotal in production, as they were in mill towns like Cornwall, where three factories in 1881 employed 133 men, 227 women, 186 boys and 190 girls, a woman–child to man ratio of about 4.6 to 1. Indeed, whole segments of the North American working class depended on the collective wages of all members of the family for survival. Children totaled 13 to 29% of the labor force in the cotton mills of Massachusetts, Pennsylvania, and South Carolina. In the face of dire need and expanding employment opportunities for women and the young, families struck reproductive strategies resonating with the new possibilities of productive labor.[145]

Whereas the birth rate per thousand native whites in the United States and industrial Ontario declined between 1850 and 1880 and continued to fall in the following years, recent studies have indicated that this precipitous drop in fertility was not shared by all classes. Professionals, agents, clerks, merchants, manufacturers, and employing craftsmen lowered their fertility rates in order to appropriate rationally the optimum in material goods and social benefits for their family units. In contrast, skilled workers increased their fertility over the same period, and laborers, especially those from the poorer immigrant groups, raised even more dramatically the number of children they were having. In cities like Montreal, in which 1 in every 4 boys aged 11–15 was engaged in wage labor, children were an economic asset to working-class families. Those social classes most constrained by economic necessity responded positively to the opportunities of an expanding teenage labor market, which could be exploited to help provide sustenance for the family. A social formation guided by manufacture's stress on expanding the work force and cutting the absolute unit costs of labor welcomed the influx of cheaply employable women and children, at least in some spheres. Production and reproduction were two halves of the same economic coin, part of the currency of class formation. "Why did you dismiss my daughters?" asked one irate mother of a cotton boss, "I have need of their assistance to live."[146]

To be sure, as capitalism moved out of manufacture and into the age of modern industry, there were signs that "the mature proletarian household" was emerging. This was a family formation characterized by dependency on the male wage, rather than on the collective wages of family members. Premised on the "family wage," or the right of the male breadwinner to remuneration capable of sustaining fathers, mothers, and children in respectable status, the mature proletarian household was characterized by declining fertility, by the termination of the practiced use of children as economic assets. Its locale was the fully industrial capitalist setting of the mine, heavy industry, or the technologically advanced factory; its children were in school; and its wives were working at unpaid domestic labor.[147] Never an option for the immigrant masses or the unskilled, such an "ideal type" of family structure was perched precariously, even for the trades, on the harsh and disruptive realities of depression, seasonality, unemployment, short time, and the blacklist. Katz and Stern, in a study of Buffalo and Erie County, New York, saw the "overproduction" of children grinding to a halt between 1855 and 1900 among just those kinds of workers likely to raise the banner of the family wage. Fertility ratios of the number of children under age 5 per 1,000 married women aged 20 to 49, establish a laborers' increase of 13.5% and a skilled workers' decrease of almost 18%. Similarly, in Hamilton, laborers and the "dishonourable" trades devastated by machines saw rising fertility ratios between 1851 and 1871, compared with stable or declining ratios for more prosperous crafts.[148] What this underscores, and what much demographic inquiry bypasses, is the reciprocity of reproduction and resistance, of class formation in the structural sphere, and of class struggle in the social relations of production.

The family wage was not simply a revival of patriarchy in the working class. It was also the locus of class struggle, of a pervasive demand on the part of skilled workers not yet fully subordinated to capital, for wages sufficient to compensate them for their labor power and provide for its replenishment on a day-to-day basis. If the wage was all that was involved in this struggle, matters might have been settled easily. But there were inevitably other issues: demeanor, dignity, and the limits that the class placed on the development of dependency.[149]

From 1850 to 1880 North America's first labor movement emerged. Led by skilled workers embedded in local communities and associational networks of fraternal orders, sporting associations, clubs, and benevolent societies, it consolidated on a bedrock of emerging class antagonism and conflict.[150] In Canada and the United States, these three decades were marked by the emergence of class struggle and parallel organization ferment. "An insurrection of labor" swept across the industrial heartland of the Canadas from Hamilton to Montreal, driving tradesmen into 62 strikes between 1851 and 1855, an unprecedented agitation followed by 11 often riotous confrontations between the unskilled and their employers in the deteriorating economic climate of the later 1850s. This early wages movement of the skilled peaked in 1853–1854, the same years that witnessed a remarkably comparable upsurge in strike activity in the United States. Four hundred labor-capital confrontations were fought in the more populous American states (a rough strike-to-population ratio in the United States would be 14.1, compared with 14.1 for the Canadas.) Alongside this escalating conflict, the trade unions developed. The 1850s were marked by the proliferation of local bodies and the faint beginnings of international organization among the shoemakers, engineers, and molders. Characterized by a high degree of mortality and localism, unions were almost entirely restricted to the skilled, and of the 30 or more active in the Canadas in the decade, only 2 were not founded on craftsmanship. Inhibited by nativism and Know-Nothingism, still disfigured in the South by slavery, and later devastated by the 1857–1859 collapse, this initial moment of class resolve foundered.[151]

The pieces were picked up in the 1860s and early 1870s as class conflict challenged the social formation; localism gave way to efforts at national organization; and labor reform consolidated a leadership and an ideological presence. Guided by a "producer ideology" that championed labor's respectability and "independence," the reform cause was premised on molders' leader William Sylvis's words that people themselves could alter their "character and condition." "*They* cut down our PRICES!" thundered Ira Steward, "We *shall cut down* THEIR HOURS!"[152] It was an argument and an orientation peculiarly suited to those skilled workers not yet brought to their collective knees by capital. Out of their growing discontent they created Eight-Hour Leagues, the National Labor Union, cooperatives, workingmen's institutes, the Knights of St. Crispin, protective associations, secret assemblies such as the Knights of Labor, brotherhoods of railway workers, and a host of craft unions that convened, over the course of the 1860s and 1870s, in city, state, national, and binational assemblies representing well over 300,000 workers. Across the industrial United States the hours of labor became the focal point of conflict, erupting in the eight-hour campaigns that rocked Massachusetts, Connecticut, Wisconsin, Missouri, Illinois, California, and New York. In Canada the nine-hour movement thrust the "labor question" to the forefront in Hamilton, Toronto, and Montreal, resulting in the legalization of labor organization in the Tory Trades Union Bill of 1872 and the formation of the first centralized labor body in 1873, the Canadian Labor Union.[153]

The shorter-hours struggles of these decades were but the episodic pinnacle of daily agitations culminating in the founding of 40 new national trade unions in the United States between 1860 and 1879; 16 similar bodies were established in Canada, embracing more than 81 locals by 1873.[154] Organization led directly into conflict, with the number of strikes in Canada almost tripling over the course of the 1860s and 1870s, rising from 72 to 276. No such data, however rudimentary, exist for the United States, but it does seem that the pattern of conflict shifted subtly over these decades. During the 1860s and early-to-mid-1870s, as the great molders' confrontations unfolded in Hamilton and Troy, strikes were fought over national issues of moment, but they were waged within local communities. By 1876 and 1877, however, with the insurrectionary railway strikes of December and July, national conflicts, fought out in local areas, were sweeping together the communities of North America, just as the lines themselves integrated larger home markets. The resulting threat to social order necessitated, on a level previously unanticipated, the intervention of a state power guarding capital's rights of property. As one contemporary noted, "the spontaneity of the movement show[ed] the existence of a widespread discontent, a disposition to subvert the existing social order, to modify or overturn the political institutions. . . . Never before in this country—perhaps in no other country in the world—have so vast a number of men taken part in riots and strikes for increased wages."[155]

By the time of the railway strikes, however, a new social formation was hammering the last nails into the coffin of the age of manufacture. The spontaneity of the first truly mass strikes in the history of North American labor merely awaited harnessing before the ambiguities of class formation partially resolved themselves in the Great Upheaval.

Everywhere the old radicalism of the 1860s and 1870s was eclipsed by the failure to cultivate a politics of opposition uncompromised by the "free labor" ideology of Republicanism, the "producer ideology" of the manufacturer-mechanic alliance, or the paternalism of astute Tories. In the work place, resistance was weakened by the tendency of those skilled advocates of the family wage to regard those who could not wrestle such concessions from capital as marginal to labor reform. But to the working women, common laborers, and immigrants so relegated to the periphery, it was the labor reform ideology itself that was marginal. What were they to make of a Boston labor paper's statement that "it is the high and holy mission of labor reform to show to men an object worthier than wealth?"[156] As industrial capitalism's relentless accumulation and concentration of wealth eroded the credibility of this free labor doctrine, materially lessening the distance among segments of the working class, new forms of collectivity emerged.[157]

THE SOCIAL FORMATION, 1880–1900

On the one hand the enormous and continuing stream of humanity, year after year driven to America, leaves behind stagnant sediments in the east of the United States, while the wave of immigration from Europe throws men on the labour market there more rapidly than the wave of immigration to the west can wash them away. On the other hand, the American Civil War brought in its train a colossal national debt, and with it, pressure of taxes, the growth of the vilest financial aristocracy, the relinquishment of a huge portion of the public lands to speculative companies . . . the most rapid centralization of capital. Thus the great republic has ceased to be the Promised Land for emigrating workers. Capitalist production there advances with giant strides. . . .

Marx, *Capital*, vol. 1 (1867)

Great change coexisted with considerable continuity in the transformation of American economic life between 1800 and 1880. The factory often remained in Nelson's words, "a congress of craftsmen's shops rather than an integrated plant."[158] But in the last two decades of the nineteenth century the dramatic shift to modern industry transformed the social relations of production. In the United States the number of wage earners in manufacturing soared from 2.7 million to 4.5 million. Factories employing more than 500 workers, of which there were but a handful in 1870, now became commonplace and by 1900 numbered over 1,500. The average number of wage earners per establishment increased sharply, growing from 65 to 333 in iron and steel, 8 to 65 in agricultural implements, and 31 to 214 in carpets and rugs between 1860 and 1900.

Technological change—the precursor of the assembly line in meat packing, Cyrus McCormick's molding machine at International Harvester, the Bessemer process in steel—extended the factory system as processes used in one industry became, with the rise of mechanized and often interchangeable machine parts, transferable to another. The expansion of installed horsepower per wage earner increased dramatically from 13% in the 1880s to 36% in the 1890s. When the first steel slabs from which nails could be cut rolled out of Pennsylvania's Wheeling's Crescent Iron Works, they were the signs of a managerial assault on labor. A disgruntled puddler responded to such technological innovation by chalking the steel with the words PUDDLERS' TOMBSTONES. But skilled workers were not the only dying breed. All of these developments sounded the death knell of competitive and patriarchal capitalism, moving the United States decisively in the direction of monopoly capital. By 1894 American industrial production ranked first in the world, and the country turned out one-third of the world's manufactured goods. Output per worker, by decade, rose significantly during both the 1880s and 1890s. Experimentation with new corporate forms and new relations with the state, in conjunction with the first attempts to restructure work itself, signaled the "turning point of capital accumulation." Small firms succumbed to the oligopolistic tendencies of the market and the devastating impact of price deflation and depression (1893–1896). The rate of business failures per 10,000 listed enterprises exceeded 100 in 13 of the 16 years from 1883 to 1898, a rate in excess of that of the Great Depression of the 1930s. In popular parlance, capitalism had arrived, and the "robber barons" were in control. As Marx noted in 1858, "when the inevitable transition to the factory system takes place in [the United States], the ensuing concentration will, compared with Europe and even England, advance in seven league boots."[159]

The Canadian social formation was outpaced by this hectic expansion to the south. But between 1870 and 1890 it too tasted the fruits, both bitter and sweet, of economic transformation. Canadian establishments capitalized at $50,000 and over increased by about 50%; employment in manufacturing rose by 76% and output in constant dollar terms by 138%; railway mileage increased from 3,000 in 1873 to over 16,000 in 1896; manufacturing's place, in terms of value added, rose from 19% of the Gross National Product in 1870 to 23.5% in 1890; the real rate of manufacturing output increased over the course of the 1880s; and many industries consolidated during the cresting fortunes of the National Policy (1880–1884). Between 1880 and 1890, for instance, the value of cotton cloth output rose by 125%. Even this dramatic increase understated the gains of the decade's first five years: the number of mills, spindles, looms, and capital investment in cotton cloth tripled in that short period.[160]

To be sure, capital still had some hurdles to overcome before it would reign hegemonic over politicians and regional interest groups, its own internal competitiveness, and its major adversary labor. On balance, however, it was between 1880 and 1900 that decisive steps were taken in just the directions demanded if capital accumulation was to proceed unchallenged. In Canada the 1880s and 1890s saw the final suppression of the Métis inhabitants of the western interior, of central Canada's penetration of the eastern coal fields, and of the colonization of west coast resources and the integration of British Columbia into the Dominion via the completion of the Canadian Pacific Railway. Although Canadian society was far from urbanized (not until the 1920s would the urban population exceed that of rural areas), the subordination of the country to the town was nevertheless a recognized feature of social relations, drawing out the organized resentments of farmers. From 1874, with the rise of the Dominion Grange of the Patrons of Husbandry, through the 1880s and into the revolt of the Patrons of Industry in the 1890s, rural Canada challenged the social formation with cooperative panaceas and eventual opposition in the political arena. The rise of the "new South" and the curbing of independence on the frontier farm, both instigating massive mobilizations of the "people" in the populist revolt of the West and the Southwest, were parallel developments in the United States. Out of them all would proceed the very uneven growth and structured underdevelopment so central to capitalist accumulation.[161]

Such momentous accomplishments were not achieved without the formalization of the increasingly prominent ties between capital and the state. Federal governments became regulatory bodies, shielding capital from cutthroat competition and price deflation, strikebreakers and agents of repression facing down unruly workers and anarchocommunist dissidents, and bagmen arranging land deals, schemes, and promotions. In an age ideologically captivated by laissez-faire and acquisitive individualism, the social formation, through the words of one of its products, John D. Rockefeller, was proclaiming that "the age of individualism is gone, never to return!"[162] For labor advocate Phillips Thompson, schooled in the class struggles of Boston and Toronto, the lessons were all too clear. "Capitalism is king," he declared and added his assessment of the prostitution of politics on the bed of powerful interests: "The real rulers are not the puppet princes and jumping-jack statesmen who strut their little hour upon the world's stage, but the money kings, railroad presidents and great international speculators and adventurers who control the money-market and highways of commerce."[163]

Thompson's words spoke of labor resistance and, implicitly, of capital's need to crush recalcitrant workers. There are indications that these years, which predated Taylorism, the rationalization of the labor process and much of the restructuring of work associated with Fordism and twentieth-century deskilling, saw labor hold considerable ground in its battles with capital. The social cost of labor may well have remained relatively high as wage rates stabilized in a context of falling consumer prices.[164] Craft unions and Knights of Labor local assemblies surged forward during the Great Upheaval, culminating in the continentwide agitations of 1886. Employers reacted with intensive applications of capital, brute force, and early drives to displace workers with machines.[165] An age of opulence and sham individualism spawned a collectivity and awareness among the working class, which came to perceive its declining status and true place in the relations of exploitation. A decidedly capitalistic social formation conditioned a class formation rooted in a mass movement of opposition and challenge.

CLASS FORMATION, 1880–1900

The Knights of Labor are the first national organization created by the American working class as a whole; whatever be their origin and history, whatever their shortcomings and little absurdities, whatever their platform and constitution, here they are, the work of practically the whole class of American wage earners, the only national bond that holds them together, that makes their strength felt to themselves not less than to their enemies, and that fills them with the proud hope of future victories.

Friedrich Engels, *Condition of the Working Class in England* (1885)

Population boomed in the last two decades of the nineteenth century. Canada and the United States grew in size by 33%, from 54.5 million in 1880 to approximately 81.4 million by 1900. Those gainfully employed in nonagricultural pursuits, however, increased their numbers by more than 50%, to almost 18.5 million, or 23% of the total population. Modern industry literally created new proletarian populations: a mere 55,000 American machinists in 1870 expanded 415% to 283,000 by 1900, whereas iron and steel workers saw their ranks expand by 1,200% between 1870 and 1910. The complex of oil, chemical, and rubber industries experienced a 1,900% growth in employment over the same years. In this latter realm, two-thirds of the labor force was immigrant. Many of them came in the post-1886 (in Canada, post-1896) wave of eastern and southern

Europeans that would "remake" the working class demographically in the opening years of the twentieth century. Between 1880 and 1900 the annual numbers of Italians immigrating to North America jumped from 12,500 to 105,000, of central Europeans (Germans, Poles, Czechs, Austro-Hungarians, and so on), from 41,000 to 144,000. These figures soared even more dramatically in the twentieth-century prewar years as the corporate octopus of monopoly capital wound its tentacles around an increasingly differentiated work force.[166]

Many distinctions prevailed within this growing working class in spite of a general drift toward the homogenization of labor.[167] New industries created new skills, and in other spheres, organization insulated some crafts from the degradations of deskilling. Regions, as well, experienced this leveling process unevenly: the large industrial cities of the East and the Midwest witnessed the most marked convergence of wage rates. Wages, however, remained the badge of respectability, so that higher rates of remuneration were the tangible material expression of privilege and status.

One loose assessment[168] suggests that approximately 40% of all working-class families hovered at or near the poverty line, many of them thrust into the depths of destitution by unemployment, disease, or the departure of the male breadwinner. Immigrants, laborers, and the unorganized most often faced such poverty directly. By overcrowding, underconsuming, and scavenging for food and fuel, they could stay alive from one year to the next, but it was often child labor that kept their economic heads above water. An 1882 New York state inquiry into child labor heard this testimony in Cohoes, a cotton mill town:

> Q. How many children have you in the mills?
> A. Four now—three girls and the old man [her husband].
> Q. Could you support your family without the help of the children?
> A. No, it would be too hard to support all of them.
> Q. How many have you?
> A. Just eleven . . .
> Q. Are you able to save any of the earnings?
> A. No, sir, not and keep clothes on them.[169]

Such words could have been heard across industrial North America between 1880 and 1900, when families unable to scrape together the $400 to $600 needed to provide the basic necessities relied on the earnings of their young.[170]

Among the more skilled trades—molding, mining, carpentry—in which as much as 45% of the working class could be located, incomes were sufficiently high, in good times, to ensure adequate food, clothing, and shelter, with the possibility for some small expenditure for recreation or luxury items. A Toronto molder's wife wrote to a Hamilton orphanage in 1889, depositing funds on her adopted daughter's account and revealing the imposed limits and cultivated resiliency of working-class family life:

> Dear Madam,
>   I am sending you $4.00 on my little daughter's account—would like to have sent more but could not on account of my Husband being sick for 2 weeks which leaves us rather short of funds however I hope to get it settled as soon as possible then on the new year pay in advance. . . . We are paying for a $300 piano for Edna and giving her a good education so that if anything should happen to her papa or I she will be able to earn a living for herself and be independent of the world. . . .[171]

Sustained by their respectable self-conception, the wage of the skilled male, the arduous domestic labor of wives, and frugal budgeting, families such as this woman's weathered the storms of a precarious life in industrial America. Their circumstances shifted with the fluctuations in the business cycle and the state of their personal good or bad fortune.[172]

Finally, among those blessed with jobs that were likely to be secure as well as skilled—locomotive engineers or glass blowers, for instance—annual income in the late nineteenth century might exceed $800, running to $1,100. Perhaps as many as 15% of working-class families were headed by craftsmen like these, proud, independent, and experienced in labor that could not be displaced. Here the wage was male terrain, the well-kept home the responsibility of the woman.

These gradations in family life had obvious ramifications in the productive and reproductive realms, with those more stable elements of the working class likely to be "protected" by unionization and smaller families, the others "dependent" on children and casual employment. Union affiliation and the family wage were thus generally paired, and one part of class formation was the divide separating those who embraced this dyad from those who could not afford it, let alone the luxury of fewer children.

On the eve of the 1880s, after pulling through the depression of the 1870s, most workers belonged to the latter category. Only 18 national or binational unions were then operative in Canada and the United States, a core group that formed the Federation of Organized Trades and Labor Unions of the United States and Canada (1881) and later the American Federation of Labor (1886). With a total membership in 1886 of no more than 350,000, the trade unions were overwhelmingly composed of male skilled craftsmen. They represented only a small minority of the North American working class, certainly no more than 3% of the nonagricultural workforce. This, of course, understates the range of organizational reach, because the large national unions were also supplemented by local unions, in which the unskilled might find more of a voice. Throughout the 1880s in Canada, for instance, purely local unions still outnumbered the locals of the internationals by 2 to 1, with over 220 surviving into the age of modern industry. American manufacturing centers, like Cincinnati had 35 unions, local and international, joined in the trades and labor assemblies that surfaced in so many cities between 1879 and 1883.[173]

If this upsurge of largely male and skilled workers had encompassed the entirety of labor's response to modern industry, the qualitative transformation of the social formation would have been unmatched in the realm of class formation: women workers would have remained marginal to the process of class struggle; the unskilled and immigrant masses would have been locked into the isolation of previous decades; and the family wage, won in sharp class conflicts over the 1860s and 1870s, would have spawned only patriarchal chauvinism and a condescending dismissal of those who could not win it for themselves. But this was not what happened. Over the course of the 1880s, women, the unskilled, and immigrants fought their way into the North American working-class movement, where they joined a skilled leadership contingent.[174] Together, these working-class elements forged an alliance that burst onto the North American industrial scene in the Great Upheaval, a moment of class formation guided by the Knights of Labor.

Formed in 1869, the Knights of Labor was initially confined by the context of its origins, restricted by its attachment to secrecy. Although committed to a broad conception of labor reform characteristic of the ideological ferment of the 1860s and 1870s, when manufacture's limitations cultivated belief in the possibilities of imminent change, the noble and holy order officially refused admittance to women until 1879. In 1881, its ranks hidden behind a facade of secrecy and still bound by gender, the Knights of Labor's North American membership was less than 20,000. Later in that year, partly as a concession to the Catholic church, the Knights abandoned the religious content of their secrecy by going public. A woman shoeworker in Philadelphia, Mary Stirling, defiantly challenged both the Knights of Labor and the largest shoe manufacturer in the city. Leading her coworkers out on strike, she organized a local assembly and successfully petitioned the Cincinnati General Assembly for admission to the order. Victorious in both confrontations, Stirling's successes and the public presence of the Knights of Labor signaled the arrival of a new vitality in working-class circles. The next five years saw a veritable transformation in class relations, culminating in the Great Upheaval, bred of at least four vital shifts in the nature of class struggle in the 1880s.[175]

Crossing the Quantitative Threshold

Organization

Organizationally, the Knights drew workers into their ranks through a relatively simple procedure and institutional apparatus. Individual members joined locals (LAs), either in mixed (diverse occupational affiliations) or trade (adhering more rigidly to specific craft categories) assemblies. Normally those who were part of a specific trade assembly followed a particular skilled calling, but occasionally the trade assembly was merely an organization of all workers employed in the same plant, shop, or factory. For an LA to be organized formally, a minimum of 10 members was required, and once established, LAs were known to swell in membership to over 1,000. Initiation fees were set by the local, but the minimum fee was $1 for men and 50¢ for women. Local dues, again, were controlled by individual assemblies, but they were to be no less than 10¢ per month. When a specific geographical region, or occasionally even a trade, contained five or more assemblies, a district assembly (DA) could be formed. Each LA then sent delegates to the DA (based on each 100 members), which in turn elected delegates to the annual general assembly, at which the national officers and the general executive board were elected. Presiding over all of these bodies was a series of leading elected officials: the master workman of the LA, the district master workman, and many lesser figures. The order, then, was a highly centralized body, with a self-defined hierarchy and structure; yet it was also egalitarian, and the LAs had a large measure of autonomy, with their own courts to prosecute those who transgressed the disciplines and regulations of knighthood.

There were approximately 15,000 LAs organized across the United States in these years and slightly fewer than 400 in Canada (which should be considered alongside the 35 lodges of the Nova Scotia–based Provincial Workmen's Association, a competing body that was nevertheless strikingly similar to the order in its ideology, rituals, and organizational form). As many as 3.5 million workers may have passed through such local assemblies over time, and at the peak of their strength, in 1886, the Knights were said to have enrolled between 700,000 and 1 million members. Some of these new recruits to labor's cause were skilled craftsmen, whose own union affiliations apparently posed no barrier to their entry into the order. But many were previously unorganized workers, often unskilled, and one advocate in ten was a woman.[176]

Such an influx of unskilled men and women into the workers' movement must have at least tripled the percentage of the organized nonagricultural work force. Among those located in that pivotal urban-based manufacturing sector, the expansion of organized labor's ranks was truly phenomenal. However cautiously the problematic figures are interpreted, it appears that at least 8% of the work force was organized by Knights and unionists at the zenith of the Great Upheaval in 1886, a figure dwarfing previous nineteenth-century levels of union affiliation and one not to be matched until the pre-1907 recession growth or the 1916–1922 upheaval.[177]

In local communities, the impact of the order was unmistakable. In New York City, 400 LAs contained at least 30,000 workers, and Boston and Cincinnati each boasted nearly 100 assemblies and 17,000 members. Detroit's 70 LAs contained roughly the same number of workers, 8,000, (the city also claimed 5,000 craft unionists) as did the combined membership of Toronto's and Hamilton's 88 assemblies, and in Montreal, both French and English flocked to the order, with approximately 60 assemblies drawing more than 3,000 men and women to the workers' cause. Oestreicher estimates that 20.5% of Detroit's manufacturing work force was organized by the combined Knights of Labor–craft union forces in 1886, compared with a mere 3.8% in 1880 and 6.2% in 1901. In Ontario, between 20 and 30% of the manufacturing work force was organized by the Knights of Labor and trade unions in a host of metropolitan centers, railway towns, and industrial communities of the hinterland.[178]

Nor were the Knights confined to the well-trod regional paths of trade unionism's previous North American journeys. They opened up new territories to organized labor, such as the Canadian prairie and coastal West, where 21 local assemblies were formed among railway laborers, miners, and urban craftsmen. In the American South the mixed assembly proved a boon in the organization of textile workers and landless laborers. The beginning of black-white unity was fostered in cities like New Orleans, where an 1892 general strike was fought by workers who had rallied to the nearly 100 labor bodies formed between 1880 and 1893, or Richmond, Virginia, where the 35 LAs were organized in two mutually supportive but socially separate district assemblies in which blacks outnumbered whites four to three. The woodlots of Michigan and Ontario were first penetrated by labor organizers in these years, as were a plethora of manufacturing hamlets in which the mixed assembly could survive where the craft union could not. The Knights of Labor had accomplished a part of what Terence V. Powerly perceived as their purpose when he proclaimed, in Providence, Rhode Island: "Something must be done to bring these people together, so that they may know that a blow struck at labor in one place affects those in another, that the evil is felt everywhere men live, from the rising to the setting of the sun."[179]

Indeed, the Great Upheaval had done much to popularize the need for solidarity, to force recognition that capital necessitated a powerful and united front of opposition. "Each for himself is the bosses plea/ Union for all will make you free," was, in 1880, a coopers' banner.[180] By 1885 to 1886 it was an ideal and a practice held high by North American labor as a whole. Engels remarked on the Knights of Labor in just this context. He described the order as "an immense association spread across an immense amount of country . . . held together . . . by the instinctive feeling that the very fact of their clubbing together for their common aspiration makes them a great power in the country." As an impressive showing of "potential energy evolving slowly but surely into actual force,"[181] the Knights of Labor were inevitably drawn into larger arenas of conflict. Just as the organization of the working class crossed a quantitative threshold in the 1880s, so too did class struggle.

Conflict

"The year 1886 was prolific in events that stirred the world from end to end," reminisced One Big Unionist Richard Kerrigan in 1927, "and particularly affected," he continued with a revolutionary's capacity to understate, "the social and political tranquility of the American continent."[182] Led by the Knights of Labor in Milwaukee, Chicago, and New York, nearly 340,000 American workers demanded an eight-hour day. As its militancy crested, the order found itself at the very center of an unprecedented explosion of class militancy, despite its leadership's pious utterances on the desirability of arbitration and the futility of strikes. Strike activity in both Canada and the United States leapt upward in the 1880s and 1890s: in Canada roughly 430 strikes were fought in the 1880s, perhaps as many as 500 over the course of the 1890s, or more in each decade than had been mounted in the entire preceding 80 years. More than three times as many strikes were fought in the United States in 1886 than in any single year between 1881 and 1884. Of the 1,432 strikes launched in that climax to the Great Upheaval, 900 were for wages and 286 for the eight-hour day. Moreover, although the number of workers involved in strikes did not exceed the 407,000 of 1886 again until 1894 (and thereafter not until 1902), the numbers of strikes fought continued to climb, totaling 7,340 between 1881 and 1889 and 12,474 over the 1890s. Many of these strikes, as Amsden and Brier have argued in the case of coal mining, were part of a process of transformation, in which workers groped through the limitations of the past and struggled to create permanent institutions of self-defense, establishing productive relations at the work place that were less exploitative and more egalitarian. As the century came to a close, increasing numbers of strikes, including such momentous clashes as the Pullman Boycott and the bituminous coal strike were planned and highly organized affairs, called and led by disciplined unionists.[183]

Many of the Knights of Labor-led battles of the 1880s and early 1890s were stepping-stones in this schoolroom of class experience, galvanizing whole communities to action. Toronto's street-railway strike, Ottawa-Hull's 1891 Chaudiére strike, or the battles at Cornwall's cotton mills were just such Canadian confrontations. Across North America the order waged countless small struggles buttressing skilled workers' attempts to secure or consolidate work-place control or acceptable wage levels. The Knights also provided the mechanism through which previously unorganized workers gained some small measure of industrial citizenship. But it was the mass strike that left its exhilarating mark so emphatically on the epoch. "One go, all go," was a Polish worker's cry in the turmoil of Detroit's eight-hour strikes of 1886. An earlier epic struggle, the 1883 telegraph operatives' unsuccessful challenge to Jay Gould's monopoly, bound North American labor into an oppositional mass:

> We're bound to fight,
> Our cause is right,
> Monopoly is sore.
> We have left our keys
> To take our ease,
> Let Jay Gould walk the floor.[184]

The massive struggles on southwestern railway lines, in Chicago's packing houses, and around sympathetic support for New York City's freight handlers, all ordered by Knights of Labor officials, were equally influential in cultivating solidarity. "All I knew then of the principles of the Knights of Labor," remembered union pioneer Abraham Bisno, "was that the motto . . . was One for All, and All for One."[185]

Workingmen's Democracy

Labour's quantitative gains in organization and concerted opposition to capital had, by 1886, transformed themselves into qualitative shifts in class experience. No less dramatic was the evolution of political practice, as workingmen turned increasingly to

> The ballot-box, the ballot box!
> There comrades, you will find the rocks

To hurl against the Giant's head;
Nor iron, dynamite or lead
Can match the ever potent knocks
Shot from our Yankee ballot box.[186]

Between 1883 and 1889, coalitions of Knights and unionists entered local politics, and after May 1886 there are references to labor tickets in 189 towns and cities in 34 of the 38 states, as well as considerable political ferment in Ontario's industrial heartland, Montreal, and New West-minster-Vancouver-Victoria, where a problematic assault on Chinese workers drew British Columbia white labor into the political arena. Running on Union Labor, United Labor, Knights of Labor, Workingman, Labor Political Association, Independent Labor Party, or Independent tickets, workers achieved considerable success, especially in municipal campaigns. There they elected representatives to authoritative posts as aldermen, mayors, councilors, and school board officials. Although national lobbying efforts on the part of the Knights of Labor have received the most attention, it was at these lower levels of government that workers were more effective in securing civic improvement, curtailing political corruption, defending work-place interests by establishing minimum wage bylaws or outlawing subcontracting, and propagandizing for a national political movement. When not demanding political independence for labor, many working-class candidates wrung concessions from the established parties. In largely rural constituencies, such tactics, although compromised, could secure victories that otherwise would have been squandered.[187] But politics was, even when weakest, most visible in the metropolitan centers. There were two sides to this metropolitan presence.

One side was the tremendous support galvanized by United Labor Party candidates, despite their losses: Henry George received 68,000 votes in the 1886 New York mayoralty campaign, or 31.2% of the vote; the United Labor ticket won more than one-quarter of the 92,000 votes cast in Chicago's 1886 election, securing seats for five judges and several prolabor assemblymen; in Cincinnati the ULP candidate, bricklayer William Stevenson, was narrowly defeated by 600 votes, losing to a Republican but gaining the support of 7,000 voters.

Beyond these impressive showings lay the second side of the working class's political impact, reform and patronage. The Knights of Labor literally stampeded the ruling parties in both Canada and the United States into concessions, changing the very character of political life. Sir John A. Macdonald, Tory leader in Canada, claimed that the Knights of Labor were one of four reefs threatening the Conservative Party ship in the 1880s, and he struck a royal commission in 1887 to investigate the conditions of labor and capital in Canada. Liberal opposition leader Edward Blake largely adopted the Knights of Labor platform in his 1887 campaign. Factory acts, suffrage extension, bureaus of labor statistics, arbitration measures, employers' liability acts, a recognized labor day, and other concessions were thrown into the ring of class struggle. Tammany Hall played a similar game in the United States, wooing labor men to the Democratic party. Patronage became the key carrot in this process, with politicians promising and delivering much in their quest to quiet dissident workers. There were more than 400 Knights of Labor on the municipal payroll of Chicago in the 1880s. In Detroit John Devlin, a Powderly loyalist and general executive board member, was put in charge of the American consulate in Windsor. He promptly filled the customs house with Knights of Labor appointees, 23 in all.[188]

Politics, as patronage revealed, was often a soiled pursuit. The Knights, many of whom rolled in the mud of this process, especially in the order's post-1887 decline, had always known this. T. W. Brosnan, the district master workman of Minnesota's DA 79 noted perceptively: "As we grow older and stronger the politicians will use their most strenuous efforts to get control of the organization." Wherever the Knights were a presence, similar words were spoken. Actions were taken, in Trevellick's phrase, to rise above "the poverty and slavery to the masses that toil"[189] that partisan political behavior produced. By creating a movement culture, a practice of solidarity and collectivity pitted against the acquisitive individualism and amorality of the age, the Knights of Labor struggled to educate men and women in the principles of labor reform.

A Movement Culture

As the Boston *Labor Leader* reflected in February 1887, one of the essential contributions of the Knights of Labor lay "in the fact that the whole life of the community is drawn into it, that people of all kinds are together . . . , and that all get directly the sense of each others needs."[190] Albert Cross of Hamilton, Ontario's LA 2481, came to the same conclusion four months later, explaining that individual Knights "were taught that in [the] home of labour there would be no distinctions . . . because all were of the Earth and with equal rights . . . and we solemnly resolved that we would do all in our power to strengthen the bonds of unity between the workers of the world. . . ."[191] Within the particular struggles and wants of specific families, ethnic groups, genders, and skill levels, then, North American workers were becoming united by the common realization that their separate strategies, however

divergent, were all pitted against bourgeois ethics and material depri-
vations. For the first time in the history of class formation, divisions
among workers were being overcome by the essential class division between bourgeois and proletarian. Workers, as George McNeill noted in
1887, were becoming cognizant of their place in the now-changed and
increasingly rigid social relations of appropriation. When at work they
saw themselves belonging to those "lower orders . . . continually under
surveillance." When out of work, however, the wage earner was reduced to the position of "an outlaw, a tramp, . . . the pariah of society."[192] Resignation could have been one response to this process of
degradation. But out of their consciousness of their social place, in conjunction with an assessment of all that was noble in the past (the Knights
extolled the chivalry of medieval times, the republican virtues of revolutionary America, and the Civil War's assault on slavery), the Noble
and Holy Order of the Knights of Labor conditioned a climate of ro-
mantic rebellion against an "age of shoddy." The result was a renewed
faith in the possibilities of the future:

> But while we dream of the chivalry of yore
> And wish for knighthood to redress all wrong.
> We know our time has braver deeds in store.[193]

The Knights of Labor prepared the way for the working class's capacity to embrace such "braver deeds" by cultivating collectivity, mutuality, and unity across the range of North American communities
where they were a public presence. In local assembly halls the symbolism and ritual of the order reverberated with the dignity of labor and
the necessity of sustaining the "Circle of Universal Brotherhood"
through mutual assistance.[194] Funerals, parades, "monster picnics" and
demonstrations proclaimed to all that:

> For well we know if sons of toil
> Will all go hand in hand
> There's none can us asunder break
> If all united stand.[195]

Soirees and balls brought families and youth together in displays of self-
organized leisure activities, liberated from both the degradations of the
saloon[196] and the confinements of commercialism or paternalism. Victory Drury of New York's Home Club commented on one such gathering:

> I have heard from the lips of those who are here that this meeting is called by
> an organization known as the Knights of Labor. It is claimed by some that the
> working classes are ignorant, that they are brutes and imbeciles, and are, in
> fact, the dregs of society. And yet what do I find? I believe that I see before

me an audience of working men and women, and the first thing I heard when I came in this hall was the excellent piano playing of two ladies . . . honest people who earn their bread by the sweat of their brow and rob not any man.[197]

Here, in a moment of recreation, leadership, radicalism, and respectability coexisted easily and without trauma.

An emerging intellectual contingent—brain workers—had in fact surfaced in almost every Knight of Labor locale,[198] editing countless labor newspapers, speechifying, and heading up local assemblies, in which, as "schoolrooms of instruction," tracts of political economy and lines of verse were read and debated:

And hosts of artisans are fired
In their industrial hives
With the same spirit that inspired
The 'Farmer of St. Ives';
Which has brought forth a great power,
Without the gun and sabre,
Before which tyrannies shall cower.
Hail to the Knights of Labor.[199]

Among the radical immigrant quarters in the United States, labor's more militant leadership might align itself with bodies such as the International Working People's Association. But the Knights of Labor were, as a mass movement, seldom isolated from such developments.[200] In Detroit, debates on the place of dynamite in the politics of class struggle (the resolution in favor of such "direct action" was defeated, but only by a vote of 100 to 95) received coverage in the Knights of Labor journal, the *Labor Leaf*, an organ not incapable of editorializing on armed struggle: "When there are robbers about it is a good thing to have a rifle handy. When you have a gun and know how to use it, you are not so likely to have trouble . . . should trouble come, the capitalists will use the regular army and militia to shoot down those who are not satisfied. It won't be so if the people are equally ready, like their forefathers of 1776." Such a stand was possible because the movement culture of labor reform had reached well past the economism of labor's battles over the wage, into a very way of life. As Oestreicher concludes in his study of Detroit, "by 1886 the movement included a weekly labour press, in both English and German, a workers' militia, the Detroit Rifles, regular debates in the Dialectical Union, a theatre group, singing societies, and almost nightly social or educational events."[201] It was precisely this mixture of the seemingly mundane and the startlingly militant that struck fear in the bosom of bourgeois America.

That fear lay behind the harsh repression of May and June 1886 as the police "shot to kill" in Chicago and Milwaukee and brought actual and threatened legal execution to bear on immigrant radicals and native-American socialists. Although the targets were individuals (Parsons—himself a Knight of Labor—Spies, Schilling, Grottkau and others), the aim was a wider suppression. In the hanging of the Haymarket martyrs, as Montgomery suggests, the ruling class found its "psychic revenge for . . . insubordination."[202] It also found a handy club to wield against the movement culture, which was thrown into a state of retreat. The pleas of Knights of Labor militants for solidarity with the Haymarket martyrs fell on too many deaf ears. The cautious leaders of the order, especially Powderly, condemned the victims to suffer their consequences at the hand of capitalist justice.[203] This abdication of solidarity was all the more tragic because the movement culture of the Knights of Labor was premised on a concern for all workers and an unprecedented entry into the entire range of working-class experience. Among women, the immigrant community, and the unskilled, the movement culture had addressed needs seldom confronted by previous unions of earlier notions of labor reform.[204]

Refusing to close the door of "brotherhood" on women workers and the confinements of a domesticity that they themselves often embraced as an ideal, the Knights of Labor entered simultaneously into the realms of production and reproduction. They provided the organizational focus for a series of women's mass strikes in Cohoes (1882), Fall River (1885), Louisville (1887), and Cornwall (1887–1889) at the same time that they demanded political rights for women. Campaigning for equal pay for equal work across North America, the order was also capable of establishing socialistic day nurseries in mill towns like Olneyville, Rhode Island. To be sure, male Knights did not universally step outside the consensual norms of Victorian gender relations. Many remained inhibited by their conventional views of femininity, adhering to a chauvinistic sentimentality and a nostalgic conception of women's role. In St. Louis, male contractors affiliated with the order's tailors' assembly were not above telling the parents of seamstresses that "no dissent girl belong to an assembly."[205] Still, there were signs of significant advance, with women organizers like Leonora M. Barry demanding "complete emancipation from political and industrial bondage."[206] A Montreal laborer recognized unpaid domestic labor as "just as essential to the well being of the workingman as the fair's day's wage itself."[207] Most dramatic was the Knights of Labor's imaginative blending of the class struggle's demand for solidarity with the social relations of domestic life. In New York City, "whenever the Knights of Labor girls went to a picnic or ball they were to tell all the brother Knights that none of the latter were to walk with a non-union girl in the opening promenade so long as a union girl was without a partner. Should any male Knight violate this rule, all the girl Knights are to step out of the promenade and boycott the entire crowd."[208] Many decades before contemporary feminists coined the phrase "the personal is political," women in the noble and holy order demonstrated an awareness of the need to infuse every day life with the practices of both equality and solidarity. "Not man's dependant will she be," declared one Richmond, Virginia, woman Knight, "But his co-worker, equal fee."[209] The Knights, as John Swinton long ago noted, recognized "the rights and principles of womanhood."[210]

Among immigrants and various ethnic groups, the Knights opened up similar possibilities. Irish workers, long divided internally by religious affiliation and isolated from English and native North American labor, were drawn into the movement culture of the 1880s. The institutional expression of this historical process was the Irish National Land League, a body that effectively wedded the North American Irish masses to the reform tradition. Upon the particular oppression of Ireland was constructed a passionate critique of power, privilege, and authority willingly embraced by the predominantly working-class Irish of North America. As Powderly noted, this swelling of Irish nationalism fed directly into the Knights of Labor. "When the public, or Land League, meeting would be over," he recalled, a "secret meeting of the Knights of Labor would follow."[211] Thus, as Foner has argued, the Knights of Labor quietly intersected with the more radical strains of Irish nationalism, providing "a social ethic that challenged the individualism of the middle class and the cautious social reformism"[212] of the established political culture and the church. Other immigrant groups experienced a similar process of integration. In Milwaukee, for instance, the Great Upheaval of 1885–1886 eroded the established skilled German workers' reluctance to rub shoulders with the newly arrived and relatively unskilled Poles, as 1,000 Polish workers entered the Polonia Assembly in one fell swoop.[213]

Both women and the immigrant masses were part of a larger contingent, the unskilled, that the movement culture also attracted. Perlman, who saw the Knights of Labor as tragically flawed in their emphasis on this segment, nevertheless captured a part of what the Great Upheaval really was:

> All the peculiar characteristics of the dramatic events of 1886 and 1887, the highly feverish pace at which organization grew, the nation-wide wave of strikes, particularly sympathetic strikes, the wide use of the boycott, the obliteration, apparently complete, of all times that divided the labouring class, whether geographic or trade, the violence and turbulence which accompanied the movement—all of these were the signs of a great movement by the class

of the unskilled, which had finally risen in rebellion. . . . The movement bore
in every way the aspect of a social war. A frenzied hatred of labour for capital
was shown in every important strike.[214]

In spite of the order's backtracking between 1887 and 1894, efforts to
revive the Knights of Labor in 1894 remained premised on the exhor-
tation that "they must stand or fall with the unskilled workers."[215]

The movement culture that so transformed the social relations of productive life and that pushed class formation in new and exhilarating
directions in the 1880s nevertheless stumbled and fell in the 1890s. Let
us conclude this discussion of social formation and class formation in
nineteenth-century North America with an attempt to understand just
why this demise took place.

CONCLUSIONS

In the United States, things go damned slowly.

Marx to Engels (1863)

During the nineteenth century the North American social and class
formations experienced two decades of profound transformation and
dissolution, the 1850s and the 1890s. Commenting on the speculation
and expansion of the productive forces in 1851, Marx asked, "Is this not
approaching a crisis? The revolution may come sooner than we wish."
Thirty years later he saw communist tendencies spreading among the
masses, the assault on "all forms of associated capital" paving the way
for a vast social transformation.[216] Indeed, these were years of great moment in the history of North American capital, and if communism did
not come in the 1880s, the next decade saw the social formation restructured in the direction of monopoly capitalism. Both the 1850s and
the 1890s were thus vital turning points that displayed striking similarities, including the prominence of major depressions that shifted the
character of productive relations and forced working-class activists to
retreat in the face of the harsh realities of the business cycle. It was in
the period between these two points of crisis that the late nineteenth-
century North American labor movement came of age.

Industrial capitalism took the final unhesitating steps toward establishing its economic supremacy in North America in the 1850s, ushering
in a late nineteenth-century context of ruthless competition among entrepreneurs. In these years as well, the labor market was transformed,
as waves of immigrants inundated North American shores, famine-Irish
finding their way to port cities in Canada and the United States, and

German Forty-eighters establishing themselves in a number of American industrial cities. Such economic and demographic change conditioned a virulent nativism that may well have helped undercut the early beginnings of working-class organization and solidarity, a process of disintegration facilitated by the onslaught of economic crisis in 1857.

The 1890s, set against the earlier background of the 1850s, appears remarkably similar. A new stage of capitalist development appeared in the increasingly close connections of finance and industrial capital, which stimulated a series of vitally important mergers, pushing the economy toward monopoly and oligopoly. Although this merger movement had attained some maturity in the United States by the 1890s, it appeared only tentatively in Canada, with significant consolidations in the textile industry, agricultural machinery production, and in the faint beginnings of the steel industry. American branch plants, especially those in nascent industries such as rubber, chemicals, and electrical products, began to invade Canadian territory, quick to reap the benefits of markets, materials, and labor. As this shift in the character of capitalism proceeded, it was strengthened by new supplies of labor, as immigration from eastern and southern Europe restructured the internal composition of the North American labor force between 1880 and 1910. Bolstered by the acquisition of plentiful supplies of unskilled labor and consolidated through the depression's impact on the small shop and the family firm, the North American political economy entered the twentieth century in its monopoly phase. Once more, this process of transformation was accompanied by a nativist reaction, centered in the American Protective Association in the United States and in its Canadian counterpart, the Protestant Protective Association. This had dramatic and debilitating consequences in former Knights of Labor strongholds like Detroit, where the retreating movement culture was challenged by nativist rhetoric threatening to "chase the Dagos back to Italy." Anti-Catholicism in Canada was further strengthened by a series of French-English disputes, beginning with the Jesuits' Estates Act and culminating in the Manitoba Schools Question in the 1890s. In this period of ethnocentrism the workers' movement suffered tangible setbacks. By the end of the 1890s jingoism was also prominent in both countries, as America's popular war with Spain and Canada's patriotic response to the Boer War undercut class solidarities and emphasized national aspirations. Although not all workers were enthralled with such militaristic adventures around the world and although a number of working-class recruits to the cause of imperialism were undoubtedly attracted by economic need and the soldier's stipend, these campaigns nevertheless enjoyed considerable support, especially among British immigrant and native American and Canadian workers.[217]

Equally significant developments in the political sphere paralleled these vast changes in the economy and society of late nineteenth-century North America. Between 1860 and 1890, the national prominence of the state was emerging, overshadowing previously dominant concerns of particular regions and specific locales. In the United States, the state developed as a vital force in the aftermath of the Civil War, as the victory of the Republicans and the forging of national parties in the throes of conflict ushered in a new age. Similarly, north of the border, the Canadian state was forged in 1867, with the 1870s and 1880s the first decades of national party activity in the newly created Dominion.

These large structural changes of the late nineteenth century are vital to an understanding of both the accomplishment and failure of the Noble and Holy Order of the Knights of Labor. The 1880s represented the culmination of an age of competitive capitalism and localism as well as the first faint beginnings of monopoly. The Knights of Labor developed within this context and embodied a working-class challenge that had been building strength for three decades. A series of perceptive studies, many of them as yet unpublished, demonstrates conclusively that in the United States, the Knights of Labor were able to unite a working class long fragmented, bridging the divisions between workers that had been the historical legacy of the 1850s and drawing them out of the cross-class alliances that had developed during the contest against slavery. In the resulting "moral universality" of the Gilded Age labor movement, as Montgomery has suggested, the Knights of Labor represented a "crusade" to "impose economic order" on a ruthlessly individualistic capitalism. A large part of the attraction of this orientation lay in its repudiation of the acquisitive egotism that the system spawned and acclaimed. This movement culture of alternative peaked, however, at precisely that moment—the 1880s—when the economic, social, political, and cultural forces that had ushered it into being were on the brink of suppression by an eminently monopolistic social formation.

The Knights of Labor thus emerged in the context of an anarchic, laissez-faire capitalism. Though the movement shook its fist at monopoly, political corruption, and the drift toward centralized control of everyday life, it found itself facing changing conditions and staunch opposition as employers united to oppose its members and the omniscient state began an open intervention in the social relations of productive life. Although the state's role in suppressing the insurrectionary railroad strikes of 1877 must have appeared as something of an aberration, by the 1890s, worker militants came to see government repression as the norm. Haymarket, Homestead, and Pullman imprinted this lesson on their consciousness. An eclectic radical critique, capable of uniting the working class around the perceived threat of an economic and political oligarchy tyrannizing labor saw its worst fears confirmed in the 1880s and 1890s. This new situation was further complicated by immigration and severe depression, both of which weakened the bonds of unity. As the crisis deepened, the whole process of forging a collective response had to be begun anew. What had been adequate in the 1870s and early 1880s was now seen to be inadequate, and as a consequence, the "moral universality" that the Knights of Labor had done so much to create began to disintegrate.[218]

Splits between socialists and Knights, eclectic radicals and unionists, and Home Clubbers and others ensued, as business unionism, revolutionary syndicalism, DeLeonite socialism, and ethnic politics vied for the allegiance of North American workers. Although the depression of the 1890s, the nationalization of politics, the increasing prominence of ethnic allegiances, and the crisis of leadership unfolding in the upper echelons of the Knights of Labor all played a part in ensuring the ultimate defeat of the noble and holy order, the demise of the Knights and the victory of the American Federation of Labor (AFL) was anything but a settled issue in the 1880s. Major leaders, later identified with the rise of the AFL and the ideological primacy of craft unionism within the American labor movement, were themselves uncertain in these years of turmoil in the 1880s. P. J. McGuire of the Carpenters' Union, for instance, was known to advocate the liquidation of the trade unions into the Knights of Labor well past the crisis of 1886; yet he is often seen as the ideological ancestor of "Big Bill" Hutcheson. Other labor leaders of the 1880s—Samuel Gompers, Thomas Morgan, Joseph Buchanan, Jo Labadie, and Frank Foster—were riding the wave of class militancy and consensus without a forceful sense of organizational direction or ideological clarity. All had been shaped in a radical milieu that contained Marxist, Lasallean, Anarchist, Greenback, Georgite, Freethinking, and Irish Nationalist influences.

Canada's labor leadership was more subdued ideologically, perhaps because capital's consolidation had not proceeded as fast north of the border. The Canadian state was therefore not compelled to utilize repression to the same extent, and finally, the demographic structure of the Canadian working class—predominantly English speaking outside Quebec—did not give rise to immigrant radicalism. Few were the Marxist or anarchist influences that swirled in the debates of the 1880s in Ontario: it was Gladstonian liberalism, Irish nationalism, and Tory paternalism that more often than not formed the backdrop against which working-class militants argued out their differing perspectives on labor activities. But the situation was also complicated by attachments to the single tax, currency reform, Bellamyite nationalism, and other reform panaceas associated with Canada's particular variant of the producer ideology. Those who want to adopt the perspective of Gerald Grob and his predecessors, arguing that business unionism in Canada was inevitable, will have difficulty explaining how the so-called father of the Canadian labor movement, Irish Dan O'Donoghue, defended and supported the Knights of Labor until its last twentieth-century days.

In short, though hindsight may facilitate North American historians' efforts to sift through the labor controversies of the 1880s, sorting out various positions and structuring them into supposedly coherent philosophical orientations, the participants themselves—Canadian and American—were far from intellectually surefooted. In the late 1880s and 1890s they were propelled in a number of different directions, especially in the United States where a more advanced economy and a radical working-class immigrant community gave rise to more precise strategies for labor in the emerging age of monopoly capital. The Canadian labor movement retreated into an effort to survive the hard years of the 1890's downturn and reemerged in the economic upswing and craft union boom of the 1898–1904 years.[219]

The structural transformations of the late nineteenth century and the attempt to come to grips with them ideologically and organizationally thus underlay the demise of the order across North America. Working themselves out evenly and in part colored by local conditions and developments, these transformations and responses wrote *finis* to the movement culture of the 1880s. Class formation was thus constantly shifting, no less so in the 1880s and 1890s than in the 1830s and 1840s, as the social formation underwent vast change. The velocity of this change in late nineteenth-century America, the quickening pace of accumulation and the rapid growth of monopoly, restructured productive relations at an unprecedented rate, literally decade by decade. As Marx predicted but could not theorize, America's rate of concentration outstripped all previous European experience, advancing "in seven league boots." With the social formation undergoing such change, class formation was characterized by just the kind of episodic struggles and chaotic disruptions that fed into labor's apparent defeats. To put it differently: things moved so damned slowly in America because they also moved so damned quickly; America was exceptional.

But slow or fast, the historical impact of the 1880s was not lost on North American workers. They looked back to that past as years in which advances had been registered. Indeed, there has historically been no moment in the experience of North American labor that weighed so heavily on the collective mind of the working-class movement in the years between 1900 and 1930 as that of the Knights of Labor upsurge of the 1880s. Until the resurgence of labor in the 1930s, workers recalled this past and drew upon its many and varied inspirations. When John L. Lewis consciously strove to create an image of himself as part of a long line of "tough people," "fighters," and class militants, he recalled (or fabricated) the story of his father's early involvement in the Knights of Labor in Lucas, Iowa, where Tom Lewis helped lead a bitter strike in 1882, an action supposedly earning him a place on the company's blacklist and exile from the town.[220] Clinton S. Golden, labor intellectual and founder of the United Steel Workers of America, first drank from the fountain of labor solidarity with "Big John" Powderly, brother of the order's central figure, Terence V. Powerly. Big John, for whom Clint tended drill at the tender age of 12, preached the gospel of the noble and holy order long after the Knights had succumbed. But even in the face of the Knights' ultimate defeat, Powderly's brother remained true to the cause of an all-embracing organization of American wage earners. He imparted his enthusiasm to his young helper, and Golden recalled of the Knights that

> their ritualism, the secrecy with which their meetings were conducted, the signs and symbols that gave notice to their members as to when and where meetings were to be held, fired my interest and imagination and in my own mind I resolved that henceforth my lot was cast with that of the wage earners. I began to see class lines and distinctions.

Moreover, in looking back on this experience years later Golden still described the Knights as "that all-embracing holy order that dared dream of a co-operative commonwealth for industrial America."[221]

Individual statements and recollections were supplemented by a more general remembrance of the place and significance of the order and the Great Upheaval. "Never since the palmiest days of the Knights of Labor," declared Toronto's *Citizen & Country* in the midst of the craft union boom from 1898 to 1904, "have trade unions taken such a firm hold of the toilers as today."[222] As these turn-of-the-century organizational gains were consolidated, however, some workers could still tar the American Federation of Labor with a brush dipped into the resentments of the 1880s and 1890s. In 1903 a Western Federation of Miners' member from Slocan, British Columbia, wrote to the *Miners' Magazine*: "Now there are thousands of old-line K of Ls in the WFM and the unsavoury acts of the AFL officials have not been altogether forgotten."[223] Twenty years later many radicals and socialists saw this newly arrived, and increasingly conservative, international craft unionism in terms even more antagonistic, characterized in their new name for it—the "American

Separation of Labor." For their part, the AFL pure and simple unionists linked the One Big Union with the Knights of Labor, the American Railway Union of Eugene Debs, and the American Labor Union. It was the latest "subtle and pernicious plea again resorted to for the purpose of severing the wage earners from their orderly and practical course of action."[224] By 1929, the radical challenge of the postwar reconstruction years had been at least partially undermined, and in this context of "normalcy" the AFL met in Toronto in October. With southern textile workers urging the organization of their mill towns, observers at the convention reported "a pitch of enthusiasm not seen in labor gatherings since the spring tide of the Knights of Labor."[225]

This collective memory brings us back to an assessment of class formation. Always situated in a particular context and a specific social setting, class formation is one part structured necessity (what the social formation determines) and one part active creation (what the particular components of the working class do within the limits imposed upon them). Struggles in the productive arena are by no means the sum total of this latter realm. The working class, while being made, has also made itself in diverse ways, many of them markedly distanced from the work place if not uninfluenced by it.[226] Nor have these conscious, if limited, choices been insignificant in their impact on the social formation itself, which they have often pushed in new directions.

Social formation and class formation are thus reciprocal developments, bound up in their own mutuality. If the former is decisive in setting the limits within which the latter unfolds, those limits are constantly changing and adapting to further accommodate and hedge in the latter. The consequences for our understanding of the historical process within which both unfold is perhaps decisive in moving us away from the tendencies in Marxist theory to situate too rigidly both social formation and class formation. Marx wrote before monopoly capitalism had emerged as an unambiguous social formation, and his periodization of primitive accumulation, manufacture proper, and modern industry implies termination and ultimate stasis. Yet the history of twentieth-century capital, of its specific modes of accumulation and of its changing social and class formations, is a history of dramatic ruptures and restructuring of the modes of appropriation. Primitive accumulation, as a process establishing the preconditions for capital accumulation, initiated the first stirrings of class formation. In an age of monopoly capital, with the constant reordering of accumulation, the process would begin anew: the original was renewed. What are we to see in twentieth-century developments such as Taylorism, the open shop drive, Fordism, neocolonialism, new waves of immigration, runaway shops, the dismantling of the welfare state, the institutionalization of labor market segmentation and job ghettoes, the expansion of the reserve army of labor, and the war economy but primitive accumulation? As new preconditions for both social and class formation are established, however, we can expect the resulting consequences to be as different as those that emerged over the course of the nineteenth century. We have only to look to the past to know how fundamentally different our future will look and how desperately necessary it is to challenge the many debasements and degradations that are now flowing in the wake of capital's project. Like the late 1840s in France and the 1880s in North America, the 1980s are one of those historical moments "which make all turning back impossible, and the conditions themselves cry out: Hic Rhodus, hic salta."[227] How and where the working class leaps will be of no small moment in determining whether it lands on Friday's feet or Crusoe's.

NOTES

1. C. L. R. James, *The Black Jacobins: Toussaint L'Ouverture and the San Domingo Revolution* (New York: Vintage Books, 1963), pp. 3–4. See also Eric Williams, *Capitalism & Slavery* (New York: Capricorn, 1966).
2. Karl Marx, *Capital*, vol. 1 (New York: International Publishers, 1967), p. 751.
3. Stephen Hymer, "Robinson Crusoe and the Secret of Primitive Accumulation," *Monthly Review* 23 (September 1971): 14–15.
4. Note, as well, Christopher Hill, "Robinson Crusoe," *History Workshop Journal* 10 (Autumn 1980): 7–24, which does not necessarily accept my view of *Robinson Crusoe*. It is not insignificant that Defoe's novel was among the bestsellers of the American revolutionary age and went through 125 American editions between 1774 and 1825. Thus, at the very time that America was experiencing a part of the process of primitive accumulation, a novel that can be read as a fictional treatment of some of the basic historical contours of such an epoch was greeted with an unprecedented popularity. See Jay Fliegelman, *Prodigals & Pilgrims: The American revolution Against Patriarchal Authority, 1750–1800* (New York: Cambridge University Press, 1982), pp. 67–82.
5. L. F. S. Upton, "The Extermination of the Beothuks of Newfoundland," *Canadian Historical Review* 48 (June 1977): 133–153.
6. Michael Rogin, *Fathers and Children: Andrew Jackson and the Subjugation of the American Indian* (New York: Vintage Books, 1975).
7. See, among many sources, A. G. Bailey, *The Conflict of European and Eastern Algonkian Cultures, 1504–1700* (Toronto: University of Toronto Press, 1969); Cornelius Jaenen, *Friend and Foe: Aspects of French-Amerindian Cultural Contact in the Sixteenth and Seventeenth Centuries* (Toronto: McClelland and Stewart, 1976); Bruce Trigger, *The Children of the Aataentsic: A History of the Huron People to 1660*, 2 vols. (Montreal: McGill-Queens University Press, 1976); Arthur J. Ray, *Indians in the Fur Trade: Their Role As Hunters, Trappers, and Middlemen in the Lands Southwest of Hudson Bay, 1660–1870* (Toronto: University of Toronto Press, 1974); Calvin Martin, "The European Impact on

the Culture of a Northeastern Algonquian Tribe: An Ecological Interpretation," *William and Mary Quarterly* 31 (1974): 3–26; Karl H. Schlesier, "Epidemics and Indian Middlemen: Rethinking the Wars of the Iroquois, 1609–1653," *Ethnohistory* 23 (1976): 129–145.

8. E. E. Rich, "Trade Habits and Economic Motivation Among the Indians of North America," *Canadian Journal of Economics and Political Science* 26 (February 1960): 35–53; Calvin Martin, *Keepers of the Game: Indian-Animal Relationships and the Fur Trade* (Berkeley and Los Angeles: University of California Press, 1978); Robin Fisher, *Contact and Conflict: Indian-European Relations in British Columbia, 1774–1890* (Vancouver: University of British Columbia Press, 1977). For a critique of Martin, see Shepard Krech, III, ed., *Indians, Animals, and the Fur Trade* (Athens: University of Georgia Press, 1981).

9. Sylvia Van Kirk, *"Many Tender Ties": Women in Fur Trade Society, 1670–1870* (Winnipeg: Watson & Dwyer, 1980); Jennifer S. H. Brown, *Strangers in Blood: Fur Trade Company Families in Indian Country* (Vancouver: University of British Columbia Press, 1980). Note the suggestive argument in Frits Pannekoek, "A Probe into the Demographic Structure of Nineteenth-Century Red River," in Lewis H. Thomas, ed., *Essays in Western Canadian History: In Honour of Lewis Gwynne Thomas* (Calgary: University of Alberta Press, 1976), pp. 83–95.

10. For an assessment of this process in the peculiar context of British Columbia, see Rolf Knight, *Indians at Work: An Informal History of Native Indian Labour in British Columbia, 1858–1930* (Vancouver: New Star, 1978).

11. See especially Rogin, "Primitive Accumulation and Paternal Authority," in Rogin, *Fathers and Children*, pp. 165–205, the Jackson quotation being on p. 3. Richard Drinnon, *Facing West: The Metaphysics of Indian-Hating and Empire-Building* (Minneapolis: University of Minnesota Press, 1980), extends Rogin's analysis.

12. The literature is now extensive. An early synthetic statement was provided by James Henretta, *The Evolution of American Society, 1700–1850: An Interdisciplinary Analysis* (Lexington: Heath, 1973). Among the best of the many specialized studies of the last two decades are Henretta, "Economic Development and Social Structure in Colonial Boston," *William and Mary Quarterly* 22 (1965): 75–92; Allan Kulikoff, "The Progress of Inequality in Revolutionary Boston," *William and Mary Quarterly* 28 (1971): 375–412; Gary B. Nash, "Urban Wealth and Poverty in Pre-Revolutionary America," *Journal of Interdisciplinary History* 6 (1976): 545–584; Nash, *The Urban Crucible: Social Change, Political Consciousness, and the Origins of the American Revolution* (Cambridge, Mass.: Harvard University Press, 1979); Billy G. Smith, "The Material Lives of Laboring Philadelphians, 1750 to 1800," *William and Mary Quarterly* 38 (1981): 163–202; Sharon V. Salinger, "Artisans, Journeymen, and the Transformation of Labor in Late Eighteenth-Century Philadelphia," *William and Mary Quarterly* 40 (1983): 62–84.

13. Consider, for instance, Eric Foner, *Tom Paine and Revolutionary America* (New York: Oxford University Press, 1976); Peter Shaw, *American Patriots and the Rituals of Revolution* (Cambridge, Mass.: Harvard University Press, 1981); Dirk Hoerder, "Boston Leaders and Boston Crowds, 1765–1776," in Alfred F. Young, ed., *The American Revolution: Explorations in the History of American Radicalism* (Dekalb: University of Northern Illinois Press, 1976), pp. 233–271. Young's work is itself the most exciting expression of this writing. See his unpublished "Pope's Day, Tar and Feathering, and 'Cornet Joyce, Jun.': From Ritual to Rebellion in Boston, 1745–1775" (Paper presented at the Anglo-American Labor Historians' Conference, Rutgers University, 1973); and "George Robert Twelves Hewes (1742–1840): A Boston Shoemaker and the Memory of the American Revolution," *William and Mary Quarterly* 38 (1981): 561–623.

14. One early attempt was Herbert G. Gutman, "Work, Culture, and Society in Industrializing America, 1815–1919," *American Historical Review* 78 (June 1973): 531–588. Michael B. Katz, Michael J. Doucet, and Mark J. Stern, *The Social Organization of Early Industrial Capitalism* (Cambridge, Mass.: Harvard University Press, 1982) present a rather cavalier, if tantilizing, periodization (pp. 18–19, 364–365). More recently, we have seen efforts from the left to address this imbalance: Michael Aglietta, *A Theory of Capitalist Regulation: The U.S. Experience* (London: NLB, 1976), a generally abstract and economistic overview; and Mike Davis, "Why the U.S. Working Class Is Different," *New Left Review* 123 (1980): 3–46, a work of powerful synthesis premised on a highly selective reading of the history and the historiography.

15. See Alan Dawley, *Class and Community: The Industrial Revolution in Lynn* (Cambridge, Mass.: Harvard University Press, 1976), especially pp. 180–184, for a critique of Commons; but for the strengths of this earlier tradition, note, in particular, John. R. Commons, "American Shoemakers, 1648–1895: A Sketch of Industrial Evolution," *Quarterly Journal of Economics* 24 (November 1909): 39–84.

16. See Theodore Hershberg, ed., *Philadelphia: Work, Space, Family, and Group Experience in the 19th Century—Essays Toward an Interdisciplinary History of the City* (New York: Oxford University Press, 1981). For critiques of social history, see Tony Judt, "A Clown in Regal Purple," *History Workshop Journal* 7 (Spring 1979): 66–94; Elizabeth Fox-Genovese and Eugene D. Genovese, "The Political Crisis of Social History: A Marxian Perspective," *Journal of Social History* 10 (Winter 1976): 205–221.

17. Pierre Vilar, "Marxist History, A History in the Making: Towards a Dialogue with Althusser," *New Left Review* 80 (1973): 101; Vilar, "Marx and the Concept of History," in E. J. Hobsbawm, ed., *The History of Marxism: Marxism in Marx's Day,* vol. 1 (Bloomington: Indiana University Press, 1982), pp. 47–78.

18. See David M. Gordon, Richard Edwards, and Michael Reich, *Segmented Work, Divided Workers: The Historical Transformation of Labor in the States* (New York: Cambridge University Press, 1982). Though attentive to certain Marxist concerns and though focusing on the long-term transformation of class relations, this book is nevertheless cast in a neoclassical repudiation of Marx's conception of capitalist development.

19. See, for instance, Marx, *Capital,* vol. 1, pp. 713–774; Marx, *Grundrisse* (Harmondsworth, England: Penguin, 1973), p. 502.

20. Paul Sweezy, "Karl Marx and the Industrial Revolution in England," in R. Eagly, ed., *Events, Ideology, and Economic Theory* (Detroit: Wayne State University Press, 1968), pp. 107–126; David Levine, "Accumulation and Technical Change in Marxian Economics" (Ph.D. diss., Yale University, 1973), pp. 119–181, 248–287.

21. Maurice Dobb, *Studies in the Development of Capitalism* (New York: International Publishers, 1973); Rodney Hilton, ed., *The Transition from Feudalism to Capitalism* (London: New Left Books, 1976).

22. See Wally Seccombe, "Domestic Labour and the Working-Class Household" and "The Expanded Reproduction Cycle of Labour Power in Twentieth-Century Capitalism," in Bonnie Fox, ed., *Hidden in the Household: Women's Domestic Labour Under Capitalism* (Toronto: Women's Press, 1980), pp. 25–99, 217–266; and, most pointedly, Seccombe, "Marxism and Demography," *New Left Review* 137 (January-February 1983): 28–29. Note the discussion in Michele Barrett, *Women's Oppression Today: Problems in Marxist-Feminist Analysis* (London: New Left Books, 1980), especially pp. 19–29.

23. Hence, Raphael Samuel's "Workshop of the World: Steam Power and Hand Technology in Mid-Victorian Britain," *History Workshop Journal* 3 (1977): 6–72 establishes the coexistence of earlier modes of production within the period of modern industry, just as Gutman, "Work, Culture, and Society" suggests that one part of the process

of primitive accumulation—the recruitment and disciplining of the wage-labor force—was not simply accomplished but was reproduced over time. In this context Gordon, Edwards, and Reich, whose *Segmented Work, Divided Workers* emphasizes the constant process of restructuring the character and mode of social accumulation, might be read as an attempt to speak to capitalism's vitality as a consequence of the persistence of forms of primitive accumulation past the epoch of manufacture into the ages of modern industry and monopoly capital.

24. Michael A. Lebowitz, "The One-Sidedness of *Capital,*" *Review of Radical Political Economy* (forthcoming); "One-Sided Marxism" (Paper presented to Conference on Marxism: The Next Two Decades, Winnipeg, March 12–15, 1983. This, as well, is central to E. P. Thompson, *The Poverty of Theory and Other Essays* (London: Merlin, 1978), pp. 247–262; and Simon Clarke, "Socialist Humanism," *History Workshop Journal* 8 (Autumn 1979): 145–150.

25. Consider E. P. Thompson, "Time, Work-Discipline, and Industrial Capitalism," *Past and Present* 38 (1967): 55–97; and John Saville, "Primitive Accumulation and Early Industrialization in Britain," in John Saville and Ralph Miliband, eds., *Socialist Register* (London: Merlin, 1969), pp. 247–271.

26. Barry Hindness and Paul Hirst, *Modes of Production and Social Formation: An Auto-Critique of Pre-Capitalist Modes of Production* (London: Macmillan, 1977), pp. 27, 62.

27. The phrases are Seccombe's ("Marxism and Demography"), although his "Reworking the Mode of Production Concept" is in fact an unacknowledged jettisoning of it in favor of analyzing the social formation.

28. Elizabeth Fox-Genovese and Eugene D. Genovese, "The Janus Face of Merchant Capital," in *Fruits of Merchant Capital: Slavery and Bourgeois Property in the Rise and Expansion of Capitalism* (New York: Oxford University Press, 1983), pp. 3–25; Dobb, *Studies*, pp. 120–122.

29. For a particularly strident and one-sided view of merchant capital's backward role in Canadian development, see R. T. Naylor, "The Rise and Fall of the Third Commercial Empire of the St. Lawrence," in Gary Teeple, ed., *Capitalism and the National Question in Canada* (Toronto: University of Toronto Press, 1972), pp. 1–42.

30. The quotations are from Dobb, *Studies*, 121, and Fox-Genovese and Genovese, "The Janus Face," pp. 6 and 7, but I am here laying greater stress on the limits of merchant capital than the latter's *Fruits of Merchant Capital* (especially in "The Slave Economies in Political Perspective," p. 36) allows.

31. See, for instance, Philip McMichael, "The Concept of Primitive Accumulation: Lenin's Contribution," *Journal of Contemporary Asia* 7 (1977): 497–512; Fox-Genovese and Genovese, "The Janus Face," pp. 24–25. This paragraph and the next draw on an as yet to be appreciated synthesis: Louis M. Hacker, *The Triumph of American Capitalism* (New York: Columbia University Press, 1940), especially pt. 2. For the Canadas, see Gerald Tulchinsky, *The River Barons: Montreal Businessmen and the Growth of Industry and Transportation, 1837–1853* (Toronto: University of Toronto Press, 1977); Gustavus Myers, *A History of Canadian Wealth* (Chicago, 1914, reprinted Toronto: James, Lewis, and Samuel, 1972); H. Clare Pentland, *Labour and Capital in Canada, 1650–1860* (Toronto: Lorimer, 1981); L. R. Macdonald, "Merchants Against Industry: An Idea and Its Origins," *Canadian Historical Review* 56 (September 1975): 263–281.

32. Witt Bowden, *Industrial History of the United States* (New York: Adelphi, 1930), pp. 231–232.

33. These forms, often conceived differently, are discussed in Charles Post, "The American Road to Capitalism," *New Left Review* 133 (May-June 1982): 30–51.

34. See Robert Brenner, "Agrarian Class Structure and Economic Development in Pre-Industrial Europe," *Past and Present* 70 (February 1976): 30–75; and Brenner, "The Agrarian Roots of European Capitalism," *Past and Present* 97 (November 1982): 16–113. I have offered some brief and overly general comments on this problem in its Canadian context in my "Town, Port and Country: Speculations on the Capitalist Transformation of Mid-Nineteenth Century Canada," *Acadiensis* 12 (Spring 1983): 131–139.

35. See Pentland, *Labour and Capital*, pp. 1–23; and Richard B. Morris, *Government and Labor in Early America* (New York: Octagon, 1965), pp. 310–512.

36. Kenneth Stampp, *The Peculiar Institution: Slavery in the Ante-Bellum South* (New York: Vintage Books, 1956), pp. 29–30; Carl N. Degler, "Starr and Slavery," *Journal of Economic History* 19 (1959): 271–277; *Historical Statistics of the United States: Colonial Times to 1957* (Washington, D.C.: U.S. Bureau of Census, 1961), p. 9; Hacker, *Triumph of American Capitalism*, pp. 287–289.

37. G. E. M. de Ste. Croix, *The Class Struggle in the Ancient Greek World* (London: Duckworth, 1981), p. 55. The quotation is from Eugene D. Genovese, *The Political Economy of Slavery: Studies in the Economy and Society of the Slave South* (New York: Vintage Books, 1965), p. 13; but see as well Eugene D. Genovese, *The World the Slaveholders Made: Two Essays in Interpretation* (New York: Vintage Books, 1971); *In Red and Black: Marxian Explorations in Southern and Afro-American History* (New York: Vintage Books, 1972); *Roll, Jordan, Roll: The World the Slaves Made* (New York: Pantheon Books, 1974); and "Yeoman Farmers in a Slaveholders' Democracy," in *Fruits of Merchant Capital*, pp. 249–264.

38. Lewis C. Gray, *History of Agriculture in the Southern States to 1860*, 2 vols. (Washington, D.C.: Carnegie Institute, 1933); Hacker, *Triumph of American Capitalism*, pp. 280–320; Robert William Fogel and Stanley L. Engerman, *Time on the Cross: The Economics of American Negro Slavery*, vol. 1 (Boston: Little, Brown, 1974), especially pp. 67–78.

39. See Elizabeth Fox-Genovese and Eugene D. Genovese, "The Debate over Time on the Cross: A Critique of Bourgeois Criticism," in *Fruits of Merchant Capital*, pp. 136–172; Herbert G. Gutman, *Slavery and the Numbers Game: A Critique of Time on the Cross* (Urbana: University of Illinois Press, 1975); Paul A. David et al., *Reckoning with Slavery: A Critical Study in the Quantitative History of American Negro Slavery* (New York: Oxford University Press, 1976).

40. Fogel and Engerman, *Time and the Cross*, vol. 1, pp. 59–63; Hacker, *Triumph of American Capitalism*, pp. 284–286.

41. See Richard D. Garrett, "Primitive Accumulation in the Antebellum Cotton South" (Ph.D. diss., New School for Social Research, 1978), chap. 4.

42. U. B. Phillips, *Life and Labor in the Old South* (Boston: Little, Brown, 1963), pp. 48, 93, 173–187, 246; Hacker, *Triumph of American Capitalism*, pp. 302–304; Genovese, *Political Economy of Slavery*, p. 264.

43. Hacker, *Triumph of American Capitalism*, pp. 299–301.

44. Note the lucid statement in Post, "American Road to Capitalism," pp. 37–38.

45. Fogel and Engerman, *Time on the Cross*, vol. 1, pp. 78–86; Richard Sutch, "The Breeding of Slaves for Sale and the Westward Expansion of Slavery, 1850–1860," in Stanley L. Engerman and Eugene D. Genovese, eds., *Race and Slavery in the Western Hemisphere: Quantitative Studies* (Princeton, N.J.: Princeton University Press, 1975), pp. 173–210.

46. Herbert G. Gutman and Richard Sutch, "Victorians All? The Sexual Mores and Conduct of Slaves and Their Masters," in *Reckoning with Slavery*, p. 155.

47. At the risk of pairing the incompatible, see Herbert G. Gutman, *The Black Family in*

Slavery and Freedom, 1750–1925 (New York: Pantheon Books, 1976), pt. 1; and Genovese, *Roll, Jordan, Roll,* especially pp. 70–75, 443–584.

48. Michel Aglietta, "Phases of U.S. Capitalist Expansion," *New Left Review* 110 (July–August 1978): 19–21.
49. John McCallum, *Unequal Beginnings: Agriculture and Economic Development in Quebec and Ontario Until 1870* (Toronto: University of Toronto Press, 1980), especially pp. 54–70, 83–92.
50. V. I. Lenin, *The Development of Capitalism in Russia* (Moscow: Progress, 1974), pp. 175–190; Rosa Luxemburg, *The Accumulation of Capital* (New York: Monthly Review Press, 1968), pp. 396–411; James O'Connor, "The Twisted Dream," *Monthly Review* 26 (March 1975); Michael Merrill, "Cash Is Good to Eat: Self-Sufficiency and Exchange in the Rural Economy of the United States," *Radical History Review* 3 (Winter 1977): 42–71; James A. Henretta, "Families and Farms: *Mentalité* in Pre-Industrial America," *William and Mary Quarterly* 35 (January 1978): 3–32; Leo A. Johnson, "Independent Commodity Production: Mode of Production or Capitalist Class Formation," *Studies in Political Economy* 6 (Autumn 1981): 93–112.
51. John J. Waters, "The Traditional World of the New England Peasants: A View from Seventeenth-Century Barnstable," *New England Historical and Genealogical Register,* 130 (January 1976): 3–22; James Henretta, "The Morphology of New England Society in the Colonial Period," *Journal of Interdisciplinary History* 2 (1971): 379–398.
52. Sigmund Diamond, "An Experiment in Feudalism: French Canada in the Seventeenth Century," *William and Mary Quarterly* 18 (1981): 3–34; L. R. Macdonald, "France and New France: The Internal Contradictions," *Canadian Historical Review* 52 (June 1971): 121–143.
53. Henretta, "Farms and Families," p. 21; Merrill, "Cash Is Good to Eat," pp. 59–57; David Gagan, *Hopeful Travellers: Families, Land, and Social Change in Mid-Victorian Peel County, Canada West* (Toronto: University of Toronto Press, 1981), pp. 50–53.
54. Mary P. Ryan, *Cradle of the Middle Class: The Family of Oneida County, New York, 1780–1865* (New York: Cambridge University Press, 1981), pp. 21–43; Joy Parr, *Labouring Children: British Immigrant Apprentices to Canada* (Montreal: McGill-Queen's University Press, 1980), p. 83.
55. See Post, "American Road," p. 43; Paul W. Gates, "The Role of Land Speculator in Western Development," in G. D. Nash, ed., *Issues in American Economic History* (Boston: Little Brown, 1964), pp. 182–196; Fred Shannon, "A Post-Mortem on the Labor-Supply Safety-Valve Theory," *Agricultural History* 19 (January 1945): 31–37; Clarence Danhof, "Farm-Making Costs and the 'Safety Valve': 1850–1860," *Journal of Political Economy* 49 (June 1941): 317–359; W. N. Parket and J. L. Klein, "Productivity Growth in Grain Production in the United States, 1840–1860 and 1900–1910," in Peter Temin, ed., *The New Economic History* (Harmondsworth, England: Penguin, 1973); R. Pomfret, "The Mechanization of Reaping in Nineteenth-Century Ontario: A Case Study of the Pace and Causes of the Diffusion of Embodied Technical Change," *Journal of Economic History* 36 (1976): 399–415. An important theoretical argument is made in Robert Sherry, "Comments on O'Connor's Review of the Twisted Dream," *Monthly Review* 28 (May 1976): 52–58
56. R. C. Harris, *The Seigneurial System in Early Canada: A Geographical Study* (Madison: University of Wisconsin Press, 1966); Pentland, *Labour and Capital,* pp. 63–78; W. H. Parker, "A New Look at Unrest in Lower Canada, 1833–1838," *Canadian Historical Review* 40 (1969): 209–218; Fernand Quellet, *Economic and Social History of Quebec, 1760–1850* (Toronto: Gage, 1980); Bernard Bernier, "The Penetration of Capitalism in Quebec Agriculture," in J. Paul Grayson, ed., *Class, State, Ideology and Change: Marxist Perspectives on Canada* (Toronto: Holt, Rinehart & Winston, 1980), pp. 71–83. For a

critical assessment of the literature on the agricultural crisis, see R. M. McInnis, "A Reconsideration of the State of Agriculture in Lower Canada in the First Half of the Nineteenth Century," in Donald H. Akenson, ed., *Canadian Papers in Rural History*, vol. 3 (Gananoque, Ontario: Langdale Press, 1982), pp. 9–49.

57. Goderich is quoted in Leo A. Johnson, *History of the County of Ontario, 1615–1875* (Whitby, Ontario: Corporation of the County of Ontario, 1973), p. 66. See also Leo Johnson, "Land Policy, Population Growth and Social Structure in the Home District, 1793–1851," *Ontario History* 63 (1971): 41–60; Graeme Wynn, "Notes on Society and Environment in Old Ontario," *Journal of Social History* 13 (Fall 1979): 51–52; Peter A. Russell, "Upper Canada: A Poor Man's Country? Some Statistical Evidence," in *Canadian Papers in Rural History*, vol. 3, pp. 138–144; Joy Parr, "Hired Men: Ontario Agricultural Wage Workers in Historical Perspective" (Paper presented to the Ontario Museum's Conference, Toronto, January 1983); Gary Teeple, "Land, Labour and Capital in Pre-Confederation Canada," in *Capitalism and the National Question*, pp. 43–55.

58. Quoted in Johnson, *County of Ontario*, p. 68.

59. Quotation from Bryan D. Palmer, "Kingston Mechanics and the Rise of the Penitentiary, 1833–1836," *Histoire Sociale-Social History* 13 (May 1980): 19. On the Home District, see Johnson, "Land Policy," 57–59.

60. Gagan, *Hopeful Travellers*; David Gagan, "Land, Population, and Social Change: The 'Critical Years' in Rural Canada West," *Canadian Historical Review* 59 (1978): 293–318. I have presented some brief critical comments on Gagan's demographic determinism in my "Town, Port, and Country."

61. Graeme Wynn, *Timber Colony: A Historical Geography of Early Nineteenth Century New Brunswick* (Toronto: University of Toronto Press, 1981), especially pp. 137, 149; Wynn, "Deplorably Dark and Demoralized Lumberers: Rhetoric and Reality in Early Nineteenth-Century New Brunswick," *Journal of Forest History* 24 (1980): 168–187.

62. Gerald M. Sider, *Christmas Mumming in Outport Newfoundland* (Toronto: New Hogtown, 1977), especially pp. 23–28.

63. Stuart M. Blumin, "Rip Van Winkle's Grandchildren: Family and Household in the Hudson Valley, 1800–1860," in Tamara K. Hareven, ed., *Family and Kin in Urban Communities, 1700–1930* (New York: New Viewpoints, 1977), especially p. 105.

64. Ryan, *Cradle and Middle Class*, pp. 52–104; Whitney Cross, *The Burned-Over District: The Social and Intellectual History of Enthusiastic Religion in Western New York* (Ithaca, N.Y.: Cornell University Press, 1950).

65. Fliegelman, *Prodigals and Pilgrims*, p. 267; Rogin, *Fathers and Children*, p. 37.

66. Hacker, *Triumph of American Capitalism*, pp. 199–226.

67. Victor S. Clark, *History of Manufactures in the United States*, vol. 1: *1607–1860* (New York: Peter Smith, 1949), p. 463.

68. Clark, *History of Manufactures*, vol. 1, pp. 438–439.

69. Christine Stansell, "The Origins of the Sweatshop: Women and Early Industrialization in New York City," in Michael H. Frisch and Daniel J. Walkowitz, eds., *Working-Class America: Essays on Labor, Community, and American History* (Urbana: University of Illinois Press, 1982), pp. 79–80; Anthony E. C. Wallace, *Rockdale: The Growth of an American Village in the Early Revolution* (New York: Knopf, 1978).

70. Nathan Rosenberg, ed., *The American System of Manufactures: The Report of the Committee on the Machinery of the United States (1855) and the Special Report of George Wallis and Joseph Whitworth (1854)* (Edinburgh: University Press, 1969), p. 209. Note the excellent documentary collection, Gary Kulik, Roger Parks, Theodore Penn, eds., *The New England Mill Village, 1790–1860* (Cambridge: MIT Press, 1982); Thomas Dublin, *Women at Work: The Transformation of Work and Community in Lowell, Massachusetts,*

1826–1860 (New York: Columbia University Press, 1979), pp. 14–22; Jonathan Prude, ''The Social System of Early New England Mills: A Case Study, 1812–1840,'' in Frisch and Walkowitz, *Working-Class America*, pp. 1–36.

71. Dawley, *Class and Community*, especially pp. 11–41, 73–96; Paul G. Faler, *Mechanics and Manufacturers in the Early Industrial Revolution: Lynn, Massachusetts, 1780–1860* (Albany: State University of New York Press, 1981), pp. 58–76; Gregory S. Kealey, ''Artisans Respond to Industrialism: Shoemakers, Shoe Factories, and the Knights of St. Crispin in Toronto,'' Canadian Historical Association, *Papers* (1973), pp. 137–158; Joanne Burgess, ''L'industrie de la chaussure à Montréal, 1840–1870: Le passage de l'artisanat à la fabrique,'' *Revue d'histoire de l'Amerique français* 31 (1977): 187–210.

72. Pentland, *Labour and Capital*, pp. 34–48; Clark, *Manufactures*, vol. 1, p. 446; Joseph E. Walker, *Hopewell Village: The Dynamics of a Nineteenth-Century Iron-Making Community* (Philadelphia: University of Pennsylvania Press, 1974); John R. Commons, ed., *A Documentary History of American Industrial Society*, vol. 2 (New York: Peter Russell, 1958), pp. 304–313.

73. Rosenberg, ed., *American System*, pp. 264–280; Clark, *Manufactures*, vol. 1, pp. 412–421; Herbert G. Gutman, ''The Reality of the Rags-to-Riches 'Myth': The Case of Paterson, New Jersey, Locomotive, Iron, and Machinery Manufactures,'' in Herbert G. Gutman, *Work, Culture, and Society in Industrializing America* (New York: Knopf, 1976), pp. 211–233; Bryan D. Palmer, *A Culture in Conflict: Skilled Workers and Industrial Capitalism in Hamilton, Ontario, 1860–1914* (Montreal: McGill-Queen's University Press, 1979), p. 10; Gregory S. Kealey, *Toronto Workers Respond to Industrial Capitalism, 1867–1892* (Toronto: University of Toronto Press, 1980), pp. 20–21; Gerald Tulchinsky, ''The Montreal Business Community, 1837–1853,'' in David S. Macmillan, ed., *Canadian Business History: Selected Studies, 1497–1971* (Toronto: McClelland and Stewart, 1972), especially pp. 130–131.

74. Clark, *Manufactures*, vol. 1, p. 464; Arthur H. Cole, ed., *Industrial and Commercial Correspondence of Alexander Hamilton* (New York: Kelley, 1968), p. 19; Rosenberg, ed., *American System*, p. 262; Richard Rice, ''Shipbuilding in British America, 1787–1890: An Introductory Study'' (Ph.D. diss., University of Liverpool, 1977), pp. 168–198.

75. Clark, *Manufactures*, vol. 1, pp. 476–479; Post, ''The American Road,'' pp. 48–49; and for Canada, note McCallum, *Unequal Beginnings*, pp. 83–107.

76. My calculations, all too problematic, are from the Occupational Census for 1851 of the colonies of Upper Canada, Lower Canada, New Brunswick, and Nova Scotia and from data on industrial distribution of gainful workers (1820–1840) in the United States. In the former I equated manufacturing with the category *industrial*, and in the latter I utilized the classification of *manufacturing and hand trades*. See *Census of Canada, 1871*, vol. 4 (Ottawa, 1876); *Historical Statistics of the United States*, pp. 7, 74.

77. The term is employed in Sean Wilentz, ''Artisan Republican Festivals and the Rise of Class Conflict in New York City, 1788–1837,'' in Frisch and Walkowitz, *Working-Class America*, especially pp. 40–43; but see as well, David Montgomery, ''The Working Classes of the Pre-Industrial City, 1780–1830,'' *Labor History* 9 (1968): 3–22; Howard B. Rock, *Artisans of the New Republic: The Trademen of New York City in the Age of Jefferson* (New York: New York University Press, 1979), pp. 235–319; George Rogers Taylor, *The Transportation Revolution, 1815–1860* (New York: Harper, 1951), pp. 215–220, 250–252; Susan E. Hirsch, *Roots of the American Working Class; The Industrialization of Crafts in Newark, 1800–1860* (Philadelphia: University of Pennsylvania Press, 1978), pp. 15–52; Tulchinsky, *The River Barons*, pp. 203–231; Peter G. Goheen, *Victorian Toronto: 1850–1900* (Chicago: Department of Geography Reserach Paper no. 127, 1970), pp. 44–57.

78. Bruce Laurie, *Working People of Philadelphia, 1800–1850* (Philadelphia: Temple University Press, 1980), pp. 3–30.
79. Stansell, "The Origins of the Sweatshop," in Frisch and Walkowitz, *Working-Class America*, p. 78.
80. Laurie, *Working People*, pp. 17, 26; Wilentz, "Artisan Festivals," in Frisch and Walkowitz, *Working-Class America*, pp. 42–43, 70.
81. Palmer, *Culture in Conflict*, p. 16; Katz, Doucet, and Stern, *Social Organization*, p. 35; Kealey, *Toronto Workers*, p. 21; Jacob Spelt, *Urban Development in South Central Ontario* (Toronto: McClelland and Stewart, 1972), p. 74.
82. Wilentz, "Artisan Festivals," in Frisch and Walkowitz, *Working-Class America*, p. 43.
83. Note the argument, however flawed, in H. J. Habakkuk, *American and British Technology in the Nineteenth Century* (Cambridge: Cambridge University Press, 1967).
84. Dublin, *Women at Work*; Howard M.Gitelman, "The Waltham System and the Coming of the Irish," *Labor History* 8 (1967): 227–253; Kulik et al., *New England Mill Village*, pp. 373–480, Frederick A. Sorge, *Labor Movement in the United States: A History of the American Working Class from Colonial Times to 1890* (Westport, Conn.: Greenwood Press, 1977), pp. 60–65.
85. The essential and pioneering statement is Pentland, *Labor and Capital*, pp. 24–60. I have elaborated upon this theme in "Producing Classes, Paternalist Authority, 1800–1850," in Bryan D. Palmer, *Working-Class Experience: The Rise and Reconstitution of Canadian Labour, 1800–1980* (Toronto: Butterworth's, 1983), pp. 7–59.
86. See Sean Wilentz, "Artisan Origins of the American Working Class," *International Labor and Working Class History* 19 (Spring 1981): 1–22.
87. Steven Langdon, *The Emergence of the Canadian Working-Class Movement* (Toronto: New Hogtown, 1975), p. 6; F. H. Armstrong, "Reformer As Capitalist: William Lyon Mackenzie and the Printers' Strike of 1836," *Ontario History* 59 (September 1967): 187–188; Friedrich Langer, "Class, Culture and Class Consciousness in Ante-Bellum Lynn: A critique of Alan Dawley and Paul Faler," *Social History* 6 (1981): 317–332.
88. *Historical Statistics of the United States*, p. 57; Mike Davis, "Why the U.S. Working Class Is Different," *New Left Review* 123 (1980): 16, 20; Donald H. Akenson, "Ontario: Whatever Happened to the Irish?", *Papers in Rural History*, pp. 111, 204–256; Pentland, *Labour and Capital*, pp. 96–129.
89. *Historical Statistics of the United States*, p. 427; Brian Young, *George-Etienne Cartier: Montreal Bourgeois* (Montreal: McGill-Queen's University Press, 1981), especially pp. 53–85; Myers, *Canadian Wealth*, pp. 168–217; Ruth Bleasdale, "Class Conflict on the Canals of Upper Canada in the 1840s," *Labour/Le Travailleur* 7 (1981): 9–39; Glenn Porter and Harold C. Livesay, *Merchants and Manufacturers: Studies in the Changing Structure of Nineteenth-Century Marketing* (Baltimore: Johns Hopkins University Press, 1971).
90. See, for instance, Bray Hammond, "Banking in the Early West: Monopoly, Prohibition and Laissez-Faire," *Journal of Economic History* 8 (May 1948): 1–25; Thomas Le Duc, "History and Appraisal of the U.S. Land Policy to 1862," in Thomas C. Cochran and Thomas B. Brewer, eds., *Views of American Economic Growth: The Agricultural Era* (New York: McGraw-Hill, 1966), pp. 299–314.
91. F. W. Taussig, *The Tariff History of the United States* (New York: Putman's, 1930), pp. 109–154; Willard Phillips, *Propositions Concerning Protection and Free Trade* (Boston: Little, Brown, 1850), pp. 18–19. See Carl Siracusa, *A Mechanical People: Perceptions of the Industrial Order in Massachusetts, 1815–1880* (Middletown, Conn.: Wesleyan University Press, 1979).

92. Note Gregory S. Kealey, *Toronto Workers Respond to Industrial Capitalism*, pp. 3–17.

93. See, for instance, Hans Medick, "The Proto-Industrial Family Economy: The Structural Function of Household and Family During the Transition from Peasant Society to Industrial Capitalism," *Social History* 3 (October 1976): 295–315; Darret B. Rutman, "People in Process: The New Hampshire Towns of the Eighteenth Century," in Hareven, ed., *Family and Kin*, pp. 16–37; Kenneth Lockridge, "Land, Population, and the Evolution of New England, 1630–1790," *Past and Present* 39 (1968): 62–80; Henretta, "Morphology," pp. 379–398; Richard A. Easterlin, "Factors in the Decline of Farm Fertility in the United States: Some Preliminary Research Findings," *Journal of American History* 63 (1976): 600–614. Figures taken from *Historical Statistics of the United States*, p. 7; Pentland, *Labour and Capital*, p. 61.

94. Marx, *Grundrisse*, p. 100.

95. For an even more forceful rejoinder to neo-Malthusianism, see Brenner, "Agrarian Class Structure," p. 31; Brenner, "The Origins of Capitalist Development: A Critique of Neo-Smithian Marxism," *New Left Review* 104 (July-August 1977): 25–92; Brenner, "Agrarian Roots," pp. 16–17. Note in Seccombe's "Marxism and Demography" the call for a softening of Brenner's suppression of demographic imperatives (pp. 23–24).

96. Edward Pessen, "Building the Young Republic," in Richard B. Morris, ed., *The U.S. Department of Labor History of the American Worker* (Washington, D.C.: Government History Office, 1976), p. 57; *Historical Statistics of the United States*, pp. 7, 57; *Census of Canada*, 1871, vol. 4.

97. Marx and Engels, "Manifesto of the Communist Party," in *Selected Works* (Moscow: Progress, 1968), p. 35.

98. G. E. M. de Ste Croix, *Class Struggle in Greek World*, pp. 42–69; E. P. Thompson, "Eighteenth-Century English Society: Class Struggle without Class?" *Social History* (1978): 133–165; Seccombe, "Marxism and Demography," p. 47. I am here ignoring Raymond Williams's insistence that there is a sharp division between class conflict and class struggle, with the latter representative of more conscious levels of class antagonism. It seems, however, that struggle conveys, semantically, a sense of pervasive, rather than episodic, activity, however strong or weak. I thus use the term *class struggle* throughout the remainder of this chapter to denote a wide range of both conscious and unconscious developments within class formation. See Raymond Williams, *Politics and Letters: Interviews with New Left Review* (London: New Left Books, 1979).

99. Susanna Moodie, *Roughing It in the Bush* (Toronto: McClelland and Stewart, 1962), pp. 140–142.

100. Ryan, *Cradle of the Middle Class*, pp. 57–58.

101. Gagan, *Hopeful Travellers*, pp. 53–60; Henretta, "Farms and Families"; Dublin, *Women at Work*, pp. 58–74; Seth Luther, *An Address to the Workingmen of New England. . . .* (Boston: 1832), especially pp. 17–23; Norman Ware, *The Industrial Worker, 1840–1860* (Chicago: Quadrangle, 1964), p. 149; Jack Goody, *Production and Reproduction: A Comparative Study of the Domestic Domain* (Cambridge, England: Cambridge University Press, 1976), pp. 86–117; E. P. Thompson, "The Grid of Inheritance: A Comment," in Jack Goody, Joan Thirsk, and E. P. Thompson, eds., *Family and Inheritance: Rural Society in Western Europe, 1200–1800*, (London: Oxford University Press, 1976), pp. 328–360; Bryan D. Palmer, "Discordant Music: Charivaris and Whitecapping in Nineteenth-Century North America," *Labour/Le Travailleur* 3 (1978): 5–63.

102. Note the suggestive comments in Merrill, "Cash Is Good to Eat," pp. 65–66; Lillian Gates, "The Decided Policy of William Lyon Mackenzie," *Canadian Historical Review* 40 (1959): 185–209; J. E. Rea, "William Lyon Mackenzie—Jacksonian?" *Mid-America*

60 (1968): 223–235; Fred Landon, "The Common Man in the Era of the Rebellion in Upper Canada," *Canadian Historical Association, Report* (1937): 79–91; D. G. Creighton, "The Economic Background of The Rebellions," *Canadian Journal of Economics and Political Science* 3 (1937): 322–334; Colin Reid, *The Rising in Western Upper Canada: 1837–1838* (Toronto: University of Toronto Press, 1982); Edward Pessen, *Most Uncommon Jacksonians: Radical Leaders of the Early Labor Movement* (Albany: State University of New York Press, 1967).

103. The verse and quotation are taken from Luther, *Address to the Workingmen of New England,* p. 25.

104. For a sampling of reform thought, see the early entries in Leon Stein and Philip Taft, eds., *Religion, Reform and Revolution: Labor Panaceas in the Nineteenth Century* (New York: Arno, 1969).

105. The literature is extensive. It commences, however, with Herbert Aptheker, *American Negro Slave Revolts* (New York: International Publishers, 1943) and has been extended in Genovese, *Roll, Jordan, Roll,* pp. 587–596; Eugene D. Genovese, *From Rebellion to Revolution: Afro-American Slave Revolts in the Making of the Modern World* (Baton Rouge: Louisiana State University Press, 1979).

106. On patriarchy and the slave South, see Bertram Wyatt-Brown, *Southern Honour: Ethics & Behaviour in the Old South* (New York: Oxford University Press, 1982).

107. Gutman, *Black Family,* p. 99.

108. Genovese, *Roll, Jordan, Roll,* p. 598; Philip D. Morgan, "Work and Culture: The Task System and the World of Lowcountry Blacks, 1700–1880," *William and Mary Quarterly* 39 (October 1982): 563–599; John O'Brien, "From Bondage to Citizenship: The Richmond Black Community, 1865–1867" (Ph.D. diss., University of Rochester, 1975); Peter Rachleff, "Black Richmond and the Knights of Labor" (Paper presented to the Knights of Labor Centennial Conference, Newberry Library, Chicago, May 17–19, 1979).

109. See Laurie, *Working People,* pp. 33–84, although Laurie's ideal typology of worker cultures is neither convincing nor unproblematic (see Bryan D. Palmer, "Classifying Culture," *Labour/Le Travailleur* 8/9 (1981–1982): 160–162); Wilentz, "Artisan Festivals," in *Working-Class America,* pp. 37–77; Gutman, "Work, Culture, and Society," pp. 533–588; Paul Faler, "Cultural Aspects of the Industrial Revolution: Lynn, Massachusetts, Shoemakers and Industrial Morality, 1826–1860"; and Alan Dawley and Paul Faler, "Working Class Culture and Politics in the Industrial Revolution: Sources of Loyalism and Rebellion," in Milton Cantor, ed., *American Workingclass Culture: Explorations in American Labor and Social History* (Westport, Conn.: Greenwood Press, 1979), pp. 121–148, 61–76. For Canada, note Eugene Forsey, *Trade Unions in Canada, 1812–1902* (Toronto: University of Toronto Press, 1982), pp. 9–31; and my own attempt at a survey in *Working-Class Experience.*

110. Verses quoted in Jack Scott, *Sweat and Struggle: Working Class Struggles in Canada, 1780–1899* (Vancouver: New Star, 1974), p. 29.

111. See, for instance, John R. Commons et al., *History of Labor in the United States,* vol. 1 (New York: Kelley, 1966), especially pp. 169–334; Leonard Bernstein, "The Working People of Philadelphia from Colonial Times to the Central Strike of 1835," *Pennsylvania Magazine of History and Biography* 74 (1950): 322–339; Laurie, *Working People,* pp. 85–106; Palmer, "Kingston Mechanics," pp. 7–32; Alden Whitman, *Labor Parties, 1827–1834: Initial Steps Independent Political Action . . .* (New York: International Publishers, 1943); Walter Hugins, *Jacksonian Democracy and the Working Class: A Study of the New York Workingmen's Movement* (Palo Alto, Calif.: Stanford University Press, 1966).

112. Dublin, *Women at Work,* especially pp. 86–164; Ware, *Industrial Worker,* pp. 125–153;

Gitelman, "Waltham System and Irish," pp. 227-253; Wallace, *Rockdale*, pp. 291-292.

113. Stansell, "Origins of Sweatshop," in *Working-Class America*, pp. 78-103; Carol Groneman, "She Earns As a Child—She Pays As a Man': Women Workers in a Mid-Nineteenth Century New York Community," in Richard L. Ehrlich, ed., *Immigrants in Industrial America, 1850-1920* (Charlottesville: University of Virginia Press, 1977), pp. 33-46.

114. Michael Cross, "The Shiners' War: Social Violence in the Ottawa Valley in the 1830s," *Canadian Historical Review* 54 (March, 1973): 1-25; Bleasdale, "Class Conflict on the Canals," pp. 9-39; H. C. Pentland, "The Lachine Canal Strike of 1843," *Canadian Historical Review* 29 (1948): 255-277; Wynn, "Demoralized Lumberers," pp. 168-187.

115. Note David Montgomery, "The Shuttle and the Cross: Weavers and Artisans in the Kensington Riots of 1844," *Journal of Social History* 5 (Summer 1972): 411-446; Hirsch, *Roots of the American Working Class*, pp. 37-132; Steven J. Ross, "Workers on the Edge: Work, Leisure, and Politics in Industrializing Cincinnati, 1830-1890" (Ph.D. diss., Princeton University, 1980).

116. Morris, *Government and Labor in Early America*, especially pp. 92-207; Rock, *Artisans of the New Republic*, pp. 205-234; Commons et al., *Documentary History of American Industrial Society*, vols. 3-4; Armstrong, "Reformer As Capitalist," pp. 187-196.

117. Canadian figures are from unpublished research I have conducted, forthcoming as a plate, "The Changing Character of Working-Class Organization and Protest, 1820-1890," in *Historical Atlas of Canada*, vol. 2. The American figures are from Commons et al., *History of Labor*, vol. 1, pp. 391, 424. Because of Commons's problematic use of early statistics on labor organization, I have utilized only the most cautious data. See Maurice Neufeld, "The Size of the Jacksonian Labor Movement: A Cautionary Account," *Labor History* 23 (Fall 1982): 599-607.

118. See Michael S. Cross and Gregory S. Kealey, eds., *Pre-Industrial Canada, 1760-1849: Readings in Canadian Social History*, vol. 11 (Toronto: McClelland and Stewart, 1982), p. 139; Michael Feldberg, *The Philadelphia Riots of 1844: A Study of Ethnic Conflict* (Westport, Conn.: Greenwood Press, 1975).

119. This is the reason for much of the ideological battle of the 1850s and 1860s. Note Eric Foner, *Free Soil, Free Labor, Free Men: The Ideology of the Republican Party Before the Civil War* (New York: Oxford University Press, 1970); Marx, *Capital*, vol. 1, p. 302.

120. Marx, *Capital*, vol. 1, p. 302.

121. Foner, *Free Soil*, p. 315.

122. Stanley B. Ryerson, *Unequal Union: Roots of Crisis in the Canadas, 1815-1873* (Toronto: Progress, 1973), p. 325.

123. A voluminous literature might be cited, but see David Montgomery, "Labor and the Republic in Industrial America: 1860-1920," *Mouvement social* 111 (avril-juin 1980): 202-203; C. Vann Woodward, *Reunion and Reaction: The Compromise of 1877 and the End of Reconstruction* (Garden City, N.Y.: Doubleday, 1956); W. E. B. Dubois, *Black Reconstruction in America, 1860-1880* (Cleveland: Meridan, 1964), p. 56.

124. Quotes in Ryerson, *Unequal Union*, pp. 320-321.

125. See Myers, *Canadian Wealth*, pp. 168-263; Young, *Cartier*, especially pp. 53-136.

126. Michael Katz, "The Entrepreneurial Class in a Canadian City: The Mid-Nineteenth Century," *Journal of Social History* 8 (Winter 1975): 1-29.

127. P. Douglas McCalla, "The Buchannan Businesses, 1834-1872; A Study in the Organization and Development of Canadian Trade" (Ph.D. diss., Oxford University, 1972); McCalla, "The Decline of Hamilton As a Wholesale Centre," *Ontario History* 65 (September 1973): 247-254.

128. My calculations, *Historical Statistics of the United States*, pp. 409, 570; Debi Wells, " 'The

Hardest Lines of the Sternest School': Working Class Ottawa in the Depression of the 1870s'' (M.A. thesis, Carleton University, 1982), pp. 5–6; Steven Joseph Ross, "Workers on the Edge: Work, Leisure, and Politics in Industrializing Cincinnati, 1830–1890'' (Ph.D. diss., Princeton University, 1980), pp. 121–124.

129. House of Commons, "Report of the Select Committee on the Causes of the Present Depression of the Manufacturing, Mining, Commercial, Shipping, Lumber and Fishing Interests,'' *Journals*, vol. 10 (Ottawa: McLean, Roger, and Company, 1876); David Montgomery, *Beyond Equality: Labor and the Radical Republicans, 1862–1872* (New York: Knopf, 1967), pp. 24, 46.

130. Sorge, *Labor Movement*, p. 123.

131. Mathew Josephson, *The Politicos, 1865–1896* (New York: Harcourt Brace, 1938), p. 118; Thomas C. Cochran and William Miller, "The Business of Politics,'' in Thomas C. Cochran and W. Brewer, eds., *Views of American Economic Growth: The Industrial Era* (New York: McGraw-Hill, 1966), pp. 4–6.

132. Myers, *Canadian Wealth*, p. 337.

133. Porter and Livesay, *Merchants and Manufacturers*, pp. 116–130; Montgomery, *Beyond Equality*, pp. 340–356, 425–447; Langdon, *Emergence of Canadian Working Class Movement*, p. 3; H. C. Pentland, "The Role of Capital in Canadian Economic Development Before 1875,'' *Canadian Journal of Economics and Political Science* 4 (November 1950): 457–474; Harold C. Vatter, *The Drive to Industrial Maturity: The U.S. Economy, 1860–1914* (Westport, Conn.: Greenwood Press, 1976), pp. 45–59; Katharine Coman, *The Industrial History of the United States* (New York: Macmillan, 1920), pp. 269–312.

134. Cited in Montgomery, *Beyond Equality*, p. 25.

135. *The Great Industries of the United States. . . .* (Harftord, Conn.: J. B. Burr & Hyde, 1872), pp. 25–26. See Herbert G. Gutman, "Reality of Rags to Riches,'' in *Work, Culture and Society*, pp. 211–233; Post, "American Road to Capitalism,'' pp. 46–49.

136. McCallum, *Unequal Beginnings*, pp. 83–114; Kealey, *Toronto Workers*, pp. 18–34; Bruce Laurie and Mark Schmitz, "Manufacture and Productivity: The Making of an Industrial Base, Philadelphia, 1850–1880,'' pp. 43–92; Montgomery, *Beyond Equality*, pp. 3–44; Vatter, *The Drive to Industrial Maturity*, p. 134; David Ward, *Cities and Immigrants: A Geography of Change in Nineteenth-Century North America* (New York: Oxford University Press, 1971), pp. 11–84; Edward Young, *Labor in Europe and America: A Special Report on the Rate of Wages, the Cost of Subsistence in Great Britain. . . . Also in the United States and British North America* (Philadelphia: S. A. George and Company, 1875), especially pp. 176–195; D. L. Burn, "The Genesis of American Engineering Competition, 1850–1870,'' in S. B. Saul, ed., *Technological Change: The United States and Britain in the Nineteenth Century* (London: Methuen, 1970), pp. 77–98; Nathan Rosenberg, "Technological Change in the Machine Tool Industry, 1840–1910,'' *Journal of Economic History* 23 (December 1983): 414–446; Carole Groneman Pernicone, " 'The Bloody Auld Sixth': A Social Analysis of a New York City Working Class Community in the Mid-Nineteenth Century'' (Ph.D. diss., University of Rochester, 1973).

137. Montgomery, *Beyond Equality*, pp. 25–44; Palmer, *Culture in Conflict*, pp. 97–122; Kealey, *Toronto Workers*, pp. 154–171.

138. Kealey, *Toronto Workers*, pp. 37–97; Palmer, *Culture in Conflict*, pp. 71–96; David Harlan Bensman, "Artisan Culture, Business Union: American Hat Finishers in the Nineteenth Century'' (Ph.D. diss., Columbia University, 1977); George Barnett, "The Printers: A Study in American Trade Unionism,'' *American Economic Association Quarterly* 10 (1909): 182–208; Solomon Blum, "Trade Union Rules in the Building Trades,'' in Jacob H. Hollander and George C. Barnett, eds., *Studies in American Trade Unionism* (New York: Henry Holt, 1907), pp. 295–319. The quotation is from David Montgo-

mery, "Workers' Control of Machine Production in the Late Nineteenth Century," in *Workers' Control in America* (New York: Cambridge University Press, 1979), pp. 9–31, especially p. 12.

139. Montgomery, "Labor and the Republic," p. 203; Laurie and Schmitz, "Manufacture and Productivity," pp. 87–88; Dawley, *Class and Community*, p. 74; Susan Beth Levine, "Their Own Sphere: Women's Work, the Knights of Labor, and the Transformation of the Carpet Trade, 1870–1890" (Ph.D. diss., City University of New York, 1979), pp. 38–43; and on price deflation, Vatter, *The Drive to Industrial Maturity*, especially pp. 243–251.

140. T. W. Acheson, "The Social Origins of the Canadian Industrial Elite, 1880–1885," in Macmillan, *Canadian Business History*, p. 162; Montgomery, *Beyond Equality*, pp. 26–27; John Merrington, "Town and Country in the Transition to Capitalism," in Hilton, *The Transition from Feudalism to Capitalism*, pp. 171, 189–190; Gordon, Edwards, and Reich, *Segmented Work, Divided Workers*, p. 88. Note the local discussions in John Herbert Cordulack, "The Artisan Confronts the Machine Age: Bureau County, Illinois, 1850–1880" (Ph.D. diss., University of Illinois at Urbana-Champaign, 1975); Ross, "Workers on the Edge," p. 126.

141. Robert Gallman, "Commodity Output, 1839–1899," in *Trends in the American Economy in the Nineteenth Century* (Princeton, N.J.: National Bureau of Economic Research, 1960), p. 34; W. S. Woytinsky, *Employment and Wages in the United States* (New York: Twentieth Century Fund, 1953), p. 29; Vatter, *The Drive to Industrial Maturity*, p. 68; Gordon, Edwards, and Reich, *Segmented Work, Divided Workers*, pp. 81–90.

142. Urquhart and Buckley, *Historical Statistics of Canada*, pp. 14–15, 23; *Historical Statistics of the United States*, pp. 7, 57; Montgomery, *Beyond Equality*, pp. 35–40; Gutman, *Work, Culture and Society*, p. 40; Kealey, *Toronto Workers*, p. 100; Ross, "Workers on the Edge," pp. 85–88; Levine, "Their Own Sphere," pp. 73, 78. Gutman's argument about the centrality of the second generation forms the core of a series of unpublished papers delivered across North America over the last three years. I heard the argument stated most thoroughly in his "Class Formation and Class Development in 19th Century America," delivered at Simon Fraser University, Burnaby, British Columbia, October 14, 1982.

143. Almost 45 years separate the publication of two magisterial treatments, Dubois, *Black Reconstruction*, and Leon F. Litwack, *Been in the Storm So Long: The Aftermath of Slavery* (New York: Vintage Books, 1980). On mobility of white labor, the pioneering work was Stephen Thernstrom, *Poverty and Progress: Social Mobility in a Nineteenth-Century City* (Cambridge, Mass.: Harvard University Press, 1964); and in a less interpretive mode, Peter R. Knights, *The Plain People of Boston, 1830–1860: A Study of City Growth* (New York: Oxford University Press, 1971). For a Canada–United States comparison, see Katz, Doucet, and Stern, *Social Organization*, pp. 102–130. On southern migrations northward, see Robert Coles, *South goes North* (Boston: Little, Brown, 1972); William M. Tuttle, Jr., "Labor Conflict and Racial Violence in Chicago, 1894–1919," *Labor History* 10 (Summer 1969): 408–432; Sterling D. Spero and Abram L. Harris, *The Black Worker: The Negro and the Labor Movement* (New York: Atheneum, 1968).

144. Quotations from Litwack, *Been in the Storm So Long*, pp. 387, 292.

145. Gordon, Edwards, and Reich, *Segmented Work, Divided Workers*, pp. 93–94; Katz, Doucet, and Stern, *Social Organization*, p. 395; Kealey, *Toronto Workers*, pp. 310–315; Gregory S. Kealey and Bryan D. Palmer, *Dreaming of What Might Be: The Knights of Labor in Ontario, 1880–1900* (New York: Cambridge University Press, 1982), pp. 43–44; Bettina Bradbury, "The Family Economy and Work in an Industrializing City: Montreal in the 1870s," Canadian Historical Association, *Papers* (1979): 71–96; Montgomery, *Beyond Equality*, pp. 33–34; Ross, "Workers on the Edge," pp. 129–130; Pernicone,

"The Bloody Auld Sixth," p. 171. On poverty, see Daniel J. Walkowitz, *Worker City, Company Town: Iron and Cotton-Worker Protest in Troy and Cohoes, New York, 1855–1884* (Urbana: University of Illinois Press, 1978), pp. 145–154.

146. *Historical Statistics of the United States*, p. 23; Bradbury, "Family Economy," pp. 71–96; Katz, Doucet and Stern, *Social Organization*, pp. 336–342; Jacques Henripin, *Trends and Factors of Fertility in Canada* (Ottawa: Government Publications, 1972); Michael Katz, "Social Class in North American Urban History," *Journal of Interdisciplinary History* 11 (Spring 1981): 579–606; Alice Kessler-Harris, *Out of Work: A History of Wage Earning Women in the United States* (New York: Oxford University Press, 1982), pp. 109–110.

147. Seccombe, "Marxism and Demography," pp. 38. 44–47.

148. Michael B. Katz and Mark J. Stern, "Fertility, Class, and Industrial Capitalism: Erie County, New York, 1855–1915," *American Quarterly* 33 (1981): especially pp. 75–78; Katz, Doucet, and Stern, *Social Organization*, p. 342. For the implications of the persistence in rural areas of what Seccombe ("Marxism and Demography," pp. 38, 43–45) terms the "early proletarian household," where fertility was higher, see Chad M. Gaffield, "Canadian Families in Cultural Context: Hypotheses from Mid-Century," Canadian Historical Association, *Papers* (1979): 48–70; Alan A. Brookes, "Family, Youth, and Leaving Home in Late Nineteenth-Century Rural Nova Scotia: Canning and the Exodus, 1868–1893," in Joy Parr, ed., *Childhood and Family in Canadian History* (Toronto: McClelland and Stewart, 1982), pp. 93–108.

149. Note Barrett, *Women's Oppression Today*, pp. 194, 204, 218–219; Jane Humphries, "Class Struggle and the Persistence of the Working Class Family," *Cambridge Journal of Economics* 1 (1977); Humphries, "The Working Class Family, Women's Liberation, and Class Struggle," *Review of Radical Political Economics* 9 (1977).

150. Palmer, *Culture in Conflict*, pp. 35–70; Palmer, *Working-Class Experience*, pp. 60–95; Kealey, *Toronto Workers*, pp. 98–123; Warren Van Tine, *The Making of the Labour Bureaucrat: Union Leadership in the United States, 1870–1920* (Amherst: University of Massachusetts Press, 1973), especially pp. 1–18, 33–40; Walkowitz, *Worker City, Company Town*, pp. 110–142, 156–170; Brian Greenberg, "Worker and Community: The Social Structure of a Nineteenth-Century American City, Albany, New York, 1850–1884" (Ph.D. diss., Princeton University, 1980), pp. 65–113, 163–186.

151. Palmer, "Changing Character of Working Class Protest and Organization, 1820–1890," forthcoming; *Historical Atlas of Canada*, vol. 11; Forsey, *Trade Unions in Canada*, pp. 31–36; Commons et al., *History of Labor*, vol. 1, pp. 601–620; Ware, *The Industrial Worker*, pp. 227–240; Roger W. Shugg, *The Origins of Class Struggle in Louisiana: A Social History of White Farmers and Laborers During Slavery and After, 1840–1875* (Baton Rouge: Louisiana State University Press, 1972), pp. 76–156; Ross, "Workers on the Edge," pp. 342–347; Douglas Vincent Shaw, "The Making of an Immigrant City: Ethnic and Cultural Conflict in Jersey City, New Jersey, 1850–1877" (Ph.D. diss., University of Rochester, 1973), pp. 48–84.

152. Silvis and Steward quoted in Montgomery, *Beyond Equality*, pp. 229, 257.

153. Norman Ware, *The Labor Movement in the United States, 1860–1890: A Study in Democracy* (New York: Vintage Books, 1964), pp. 1–54; John R. Commons et al., *Documentary History of American Industrial Society*, vol. 10; John Battye, "The Nine-Hour Pioneers: Genesis of the Canadian Labour Movement," *Labour/Le Travailleur* 4 (1980): 25–56; Ross. "Workers on the Edge," pp. 368–458.

154. Commons et al., *Documentary History*, vol. 10, p. vii; Forsey, *Trade Unions in Canada*, p. 61.

155. Bryan D. Palmer, "The Changing Character of Working-Class Organization and Protest, 1820–1890," forthcoming; *Historical Atlas of Canada*, vol. 2; Palmer, *Culture in*

Conflict, pp. 78–82; Walkowitz, *Worker City, Company Town*, pp. 95–98, 183–218; Montgomery, "Labor and the Republic," p. 203; Montgomery, "Strikes in Nineteenth-Century America," *Social Science History* 4 (February 1980): 81–104; Desmond Morton, "Taking on the Grand Trunk: The Locomotive Engineers Strike of 1876–1877," *Labour/Le Travailleur* 2 (1977): 6–34; Marianne Debouzy, "Workers' Self-Organization and Resistance in the 1877 Strikes," in Dirk Hoerder, ed., *American Labor and Immigration History, 1877–1920: Recent European Research* (Urbana: University of Illinois Press, 1983), pp. 61–77; Jeremy Brecker, *Strike!* (San Francisco: Straight Arrow, 1972), pp. 1–24. The quotation is from J. A. Dacus, *Annals of the Great Strikes in the United States. . . .* (Chicago: Palmer & Company, 1877), pp. 16–17. On military intervention, see Jerry M. Cooper, *The Army and Civil Disorder: Federal Military Intervention in Labor Disputes, 1877–1900* (Westport, Conn.: Greenwood Press, 1980), pp. 43–98.

156. The quotation is from David Montgomery, "Labor in the Industrial Era," in Morris, ed., *The American Worker*, p. 120.

157. Montgomery, *Beyond Equality*, pp. 335–386; Palmer, *A Culture in Conflict*, pp. 97–152; Kealey, *Toronto Workers*, pp. 124–153.

158. Daniel Nelson, *Managers and Workers: Origins of the New Factory System in the United States* (Madison: University of Wisconsin Press, 1975), pp. 3–10.

159. Gordon, Edwards, and Reich, *Segmented Work, Divided Workers*, pp. 84, 94–106; Joseph Steindl, *Maturity and Stagnation in American Capitalism* (New York: Monthly Review, 1976), p. 191; Philip S. Foner, *History of the Labor Movement in the United States*, vol. 1 (New York: International Publishers, 1962), p. 58, where Marx is quoted; Gabriel Kolko, *Railroads and Regulations, 1877–1916* (Princeton, N.J.: Princeton University Press, 1965); Vatter, *The Drive to Industrial Maturity*, pp. 132–140; John William Bennett, "Iron Workers in Woods Run and Johnstown: The Union Era, 1865–1901" (Ph.D. diss., University of Pittsburgh, 1977), pp. 34–35.

160. Drawn from more extensive data/sources cited in Kealey and Palmer, *Dreaming of What Might Be*, pp. 29–35.

161. Joseph Kinsey Howard, *The Strange Empire of Louis Riel* (Toronto: Swan, 1965); David Frank, "The Cape Breton Coal Industry and the Rise and Fall of the British Empire Steel Corporation," *Acadiensis* 7 (Autumn 1977): 3–34; Martin Robin, *The Rush for Spoils: The Company Province, 1871–1933* (Toronto: McClelland and Stewart, 1972), pp. 49–86; C. Vann Woodward, *Origins of the New South* (Baton Rouge: Louisiana State University Press, 1951); Vatter, *The Drive to Industrial Maturity*, pp. 87–130; Norman Pollack, *The Populist Response to Industrial America* (New York: Norton, 1968); Lawrence Goodwyn, *Democratic Promise: The Populist Movement in America* (New York: Oxford University Press, 1976); J. D. Hicks, *The Populist Revolt* (Minneapolis: University of Minnesota Press, 1931); Russell Hann, *Farmers Confront Industrialism: Some Historical Perspectives on Ontario Agrarian Movements* (Toronto: New Hogtown, 1975); Louis Aubrey Wood, *A History of Farmers' Movements in Canada: The Origins and Development of Agrarian Protest, 1872–1924* (Toronto: University of Toronto Press, 1975), pp. 9–146.

162. Kolko, *Railroads and Regulation*; Joe S. Bain, "Industrial Concentration and Anti-Trust Policy," in Harold Williamson, ed., *Growth of the American Economy* (Englewood Cliffs, N.J.: Prentice-Hall, 1964), p. 623; Vatter, *The Drive to Industrial Maturity*, pp. 168–212; Cooper, *The Army and Civil Disorder*; Myers, *Canadian Wealth*, pp. 301–337.

163. T. Phillips Thompson, *The Politics of Labor* (New York: Belford Clark, 1887), p. 93.

164. Kealey and Palmer, *Dreaming of What Might Be*, pp. 30–32; Montgomery, "Labor in the Industrial Era," p. 113.

165. Clark, *Manufactures*, vol. 2, pp. 79, 106; Robert Ozanne, *A Century of Labor-Manage-*

ment Relations at McCormick and International Harvester (Madison: University of Wisconsin Press, 1967), pp. 22–26; Gordon, Edwards, and Reich, *Segmented Work, Divided Workers*, pp. 115–116; Bennett, "Iron Workers in Woods Run and Johnstown," pp. 10–39.

166. *Historical Statistics of the United States*, pp. 7, 56–57; Urquhart and Buckley, *Historical Statistics of Canada*, pp. 12, 27–28, 59; Montgomery, "Labor in the Industrial Era," pp. 109, 111; Montgomery, "Immigrant Workers and Managerial Reform," in *Workers' Control in America*, p. 35; Donald Avery, *'Dangerous Foreigners': European Immigrant Workers and Labour Radicalism in Canada, 1896–1932* (Toronto: McClelland and Stewart, 1979); Neufeld, "The Size of the Jacksonian Labor Movement," p. 606.

167. The term is employed and the process is outlined in Gordon, Edwards, and Reich, *Segmented Work, Divided Workers*, pp. 106–132. Note the discussion of wage convergence in the Northeast in Sari J. Bennett and Carville V. Earle, "Labour Power and Locality in the Gilded Age: The Northeastern United States, 1881–1894," *Histoire Sociale/Social History* 15 (November 1982): 383–405.

168. The following general description of working-class family incomes comes from Montgomery, "Labor in the Industrial Age," pp. 117–118. But see, as well, the particular study of family life in three groups (carpenters, teamsters, and day laborers) in Jules Evertt Tygiel, "Workingmen in San Francisco, 1880–1901" (Ph.D. diss., University of California at Los Angeles, 1977), pp. 179–227.

169. Walkowitz, *Worker City, Company Town*, p. 150.

170. Kessler-Harris, *Out of Work*, p. 121; Donald Cole, *Immigrant City: Lawrence, Massachusetts, 1845–1921* (Chapel Hill: University of North Carolina Press, 1963), p. 118; Gregory S. Kealey, "Hogtown: Working Class Toronto at the Turn of the Century," in R. Douglas Francis and Donald B. Smith, eds., *Readings in Canadian History: Post-Confederation* (Toronto: Holt, Rinehart & Winston, 1982), pp. 177–180.

171. Record of Orphan's Apprenticeships, Hamilton Orphan Asylum, April 1881–1905, Hamilton Collection, Hamilton Public Library.

172. Susan J. Kleinberg, "Technology and Women's Work: Lives of Working-Class Women in Pittsburg, 1870–1900," *Labor History* 17 (Winter 1976): 61.

173. Neufeld, "The Size of the Jacksonian Labour Movement," p. 606; Mary Ritter Beard, *The American Labor Movement* (New York: Macmillan, 1931), pp. 86–89; Foner, *History of the Labor Movement*, vol. 1, pp. 497–524; Bryan D. Palmer, "The Changing Character of Working-Class Organization and Protest, 1820–1890," forthcoming *Historical Atlas of Canada*, vol. 2; Ross, "Workers on the Edge," p. 396; Forsey, *Trade Unions in Canada*, pp. 169–290.

174. See Leon Fink, "Workingmen's Democracy: The Knights of Labor in Local Politics, 1886–1896" (Ph.D. diss., University of Rochester, 1977), pp. 389–409.

175. Kessler-Harris, *Out of Work*, p. 86; Ware, *The Labor Movement in America*, p. 93; Montgomery, "Labor in the Industrial Age," p. 107.

176. On the general organizational contours, see Jonothon Garlock, "A Structural Analysis of the Knights of Labor: A Prolegomenon to the History of the Producing Classes" (Ph.D. diss., University of Rochester, 1974); Kealey and Palmer, *Dreaming of What Might Be*, pp. 57–91; Forsey, *Trade Unions in Canada*, pp. 138–166; Palmer, *Working-Class Experience*, chap. 3; Palmer, "The Changing Character of Working-Class Organization and Protest, 1820–1890," forthcoming *Historical Atlas of Canada*, vol. 2. On women, see Kessler Harris, *Out of Work*, p. 86; Kealey and Palmer, *Dreaming of What Might Be*, pp. 316–326. For an assessment of one critical uprising, note Michael J. Cassity, "Modernization and Social Crisis: The Knights of Labor and a Midwest Community, 1885–1886," *Journal of American History* 66 (June 1979): 41–61.

177. Problems of realistically defining the work force, of estimating the size of organized

306 BRYAN D. PALMER

labor's ranks, and of dealing with the volatility of labor's episodic organizational history intrude on efforts to gauge the impact of bodies such as the Knights of Labor. See Neufeld, "The Size of the Jacksonian Labor Movement," p. 606; and the debate flowing from our preliminary statement in Kealey and Palmer, "The Bonds of Unity: The Knights of Labor in Ontario, 1880–1900," *Histoire Sociale/Social History* 28 (1981): 369–411, outlined in Michael J. Piva, "The Bonds of Unity: A Comment"; and Kealey and Palmer, "The Bonds of Unity: Some Further Reflections," *Histoire Sociale/Social History* 31 (May 1983): 169–189.

178. See Kealey and Palmer, *Dreaming of What Might Be*, pp. 63–64; Steven J. Ross, "Strikes, Knights, and Political Fights: The May Day Strikes, the Knights of Labor, and the Rise of the United Labor Party in Nineteenth-Century Cincinnati" (Paper presented to the Knights of Labor Centennial Conference, Newberry Library, Chicago, May 17–19, 1979; Richard J. Oestreicher, "Solidarity and Fragmentation: Working People and Class Consciousness in Detroit, 1877–1895" (Ph.D. diss., Michigan State University, 1979), pp. 228, 492–495; Jacques Martin, "Les Chevaliers du Travail et le Syndicalisme international a Montreal" (M.A. Thesis, Université de Montreal, 1965), app.

179. Terence V. Powerly, *Address Delivered in Music Hall, Providence, Rhode Island* (Boston: 1886), pp. 19–20; Palmer, *Working-Class Experience*, chap. 3; Melton McLaurin, *The Knights of Labor in the South* (Westport, Conn.: Greenwood Press, 1978); Leon Fink, "Irrespective of Party, Color, or Standing: The Knights of Labor and Oppositional Politics in Richmond, Virginia," *Labor History* 19 (1978): 324–349; Rachleff, "Black Richmond and the Knights of Labor"; Kenneth Kann, "The Knights of Labor and the Southern Black Worker," *Labor History* 18 (1977): 49–70; Kealey and Palmer, *Dreaming of What Might Be*, pp. 359–361; David Paul Bennetts, "Black and White Workers: New Orleans, 1880–1900" (Ph.D. diss., University of Illinois at Urbana-Champaign, 1972), especially pp. 313–392.

180. Oestreicher, "Solidarity and Fragmentation," p. 122.

181. Friedrich Engels, "Preface to the American Edition of 1887," in W. O. Henderson and W. H. Chaloner, eds., *The Condition of the Working-Class in England* (Oxford, England: Allen & Unwin, 1958), pp. 356–357.

182. Richard J. Kerrigan, "The Dynamic Year of 1886," *One Big Union Monthly*, September 23, 1927, courtesy of Allen Seager.

183. Palmer, "Changing Character of Working-Class Organization and Protest, 1820–1890"; research notes for *Historical Atlas*, vol. 3, courtesy G. S. Kealey and Doug Cruikshank; David Montgomery, "Strikes in Nineteenth-Century America," pp. 92–100; Van Tine, *Making of Labor Bureaucrat*, p. 59; Jon Amsden and Stephen Brier, "Coal Miners on Strike: The Transformation of Strike Demands and the Formation of a National Union," *Journal of Interdisciplinary History* 9 (1977): 583–616. See P. K. Edwards, *Strikes in the United States, 1881–1974* (New York: St. Martin's Press, 1981); Bennett and Earle, "Labour Power and Locality," pp. 383–405.

184. Kealey and Palmer, *Dreaming of What Might Be*, pp. 116–126, 330–375, verse on p. 147; Oestreicher, "Solidarity and Fragmentation," p. 335; Eugene Forsey, "The Telegraphers' Strike of 1883," *Transactions of the Royal Society of Canada*, 4th ser., vol. 9 (1971): 245–259; Edward McKenna, "Unorganized Labor Versus Management: The Strike at the Chaudiere Lumber Mills, 1891," *Histoire Sociale/Social History* 5 (1973): 186–211.

185. Abraham Bisno, *Abraham Bisno, Union Pioneer* (Madison: University of Wisconsin Press, 1967).

186. Fink, "Workingmen's Democracy," pp.10–11.

187. Palmer, *Working Class Experience*, chap. 3; Kealey and Palmer, *Dreaming of What Might Be*, pp. 204–276; Leon Fink, "The Uses of Political Power: Toward a Theory of the

Labor Movement in the Era of the Knights of Labor," in Frisch and Walkowitz, *Working-Class America*, pp. 104–122.

188. Sorge, *Labor Movement*, pp. 218–229; Oestreicher, "Solidarity and Fragmentation," pp. 374; 483; Ross, "Knights, Strikes, and Political Fights"; Montgomery, "Labor and the Republic," p. 14; Kealey and Palmer, "The Bonds of Unity," pp. 397–401, 410–411.

189. Quotations from Kealey and Palmer, *Dreaming of What Might Be*, p. 203.

190. *Boston Labor Leader*, February 5, 1887, cited in Leon Fink, "Class Conflict in the Gilded Age: The Figure and the Phantom," *Radical History Review* 3 (1975): 56–74.

191. Cross is quoted in Kealey and Palmer, *Dreaming of What Might Be*, p. 312.

192. George McNeill, *The Labor Movement: The Problem of Today* (New York: 1887), p. 455, cited in Montgomery, "Labor and the Republic," p. 205.

193. McNeill, *Unfrequented Paths: Songs of Nature, Labor, and Men* (Boston: 1903), pp. 111–112.

194. See the argument in Kealey and Palmer, *Dreaming of What Might Be*, pp. 227–329.

195. *Trade Union Advocate*, July 20, 1882.

196. On saloons, see Peter de Lottinville, "Joe Beef of Montreal: Working Class Culture and the Tavern, 1869–1889," *Labour/Le Travailleur* 8–9 (1981–82): 9–40; David Brundage, "The Producing Classes and the Saloon: Denver in the 1880s" (Paper prepared for the Knights of Labor Centennial Conference, Newberry Library, Chicago, May 17–19, 1979).

197. *Palladium of Labor*, April 24, 1886.

198. See Russell Hann, "Brainworkers and the Knights of Labor," in Gregory S. Kealey and Peter Warrian, eds., *Essays in Canadian Working Class History* (Toronto: McClelland and Stewart, 1976), pp. 35–57.

199. *Canadian Labor Reformer*, May 22, 1886.

200. Fink, "Workingmen's Democracy," pp. 399, 335–341; *National Labor Tribune*, August 1, 1885; Andrew Roy, *A History of the Coal Mines of the United States* (Westport, Conn.: Greenwood Press, 1970), p. 262; Montgomery, "Labor and the Republic," pp. 207–208.

201. Oestreicher, "Solidarity and Fragmentation," pp. 258, 280; Commons et al., *History of Labor*, vol. 2, pp. 386–394.

202. Montgomery, "Strikes in America," pp. 98–99.

203. Ware, *The Labor Movement in the United States, 1860–1890*, pp. 299–319; Sorge, *Labor Movement in the United States*, pp. 209–218.

204. Kealey and Palmer, *Dreaming of What Might Be*, pp. 19–20.

205. Quoted in Montgomery, *Workers' Control in America*, p. 21; Philip S. Foner, *Women and the American Labor Movement: From Colonial Times to the Present* (New York: International University Press, 1976), p. 206; Nancy Dye, "Louisville Woolen Mill Operatives and the Knights of Labor" (Paper prepared for the Knights of Labor Centennial Conference, Newberry Library, Chicago, May 17–19, 1979); Paul Buhle, "The Knights of Labor in Rhode Island," *Radical History Review* 18 (Spring 1978): 58; Walkowitz, *Worker City, Company Town*, p. 299.

206. Kealey and Palmer, *Dreaming of What Might Be*, p. 317.

207. *Palladium of Labor*, April 25, 1885.

208. Montgomery, "Labor and the Republic," pp. 204–205.

209. Quoted in Kealey and Palmer, *Dreaming of What Might Be*, p. 320.

210. The essential source on women and the Knights of Labor is Levine, "Their Own Sphere," where Swinton is quoted on p. 133.

211. Terence V. Powerly, *The Path I Trod* (New York: Columbia University Press, 1940), p. 179.

212. Kealey and Palmer, *Dreaming of What Might Be*, pp. 313–316; John W. Bennett, "The

Knights of Labor and the Clan-Na-Gael'' (Paper presented to the Knights of Labor
Centennial Conference, Newberry Library, Chicago, May 17–19, 1979); Eric Foner,
''Class, Ethnicity, and Radicalism in The Gilded Age: The Land League and Irish
America,'' *Marxist Perspectives* 1 (Summer 1978): 6–55, especially 46.

213. Fink, ''Workingmen's Democracy,'' pp. 308–388.
214. Commons et al., *History of Labor,* vol. 2, pp. 350–354.
215. Joseph R. Buchanan to Powderly, December 7, 1893, Powderly Papers, Catholic University, Washington, D.C.; Joseph Buchanan, *The Story of a Labor Agitator* (Freeport, N.Y.: Books for Libraries Press, 1971), p. 439.
216. Quoted in Saul K. Padover, ed., *Karl Marx on America and the Civil War* (New York: McGraw-Hill, 1972), pp. 38, 46.
217. On the rise of nativist groups like the American Protective Association and the Canadian variant, the Protestant Protective Association, both products of the 1890s and not without impact in working-class circles, see Donald C. Kinzer, *An Episode in Anti-Catholicism: The American Protective Association* (Seattle: University of Washington Press, 1964); John Higham, *Strangers in the Land: Patterns of American Nativism, 1860–1925* (New York: Vintage Books, 1963), pp. 81–82; Davis, ''Why the Class Is Different,'' p. 34; Oestreicher, ''Solidarity and Fragmentation,'' pp. 56–61; James T. Watt, ''Anti-Catholicism in Ontario Politics: The Role of the Protestant Protective Association in the 1894 Election,'' *Ontario History* 59 (1967): 57–67; Watt, ''Anti-Catholic Nativism in Canada: The Protestant Protective Association,'' *Canadian Historical Review* 48 (1967: 45–58. On the Jesuits Estates Act, see Roy Dalton, *The Jesuits' Estates Question, 1760–1888: A Study of the Background for the Agitation of 1889* (Toronto: University of Toronto Press, 1968); J. R. Miller, ''The Jesuits' Estate Act Crisis,'' *Journal of Canadian Studies* 9 (August 1974): 36–50. On the Manitoba Schools Question, see Paul Crunican, *Priests and Politics: Manitoba Schools and the Election of 1896* (Toronto: University of Toronto Press, 1976). Jingoism deserves further study, but note Montgomery, ''Labor and the Republic,'' p. 210; Carman Miller, ''A Preliminary Analysis of the Socio-Economic Composition of Canada's South African War Contingents,'' *Histoire Sociale/Social History* 8 (November 1975): 219–237.
218. See Ross, ''Workers on the Edge,'' p. 596; Oestreicher, ''Solidarity and Fragmentation,'' p. 193; Levine, ''Their Own Sphere''; Bensman, ''Artisan Culture, Business Union''; Michael Gordon, ''Studies in Irish and Irish-American Thought and Behaviour in Gilded Age New York City'' (Ph.D. diss., University of Rochester, 1977); Clare Dahberger Horner, ''Producers' Co-operatives in the United States, 1865–1890'' (Ph.D. diss., University of Pittsburgh, 1978); Montgomery, ''Labor and the Republic,'' p. 204; Davis, ''Why the U.S. Working Class Is Different,'' pp. 26–30; Fink, ''Workingmen's Democracy.''
219. Grob's *Workers and Utopia* is challenged by a range of other work, aside from sources cited frequently throughout this chapter: David Lyon, ''The World of P. J. McGuire: A Study of the American Labor Movement, 1870–1890'' (Ph.D. diss., University of Minnesota, 1972), especially p. 271; Ralph W. Scharnau, ''Thomas J. Morgan and the Chicago Socialist Movement, 1876–1901'' (Ph.D. diss., University of Northern Illinois, 1969); Gene Marlatt, ''Joseph Buchanan: Spokesman for Labor During the Populist and Progressive Eras'' (Ph.D. diss., University of Colorado, 1975); George Cotkin, ''Working Class Intellectuals and Evolutionary Thought in America, 1870–1915'' (Ph.D. diss., Ohio State University, 1978); Stuart B. Kaufman, *Samuel Gompers and the Origins of the American Federation of Labor, 1848–1896* (Westport, Conn.: Greenwood Press, 1973).
220. Melvyn Dubofsky and Warren Van Tine, *John L. Lewis: A Biography* (Chicago: Quadrangle, 1976), p. 12.

221. Thomas R. Brooks, *Clint: A Biography of a Labor Intellectual—Clinton S. Golden* (New York: Atheneum, 1978), pp. 17–18, ix.

222. *Citizen and Country*, May 4, 1900.

223. Melvyn Dubofsky, "The Origins of Western Working Class Radicalism, 1890–1905," in Peter Stearns and Daniel Walkowitz, *Workers in the Industrial Revolution: Recent Studies of Labor in the United States and Europe* (New Brunswick, N.J.: Transaction Books, 1974), p. 383.

224. David J. Bercuson, *Fools and Wise Men: The Rise and Fall of the One Big Union* (Toronto: McGraw-Hill, 1978), p. 120.

225. Irving Bernstein, *The Lean Years: A History of the American Worker, 1920–1933* (Baltimore: Penguin, 1960), p. 34.

226. See, for example, Tamara Hareven, *Family Time and Industrial Time: The Relationship Between the Family and Work in a New England Industrial Community* (Cambridge, England: Cambridge University Press, 1982).

227. Marx, "The Eighteenth Brumaire of Louis Bonaparte," in Marx and Engels, *Selected Works*, p. 100.

Index

311

STUDIES IN SOCIAL DISCONTINUITY

DATE DUE